*Many times I have heard people say 'Teach the real history of this country', in regard to the uninvited arrival of the Europeans and their mistreatment of the Aborigines. I agree, the real history should be taught – but in its entirety. This means teaching those parts which some people may not enjoy hearing, such as the mistreatment (violence) of Aborigines against themselves, both after and before colonisation. This book aims to teach that part as well as provide solutions to the problems of violence facing Aborigines today.*

**Dr Anthony Dillon, University of Western Sydney**

*Stephanie Jarrett is the voice of reason among the dissemblers in Aboriginal policy. She has had the strength to tell the truth about Aboriginal culture. For those who want Aborigines to reach a better life, they should begin with Jarrett's superb analysis.*

**Gary Johns, author of**
***Aboriginal Self-Determination: The Whiteman's Dream.***

*Both racism and political correctness deny truth and deal in stereotypes. All stereotypes, positive or negative, dehumanise. Truth is the most useful of problem-solving tools. If we want to solve the problem of violence we must search honestly for its causes. Stephanie Jarrett rejects stereotypes and by doing so she welcomes Aboriginal Australians into the rest of poor, vexed, complex humanity. We're all in this together, now let's find some answers.*

**Dave Price, cross-cultural trainer and consultant**

*Stephanie Jarrett is driven by a combination of three things rarely seen, let alone seen together, amongst scholars in the field of Aboriginal Australia: she genuinely wants to liberate Aboriginal women, not just to apply discursive frameworks to their suffering; she is careful, thorough and shockingly detailed in her research; and most strikingly, she is persistently courageous in confronting us all with the truth about ourselves and what we are doing to our own Indigenous people.*

**Rev Steven J. Etherington PhD, language researcher for 30 years in the Kunwinjku Language Speaking communities of Western Arnhem Land**

# Liberating Aboriginal People from Violence

Stephanie Jarrett

Connor Court Publishing
Ballan, Australia

Published in 2013 by Connor Court Publishing Pty Ltd

Copyright © Stephanie Jarrett 2013

ALL RIGHTS RESERVED. This book contains material protected under International and Federal Copyright Laws and Treaties. Any unauthorised reprint or use of this material is prohibited. No part of this book may be reproduced or transmitted in any form or by any means, electronic or mechanical, including photocopying, recording, or by any information storage and retrieval system without express written permission from the publisher.

Connor Court Publishing Pty Ltd.
PO Box 1
Ballan VIC 3342
sales@connorcourt.com
www.connorcourt.com

ISBN: 9781922168139 (pbk.)

Printed in Australia

# CONTENTS

Foreword ........................................................................... vii
Acknowledgements ........................................................... ix
Introduction ....................................................................... 1

**Barriers to solutions**

1. Misleading statistics ................................................... 23
2. Interrupted memories ................................................. 53
3. Mitigating circumstances:
   judicial emphasis on traditional violence ................... 65

**Legitimacy of violence in Aboriginal traditional cultures**

4. "Necessity" of violent punishment for Dreamtime sacrilege ........... 105
5. Interpersonal violence in traditional times ............... 121

**Continuity of traditional violence**

6. Dangerous lands ....................................................... 143
7. Outstations ............................................................... 173
8. The Yolngu of north-east Arnhem Land .................. 197
9. Towns and cities ...................................................... 255

**Shedding tradition's violent shackles**

10. Aboriginal men's apology for violence .................. 279
11. Income Management as a pathway to the mainstream ......... 295
12. From cultural compliance to personal choice ........ 313

Bibliography .................................................................... 356
Index ................................................................................ 375

# Foreword

## Bess Nungarrayi Price

I have lived with violence all of my life. Many of my relatives have been either the victims or perpetrators of what is called grievous bodily harm, some of homicide. My own body is scarred by domestic violence. Some of this violence comes from our traditional way of life.

When we lived in the desert we had no armies, police forces or courts. Every family had to defend itself. Everybody, male and female, knows how to fight in their own defence and to defend their families. Men had the right to beat their wives. Young women had very few rights. Men had the right to kill those who they thought had broken the law. We all know this but won't talk about it.

Things are now much worse because the good things about the old law are dying with the old wise ones who were born and raised in the desert and knew how the old law should work to make sure it was just. Now we have alcohol and drugs and our young people are confused and frightened. When they follow our old law they break the new, when they follow the new law they break the old. That is why the jails are full of our young men, and more and more, our young women.

We Aboriginal people have to acknowledge the truth. We can't blame all of our problems on the white man. The best thing about acknowledging that we have our own traditional forms of violence is that this is our problem that we can fix ourselves. We don't need to be told what to do by the white man.

In Alice Springs the courageous Aboriginal men of the Ingkintja Male Health Unit in Alice Springs admitted that there was too much violence and apologised to their women and children for the violence inflicted by men. They were brave enough to admit the truth, strong and decent enough to apologise.

Governments and human rights activists have ignored them. They are heroes who should be supported. I know Stephanie Jarrett to be decent, caring and hard working. I commend her work to you. We need to support those who tell the truth, acknowledge it and start solving our own problems.

**Bess Nungarrayi Price**
**Alice Springs**
**February, 2012**

# Acknowledgements

Writing a book on Aboriginal violence is a confronting and demanding task, and I doubt if I could have accomplished it without the support of my family, friends and colleagues.

Professor James Franklin has been my steadfast mentor, editor and guide throughout this endeavour. Because of James Franklin's encouragement and support, I embarked on the writing of this book, and his commitment to the book has sustained my courage, and I express my gratitude. I also thank Irene and James Franklin for their warm and welcome hospitality.

For more than a decade, the dedicated encouragement and support of the Honourable Doctor Gary Johns was crucial to me in keeping to the difficult endeavour of speaking and writing about Aboriginal violence. I express my gratitude to Gary Johns for these years of being my mentor and editor, especially for this book.

I thank Dr Anthony Cappello and his team at Connor Court Publishing for their invaluable support for the book and George Thomas for his professional editing.

I am grateful for the valued, small amount of support from ARC DP Grant DP066401 "Restraint: Recovering the Virtue of Self-Control or Temperance to Strengthen the Australian Social Fabric".

Bess Nungarrayi Price and Dave Price have extended invaluable support and feedback for the book, and I express my gratitude. Bess Price's courage and commitment to improving the lives of remote Aboriginal communities is inspirational, and I am privileged that Bess Price has written the Foreword.

Inspirational members of the Bennelong Society provided much appreciated encouragement and assistance for the book. I thank Rev Dr Steve Etherington for his invaluable feedback and his insights based on decades of first-hand experience in a remote community.

With my Left-leaning perspectives on economic and social justice, feminism, and environmental issues, sustained critique of Aboriginal violence could have been an isolating task, because to express misgivings about minority cultures' treatment of women can create dissonance within the Left, with its prioritisation of cultural "rights". The Bennelong Society extended overwhelming support to me and my prioritisation of Aboriginal women's universal human right to be free from violence. For this support over the past decade and more, I am truly grateful.

I extend a special thank you to Dr Anthony Dillon, Joe Lane and Alistair Crooks for their encouragement and inspiration to express critical perspectives when it is not always easy to do so.

I extend my appreciation to my university teachers and colleagues, service providers, and families who have over the years provided invaluable support and insights into Aboriginal policy.

My own dear family and friends have loyally supported me with their caring interest and patience over the years regarding this project, and I express my heartfelt gratitude to them all. In particular, I express my love and gratitude to my mother and to my daughter.

**Stephanie Jarrett**
**October 2012**

# Introduction

## The importance of acknowledging the links of today's violence with the past

Aboriginal people suffer violence more than other Australians. This was so in pre-contact times, as it is today. It is important to acknowledge this link between today's Aboriginal violence and a violent, pre-contact tradition, because until policymakers are honest in their assessment of the causes, Aboriginal people can never be liberated from violence. There are now a number of authors urging us to understand the severe violence of traditional Aboriginal culture. This book is another contribution, but it goes further, in linking the fact of traditional violence to the need for fundamental policy reform now. The nation needs to understand that to liberate Aboriginal people from violence, deep cultural change is necessary, away from traditional norms and practices of violence. Such fundamental change is unlikely to occur in separate, self-determined communities which are premised on maintaining traditional culture.

Our courts also need to acknowledge the link between today's Aboriginal violence and a violent, pre-contact tradition. Securing justice and safety for Aboriginal victims of Aboriginal violence depends upon it. "Cultural rights" thinking favours Aboriginal perpetrators, so Aboriginal victims need the full force of liberal-democratic law, which disallows the private use of violence. Our legal system currently gives some allowance for heinous acts committed by "others" as part of their tradition. This renders Aboriginal victims vulnerable, because our law can reach back past living memory to anthropological, judicial, and other colonial records, to validate a perpetrator's claim that his act is consistent with pre-contact tradition. This specious, perpetrator-favouring situation should be anathema within our liberal democracy.

Above all, the safety of Aboriginal women depends on our governments understanding and responding to the reality of the brutal side of Aboriginal traditional culture. It should be self-evident that a program of self-determination is a high-risk enterprise in cases where the traditional culture is inherently unsafe for women; but post-Enlightenment principles have successfully rendered it not self-evident, and Aboriginal women have been condemned to suffer.

**A slow and reluctant awakening**

A number of coalescing forces have contributed to the growing – albeit belated – alarm regarding violence among Aboriginal Australians, particularly against women. First, Australia took centuries to recognise that all women had the right to be free from violence within the home, and full recognition of this right was not delivered until the 1970s. The 1980s and 1990s witnessed a growing awareness of the level of Aboriginal men's violence against Aboriginal women. There was a reticence about extending equivalent protection, however, to Aboriginal women victims. One early voice was Aboriginal author and anti-violence campaigner Judy Atkinson, who pointed to the discrepancy between the huge national outrage over Aboriginal male deaths in custody, while the nation remained ignorant about – or chose to ignore – the appalling number of Aboriginal women who were injured or murdered by Aboriginal men. Atkinson sounded a wake-up call:

> more women have died from violent assault in a number of communities than all the deaths in custody in the states concerned ... and too often no charges are laid.[1]

Other early voices include Diane Bell and Topsy Napurrula Nelson in

---

1  Judy Atkinson, "Violence in Aboriginal Australia Part 2", *The Aboriginal and Islander Health Worker*, 14 (3), September 1990, 9.

"Speaking about rape is everyone's business"[2], and Audrey Bolger in *Aboriginal Women and Violence*.[3]

Only a few pointed to a link between pre-contact culture and present high rates of violence. The scholarship of those who made the link and emphasised its dangers – particularly Joan Kimm, Louis Nowra and Peter Sutton – is substantive and of high quality.[4] Nevertheless, even among these brave writers is a reluctance to suggest strategies that fall outside the tenets of community self-determination.

In the concluding chapter of *Bad Dreaming*,[5] while Louis Nowra gets close to the idea that integration is necessary to end male violence against women, he evades recommending this as policy. He advocates critically necessary *in situ* interventions such as the end to lighter sentences for Aboriginal perpetrators, improved health, child protection and education services, more policing, more women's shelters, better protection of whistleblowers, and the end of the permit system. He urges violent men on indigenous communities to change, assuming that violent men on the communities can be taught "that their behaviour towards women is wrong, just as is happening in non-indigenous Australia"[6] and that they can be persuaded to take responsibility for their own deep cultural and behavioural changes.

---

2  Diane Bell and Topsy Napurrula Nelson, "Speaking about rape is everyone's business", *Women's Studies International Forum*, 12 (4), 1989, 403-10.

3  Audrey Bolger, *Aboriginal Women and Violence*, A Report for the Criminology Research Council and Northern Territory Commissioner of Police, Australian National University Research Unit, Darwin, 1991. See also Joan Kimm, *A Fatal Conjunction: Two Laws Two Cultures*, The Federation Press, Sydney, 2004, Chapter 14, where she outlines some key Aboriginal people, particularly Aboriginal women, who have spoken out against "intra-communal" violence and misogyny.

4  Pre-contact origins of present-day Aboriginal violence were also highlighted more than a decade earlier by Dr Jock McLaren, a psychiatrist with years of experience in the Kimberley. See Margaret Harris, "Black violence: why whites shouldn't feel so guilty", *Herald (Spectrum)*, 16 February, 1991.

5  Louis Nowra, *Bad Dreaming: Aboriginal men's violence against women and children*, Pluto Press, North Melbourne, 2007, Chapter 7.

6  Ibid, 91.

Nowra concludes:

> Indigenous communities have to recognise that they are part of Australian society and integrate into their cultural sensibility the idea of personal and individual responsibility for their actions. Furthermore, they need to accept that certain aspects of their culture – such as promised marriages, polygamy, violence towards women and male aggression – are best forgotten. There has to be an acknowledgement by the men that women have human rights and that murder and violence are to be judged not by their standards but by the standards of the general community. If men refuse to do anything then they are responsible for the slow death of the many wonderful aspects of their culture, traditions and customs, and their communities will continue to be on a nightmarish treadmill to cultural oblivion.[7]

This is a moving and exemplary plea, and one hesitates to challenge it, particularly as it contains the difficult but unavoidable term, "integrate". Nevertheless, Nowra's conclusion is predicated on two uncertain ideas that need greater exploration than he provides: first, that people in the more traditional remote communities generally want to be part of mainstream Australian society; and second, that these communities will respond to persuasion to view violence as unwanted behaviour, when it is an integral aspect of traditional life, values and belief.

Can such change happen when mainstream impacts are deliberately limited through self-determination, extreme isolation even without a permit system, and the brutal silencing of whistleblowers? If so, how? Who says that these norms should change? Certainly many Aboriginal people do, particularly those leading more mainstream lives, and those in communities whose tolerance for subjection to violence is perhaps less than in pre-contact times when there was no escape and no alternative perspective or way of life. However, are these Aboriginal people's calls and campaigns for change strong enough

---

7 Ibid, 92-3.

to counter resilient cultural norms that include a legitimised place for interpersonal violence? And how do we counteract the frequent claims that violence is "not part of our culture" when it very much is, thereby protecting the culture from direct challenge, and keeping interventions focused on exacerbators such as alcohol, drugs and petrol-sniffing?

Nowra's argument that Aboriginal communities need to integrate "the idea of personal and individual responsibility for their actions", and that promised marriages, polygamy, violence towards women and male aggression are "best forgotten", is a critical breakthrough. Here, Nowra moves us beyond the general position in report after report that the violence and injustice in Aboriginal communities are due to post-contact causes, and raises the reality that solutions will require changes to Aboriginal cultural practice itself. However, his book does not tackle the problem that the scope for such change within traditional communities is limited. In remote communities plagued by violence, Nowra recommends outside intervention to secure the safety of women and children. But is that what we want for Aboriginal communities: remote places where the services are controlled by outside authorities who supervise every family every day and every night, to make sure another woman is not killed, another child is not abused, another young man does not suicide, and where a key instrument of success is the presence of a women's shelter?

In her seminal book on pre-contact origins of Aboriginal violence, *A Fatal Conjunction* (2004), Joan Kimm is critical of a generalised failure, as in the Gordon Inquiry, to acknowledge the existence of pre-contact violence.[8] Kimm urges the need in law to place women's rights above cultural rights. Nevertheless, the powerful implications

---

8 Kimm, 2004, 148, referring to S. Gordon, K. Callahan, and D. Henry, *Putting the Picture Together, Inquiry into the Response by Government Agencies to Complaints of Family Violence and Child Abuse in Aboriginal Communities*, Dept. of Premier and Cabinet, Western Australia, 2002: http://www.slp.wa.gov.au/publications/publications.nsf/DocByAgency/FEB7D71FB3A6AF1948256C 160018F 8FE/$file/Gordon+Inquiry+Final.pdf

of her book – that addressing Aboriginal violence requires strategies that tackle its traditional, cultural roots – are circumvented in the concluding chapter by her priority to uphold self-determined strategies, in particular community consultation, community initiatives, and community control of programs. She highlights communities where such tenets are meeting with success, including Lajamanu[9] and Ali Curung[10] – where significant reductions in violence and other benefits such as increased school enrolments have occurred with community-controlled services, including women's shelters, under the trial Aboriginal Law and Justice Programs.[11]

The communities deserve recognition for these changes. However, night patrols[12] and safe houses[13] remain required instruments of safety in these communities, and alcohol and gambling are still scourges.[14] Moreover, there have always been some communities with the

---

9 Lajamanu Population 2006 = 790; classified "very remote". Source: Australian Bureau of Statistics (ABS), *National Regional Profile: Lajamanu (CGC) (Local Government Area)*, 2008: http://abs.gov.au/AUSSTATS (link to Population for Local Government Area)

10 Ali Curung population = 320-450. Source: Central Land Council, 2008. *Reviewing the Northern Territory Emergency Response: Perspectives from six communities*, 2008, 10: http://www.clc.org.au/Media/issues/intervention/CLC%20_REPORTweb.pdf Note: Kimm, 2004, 156, refers to Ali *Curang*. Usually, the spelling is Ali *Curung*, but both spellings are used. Formerly it was known as Warrabri.

11 Kimm, 2004, 156.

12 Central Land Council, 2008, 46; Attorney-General's Department, Indigenous Justice and Legal Assistance Division, 2008. *Night Patrol Services – Frequently Asked Questions*, Australian Government, Canberra, 2: www.ag.gov.au

13 Russell Skelton, "Violence Behind the Silence", *The Age*, 7 July 2007: http://www.theage.com.au/news/violence-behind-the-silence/2007/07/06/1183351448912.html; and The Hon. Jenny Macklin MP, "Doors begin to open on safe places across the NT," *Media Releases*, Joint Media Release with Malarndirri McCarthy, NT Minister for Children and Families – Minister for Child Protection, and The Hon Warren Snowdon MP, Member for Lingiari, 30 January 2009:http://www.jennymacklin.fahcsia.gov.au/m ediareleases/2009/Pages/safe_places_30jan09.aspx

14 Central Land Council, 2008, 25; Northern Territory Emergency Response (NTER) Review, 2007. Section A – Summary of Task Force Findings as at September 2007, Commonwealth of Australia: http://nterreview.gov.au/subs/nter_review_report/177_drug_free/177_Drug_Free_2.htm

commitment and human capital to secure progress, whatever the policy regimen, and it is too easy to get diverted, complacent, or even guilty for remaining critical in the face of gains here and there. Too many remote communities remain chronically dysfunctional despite decades of dedicated people working in community-based programs and consultation including Aboriginal women's input.

An investigation a few years later in 2007 by *The Age* journalist Russell Skelton paints a very different picture of Ali Curung.[15] When Rex Wild and his team made a two-hour visit, it was tea and biscuits and assurances from the men that "child abuse was not a problem, and faced with silence from the women, the team left". Skelton continues,

> The visit by the author of the landmark *Little Children are Sacred* report into sex abuse of Aboriginal children in the Northern Territory dismayed some of those present who had been fighting a losing battle to contain a generation of violent young men. In Ali Curung, followers of gangsta rap have imposed a mindless culture of terror on women, the elderly and children.
>
> When the Federal Government's team of soldiers, federal police and social workers visits the community next week to assess infrastructure needs, violence and abuse, NT officials hope they will stay long enough to penetrate the silence and denials. One person they won't be able to interview is the woman who supervised the woman's shelter, a small, vulnerable building surrounded by a cyclone fence and located next to the police station.
>
> *The Age* believes that she abruptly left last week after two years working in the "Ali Curung war zone". She told colleagues before she left that it was not uncommon for the safe house, staffed by local women, to be attacked at night by men attempting to extract revenge on the women who fled there. She described how they would scale the rear fence, bash on the door, demand entry and threaten reprisals.[16]

---

15 Skelton, 2007.
16 Ibid.

The article paints a bleak picture of community life, high levels of sexually transmitted disease, and a football carnival that descended into a brawl involving "several hundred people going at each other with nulla-nullas, axes and rocks". Perhaps most directly related to Kimm's observations, anthropologist Jenny Walker said that while the older women of Ali Curung made progress in containing violence with a night patrol vehicle, "the change was short-lived when the men commandeered the vehicle, which was in turn confiscated by police when men were caught smuggling grog".[17]

The Ngaanyatjarra Pitjantjatjara Yankunytjatjara Women's Council (NPYWC) of Central Australia, which Kimm also points to in a positive context, is another sad example.[18] Established in 1980, the NPYWC has long been a celebrated and hard-working institution, providing scope for more women's input into community decisions and government reports on a wide range of community issues, including child protection and domestic violence across the vast NPY Western Desert lands. These lands cover 350,000 square kilometres in the Northern Territory, South Australia and Western Australia. The total population is about 6000, and includes a number of towns and dozens of homelands.[19] Their 10-year celebratory book declares that the NPYWC has enabled NPY women to "speak as forceful, confident persons who back their words with action".[20]

Jane Lloyd's figures compiled for the Australian Crime Commission indicate that 28 years after the establishment of the NPYWC, violence

---

17 Ibid.
18 Kimm, 2004, 155.
19 Ngaanyatjarra Pitjantjatjara Yankunytjatjara Women's Council (NPYWC) (Aboriginal Corporation), 2007. "About us": http://www.npywc.org.au/html/about_us.html
20 NPYWC, *Minyma Tjuta Tjunguringkula Kunpuringanyi: Women Growing Strong Together, NPYWC 1980-1990*, 1990, 3. See also NPYWC (Aboriginal Corporation), 2007.

in the NPY lands remains catastrophic.[21] Domestic homicide figures from Central Australia are a clear indication that women's initiatives and other responses are not working. Between 2000 and 2008, 14 (probably 16, with two missing presumed killed) women on these lands were killed by their husband or boyfriend. Six of the homicides occurred in the eighteen months between May 2007 and November 2008. Women from the NPY regions are "67 times more likely to be a domestic violence related homicide victim".[22] Lloyd's report indicates the deliberate nature of these homicides, including injuries to "head, face and torso"; "multiple episodes of trauma"; "injuries are inflicted in isolated places"; and "offender delayed seeking help or medical attention for victim in all cases". Victims, fearing the risk, sought "direct help from outside authorities in 9 of the 16 cases". Perhaps the most telling information is found under Lloyd's heading, "Externalisation of blame and normalisation of violence", with its following list,

- Offender blamed victim for the violence
- Outside authorities blamed the woman for [her] death
- Family, community, and outside authorities fear retribution if they report
- Offender deliberately downplayed the injuries and did not express remorse
- Witnesses, including family and those non-related, did not report or seek help for the victim.[23]

What is happening here? Even outside authorities are not resilient

---

21 Jane Lloyd, "Domestic Violence Related Homicide Cases in Central Australia", Australian Crime Commission, paper given at *International Conference on Homicide – Domestic-Related Homicide*, 3-5 December 2008: http://www.aic.gov.au/events/aic%20upcoming%20events/2008/~/media/conferences/2008-homicide/lloyd.ashx
22 Ibid. It is presumed that this "67 times more" means "more than mainstream Australian figures".
23 Ibid.

enough to defend victims in these communities: how much harder it must be for community people themselves. Clearly commentators and governments have expected too much from such troubled communities steeped in the tradition that male violence is a right. To promote such initiatives as the NPYWC into key solutions traps us within orthodox thought, thereby sapping the crucial energy needed to embark on essential but more difficult strategies.

An attraction of strategies such as the NPYWC where community women initiate and control processes, is their fit within "empowerment" ideology. Surely they empower women, and so reduce their vulnerability to violence? Surely outside intervention reduces the voice and power of minority women, the opposite of what our goals are? In fact, too often the women themselves share in the victim-blaming against other women, or are themselves violent, including against each other. Even among urban, educated Aboriginal women, victim-blaming and defence of male perpetrators can remain a prohibitive force, to the frustration of service providers grappling with the policy of Aboriginalisation of services, even if it might compromise victim safety.[24] Kimm's commitment to self-determined strategies pulls her short of exploring what it means to give choice and voice to women victims in communities where even the women see violence as part of culture, a tolerable normality, and where silence reigns because to speak out is too dangerous. The vital question is: how do we best empower Aboriginal women *victims*, when so many of the women themselves tolerate or perpetrate the violence of the culture?

Staying within the self-determination framework even in cases of promising results can mean tacitly condoning other culturally embedded behaviours that by mainstream standards are disturbing and dysfunctional. An example is the Indigenous Family Violence

---

24 Stephanie Jarrett, "'This is as much as we can do': Aboriginal domestic violence", in Gary Johns, (ed), *Waking Up To Dreamtime: The Illusion of Self-Determination*, Media Masters, Singapore, 2001, 106, 115.

Offender pilot program at Nguiu.[25] The reason victims were less afraid of attracting blame here was because offenders were less likely to be jailed, and could remain in the community. Another claimed reason for the program's success is its process.

> The commitment of the Nguiu facilitators, ACCO, and community to address family violence in their community has been integral to the success of the program. The facilitators are from 4 different skin groups which allows for diversity when dealing with cultural issues such as avoidance relationships. If a facilitator is not allowed to directly address an offender then one of the other facilitators will do this.[26]

Avoidance as described is disturbing enough. The possibility in some communities of invoking violence when avoidance is breached makes it more disturbing. Furthermore, avoidance relationships can mean that a witness cannot give evidence against a defendant if they have an avoidance relationship with that defendant, or may even deny what they saw, with serious judicial consequences. In one example of a young witness in an assault case, "Her evidence was she didn't see the defendant assault Ms (N) although she saw the whole incident". The interpreter advised the Court that the witness "could not give evidence as there was an avoidance relationship between herself and the defendant".[27] Regarding the impact of avoidance on court cases, Jenny Blokland CM writes,

> It is unlikely to be a matter that can be dealt with simply by the usual vulnerable witness procedures ... Despite significant energy and expertise being devoted to Indigenous People in the Criminal Justice System in both the "Little Children are Sacred"

---

25 Debra White of Casuarina Community Corrections, and Melissa and Gilbert Alimankinni, Facilitators at Nguiu, *Indigenous Family Violence Offender Program: The Nguiu Experience*, September 2006: sitebuilder.yodelaustralia.com.au/sites/5530/Debra%20White.doc

26 Ibid, 5.

27 Jenny Blokland CM: *Chambers v Kerr* [2007] NTMC 055. 2007: www.nt.gov.au/justice/ntmc/judgements/2007/pdf/20070821ntmc055.pdf. Name given in original.

report (2007) and a legislative response in the *Northern Territory National Emergency Response Bill 2007* (CW), no strategy has been developed as far as I am aware to solving or mitigating this problem. The inability of witnesses to give evidence because of cultural constraints serves neither party nor the community well.[28]

Despite the power of Kimm's book, and its call for greater recognition of Aboriginal victim rights in law, one is left with the sense that while we can secure some reductions here and there, community violence at higher than the mainstream rate is inevitable, and Aboriginal women's empowerment is about community women themselves running the sadly necessary community women's shelters and night patrols and legal centres to secure some safety. There is no breakthrough here and it sounds little better than surrender. Is this the best Australia can do for remote Aboriginal victims? And what about the children?

Should Peter Sutton's *The Politics of Suffering* have offered more in the way of solutions?[29] This incisive critique of how policy since the 1970s has failed Aboriginal people takes us closer to solutions for Aboriginal community dysfunction and interpersonal violence. As Rosemary Neill points out,

> Through his observations and careful marshalling of historical and anthropological evidence, Sutton demonstrates how traditional approaches to violence, hygiene, sorcery and child-rearing persist in many indigenous communities. He argues that together with recent, destructive impacts such as welfare dependence and substance abuse, these cultural practices often have a detrimental effect on indigenous health, housing and wellbeing.
>
> Yet he discovers that the complex question of culture is still

---

28 Ibid.
29 Peter Sutton, *The Politics of Suffering: Indigenous Australia and the end of the liberal consensus*, Melbourne University Press, Carlton, Victoria, 2009.

being quarantined from discussions of indigenous advantage through what he calls "untruth by omission".[30]

Neill signals, however, a shortage of precise strategies:

> He believes "deep – rather than superficial – cultural redevelopment is necessary" and that "the cycle of childhood socialisation needs to be regeared" if there is to be radical improvement. However, *The Politics of Suffering* offers few concrete suggestions as to how this might be achieved.[31]

Nevertheless, Sutton's book adds valuable insights into why self-determination has produced such disappointing results for Aboriginal well-being and safety.

For over 20 years, some analysts of Aboriginal suffering and disadvantage have tried to alert us that something is awry with self-determination itself. Colin Tatz's powerful 1990 article "Aboriginal Violence: a Return to Pessimism" sounded an early alarm.[32] The late Peter Howson, Minister for Aboriginal Affairs in the McMahon government, for years expressed his alarm about the separatist direction of Aboriginal policy, including the harm it presented to Aboriginal women.[33] For the last decade policy analyst Gary Johns has argued powerfully for a shift away from self-determination if we are to address Aboriginal disadvantage, suffering and violence.[34] In his 2011 book, *Aboriginal Self-Determination: The Whiteman's Dream*, Johns delineates key elements of the self-determination agenda, which

---

30 Rosemary Neill, "Untruth by Omission", *Mission and Justice: Justice and Peace News from the Asia Pacific Region*, 11 July 2009: http://www.missionandjustice.org/untruth-by-omission/

31 Ibid.

32 Colin Tatz, "Aboriginal Violence: a Return to Pessimism", *Australian Journal of Social Issues*, Vol. 25, No. 4, November 1990, 245-259.

33 For example, Peter Howson, "Why we desperately need new Aboriginal policies", *The Age*, 10 May 2002: http://www.theage.com.au/articles/2002/05/09/1020914030021.html

34 In particular, see Gary Johns, *Aboriginal Self-Determination: The Whiteman's Dream*, Connor Court, Ballan, 2011.

are "given life in the recommendations of the Royal Commission into Aboriginal Deaths in Custody" (RCADC).[35] Among these are

- Disadvantage is the product of domination of Aborigines by non-Aboriginal society
- The broader society to supply assistance and Aboriginal society to maintain its independent status
- Aboriginal people have the right to retain culture and identity ...
- National Aboriginal Language Policy should be compulsory. English, arithmetic and science not so
- Restoring unalienated Crown land to Aboriginal claimants on an inalienable freehold basis with the right of the Aboriginal owners to determine entry[36]

Johns argues that the self-determination assumption – non-Aboriginal society is the central cause of Aboriginal people's present-day suffering – is causing great harm, because it is unable to recognise or address the main causes of their suffering including violence, such as cultural generators, poor English, welfare dependency, and the poor economic potential of their remote lands.[37]

David Pollard[38], Geoffrey Partington[39] and Ron Brunton[40] have written books presenting their critical perspectives. Their critiques secured little traction, perhaps dismissed as too "politically incorrect" with their call for a move away from self-determination. As early as 1988, Pollard, an experienced practitioner in New South Wales Aboriginal policy, argued that an emergent Aboriginal desire for

---

35 Ibid, 45.
36 Ibid. Johns' data source: RCADC, 1991, Volumes 1 and 5.
37 Ibid, 44-49.
38 David Pollard, *Give and Take: The losing partnership in Aboriginal poverty*, Hale and Iremonger, Sydney, 1988.
39 Geoffrey Partington, *Hasluck versus Coombs, White Politics and Australia's Aborigines*, Quakers Hill Press, Quakers Hill, 1996.
40 Ron Brunton, *Black Suffering, White Guilt: Aboriginal Disadvantage and the Royal Commission into Aboriginal Deaths in Custody*, Institute of Public Affairs, Current Issues, February 1993.

greater participation in mainstream society should receive more consideration in policy making.[41] In his 1993 book, *Black Suffering, White Guilt*, Brunton asked the following questions:

> Can people achieve their aspirations for individual and social efficacy without some commitment to the Western liberal virtues, such as a strong sense of personal responsibility and self-control, or a capacity to trust and cooperate productively with non-kin and strangers, or an ability to take advantage of new opportunities without being "brought back into place" as a "high flyer"? To what extent can these virtues co-exist with traditional values and dispositions – or the values of the "oppositional culture"?[42]

Brunton wrote in his conclusion:

> Throughout the two centuries of European settlement in Australia, one principle has remained intact: the administrative and legislative dichotomy between Aborigines and non-Aborigines ... [This dichotomy] provides incentives for maintaining and strengthening boundaries which might otherwise be blurred or corroded as a consequence of individuals choosing to take advantage of the social and economic opportunities that a free and comparatively tolerant society could provide. Ameliorative policies formulated in terms of this dichotomy tend to benefit those least in need of assistance, while the most disadvantaged remain largely unaffected or become even worse off.[43]

Rosemary Neill's 2002 book, *White Out: How Politics is Killing Black Australia*, speaking more from a middle ground, sounds the alarm with her thorough examination of the self-determination era's devastating

---

41 Pollard, 1988, 133.
42 Brunton, 1993, 55.
43 Ibid, 61-2.

failures.[44] More recently, Helen Hughes' book *Lands of Shame* depicts how "30 years of exceptionalist policies" have inflicted great harm onto remote Aboriginal people.[45]

In 2001 Sutton discussed the dichotomy between the Australian mainstream and its nation state, and the culture and localised political entities of discrete Aboriginal communities.[46] This is further developed in his 2009 book, which includes an exploration of the potential hazards of undertaking reconciliation:

> The difference between the state and the Indigenous realm that matters most here is that the modern state is the concrete outgrowth of centuries of movement along the road, whereby belonging to the wider nation brings with it both the fee of self-subordination to the collective and the right to national protection in return. Although among Aboriginal people there is general acceptance of the rule of Australian law, much of the informal Indigenous domain within the Australian state actually operates on different and previous principles, including those of local sovereign autonomy, the commitment of primary loyalty to one's kin, and, when needed, an assertion of the right of physical redress as a means of dealing with conflict. In this realm the state is not held to own a monopoly on violence.[47]

On the limits of reconciliation as a means to address Aboriginal suffering, Sutton writes that in "so many of the Indigenous communities",

---

44 Rosemary Neill, *White Out: How Politics is Killing Black Australia*, Allen and Unwin, Crows Nest, NSW, 2002. Neill is a journalist who has for years written powerfully on the plight of Aboriginal women victims of domestic violence. Her 1994 article, "Our Shame: How Aboriginal women and children are bashed in their own community – then ignored", *The Weekend Australian Review*, 18-19 June 1994, I read while doing my own field work. Neill 2002 also contains valuable pages (88-105) on Aboriginal violence against women.

45 Helen Hughes, *Lands of Shame: Aboriginal and Torres Strait Islander "homelands" in transition,* Centre for Independent Studies, St Leonards, 2007.

46 Peter Sutton, "The Politics of suffering: Indigenous policy in Australia since the 1970s", *Anthropological Forum* Vol. 11. No. 2, 2001, 152-153.

47 Sutton, 2009, 198.

the more important, visible, daily and emotionally consuming ties and conflicts are not with 19.5 million non-Indigenous people, most of whom they will never meet, but with the other Indigenous families and neighbourhoods of their own kindred and township and district.[48]

While most conflict occurs within Aboriginal families and communities, and not between Aboriginal and non-Aboriginal people, the idea that Aboriginal people are responsible for their own negative behaviours is still resisted. As Partington emphasised in his critique of the Coombsian self-determination project,

> The refusal to help Aboriginal women subjected to violence from Aboriginal men stemmed at heart from the determination that all Aborigines must be seen as victims, that no Aborigines can seriously be held responsible for their own actions.[49]

## Mission out, self-determination in, and the task is harder now[50]

There is evidence that under mission regimes, Aboriginal violence was considerably less than in both pre-contact communities and the self-determined communities of the present, post-mission era. Richard Trudgen shows in his book *Why Warriors Lie Down and Die* that well-run, compassionate missions provided a supportive, effective, bridging environment, often on or close to their own country, enabling Aboriginal people to gain many essential skills – education, trades, work culture, English language – required to participate in

---

48  Ibid, 199.
49  Partington, 1996, 137.
50  See Johns, 2011, 67.

the mainstream economy and society.⁵¹ It seems too that well-run missions provided a mainstream cultural context that could effectively suppress Aboriginal violent practices. It is possible that together with other reforms that gave Aboriginal people equal citizenship status, a relatively benign process from tradition to mission to mainstream was taking place, until about forty years ago. Had it continued, this process could have secured greater opportunity, assured by a later moderate, pluralist polity, for Aboriginal people to retain any aspects of Aboriginal culture including country, compatible with mainstream integration. Back then, perhaps the most difficult challenges existed less within Aboriginal Australia than with white Australia, with the main task being to break down the raw racism and racial segregation of those earlier years.

Years later most of us are in despair as we search for solutions. This includes those who acknowledge the need to dismantle the latter-day racial separatism of self-determination, that legacy of a progressive politics that went way beyond the moderate. Brunton, arguing that separate, Aboriginal policy-making should be replaced by non-racial policies that assist people on the basis of need, wrote in 1993,

> Unfortunately, there are few grounds for optimism that change along the lines suggested in [Brunton's] monograph is likely to take place in the near future ... Too many people with influence over the direction of Aboriginal affairs have an interest – economic, political, psychological – in maintaining the *status quo*.⁵²

---

51 For examples, see F. X. Gsell, *"The Bishop with 150 Wives": Fifty Years as a Missionary*, Angus and Robertson, Sydney, 1956, Chapters V and VI; Mary Durack, *The Rock and the Sand*, Constable, London, 1969, Chapter 25; Graham Jenkin, *The Conquest of the Ngarrindjeri*, Raukkan Publishers, Point McLeay, 1985 (first edition 1979), Chapter 3; Richard Trudgen, *Why Warriors Lie Down and Die*, Aboriginal Resource and Development Services (ARDS), Darwin, 2000, Chapter 2; David McKnight, *From Hunting to Drinking: The Devastating Effects of Alcohol in an Australian Aboriginal Community*, Routledge, London, 2002, 47-51; 60-61; James Franklin, "The Cultural Roots of Aboriginal Violence", *Quadrant* 52 (11) (Nov, 2008), 22-25.
52 Brunton, 1993, 63.

Sutton expounded the need for a better ethnography of Aboriginal violence, while hinting that the best window of opportunity to benefit from such an ethnography may have passed:

> If in our time we try to understand phenomena like the reproduction of violence over time, we cannot start just with yesterday, and we cannot begin by excluding violence from "culture" and confining it to pigeonholes such as "criminality" or the emotional "pathology" of individuals. The in-depth methodology of anthropology and its encompassing theoretical base, not mere assemblages of medical or criminal facts alone, can assist official policies and practices to move beyond their present, tragically ineffectual standing to a point where communities have a chance of a better life. Yet one should not exaggerate the value of anthropology in this highly politicised context – its role is now always likely to be minor, and indeed we may have seen the end of the era in which it was otherwise.[53]

Sutton expressed a hope that communities might be able to reform violent aspects of their culture:

> Aboriginal people have abandoned many past practices voluntarily. Are the practices of "cruelling" infants and tolerating violent demanding behaviour in boys, just to give two examples, beyond being brought to consciousness for critical assessment within the relevant communities? Here is a case where "rethinking culture" might prove beneficial, in a context where community members, not their critics or enemies, do the judging and produce the initiative for change.[54]

This however, is followed by a less hopeful passage:

> Yet rethinking a culture is never an easy matter, especially if we are not in the habit of objectifying it. Also, would this kind of cultural re-assessment just be tinkering? A deeper approach is warranted if such things are to change ... In particular, I am

---

53 Sutton, 2001, 154-5.
54 Ibid, 156.

unable to see how problems that have deep-seated historical and cultural foundations can be seriously challenged in the absence of a radical shift in the political economy – with an emphasis on the economy – even though this alone may never be enough. Any truly significant shift in an Indigenous political economy, in the non-agrarian and technologically complex context of Australia, is likely to involve much greater social integration with non-kin than occurs at present, even though this kind of integration may have long been advancing because of, among other things, urban drift. So long as kinship remains a major basis rather than a mainly private aspect of the political economy of a people, it is unlikely that they will pursue the desired benefits of the post-industrial world very effectively or at great speed.[55]

Evidence suggests that urban drift does not alone secure a strong enough "integration with non-kin" or privatisation of kinship. The poor match between kin obligations such as demand-sharing, with the bounteous urban supply of goods, services and employment acquirable through individual effort or need, can continue as sources of conflict and violence in ghettoised urban Aboriginal populations. Such is the legacy of forty years of encouraging cultural distinction and separatism.

---

55 Ibid, 156.

# Barriers to solutions

A primary ideological barrier to overcoming Aboriginal violence is the denial that violence is linked with tradition. Sutton argues that "it is not so much the listed causes" that he objects to in official documents about Aboriginal disadvantage, but what is "nothingised": "What is repeatedly missing in officialese accounts of what lies behind 'disadvantage' is the very thing that everyone in such circles is usually quick to say needs proper recognition: Indigenous culture and society."[1] Referring to the Reconciliation document "and those multitudinous statements that resemble it", Sutton argues that

> there seems to be a wilful blindness to the role of past and present Indigenous egalitarian social organisation and the challenge this offers to performing in accordance with the expectations of a modern corporatist society. There is a blindness to the role of traditional power structures in setting some of the conditions for dependency. There is a blindness to the ancient need to pursue family loyalties over essentially foreign ideologies such as the doctrine of "the common good" ... There is a blindness to the legacy of a formerly and in some places very recently stateless society and its perfectly expectable system of self-help or self-redress during conflict, including frequent recourse to physical means.[2]

With the silence of victims, the interrupted memories of a violent past, and tradition as a mitigating circumstance in our courts, any blindness in "officialese" accounts is a travesty to victims. Securing safety for Aboriginal violence victims requires open and rigorous research and reporting of the highest order.

---

1 Ibid, 148.
2 Ibid, 148.

# 1
# Misleading statistics

## National Aboriginal and Torres Strait Islander Social Survey, 2002[1]

Government statistics are hiding Aboriginal victims of violence. The 2008 article "Theories of Indigenous Violence: A Preliminary Empirical Assessment", by Lucy Snowball and Don Weatherburn, has a seminal quality due to its presentation of pioneering work. It uses the Australian Bureau of Statistics (ABS) National Aboriginal and Torres Strait Islander Social Survey 2002 (NATSISS)[2] of 9359 Indigenous Australians from across Australia to test theories on Aboriginal violence via multivariate analysis. In the words of Snowball and Weatherburn,

> A number of theories have been put forward to explain the high level of violence among Australia's indigenous population. Up until 2002, lack of suitable data on the risk factors associated with Indigenous violent victimisation made it very difficult to assess adequacy of these theories.[3]

The problem is that their uncritical use of data hides the very phenomena they purport to study. Theories tested by Snowball and Weatherburn are Cultural Theory, Anomie Theory, Social

---

[1] I am indebted to James Franklin and Jenness Warin for their invaluable dialogue, assistance with sources, and contributions for this chapter, and to Gary Johns for his invaluable encouragement.

[2] ABS, *National Aboriginal and Torres Strait Islander Social Survey 2002*, 2004, ABS Catalogue No 4714.0. Referred to as "NATSISS" in this chapter.

[3] Lucy Snowball and Don Weatherburn, "Theories of Indigenous Violence: A Preliminary Empirical Assessment", 2008, *Australian and New Zealand Journal of Criminology*, Vol. 41 No. 2, 2008, 216.

Disorganisation Theory, Social Deprivation Theory, and Lifestyle/Routine Activity Theory. The dependent variable was "whether the respondent had experienced threatened or physical violence at least once in the 12 months preceding the survey". This was tested against NATSISS independent variables.[4]

According to the authors, the results refute the Cultural Theory argued in this book: that pre-contact, traditional culture is the key cause of today's high rates of Indigenous violence. They argue in their multivariate analysis that the dependent variable, "whether the respondent had experienced threatened or physical violence at least once in the 12 months preceding the survey", did not correlate significantly with cultural factors:

> If cultural theory is correct, for example, one might expect higher rates of violence among Indigenous Australians who:
> - live on traditional homelands
> - identify with a clan or speak an Indigenous language
> - have difficulties speaking English
> - live in a remote community [5]

The highest correlation was found mostly among factors expected within Lifestyle/Routine Activity Theory:

> [O]ur findings provide strong support for lifestyle/routine activity theory, moderate support for social deprivation and social disorganisation theories, but little or no support for cultural theories of violence.
>
> The salience of lifestyle/routine activity theory is attested to by the fact that high-risk alcohol consumption has the highest odds ratio (odds ratio 2.23) among all our predictors. Significant effects were also found for most other lifestyle/routine activity variables including residing in an area with neighbourhood problems (odds ratio 1.61), substance abuse (odds ratio 1.49),

---

4 Ibid, 217-21, 224-6.
5 Ibid, 2008, 222.

having a severe or profound disability (odds ratio 1.31), and living in a household with someone who has been charged with an offence (odds ratio 1.15).[6]

However, as noted by James Franklin, it is debatable whether Lifestyle/Routine Activity is an alternative "theory" in the sense of a causal theory. It is unsurprising that one indication of dysfunction, such as violence, will be highly correlated with others, such as risky drinking or criminal behaviour. That says nothing about the causal relations between those variables. Lifestyle/Routine Activity "theory" is just a name for "things go wrong together".[7]

Another theory does point to a variable that appears to be causal. The categorised Social Disorganisation Theory factor, "are members or have relatives who are members of the stolen generation", was found to be significantly correlated with the dependent variable " ... experienced threatened or physical violence ..."[8]

Indeed, by reading through the NATSISS tables, correlations identified by Snowball and Weatherburn are often readily apparent. For example, in the Northern Territory, the dependent variable "... experienced threatened or physical violence ..." in non-remote areas was 24.9%. While higher than in Northern Territory remote areas at 15.9%, the difference was "not significant", in line with the general finding that remoteness status was not a significant factor.[9] Nevertheless, the lower rate of "... experienced threatened or physical violence ..." in remote Northern Territory fits other factors identified by multivariate analysis, in particular the NATSISS finding of remote Northern Territory's lower levels of being a member of the stolen generation, lower levels of risky alcohol consumption, and lower levels of total neighbourhood/community problems.

---

6 Ibid, 230.
7 James Franklin, pers. comm., 2010.
8 Snowball and Weatherburn, 2008, 227.
9 ABS, *NATSISS 2002*, Cat. No. 4714.8.55.001. NT figures, "revised_4714_0 tables_nt".

The Australian Capital Territory pattern provides another depiction of the multivariate findings, where the dependent variable "... experienced threatened or physical violence ..." is higher at 33.3% than remote or non-remote Northern Territory. NATSISS also found that in the Australian Capital Territory, being a member of the stolen generation is nearly twice as high as the Northern Territory average; Australian Capital Territory's risky drinking is nearly twice as high as the Northern Territory average; and Australian Capital Territory's level of total neighbourhood/community problems is also above the Northern Territory average.[10]

Accordingly, a typical profile of an Indigenous person with a lower likelihood of having "experienced threatened or physical violence at least once in the 12 months preceding the survey" is a Northern Territory woman of a remote community. A typical profile of an Indigenous person with a higher likelihood of having "experienced threatened or physical violence at least once in the 12 months preceding the survey" is a man or woman living in the Australian Capital Territory.

To quote these NATSISS results or their Snowball and Weatherburn multivariate analysis as if reflecting a direct truth is an unwitting betrayal of violated remote Indigenous women, because it adds further to their invisibility and imperilled situation. This is happening in repeated echoes, with NATSISS results used repeatedly in major reports to inform us that the rate of having "experienced threatened or physical violence at least once in the 12 months preceding the

---

10 ABS, *NATSISS 2002*, "revised_4714_0 tables_nt", and "revised_4714_0 tables_act".

survey" is the same for remote and non-remote locations.[11] Hence it is important to correct this misleading conclusion by emphasising that more objective measures paint an almost opposite picture.

Anyone having some familiarity with more objective figures should be readily alerted to those NATSISS statistics. Of most concern, results for the dependent variable itself appear particularly anomalous, with NATSISS results relating to remoteness, gender and Indigenous identity (Northern Territory) being the opposite to those found by more objective measures. The following selected figures portray some anomalies here, with high levels in bold.

---

11 Examples,
– Brian Pink and Penny Albion, *The Health and Welfare of Australia's Aboriginal and Torres Strait Islander Peoples*, Australian Bureau of Statistics-Australian Institute of Health and Welfare (ABS-AIHW), 2008, Canberra, 147
– "Section 1: Overview of the Northern Territory Emergency Response", *Submission of Background Material to the Northern Territory Emergency Response Review Board*, 2008: http://www.fahcsia.gov.au/sa/indigenous/pubs/nter_reports/Documents/nter_review_submission/sec1.htm
– This "Section 1" source for remote/non-remote violence is: Fadwa Al-Yaman, Mieke Van Doeland and Michelle-Wallis, *Family Violence among Aboriginal and Torres Strait Islander Peoples*, AIHW, Canberra, Nov 2006, AIHW cat. no. IHW 17 (page 42). However, Al-Yaman *et al* provide important cautionary passages regarding NATSISS data collection on violence, see 8.3 Recommendations: http://www.aihw.gov.au/publications/ihw/fvaatsip/fvaatsip.pdf
– *A Social and Cultural Profile of Aboriginal and Torres Strait Islander People in Canberra*, authorised by Lincoln Hawkins, Australian Capital Territory Chief Minister's Dept, Canberra City, August 2004, 65: http://www.actdgp.asn.au/content/Document/Social%20and%20cultural%20profile %20of%20Aboriginal%20and%20Torres%20Strait%20Islander%20people%20in%20Canberra.pdf

## 1. NATSISS 2002 "whether the respondent had experienced threatened or physical violence at least once in the 12 months preceding the survey" (15+ years of age unless stated)[12]

NT Indig remote = 15.9%　NT Indig non-remote = **24.9%**　ACT Indig = **33.3%**
Aust Indig remote = 22.7%　　　Aust Indig non-remote = 25%
NT Indig male = **21.6%**　　　　NT Indig female = 13.5%
Aust Indig male = 25.7%　　　　Aust Indig female = 23.1%
NT Indig total (18+ years) = 14.2%　NT non-Indig total (18+ years) = **16.0%**

## 2. Productivity Commission murder and assaults per 100,000 (police figures)

2005[13] (for Northern Territory)

NT Indig total victims murder = 18.2　　NT Indig female victims murder = 19.9

NT non-Indig total victims murder = 0.7 NT non-Indig female victims murder = nil or rounded to zero

NT Indig total victims assault = 3783.1　　NT Indig female victims assault = **6211.3**

NT non-Indig total victims assault = 913.8　NT non-Indig female victims assault = 780.2

1999-2000 to 2004-2005[14] (for Australia)

Aust Indig homicide remote + very remote = **13.1-16.7**
Aust Indig homicide major cities and inner regional = 4.6-4.9
Aust non-Indig homicide across all areas ranged from 1.4-2.4

---

12　ABS, *NATSISS 2002*, "revised_4714_0 tables_nt" , and "revised_4714_0 tables_act" .
13　Productivity Commission, *Overcoming Indigenous Disadvantage: Headline Indicators 2007*, Canberra, 3.119: www.pc.gov.au/gsp
14　Ibid, 3.100.

3. MJA Indigenous hospitalisation for head injury due to assault per 100,000, 1999-2005 (Q, WA, SA and NT hospital data)[15]

Rural + remote = 1499.7

Metropolitan = 214.8

Male = 767.4

Female = 940.4

NATSISS itself contains often divergent results between remote versus non-remote participant reportage of more direct, personal experiences of violence, and for reportage of more indirect violence on others in the family, neighbourhood or community. The following comparisons show this, with Snowball and Weatherburn's dependent variable in bold to illustrate the problem.

|  | NT | | Qld | | ACT[16] |
|---|---|---|---|---|---|
|  | remote | non-remote | remote | non-remote | |
| 1. % Victim of physical or threatened violence in last year | **15.9** | **24.9** | **29.7** | **25.4** | **33.3** |
| 2. % Experienced personal stressors – Abuse or violent crime | 12.9 | 9.0 | 33.1 | 6.5 | 21.0 |
| 3. % Experienced personal stressors – Witness to violence | 33.9 | 8.7 | 42.0 | 10.9 | 17.2 |
| 4. % Neighbourhood/community problems – Family violence | 36.2 | 16.9 | 64.5 | 13.6 | 7.5 |
| 5. % Neighbourhood/community problems – Assault | 42.4 | 11.7 | 58.4 | 8.4 | 9.1 |
| 6. % Neighbourhood/community problems – Sexual assault | 9.5 | 3.1 | 37.9 | 4.4 | 2.6 |

Apart from the dependent variable, nearly every violence measure is higher in remote areas, in most cases markedly. A partial

---

15 Lisa M. Jamieson, James E. Harrison and Jesia G. Berry, "Hospitalisation for head injury due to assault among Indigenous and non-Indigenous Australians, July 1999-June 2005", *Medical Journal of Australia (MJA)*, Vol. 188, No. 10, 19 May 2008, 576-579: http://www.mja.com.au/public/issues/188_10_190508/jam11393_fm.html

16 ABS, *NATSISS 2002*, "revised_4714_0 tables_nt"; "revised_4714_0 tables_qld"; and, "revised_4714_0 tables_act"

explanation might be that non-remote participants with predominantly white neighbours would tend to have less exposure to "neighbourhood problems" of violence. However, the lower level of "personal stressors" of violence reported by non-remote Indigenous participants suggests that factors independent of "(white) neighbourhood", such as less violent household or family lives, are also key to their lower experience of violent personal stressors.

Above all, these personal and neighbourhood violence stressors portray a picture of a very violent remote Aboriginal Australia. Hence, the overall result indicated by the NATSISS figures that people tend *less* likely to be victims of violence in locations of *higher* levels of violence in the family, household, community or neighbourhood is just not credible. According to NATSISS, the locations and gender with the *lowest* "victimisation to violence" are those that generate the *highest* objective levels of violence including homicide as recorded by police and hospitals – viz. remote Northern Territory and Northern Territory women – a conclusion which just defies credibility. Is the manner in which these figures are so disparate, plus the fact that the more indirect NATSISS violence results – witness, family, neighbourhood and community – are aligned with police and hospital data, revealing to us the remote victims' silence? Just as a dimming star reveals an invisible planet, perhaps these beclouded NATSISS victim figures catch the silence of the most voiceless and victimised.[17]

To add to the beclouding of victims' voices, NATSISS also produced results that appeared to indicate that remote Northern Territory has a *lower* overall level of neighbourhood stressors, in alignment with its lower level of the dependent variable "... experienced threatened or physical violence ...". The Australian Capital Territory was found to have *higher* neighbourhood stressor levels than remote Northern

---

[17] See ABC News, "Many Indigenous too scared to report abuse", 21 January 2011: http://www.abc.net.au/news/stories/2011/01/21/3118796.htm

Territory, in alignment with the Australian Capital Territory's higher level of the dependent variable " ... experienced threatened or physical violence ...". NATSISS results for "Total with neighbourhood/community problems" for remote Northern Territory, non-remote Northern Territory, and Australian Capital Territory are as follows:

**Total with neighbourhood/community problems (%)** [18]

| | |
|---|---|
| NT remote: | 67.8 |
| NT non-remote: | 81.9 |
| ACT | 77.6 |

Given the higher remote Northern Territory *violence* results in the "neighbourhood community problems" list, how could this have happened? NATSISS has thirteen rather wide-ranging sub-factors placed under the heading "Neighbourhood/community problems", courageously defined as available for cumulative treatment. These sub-factors vary in results, so that their cumulative treatment presents a hazardous interpretive undertaking.

Making the situation even more befuddled and misleading, for four of these sub-factors, data was not collected for the remote Northern Territory tally. This would tend to deflate the cumulative results for remote Northern Territory, further shrouding the critically important, high violence sub-factors for remote Northern Territory within the sum "Total with neighbourhood/community problems" and "No neighbourhood/community problems reported". This has remote Northern Territory looking pretty good. The neighbourhood/community problems list, with the highest tally out of the three locations in bold, readily shows this issue.

---

18 ABS, *NATSISS 2002*, "revised_4714_0 tables_nt" , and "revised_4714_0 tables_act" .

**Neighbourhood/community problems**[19]

(Data for these problems marked * collected for non-remote areas only)

|  | NT Remote | NT Non-remote | ACT |
|---|---|---|---|
| Theft | 35.5 | 47.4 | 53.4 |
| Problems involving youth | 47.6 | 25.1 | 22.8 |
| Prowlers/loiterers* | – | 17.0 | 12.5 |
| Vandalism | 39.6 | 26.4 | 31.3 |
| Dangerous or noisy driving* | – | 49.3 | 46.3 |
| Alcohol | 45.4 | 33.7 | 15.7 |
| Illegal drugs | 36.8 | 18.4 | 22.8 |
| Family violence | 36.2 | 16.9 | 7.5 |
| Assault | 42.4 | 11.7 | 9.1 |
| Sexual assault | 9.5 | 3.1 | 2.6 |
| Problems with neighbours* | – | 17.6 | 15.7 |
| Levels of neighbourhood conflict | 30.7 | 10.5 | 9.0 |
| Level of personal safety day or night* | – | 9.2 | 7.4 |
| Total with neighbourhood/community problems | 67.8 | 81.9 | 77.6 |
| No neighbourhood/community problems reported | 31.1 | 15.4 | 20.1 |

(Respondents may have included more than one response category)

How did NATSISS, and Snowball and Weatherburn's analysis of it, produce such discordant results? Franklin argues,

> It is a platitude that the robustness of a statistical analysis relies on the quality of the variables. The NATSISS is a "nationally representative survey of over 9000 Indigenous Australians" (p.217), who fill out the ABS questionnaire. It is a self-reporting, voluntary survey, with unavoidably more scope for subjectivity and variations in willingness and ability for participation and disclosure than other more objective measures such as police and hospital statistics. In particular, the variable, "whether the

---

19 Ibid, "revised_4714_0 tables_nt", and "revised_4714_0 tables_act".

respondent had experienced threatened or physical violence" as reported by the respondent, is not the same as violence. That is for two reasons: the mismatch between threatened and actual violence, and the mismatch between report and reality.[20]

First, there is no indication in the dependent variable regarding what proportion is threatened, or actual, violence. That is significant, given the likelihood of different perceptions of the seriousness of threats, depending on cultural factors.[21] These were asked as two questions but "the ABS collapsed responses from these two questions into a single variable".[22] We need to consider the possibility that in urban populations, a more mainstream intolerance for violence means that being threatened with violence is a memorable devastating event, while in some remote communities actual, physical violence might be so high that threatened violence barely registers. Where the threat of violence is pervasive and "normal", reporting of perceived threats is less likely.[23] Also violence is still an accepted instrument of punishment and payback in much of remote Australia. Do the victims of such violence view themselves as victims of violence, or as transgressors who received justly deserved punishment? Perhaps there are cultures and circumstances where the more subject to violence a person is, the less able they are to "name" it?

The 1994 NATSISS reported only half the level of threatened or physical violence of the 2002 NATSISS (13%). Researchers suspected under-reporting in 1994, which if true suggests very large shifts or inconsistency in reporting of this "furry" variable.[24]

The second dubious feature of the dependent variable concerns

---

20 Franklin, pers. comm., 2010.
21 Ibid, 2010.
22 Kyllie Cripps, Catherine Bennett, Lyle Gurrin and David Studdert, "Victims of violence among Indigenous mothers living with dependent children", *MJA*, 191 (9), 2009: http://www.mja.com.au/public/issues/191_09_021109/cri10621_fm.html
23 Franklin, pers. comm., 2009.
24 Ibid.

the reliability of reporting the threatened or physical violence. Did conditions assist respondents to answer openly? NATSISS describes the conditions of interviews in communities:

> In communities, the interviewers were accompanied, wherever possible, by local Indigenous facilitators, who assisted in the conduct and completion of the interviews. The Indigenous facilitators explained the purpose of the survey to respondents, introduced the interviewers, assisted in identifying the usual residents of a household and in locating residents who were not at home, and assisted respondents in understanding questions where necessary.[25]

Local Indigenous facilitators may hamper victim reportage of violence. Jenness Warin states that these facilitators are likely to "have a better understanding of English" and thus would tend to have higher status, which could hamper a vulnerable victim's openness.[26] Moreover, the community setting itself is problematic. As Warin emphasises, people living in remote communities, and people who have experienced extremely violent environments, are unlikely to respond in communal settings.[27] Furthermore, as Franklin points out, in small communities the interview is likely mediated by someone who has close kin connections with both the victim and perpetrator of any violence. It is likely that in many cases the "blow-in" interviewer takes away an inaccurate report of any violence that may be occurring. In short, taking reported violence, either threatened or actual, as indicating the true level of violence is naïve. Add the mismatch

---

25 ABS, *NATSISS 2002*, 4714.0.55.002 *NATSISS: Data Reference Package* 2002, "Explanatory Notes", par. 22.

26 Warin, pers. comm., 2009. Also, Hughes wrote in relation to "homeland" dwellings, "NATSISS gave surprisingly high figures for ... adequate kitchen and bathroom equipment". Hughes comments, "Because of widespread illiteracy, census forms have typically been filled in by the consultants who contract census work" who may well not have seen the many sickness-inducing, derelict, toilet and kitchen facilities: Hughes, 2007, 135.

27 Warin, pers. comm., 2009.

between this dependent variable and the harder crime and hospital data, and any conclusions based on it are misinterpretation.[28]

Furthermore, this variable's questions were worded differently for remote areas in most states, to "minimise language and comprehension difficulties".[29] For remote areas:

> 608. In the last year, did anybody start a fight with you or beat you up?
>
> 609. In the last year, did anybody try to or say they were going to hit you or fight with you?[30]
>
> In non-remote areas:
>
> Q01VIC. In the last 12 months, did anyone, including people you know, use physical force or violence against you?
>
> Q02VIC. In the last 12 months, did anyone, including people you know, try to use or threaten to use physical force or violence against you?
>
> Q03VIC. Were any of those threats made in person?[31]

While these word differences between the remote and non-remote questionnaires were aimed to maximise comparable results, there is room for doubt. Nicholas Biddle and Boyd Hunter observe that "[t]here are arguments made for and against the results from the two questions being comparable or not".[32] In particular, the terms "fight" and "beat you up" can evoke a range of meanings and responses in remote Australia. Up north, observes Warin, "did anyone start a fight"

---

28 Franklin, pers. comm., 2009.
29 Cripps *et al*, 2009.
30 Ibid; and ABS, *NATSISS 2002, Indigenous Social Survey 2002 Remote Areas Questionnaire*, 37 (ABS underlining).
31 ABS, *NATSISS 2002, Indigenous Social Survey 2002 Non-Remote Areas Questionnaire*, 62 (ABS underlining).
32 Nicholas Biddle and Boyd Hunter, "Selected methodological issues for analysis of the 2002 NATSISS", in B.H. Hunter (ed), *Assessing the Evidence on Indigenous Socioeconomic Outcomes: A focus on the 2002 NATSISS*, CAEPR, Research Monograph No. 26, 2006 Canberra, 39: http://epress.anu.edu.au/caepr_series/no_26/pdf/c26-whole.pdf

is a colloquialism for "someone has initiated a response so as (1) to get what they want – called humbugging, bullying, harassment; or (2) to diffuse a situation eg 'are you trying to fight with me ...'"[33]

Mick Dodson and Boyd Hunter observe that,

> [t]he use of plain English in such a sensitive area might be seen as more emotive by some respondents, and open to subjective interpretation of what a "real" fight is by other respondents. While there are likely to be substantial variations in the cultural standards of what constitutes a "fight" (or a "beating") in the Indigenous and other Australian communities ... [34]

These observations are important. Perhaps the broad meaning and raw emotionality of these terms were enough to close down responses to this question among some remote area participants.

Two other factors identified by Snowball and Weatherburn's multivariate analysis as being significantly correlated with victimisation to violence – the social disorganisation factor "membership of the stolen generation", and the lifestyle/routine activity factor "risky alcohol consumption" – also warrant assessment. One of the lowest NATSISS areas for identifying as part of the stolen generation, either as self or a relative, is remote Northern Territory.

Significant correlation between the same 2002 NATSISS variants "victim of physical or threatened violence in last 12 months" and "removal from natural family" was also emphasised recently by Kyllie Cripps et al.[35] Cripps et al focused their univariate and multivariable analyses on the 3589 NATSISS participating mothers who "reported

---

33 Warin, pers. comm., 2009.
34 Mick Dodson and Boyd Hunter, "Crime and Justice Issues", in Hunter, 2006, 255.
35 With thanks to Warin for informing me of the video interview of Cripps where she speaks about the findings presented in Cripps et al 2009: "A violent wake up call: the lasting impact of removal", *From the Studio*, The Melbourne Newsroom, The University of Melbourne, 9 November 2009: http://newsroom.melbourne.edu/studio/ep-17?video=1&play=1 which led to my analysis of Cripps et al, 2009.

living with dependent children younger than 15 years". They write:

> There was a strong positive association between being a victim of violence and having been removed from one's natural family during childhood ... In non-remote areas, mothers with this history had 72% greater odds of being a victim of violence than those without this history ... and in remote areas, the odds were nearly three times greater ...
>
> Our study breaks new ground by identifying statistically significant characteristics of victims of violence from a national sample. Our finding that removal from natural family is strongly associated with increased risk of victimhood in both remote and non-remote areas ... is especially troubling ... this result highlights the formidable and complex challenges that confront efforts to combat violence in Indigenous communities.[36]

Cripps *et al* emphasise the "strong positive association between being a victim of violence and having been removed from one's natural family during childhood". They could have provided a more complete, contextualised picture had they pointed out that a large majority of participants did not report being removed as a child. Out of their sample of 3589, only 276 (7.7%) reported removal from their natural family as a child, while 3313 (92.3%), did not. In remote and non-remote areas, this rises to 96.1% of participants who did not report being removed as a child. Overall, 86% of those reporting violence reported no experience of removal of self as a child.[37]

However, the 276 who reported removal did report victimisation to violence at a significantly higher rate,. Of these 276, 129 (46.8%) reported victimisation to violence in the last year. Of the 3313 who did not report removal as a child, 793 (23.9%) reported victimisation to violence in the last year. That is, from those who reported removal as a child, this 7.7% included 14% of those who reported victimisation

---

36 Cripps *et al*, 2009.
37 Ibid.

to violence, or nearly double the overall rate.[38]

Of the 1713 remote and very remote area participants in their sample, only 67 (3.9%) reported removal from their natural family as a child, while 1646 (96.1%), did not. Of the 1646 who did not report removal as a child, 359 (21.8%) reported victimisation to violence in the last year. Of the 67 who reported removal as a child, 27 (40.3%) reported victimisation to violence in the last year. That is, those who reported removal as a child, reported victimisation to violence at nearly double the overall rate.[39]

Presentation of these raw percentages conveys the strong positive association found by Cripps *et al*, between reporting of removal as child and reporting of victimisation to violence as an adult, among NATSISS participant mothers with children younger than 15. However there are major difficulties with Cripps *et al*'s assertions. As with Snowball and Weatherburn's claims regarding the NATSISS results for "victim to violence" and "stolen generation" membership, the first problem concerns the key "victim to violence" variant. To state it again, remote Northern Territory, which records one of the lowest levels of removal from natural family in NATSISS, is the region with the *highest* objective measures for Indigenous violence including homicide. The conspicuous deviation of the NATSISS "victim to violence" measure from more objective Indigenous violence measures renders this variant worse than useless for analysis with any other correlate, including removal from natural family. Indeed, this anomaly's only value may be its provision of a rare glimpse at a massive victim silence in remote areas. But who knows the pattern of this silence, what variants compound this silence, beyond its seeming association with remote areas, and perhaps femaleness? Any results derived from this NATSISS "victim to violence" variant, including

---

38 Ibid.
39 Ibid.

those asserted by Cripps *et al*, are either meaningless, not credible, or worse, misleading.

Another major problem is that Cripps *et al* promote the idea that this statistical association of removal as a child with later victimisation to violence, means that removal is causal of the later victimisation.[40] It is well-documented that in the last three or four decades our governments have been reluctant to remove Indigenous children from their natural families, in an effort to avoid the damage, guilt or accusation of undertaking the race-based child removal of earlier eras. Nevertheless, the rate of Indigenous child removals from the 1970s until today is still extremely high, because the alarming rate of severe neglect and physical and sexual abuse of Aboriginal children within their families has given government workers no other safe option for these children. To portray such child removal as the primary villain as Cripps *et al* do is a breathtaking avoidance of acknowledging the family situations that have led to these more recent child removals. Further, it is a breathtaking avoidance of discussing even the possibility that it is the toxic family situations that lead to child removal that might be a primary cause of vulnerability to violence in adult life. As Franklin states, "it is hardly surprising that those who spent their early years in conditions of extreme neglect and violence should grow into adults with many problems".[41]

Avoidance of discussion of family violence as a cause of child removal is a significant policy problem. Indeed, Rosemary Neill wrote that the *Bringing Them Home* report

> is vague ... about the circumstances that led to so many abused, neglected or alienated indigenous children ending up in foster homes or the juvenile justice system during the same decade [the 1990s]. Its section on family violence as a cause of removals takes up less than a page. Yet such violence is endemic among

---
40 Franklin, pers. comm., 2009.
41 Ibid.

> so many indigenous communities ... In this uneasy silence, one shocking fact has gone almost unnoticed: since the BTH was released, the rate of removals of indigenous children has actually *risen*. Indeed, it has soared.[42]

Removing children from their natural family is one of the saddest events, and the pain that children suffer due to the removal itself, even when they are placed in a loving home, is undeniable. However, there is one even sadder event, and that is when a child receives permanent psychological, mental or physical damage or worse, loses their life, because they were not removed in time from their dangerous family environment.

Articles like Cripps *et al*'s that do not acknowledge the sad necessity for child removal but only condemn it, fuel the potent ideological idea that removing Aboriginal children is an intrinsically racist act. This ideology has caused authorities to fail Aboriginal children by not rescuing them from dangerous families.[43] Such articles imply that the solution to the pain of Indigenous child removal resides in simply no longer removing Indigenous children, when what is actually needed is a better understanding of how to prevent the dangerous Indigenous family situations that necessitate child removal.[44] Furthermore, Cripps *et al*'s and Snowball and Weatherburn's granting of undeserved credibility to 2002 NATSISS data leads us further away from a proper understanding.

Regarding the higher percentage of "removal from natural family" in cities and regional areas (both victims and "non-victims"), we need to consider that a significant percentage of remote area children removed from family might be taken to non-remote locations (and less often perhaps, from non-remote to remote locations). This further compounds the difficulty of comparative analysis regarding

---

42 Neill, 2002, 166-7.
43 See Ibid, esp. 156-7.
44 Ibid, 156-7.

remote and non-remote locations, child removal, and victimisation to violence. Knowing where the child removal occurred, and where the child was taken, is essential to understanding.[45]

Cripps et al highlight another NATSISS result, that "having a partner or husband residing in the dwelling" is associated with "lower risk of victimhood". In cities plus regional areas, 28% of those who reported victimisation to violence had their partner/husband in the household, while 46% of those who did not report violence had a partner/husband in the household. In remote and very remote areas, 45% of those who reported victimisation to violence had their partner/husband in the household, while 58% of those who did not report violence had a partner/husband in the household.[46] Cripps et al write:

> Multivariable analysis showed that the presence of a male partner in the house reduced mothers' odds of experiencing violence by half in both remote and non-remote areas. This is a novel finding in Australian research on Indigenous violence, although previous international research has shown higher rates of violence among divorced and separated women. One explanation is that a regular male presence, a stable relationship, or both, deter attackers. An alternative explanation that warrants serious consideration and research is under-reporting: respondents may have been reluctant to report their experiences of violence if their partner was the perpetrator. A third explanation, given that we observed a correlation but cannot infer causality, is that women harmed by cohabiting partners are less likely to continue living with them.[47]

While Cripps et al's presentation and discussion of these NATSISS results is accurate, precision would have increased had they written "... reduced mothers' odds of *reporting* experience of violence ...". This "imprecision" exacerbates the main problem here, namely Cripps et al's brief and underdeveloped discussion of this result, especially

---
45  Franklin, pers. comm, 2009.
46  Cripps et al, 2009, Table 2.
47  Ibid.

given that it concerns the critically important and widespread problem of Aboriginal domestic violence. In particular, given that numerous papers on Aboriginal violence have uncritically drawn on NATSISS data, the issue of under-reporting warrants major discussion in such a keynote article as Cripps *et al*'s, rather than their brief albeit respectful mention of under-reporting as a possible explanation.

It has been known for decades that violence from a partner or spouse is under-reported by the victim, particularly while still living with the violent partner. This renders research and accurate data collection regarding partner and spousal assault especially difficult. In 1994, Elizabeth Stanko wrote that all crime surveys "should be considered to be under-reporting incidence and prevalence of violence within families".[48] In 1986, the Western Australian Task Force on Domestic Violence identified under-reporting by victims as a major problem regarding data collection for domestic violence. As stated in the 1987 Report of the South Australian Domestic Violence Council,

> Women, as victims, are reluctant to inform anyone of the behaviour of their violent partners. Thus such sources will only include those who have presented for assistance and have identified themselves or have been identified as victims of domestic violence.[49]

In 2009, the Queensland Commissioner of Police, Bob Atkinson, made a similar observation:

> Domestic and family violence is difficult to accurately measure – due to the complex cyclic and private nature of domestic and

---

48  Elizabeth Stanko, *Looking Back, Looking Forward: Two Decades and Shifting Perspectives on Familial Violence,* 42, in Chris Sumner, Mark Israel, Michael O'Connell and Rick Sarre (eds), *Proceedings of a symposium held 21-26 August 1994,* AIC, Canberra, January 1996: http://www.aic.gov.au/en/publications/previous%20series/proceedings/1-27/27.aspx

49  South Australian Domestic Violence Council (SADVC), *Report of the South Australian Domestic Violence Council,* 1987, Women's Advisers' Office, Dept. of the Premier and Cabinet, South Australia, 1987, 187.

family violence, it is difficult to accurately measure how many Queensland families are affected. It is not until the threat of violence escalates to actual physical or sexual violence, that the hidden nature of domestic and family violence may be revealed.[50]

In my field work interviews there were both Aboriginal and non-Aboriginal women who spoke about their experiences of domestic violence from a previous partner or spouse. However no women, with perhaps one exception, spoke of violence from a present spouse or live-in partner, although I knew that domestic violence with present spouses or live-in partners was occurring in these neighbourhoods. At a nightclub I was attending, one Aboriginal woman in a drunken and apologetic state for punching another woman for dancing with "her man", did reveal to us that

> she was feeling very jealous and insecure, and that's why she lashed out ... She said that her boyfriend had beaten her up badly at another club the night before, bashed her face up against the toilet door there, until blood poured out of her forehead and nose, and ran down all over her face. She did not say why he did this to her.[51]

I do not know if her boyfriend was a live-in partner. Also, her revelation occurred in emotionally charged circumstances, and the woman initiated the revelation in an attempt to gain some understanding for her own violent actions.

Since the 1980s, phone-in surveys for domestic violence have been identified as having some advantages, in particular because

> they provide the anonymity which lessens women's fear of reprisal and allows them to disclose information regarding family violence. Anonymity is a key element in encouraging a

---

50 Bob Atkinson, "A Message from Commissioner of Police", Queensland Police Service Domestic Violence page, 2009: http://www.police.qld.gov.au/programs/crimePrevention/dv/

51 Field work, mid 1990s.

woman to feel it is safe to disclose that she or her children are victims of violence in the home. Their success can be gauged by the numbers of women who make use of the opportunity to disclose a situation of family violence.[52]

This raises the issue of reduced privacy, anonymity and phone access facing Aboriginal women victims in small, isolated communities. Remote area Indigenous women have less access to home phones, and if they did, could they call in secret as readily as those in urban areas? Mobile phones are increasing remote phone access, but secrecy is still difficult, as mobile phones record phone numbers and the times of calls made and received, texts and more, and can easily be taken from their owner. Kimm wrote of further phone difficulties faced by remote area Aboriginal women, such as the deliberate wrecking of community telephones.[53]

Regarding NATSISS face-to-face interviews, the structure of the interview process rendered it less secret than in non-remote areas.[54] The fear that Aboriginal women have of violent reprisals if they speak out or seek help,[55] feelings of self-blame, loyalty to their men, and women's community powerlessness, can have profound silencing effects upon victims. Anonymity is often the essential enabling factor regarding speaking out about victimisation to violence. Hence, the very process that no doubt assisted remote area people to participate in the survey – the provision of a local Indigenous facilitator – might also be a cause of increased silencing among remote area participating women about one variable – their experience of violence from their partner.

---

52 Family Violence Professional Education Task Force, *Family Violence: Everybody's Business, Somebody's Life,* The Federation Press, Leichhardt, NSW, 1991, 68-69.
53 Kimm, 2004, 23.
54 See ABS, *NATSISS 2002*, "Explanatory Notes", 4712.0.55.002- *National Indigenous Social Survey: Data Reference Package, 2002,* par. 22; Warin, pers. comm., 2009.
55 See Kimm, 2004, 18-19.

Perhaps the most telling suggestion of silencing, and the need for more discussion than provided by Cripps *et al*, can be deduced from the police and hospital statistics regarding the relationship of victim to perpetrator in homicides and assaults. In 2006-07,

- 45.2% of Indigenous homicides involved "intimate partners",
- 32.3% involved "other family members",
- 22.6% involved "friends and acquaintances", and
- 0% involved strangers.

The profile for non-Indigenous homicides in 2006-07 is:

- 22.5% of non-Indigenous homicides involved "intimate partners",
- 19.5% involved "other family members",
- 29% involved "friends and acquaintances", and
- 16.5% involved strangers.[56]

For Indigenous victims, the main source of lethal violence is from their intimate partner and family.[57] While "intimate partner" does not necessarily mean live-in partner or spouse, these figures portray higher lethal victimisation of Indigenous people from Indigenous partners and other family members – which would include those residing in the same house – compared with mortal danger from non-intimate, non-family members. Furthermore, there were more domestically motivated Indigenous killings than for non-Aboriginal homicides. In the same year, 77% of Indigenous homicides involved the key factor "domestic altercation", while for non-Indigenous homicide the rate for "domestic altercation" was 42%. However, "domestic altercation" here includes "jealousy, *desertion/termination* and argument of a

---

[56] Productivity Commission, *Overcoming Indigenous Disadvantage: Key Indicators*, 2009, Table 4A.11.19.
[57] Note that the Productivity Commission, 2009, Table 4A.11.19 and 4A.11.22. do not provide separate data for male and female homicide victims according to type of relationship.

domestic nature" (my emphasis), and so these high figures include cessation of intimate relationships, which would include cessation of live-in partnerships.[58] The extent to which Cripps *et al*'s findings from NATSISS here might be reflecting the notoriously dangerous days and months immediately after a woman leaves a violent partner is unknown.

Non-fatal hospitalisation for assault figures include a category "Family violence assaults – Spouse/domestic partner", thereby suggesting a more direct picture of live-in partner violence. It is here that we see the high vulnerability of Indigenous females to severe spouse/domestic partner assault. In 2006-07, 39.3% of the total 3268 non-fatal hospitalised assaults for Indigenous females were perpetrated by a spouse/domestic partner. For non-Indigenous ("other") females, it was 39.0% of the total 3858. While relationship category percentage distribution is very similar across identities here, the rate of violence victimisation is very much greater for Indigenous women. Hence in 2006-07, Indigenous women experienced a "non-fatal hospitalisation assault by spouse/domestic partner" rate of 5.4 per 1000, which is recorded by the Productivity Commission as 34.8 times the non-Indigenous ("other") female rate of 0.2 per 1000. For total non-fatal hospitalised assaults, the Indigenous female victim rate was 13.6 per 1000, which is 34.4 times higher than the rate of 0.4 per 1000 for non-Indigenous ("other") females.[59]

It is noteworthy that 47.6% of non-fatal hospitalised assaults for Indigenous females (49.9% for non-Indigenous ["other"] females) were not family or partner assaults.[60] In the light of anthropologist M.J. Meggitt's observation that among the "Walbiri" people, a man is obliged to physically defend his wife in her fights with other people,

---

58 Ibid, Table 4A.11.22, including especially, note (h).
59 Ibid, Table 4A.11.2. Note that 5.4/0.2 = 27, so it is assumed that "0.2" is rounded upwards in Table 4A.11.2.
60 Calculations derived from Ibid, Table 4A.11.2.

and the traditional role of male as protector in most cultures,[61] perhaps Indigenous women with the deterrence of a live-in partner are less subjected to outsider violence. Further to this, the Mullighan Inquiry records the following from a police report regarding a "sex-for-petrol suspect" from a remote community:

> The girls are believed to have been chosen by him due to their petrol sniffing and because they do not have fathers or older male family members in the community to protect them. [62]

Perhaps Cripps *et al*'s identification of recorded reduction in a woman's victimisation to violence when a male partner resides in her home reflects these protective roles. However, this is shifting into conjecture, relying as it does on the highly anomalous NATSISS results for the variable, "victim of physical or threatened violence in last 12 months".

Most critically, the homicide and hospitalisation figures recorded by the Productivity Commission signal a clear caution regarding interpretation of Cripps *et al*'s finding of lower victimisation to violence if the Indigenous woman lives with a partner. Objective statistics indicate that the domestic sphere is the most likely realm for victimisation to serious injurious and lethal violence for Indigenous women, and in this most dangerous sphere, the most likely offender is her partner.[63]

The NATSISS result of a high connection between alcohol and violence is also dubious.[64] Risky alcohol consumption is shown in

---

[61] M.J. Meggitt, *Desert People: A study of the Walbiri Aborigines of Central Australia*, Angus and Robertson, Sydney, 1962, 95.

[62] Hon. E.P. Mullighan QC, *Children on Anangu Pitjantjatjara Yankunytjatjara (APY) Lands: Commission of Inquiry: A Report into Sexual Abuse* (Mullighan Inquiry), presented to the South Australian Parliament, April 2008, 51: http://www.sa.gov.au/subject/Crime,+justice+and+the+law/Mullighan+Inquiry/Children+on+the+APY+Lands#Commission

[63] Productivity Commission, 2009, Table 4A.11.2.

[64] For a valuable critique of NATSISS 2002 regarding its alcohol consumption data, see Tanya Chikritzhs and Maggie Brady, "Substance use in the 2002 NATSISS", Chapter 18 in Hunter (ed), 2006, 231-247.

both NATSISS and other studies to be similar across remote and non-remote locations. In NATSISS, remote Australia records a risky alcohol consumption level of 16.8%, and for non-remote Australia, 14.5%, with abstinence levels much higher in remote locations (46.4% as opposed to non-remote at 24.7%). The Productivity Commission also depicts similarity across locations for high-risk drinking, although both risky drinking and abstinence results are much lower for both locations than in NATSISS.

**Indigenous alcohol consumption levels by location 2004-05 (%)**[65]

|  | high risk | low risk | never |
|---|---|---|---|
| major cities | 8.0 | 36.5 | 7.0 |
| remote | 8.2 | 31.4 | 10.6 |

In NATSISS, remote Northern Territory records both low victimisation to violence and a low risky alcohol consumption result of 7.8% (low compared with other NATSISS risky alcohol consumption results). However, this is a "default" result, as the NATSISS subjective measure of victimisation to violence is a flawed instrument, and more objective measures confirm that violence is actually *high* in remote Northern Territory.

Hence to claim, as Snowball and Weatherburn do, that alcohol as a major factor in Indigenous violence is confirmed by NATSISS is highly problematic. I urge you to read Tanya Chikritzhs and Maggie Brady's solid critique of the 2002 NATSISS regarding its alcohol data. At one point, Chikritzhs and Brady state:

> The ability to corroborate findings between various sources of information is indicative of the level of confidence that can be placed in the results of any particular study. In the case of the 2002 NATSISS and its findings on substance use, the corroborative evidence is weak.[66]

---

65 Productivity Commission, 2009, Table 10A.3.9.
66 Chikritzhs and Brady, 2006, 245.

They express strong misgivings regarding accurate reportage in situations of non-confidentiality:

> The questioning in the 2002 NATSISS on alcohol and tobacco use was neither confidential nor self-completed. Respondents were asked whether they would like a one-on-one interview but, in practice, they often answered questions in the presence of other family members. With alcohol and drug use being highly personal, potentially embarrassing and inevitably sensitive, and with family members listening in, it is hardly surprising that many respondents would have been unwilling to provide accurate estimates.[67]

I now ask you to wonder anew about the widespread, seemingly naive acceptance among other analysts and report writers, of the 2002 NATSISS data on *violence*. Above all, Snowball and Weatherburn's, and Cripps *et al*'s central, dependent variable – the NATSISS subjective measure of victimisation to violence "experienced threatened or physical violence at least once in the 12 months preceding the survey" – is a face-to-face survey question demonstrably incapable of reflecting the harsh frequency and brutality of violence against Aboriginal women in remote Northern Territory. Hence, Snowball and Weatherburn's conclusion that the 2002 NATSISS does not support Cultural Theory for Aboriginal violence is rendered to be in my opinion dangerously misleading and meaningless.

## NATSISS, 2008

The Law and Justice figures of the 2008 NATSISS were released in December 2010. As recent reports, analyses and debates referring to NATSISS violence data have drawn from its 2002 survey, the 2002 data remain the main focus for this chapter. However, 2008 NATSISS statistics for Aboriginal violence again display puzzling results.[68]

---

67  Ibid., 246.
68  ABS, *NATSISS 2008*, 2010, 4714.0. Law and Justice excel cube.

For example in the Northern Territory, for the variable "Victim of physical or threatened violence in the last 12 months", the non-remote figure was 32.3%, and the remote/very remote figure was 20.0%. In apparent contrast, under the heading "Neighbourhood and Community problems/At least one neighbourhood/community problem present", the variable "Family violence" figure was 24.3% non-remote, and 34.1% remote/very remote; and the variable "Assault" figure was 21.6% non-remote, and 32.9% remote/very remote.[69]

Regarding Australia-wide, for the 2008 NATSISS variable "Victim of physical or threatened violence in the last 12 months", the scores were similar between non-remote (23.8%) and remote/very remote regions (21.3%).[70] These results do not alert us to the greater lethality of violence in remote areas. In the year 2006-07, the Australia-wide rate per 100,000 of Indigenous homicide victims in major cities was 1.8; in very remote areas it was 22.0.[71]

Moreover, the 2008 NATSISS has similar conditions for interviews in communities, such as "local Indigenous facilitators" and lack of privacy, that tend to dampen disclosure of violence. As alerted to me by Warin, the 2008 NATSISS has similar, significant exclusions:[72]

> The scope of the survey is all Indigenous people who were usual residents of private dwellings in Australia. Private dwellings are houses, flats, home units and any other structures used as private places of residence at the time of the survey. People usually resident in non-private dwellings, such as hotels, motels, hostels, hospitals, nursing homes, and short-stay caravan parks were not in scope. Usual residents are those who usually live in a particular dwelling and regard it as their own or main home.[73]

---

69 ABS, *NATSISS 2008*, Law and Justice Tables 1a, and 10.
70 Ibid, Law and Justice Table 1a.
71 Productivity Commission, 2009, Table 4A.11.15.
72 Warin, pers. comm., 2009, regarding ABS, *NATSISS 2008, Explanatory Notes*: http://www.abs.gov.au/AUSSTATS/abs@.nsf/Lookup/4714.0Explanatory%20Notes12008?OpenDocument
73 ABS, *NATSISS 2008, Explanatory Notes*, Par. 10.

Adds Warin, what about "those living in the long grass",[74] and what about women's shelters? While resulting in less than 6% under-coverage nationally,[75] the exclusions would fall more heavily on victims such as women fleeing violent husbands. Additionally, the 2008 NATSISS excluded household visitors, restricting inclusion to residents of six months or longer.[76] Transience is all too common among disaffected Aboriginal populations. Moreover, as identified by Franklin, how easy is it to answer questions about violence in a household overcrowded with uninvited, possibly troublesome kin?[77]

Other critical 2008 NATSISS exclusions relate to "issues arising in the field", resulting in under-coverage of 3.7% nationally due to:

- overlap with the Monthly Population Survey; and
- occupational, health and safety issues.[78]

This under-coverage might seem small, but concentrated exclusion of those at highest risk is likely. The most violent of households cause more than victim silence, but present occupational, health and safety issues that place the most vulnerable victims beyond even the chance of a household interview, as their homes are too dangerous for surveyors to enter.

**Conclusion**

The institutions that can and should assist remote community Aboriginal victims of violence with exemplary statistical collection and analysis are letting these victims down. Through poor design of survey collection and failure to adequately scrutinise results, they are collaborating in keeping these victims silent and invisible.

---

74  Warin, pers. comm., 2009.
75  ABS, *NATSISS 2008, Explanatory Notes*, Pars. 15 and 16.
76  Ibid, Par. 12.
77  Franklin, pers. comm., 2009.
78  ABS, *NATSISS 2008, Explanatory Notes*, Pars. 89 and 90.

Serious interpersonal violence in remote Aboriginal communities is catastrophically high, while Aboriginal people commit and suffer less violence in mainstream locations and amidst mainstream cultures. These facts sit uncomfortably with the ideology that Aboriginal suffering can be alleviated by returning to a more traditional lifestyle in self-determined communities. Such discomfort is blunting critical scrutiny of Aboriginal violence statistics even at the highest echelons of data analysis and report-writing. This is a national travesty.

# 2
# Interrupted memories

Few if any Aboriginal communities have a direct living memory or unbroken oral link with their pre-contact past. To a large extent, this applies to us all. British philosopher Kenan Malik argues that culture is just what we do. We are not fully mindful that we are practising our culture, or even "having" a culture.[1] Indeed, Malik suggests that a conscious, group culture that every people "wants to defend against the depredation of Western cultural imperialism" is a Western and recent concept.[2] Nevertheless, Aboriginal peoples' greater cultural upheaval and loss create problems of – some might say opportunity for – uncertainty and dispute regarding violence in pre-contact times, and whether traditional violence is a key factor today.

Has the relative peace and lower violence of the Mission era generated the living memory idea of a less violent pre-contact time? The Mission era and white law imposed decades-long suppression – though not elimination – of pre-contact violence. This has no doubt contributed to conflicting memories about Aboriginal life in times past. Aboriginal people interviewed one or two decades after Mission times tend to recall frequent and severe traditional violence. The following Aboriginal people's memories of violence in times past, mostly 1940s

---

[1] Kenan Malik, "Identity is that which is given", 2008: http://www.kenanmalik.com/essays/butterflies_identity.html (first published on butterfliesandwheels.com, 9 July 2008).
[2] Kenan Malik, "Mistaken identity", 2008: http://www.kenanmalik.com/essays/humanist_culture.html (first published in *New Humanist*, July/August 2008).

and earlier, were collected during or within two decades after Mission days, from the 1960s to the 1980s.

> *Waipuldanya, also named Phillip Roberts, of the Alawa people, Roper River.*
>
> a. A cuckolded husband is redressed by his sons and nephews. Twenty years ago they would have murdered both the woman and her lover. Today, having experienced the application of white-feller law to blackfeller crimes, they are content after a thorough beating with sticks.[3]
>
> b. Aboriginal children like watching fights, whether they are between women or men. In this way they acquire early knowledge of how to carry a spear, a boomerang, or a nulla-nulla. I must admit that the women were better teachers, if only because they fought twice as often.
>
> But being in a fight is better than watching one, and we attacked the girls – and were attacked – on the slightest pretext. Our stick fights were classics in canine ferocity ... and stopped only when threatened by the Elders.
>
> The lurid imprecations which accompanied these fights were learnt mostly from the women.
>
> "Rip ... with a yam stick!"
>
> "Brain ... with a boomerang!"
>
> "Break her legs with a nulla-nulla!"
>
> I often wondered what the missionaries thought – and especially their wives – when they saw us go to war, and overheard our battle cries. Perhaps they believed we were playing a game? Perhaps they didn't understand the words? There must have been some explanation for the fact that they did not interfere.
>
> I understand that white boys and girls overcome mutual enmity in their early teens and then show a disposition to pet and cuddle. There is no cuddling in the Alawa. We would rather fight than flirt.[4]

---

3 Waipuldanya (Phillip Roberts), narrated in Douglas Lockwood, *I, The Aboriginal*, Readers Book Club, Colorgravure Publications, 1964, 119.

4 Ibid, 106-7.

> c. It also happens that two men from eligible skins want the same unattached woman. Several men were Right-Side for Hannah when she was given to me. I was lucky that my inheritance was not disputed. Inevitably, a brutal fight with spears, boomerangs and nulla-nullas must have followed.
>
> There is just one solution to tribal triangles: the two men go to war until one is either killed or so badly injured that he loses his appetite for women for a long time. I remember one fight in which a man's spine was laid bare by a shovel-spear. And I have seen Wailbri and Pitjantjarra tribesmen in Central Australia whose bodies were a patchwork of scars from wounds inflicted in women-trouble fights.[5]

However, even these accounts would probably not faze those seeking to suppress traditional causes. Key Aboriginal violence reports including those by Bolger, Gordon *et al*, Paul Memmott *et al*, and Boni Robertson dismiss continuity by differentiating traditional from present-day violence. They emphasise that pre-contact violence was governed by rules, and operated within a level of safety and limitation. Colonisation did harm, they argue, by breaking down institutions of, and respect for, traditional law, thereby unleashing unrestricted, alcohol-fuelled violence. Bolger writes in her 1991 report:

> By traditional violence is meant the punishments for transgressions which were part of the means of social control in Aboriginal society and were meted out to both male and female offenders. Such physical punishments, which could involve spearing, beating, or even death, were not between individuals but were the responsibility of whole communities, both men and women. There were recognised punishments for specific transgressions and they were carried out by particular people under community control.[6]

A review undertaken for the Gordon Inquiry of 2002 offers a similar perspective:

---

5 Ibid, 114.
6 Bolger, 1991, 49.

> our review of the anthropological literature reveals examples of what, on the face of it, might be taken as instances of family violence or child abuse. But the literature also shows that such actions are invariably within the sphere of traditional practice, ritual or the operation of customary law. We have found little material which suggests that violence or abuse per se are condoned, or took place with impunity, outside traditionally regulated contexts.[7]

Kimm has well noted the reluctance in the Gordon Inquiry to acknowledge that customary law contained aspects that were abusive to the rights of young women and girls.[8]

The Memmott *et al* 2001 report, *Violence in Indigenous Communities*, records that "several researchers take the view that 'it is difficult to accept that wife beating is justified by tribal custom and such suggestions are misleading and defamatory'".[9] Regarding legal cases and whether a particular act of violence is traditional, Memmott *et al* write that

> while acknowledging that in many Indigenous communities an extention [sic] of the traditional concept of and acceptance of fighting behaviour still exists, for example, in the use of violence as payback, and as a way of redressing wrongs, there are other types of violence that should be classified outside of the defined

---

[7] K. Apted and M. Robinson, *Review of Anthropological Literature on Family Violence and Child Abuse in Aboriginal Communities*, Centre for Anthropological Research, Uni. of Western Australia, 2002, for and q. in Gordon *et al*, 2002, 69.

[8] Kimm, 2004, esp. 63-4, 87-9, 148.

[9] Paul Memmott, Rachael Stacy, Catherine Chambers and Catherine Keys, *Violence in Aboriginal Communities*, Report to the Crime Prevention Branch of the Attorney General's Dept, Canberra, 2001, 25: http://www.ema.gov.au/agd/www/rwpattach. nsf/viewasattachmentPersonal/(E24C1D4325451B61DE7F4F2B1E155715)~viol enceindigenous.pdf/$file/violenceindigenous.pdf quoting M. Brady, "Alcohol Use and Its Effects Upon Aboriginal Women", 1990, http://www.aic.gov.au/publications/previous%20series/proceedings/1-20/~/media/publications/proceedings/01/brady. ashx (Previously published in J. Vernon, (ed), *Alcohol and Crime*, AIC, Canberra, 1990 (AIC conference proceedings; no.1, 135-147).

boundaries of traditional violence, for example, child abuse and rape, spousal violence, gang rape, suicide and psychological violence.[10]

There are problems with these assertions on several fronts.

## Problem One. There are traditional precedents for a range of interpersonal violence

The assertion that spousal violence cannot be classified as part of traditional violence is wrong. Child abuse and rape, and gang rape, also have traditional, formalised precedents, as well noted by Kimm and Nowra.[11] The tragic commonality of suicide is a recent phenomenon, but suicide too had a particular form in traditional times, when under the harsh psychological violence of sorcery, victims could lose the will to live.[12]

## Problem Two. Boundaries to interpersonal violence in traditional times provided limited protection

Literature shows "that such actions are invariably within the sphere of traditional practice, ritual or the operation of customary law"[13] but this means violence of unacceptable levels by Western standards was formally condoned, including between spouses. Traditionally there was an array of misdemeanours for which spouses and other family or community members had a right, indeed obligation, to physically punish the offender. Extracts from Meggitt's account of "Walbiri" spousal obligations demonstrate the tangle when trying to differentiate domestic violence from traditional violence that was

---

10 Ibid, 2001, 25.
11 See Kimm, 2004, 63-4, 76; Nowra, 2007, 14-18, 20-22.
12 See David McKnight, *Of Marriage, Violence and Sorcery: The quest for power in northern Queensland*, Ashgate Publishing, Aldershot, England, 2005, 206; and W. Lloyd Warner, *A Black Civilization: A Social Study of an Australian Tribe*, Harper and Brothers, New York and London, 1958, revised edition, (first edition, 1937). 240-242.
13 Apted and Robinson, in Gordon *et al*, 2002, 69.

"sanctioned through formal societal mechanisms".[14] While the Walbiri of the 1950s had interactions with white society and law, and some were employed, particularly on cattle stations, they were proud and powerful tribal people and strong adherents to traditional law and culture: "Our laws are true laws; other blackfellows have inferior laws which they continually break":[15]

> when a woman marries, her parents and close maternal kinsmen surrender to her husband certain personal claims on her services, but they retain the privilege of ensuring that she meets her obligations to him. At the same time, the husband assumes duties towards the woman (and her subsequent offspring) and towards her maternal kin. The latter also have the privilege of enjoining him to discharge these duties.
>
> In this society the sexual division of labour is clearly marked ... If either fails to honour the obligation, the other is entitled to penalise the offender. A man should always berate his wife for such shortcomings (although he should not swear at her) and he may occasionally beat her. But, if he strikes her too often or too heavily, or sheds her blood, her father should upbraid him ...
>
> A married woman who frequently neglects her domestic duties may also be reprimanded by her mother. Should the warning prove ineffective, her father, elder brother, or mother's brother may beat her.[16]

Meggitt adds that while men may also be subject to censure, "[t]his would attack the conventional belief in male superiority; and most men are more concerned to maintain male solidarity than to redress the wrongs done to women":[17]

> although husband and wife have in theory reciprocal claims on

---

14  Meggitt, 1962.
15  Ibid, 34-5.
16  Ibid, 92.
17  Ibid, 93.

each other's economic services, there is often in fact marked inequality. The rights of the wife, both in the satisfaction of her just claims on her husband and in the rejection of his unjust demands, may be seriously infringed.[18]

This imbalance is also evident regarding parental care of young children:

> The negligent father (who is indeed rare) receives little more than scoldings from his wife and diffuse censure from the rest of the camp. The negligent mother, on the other hand, is sure to be beaten by her husband and very probably by her own mother as well.[19]

Regarding the prohibition of swearing:

> Spouses should not swear at each other. Although this prohibition is a rule of etiquette, it is also intended to protect jural rights. The people are aware that swearing usually leads to blows, and often to bloodshed. A woman's abusing her husband, however, is felt to be more culpable than the converse, for her action is also an attack on the basic stereotype of male superiority. It positively forces the husband to reply with physical violence.[20]

Meggitt tells of instance of a man who,

> aged about 30, was playing poker when his wife appeared at a distance and berated him for some slight, real or fancied. He said nothing, although his expression became thunderous, and the other men ostentatiously ignored the woman's outcry. She then began to swear obscenely at him. [He] immediately seized a boomerang, strode across without a word and felled her with several powerful blows to the back of the head. Without a backward glance, he returned and took up his game. The other men exchanged winks and kept silent. [The man] drew me aside afterwards and said, "I had to hit her. A woman cannot swear

---

18  Ibid, 93.
19  Ibid, 93.
20  Ibid, 90.

at an initiated man and order him about as though he were a child!"²¹

A woman is severely bashed on her head, but at least an initiated man did what an initiated man had to do: "I had to hit her". In an attempt to validate its urging that spousal violence was not traditionally condoned, the Gordon Inquiry draws from this same chapter of Meggitt, as well from Memmott *et al* and Robertson.²² As occurred with the 2002 NATSISS misleading violence data, key reports draw upon each other uncritically, this time to reinforce the idea that domestic violence is not traditional. Of course, an overlapping range of sources is common, given that the same issue is being addressed. However, there is a reinforcing circularity in these reports which contributes to a stifling of critical debate and search for truth. The following Gordon Inquiry extracts draw upon these references:

> Acts of violence that are beyond the bounds of customary violence include "child abuse and rape, spousal violence, gang rape, suicide and psychological violence". (Gordon *et al*, 70, quoting Memmott *et al*, 25)
>
> Meggitt notes that there is a duty to protect one's spouse and children from the attacks of another. He adds that the angriest Walbiri men he had encountered were those whose spouses and/or children had been injured at the hands of another. (Gordon *et al*, 70, referring to Meggitt, 95)
>
> The material consulted by the review suggests instances of customary sanctioned violence were isolated instances of punishment governed by strict rules and regulations. Society was regulated through principles and values that determined everyone's cultural and social responsibilities and breaching those responsibilities attracted punishment. (Gordon *et al*, 70, referring to Robertson, 2000)

---

21 Ibid, 90-1. In Meggitt, names are given. To preserve anonymity, names in quotation removed, and replaced by bracketed.
22 Boni Robertson (ed), *Aboriginal and Torres Strait Islander Women's Task Force on Violence Report*, State of Queensland, 1999.

If such "principles and values" were operating to govern the brawls depicted by Meggitt, they seemed to inflame rather than subdue violence, or perhaps they were just ineffective. When I read Meggitt's passages surrounding the reference in Gordon, I was shocked by the chaos, the severe violence, and the escalation. These reports' depiction of pre-contact violence as orderly and less lethal suggests an unwillingness to broadcast the harsh reality of traditional interpersonal violence. I quote Meggitt at length to provide a comprehensive sense of his portrayal:

> Spouses are expected to protect each other from the verbal and physical attacks of outsiders. This ideal seems to me to aim at the defence of the personal claims that each other has on the other's services. It might perhaps be argued that in this case the spouse is merely a possession to be shielded from injury, or that each spouse is concerned to safeguard his or her own social status and self-esteem, of which the partner is thought to be an extension; but I doubt that the people would think in these terms.
>
> A person whose own spouse is attacked may often retaliate by falling upon the aggressor's spouse as well. Thus when one man is struck by another, the victim's wife first tries to belabour the assailant from the rear with a club; if she is prevented, she is likely to turn on his wife. Although women are not positively enjoined to assist their husbands in this way, they are usually quick to do so. Such subsidiary engagements are often far more sanguinary than are the quarrels in which they originated, and in a matter of minutes they may transform a half-hearted altercation between two men into a wild brawl that involves half the camp.
>
> Men frequently told me that many disputes among them would end with only an exchange of insults were it not for the wives' urging them to violence, and the development of most fights that I saw certainly supported this statement. Husbands generally try to keep out of quarrels that begin among women. This is a sensible precaution, for, as I have observed, the women frequently sink their differences and join forces to attack any man who intervenes. Sometimes, however, a man whose wife

is in the wrong in a dispute drags her from the melee before the weakness of her case exposes her to serious injury.[23]

The Gordon Inquiry also omits Meggitt's observations of incidents where European intervention and influence reduced the severity of husbands' violence:

> (LH) had two wives, (LW) and (LLW), who were actual sisters. For some months the women had been involved in a liaison with two bachelors, (JB) and (KB), who were not (LH)'s countrymen. (LH) knew this but, because of (LW)'s poor reputation, was in no hurry to make an issue of it. Eventually (LLW) became pregnant, so retired to the bush one day, where (LW) helped her procure an abortion. Somehow the news reached the camp and some well-meaning friends told (LH), not only of the abortion, but also of the names of the women's lovers. This forced him to take action. He enlisted the support of several countrymen who were close brothers of his wives and then attacked the two women and their lovers. He speared (KB) through the knee and (LLW) through the arm; (JB) he stabbed in the back with a long knife, and only European intervention prevented him from cutting (LW)'s throat. At the same time his djambijimba countrymen thrashed all four of the offenders with clubs and boomerangs.[24]

To differentiate current Aboriginal domestic violence by arguing that traditionally it was, and today it is not, traditionally rule-governed, is a largely futile, hair-splitting endeavour. Worse, such differentiation deflects from developing real remedies for Aboriginal women. For when men, their supporters and lawyers claim in Western courts that men have traditional rights to beat wives for domestic misdemeanours, their claim is true. Tradition might have specified limits on frequency and severity, but it was family through more violence, not a detached

---

23 Meggitt, 1962, 94-5.
24 Ibid, 98-9. In Meggitt, names are given. To preserve anonymity, I have replaced these with fictitious initials, with surname initials "H", "W", and "B" signifying "Husband', "Wife" and "Bachelor".

State, that was the instrument of containment, and evidence suggests it was not very protective. From across the continent, early contact evidence points to harsh injurious punishment of wives at the hands – and weapons – of husbands. The tautologous denial in key reports of pre-contact origins of today's domestic violence, and their suggestion that traditional societies' formally sanctioned violence was a more favourable situation, contributes to serious delays in tackling the problem. At core too, their position permits a morally bankrupt question: should we explore the scope for improving the situation for victims by allowing limited spousal violence as condoned and formalised by classical, traditional culture?

## Problem Three. Traditional violence as a means to set things right can be devastating

These reports overlook or downplay another central feature, the traditional normality and acceptability of violence as a means to set things right. Violence was seen as an accessible healing instrument, a means of settling scores, of getting relationships back onto a correct standing. This traditional, radically different, positive view of violence is still operating, and holds great dangers for today's Aboriginal people. The problem is the reverse of what key reports urge upon us. The problem is not that interpersonal violence including spousal and family violence is *not* sanctioned by traditional norms, but that it *is* sanctioned by traditional norms.

# 3

# Mitigating circumstances: judicial emphasis on traditional violence

> Customary law is presently under siege. We have politicians who want to abolish it. We have a media who demonise it. We have a general population who seem content to either ignore it or denigrate it. And then we have that small, but proud, percentage of the population who understand it, cherish it and live it.
> Somewhere in the middle we have a legal system that has made and is making some effort to acknowledge and respect it. However, much more needs to be done, now more than ever.
> – Stewart O'Connell, NILC, 2006.[1]

### Violence as virtue

In Australia's judicial system, establishing a link between an incidence of violent behaviour and a pre-contact custom can work in an Aboriginal offender's advantage by shortening the sentence. The reduction in sentencing can be so extreme that it mocks the suffering of the Aboriginal victim, and effectively dismisses the victim's right to legal redress and safety. This injustice is particularly severe for Aboriginal women in remote, more traditional communities.

To some extent, it does not matter whether pre-contact Australia was violent or otherwise, because if a return-to-culture path consistently fails to adequately reduce violence, no matter what the cause, the alternative path – towards mainstreaming – needs to be embarked upon. If pre-contact culture is a potent source of today's interpersonal

---

[1] Stewart O'Connell, "Aboriginal Customary Law under Siege", National Indigenous Law Conference (NILC), 22-23 September 2006, Sydney, 11: http://www.nswbar.asn.au/docs/professional/eo/indigenous/docs/NILC_paper1.pdf

violence, the need for mainstreaming becomes all the more clear and urgent. Despite little difference in policy directions implicit in these two scenarios, the stakes remain high regarding the possible connection between pre-contact culture and post-contact violence.

This is because if there is a connection, the self-determination model needs to step away from the Enlightenment commitment to individual safety to "justify" its case. Thus, instead of violent customs signalling the need to abandon the self-determination project, such "stepping away" provides scope to recast Aboriginal violence as a cultural feature warranting some level of allowance, at times even a cultural virtue. Within the post-Enlightenment Australian polity there are signs of this happening. This is evident in some troubling public statements in recent years. One such statement criticises the Minister for Indigenous Affairs Jenny Macklin's strong advocacy for Aboriginal children's rights to safety:

> For me, when it comes to human rights, the most important human right that I feel as a Minister I have to confront, is the need to protect the rights of the most vulnerable, particularly children and for them to have a safe and happy life and a safe and happy family to grow up in.[2]

The retort on *Songlines: A People's Well-Being Movement*, to Macklin's statement, is disturbing:

> But she is clearly very wrong. There are more important human rights, and they are People's Rights – as now recognised by the United Nations Declaration on the Rights of Indigenous Peoples.
> **"Peoples Abuse" is a far more serious crime against life than child abuse.**

---

2 Jenny Macklin, Minister for Indigenous Affairs, speaking on ABC, *PM*, 28 August 2009, q. by songlinesoz, in "'Peoples abuse' – why Jenny Macklin must now resign as Minister for Indigenous Affairs", *Songlines: A Peoples Well-Being Movement*, 8 September 2009: http://songlines.org.au/2009/09/08/peoples-abuse-why-jenny-macklin-should-now-resign-as-minister-for-indigenous-affairs/

> Institutionalised racism of the kind Jenny Macklin relies upon to pursue her high handed Western woman's agenda against Australia's First Peoples is no longer acceptable in the 21st Century. Combating child abuse can only work within a context set by respecting First Peoples.
>
> People attacking First Peoples have to learn to stop hiding behind indigenous children![3]

Of course, people have rights, but not primarily as a group: the possessor of a human right is the individual. It is the individual whose rights to safety must be protected, and their rights to these are equal and universal, irrespective of what group, culture or people they have connection to. Hence, a child's rights are more important than a "people's rights". Other troubling statements reveal a willingness among some of our legal profession to extend a tolerance for Aboriginal violence far beyond compatibility with Enlightenment norms. A 2006 National Indigenous Legal Conference paper by Stewart O'Connell presented a case of payback violence which resulted in unconsciousness after four blows to the head from a *waltha*, "a big stick that is specifically used in carrying out physical punishment in payback".[4] The Northern Territory Supreme Court delivered a fully suspended sentence, having understood the traditional healing role of such payback. O'Connell provides court transcript extracts, including an elder's evidence.

> it is a common practice, it's a practice of healing. It's a practice of keeping relationships on a cordial and a workable everyday relationship ...
>
> *So this type of payback amongst the Alyawarra people is not seen so much as retribution but more as a healing? ...*
>
> It's definitely not a retribution. It's one of cleansing and forgiveness.[5]

---

3 songlinesoz, 8 September 2009 (emphasis on *Songlines* site).
4 O'Connell, 2006, 11.
5 Ibid, 12.

O'Connell posits this case as an example of "how customary law can impact positively on the law and order of the communities involved and how the courts have acknowledged and respected this positive impact." He concludes:

> The Judge in that case was very impressed with the elder's evidence. In particular it challenged the misconception of "payback" (which is a non-Indigenous label) as being a practice of violent retribution and described it in terms of being part of an overall system of law that is aimed at maintaining balance and harmony within the community. It was not violence for violence sake. The end result was a fully suspended sentence of imprisonment.[6]

Malik argues that multiculturalism does away with the Enlightenment idea of the autonomous individual requiring equal rights and equal treatment, replacing it with the idea of cultural identity, where an individual is defined primarily by their culture. Thus their well-being and rights are contingent upon public respect for their culture:

> We cannot, in other words, treat individuals equally unless groups [are] also treated equally. And since, in the words of the American scholar Iris Young, "groups cannot be socially equal unless their specific experience, culture and social contributions are publicly affirmed and recognised", so society must protect and nurture cultures, ensure their flourishing and indeed their survival.
>
> One expression of such equal treatment is the growing tendency in some Western nations for religious law – such as the Jewish halakha and the Islamic sharia – to take precedence over national secular law in civil, and occasionally criminal, cases. Another expression can be found in Australia, where the courts increasingly accept that Aborigines should have the right to be treated according to their own customs rather than be judged by "whitefella law". According to Colin McDonald, a Darwin

---
6 Ibid, 13.

barrister and expert in customary law, "Human rights are essentially a creation of the last hundred years. These people have been carrying out their law for thousands of years ..."[7]

Within liberal democracies, multiculturalism, pluralism and diversity are rightly recognised and celebrated enhancers of individual and societal freedom. They also, ironically, provide scope for human rights violations unless restrained from doing so. An unfettered multiculturalism can have such a commitment to cultural rights that the idea of individual well-being and autonomy becomes surrenderable to the survival of the culture that the individual was born into. Malik observes:

> The demand that because a cultural practice has existed for a long time, so it should be preserved – or, in Charles Taylor's version, the demand that because I am doing X so my descendants, through "indefinite future generations", must also do X – is a modern version of the naturalistic fallacy, the belief that "ought" derives from "is". For nineteenth century social Darwinists, morality – how we ought to behave – derived from the facts of nature – how humans are. This became an argument to justify capitalist exploitation, colonial oppression, racial savagery and even genocide. Today, virtually everyone recognises the falsity of this argument. Yet, when talking of culture rather than of nature, many multiculturalists continue to insist that "is" defines "ought".[8]

Enlightenment and human rights activist Ayaan Hirsi Ali signals the problem of an uncritical multiculturalism's response to abusive customs among minority groups. She argues that "by creating the illusion that one can hold on to tribal norms and at the same time become a successful citizen", the West delays "their transition to modernity". Further, she writes that "what comes packaged in

---

7 Malik, 9 July 2008.
8 Ibid.

a compassionate language of acceptance is really a cruel form of racism. And it is all the more cruel because it is expressed in sugary words of virtue."⁹

**Judicial debates regarding different "ordinary" behaviours**

The cultural relativism of "is" being "ought", as identified by Malik, is present in debates around what constitutes tolerated behaviour in different cultures. At least, judicial debates raise the idea that Australian courts when determining sentencing need to be flexible regarding the kind of self-control an "ordinary person" might be expected to have in a given culture. In his submission to the Senate Select Committee on Indigenous People and Mental Health on Cape York Peninsula, Roger Cribb makes the following observation:

> In Aboriginal societies on Cape York Peninsula people are raised to be very personally and physically assertive, including the women. This kind of behaviour is tolerated, even encouraged within Aboriginal society but often leads to problems with the mainstream legal system. It could greatly enhance paranoid or manic-type behaviour.¹⁰

A similar "ordinariness" is reported for Palm Island. G.M. Eames QC noted its deadly consequences.¹¹ In his 1993 article, Eames comments that "[i]t is tragic and commonplace for there to be so many homicide cases involving Aboriginal people as victims and for the person accused to also be Aboriginal and to be the male spouse of the

---

9 Ayaan Hirsi Ali, *Nomad: A Personal Journey Through the Clash of Civilizations*, Fourth Estate, Sydney, 2010, xviii.

10 Roger Cribb, *Indigenous People and Mental Health on Cape York Peninsula*, Individual Submission from Dr Roger Cribb, Submission to Senate Select Committee, 12 May 2005, 3: http://www.aph.gov.au/senate/committee/mentalhealth_ctte/submission/sub261.pdf

11 G.M. Eames QC, "Aboriginal Homicide: Customary Law Defences or Customary Lawyers' Defences?", in H. Strang, and S-A. Gerull, (eds), *Homicide: Patterns, Prevention and Control: proceedings of a conference held 12-14 May 1992*, AIC, Canberra, 1993, 150-165: http://www.aic.gov.au/publications/previous%20series/proceedings/1-27/~/media/publications/proceedings/17/eames.pdf

deceased."[12] Eames examines two cases of spousal homicide, where the defence was that the woman behaved in a manner that would provoke an "ordinary person" of the community, in the context that husbands have the right to physically punish wives under customary law.[13] The following is an extract from Eames' account of a Palm Island case, heard in a Brisbane court in 1986.

> The appellant was convicted of murder of "his woman" by stabbing her with a knife which penetrated 15 cm, passing through the liver, bladder and aorta. The defence was that the accused had not formed an intention to kill or cause serious bodily harm but intended to "cut" the victim on the arm or her side so as to make her go home with him, which she was refusing to do. The appeal was concerned with the refusal of the trial judge to allow an expert witness to be called to give evidence of what were said to be the cultural practices of Aboriginal people on Palm Island. It was said that it was consistent with conduct on the Island for a person to use a knife in the way the accused did and yet not be intending any serious harm.
>
> In a statement supplied to the appeal court, it was noted that the evidence which the expert, a sociologist, would have given was to this effect:
>
> "In general terms, the distinctions in our culture between discipline, punishment, violence, and assault – including the use of weapons – have little impact on a very large section of the Palm Island community – male or female."[14]

The witness said that whereas a non-Aboriginal person brandishing a knife in Brisbane would be presumed by onlookers to have the intention of harming someone, that would not be the perception of Palm Islanders witnessing such a scene on the Island. The witness said:

---

12  Ibid, 154.
13  Ibid, 154-58.
14  Ibid, 152.

> Assuredly, some offences on the Island are motivated the same as the above example. However, a very large proportion of such uses are, as their motivation, a desire to discipline and punish a person for violation of a code of behaviour or conduct. And this code, as it applies to heterosexual relationships, is based on a traditional sense of male superiority and feminine subservience. While not ritualistic, the men very often feel it is their "right" to discipline "their women" ... Even the severity of the injuries is seen differently on the Island. "I intended to cut her" is a phrase often heard, and we may be mortified at the prospect of being "cut". However this is readily accepted by Palm Island people as attested to by the very large number of scars on these people.[15]

The judges rejected an appeal and agreed that such evidence was not admissible. In this case, contemporary law based on individual rights won through.

Justice McPherson noted that if there was such a practice and custom, it was in contravention of the Racial Discrimination Act, which incorporated the right to security of individuals from violence provided by Article V of the Covenant on Civil and Political Rights.[16] Eames notes that while such evidence based on customary law "more often than not" does not "succeed in allowing a defence", "similar arguments have been frequently successful when advanced during the sentencing process", resulting in a tendency for courts to bestow shorter sentences for violent crimes when the accused is Aboriginal.[17]

In relation to crimes of rape, Eames wrote:

> As a result of submissions made on behalf of accused people, similar comments to the following observations of Gallop J. have been repeated many times by sentencing tribunals:
>
>> "I cannot ignore the fact that whether the European society likes it or not, rape is not as seriously regarded in the

---

15 Ibid, 153.
16 Ibid, 152-153.
17 Ibid, 153.

Aboriginal community as it is in the European community."[18]

Eames concluded by emphasising the competing civil liberties between Aboriginal perpetrators and victims, and the need to address the legal system's failure "to represent the opinions of Aboriginal women". Nevertheless, Eames' key message is that courts are too restrictive in their definition of an "ordinary person" when it comes to violent acts committed by traditional Aboriginal people, and a more relativist approach would be fairer. This might be as "expounded by Kearney J. in *Jabarula v. Poore* (68 ALR 26)", who said that

> the ordinary person was one on the remote community where the killing occurred and was a person "who possesses such powers of self-control as everyone is entitled to expect an ordinary person of that culture and environment to have".[19]

## Where's your bargaining power? Judicial promotion of traditional causes

Lawyers are expected to represent their individual clients to the utmost. There have long been pressures upon our judiciary to emphasise the traditional roots of violence, arising from its inherent task to justly apply Western law, which includes taking into account a perpetrator's individual circumstances. As stated by O'Connell:

> Lawyers who work for Indigenous people have a responsibility to "discover" the customary law applicable in the cases they deal with. These lawyers then must strive to have the relevant customary law acknowledged and taken into account by the court or other relevant legal body.[20]

There is also a reasonably robust consensus in our polity that we should not recognise customary practices that abuse human rights.

---

18 J. Gallop, *R v Gus Forbes*, Northern Territory Supreme Court, Unreported, 29 August 1980, q. in Eames, 1993, 154.
19 Eames, 1993, 156.
20 O'Connell, 2006, 1.

This still provides scope for defence lawyers to posit as mitigating circumstances a perpetrator's cultural context that allows – in some contexts, demands – violence in traditional Aboriginal Australia. So perpetrators of violence and their defence lawyers will tend to emphasise where possible the traditional nature of the act. This can set up a confusing and conflict-ridden situation wherein different individuals in the same community have an interest in either promoting or denying that an act of violence has a traditional component. Hence a male perpetrator and his defence claim "tradition", while supporters of female victims claim, as in the well-known quote in Bolger's report, "bullshit tradition".[21] These opposing sides are engaging in high-stakes bargaining with the Western legal system. This bargaining is a rational, predictable response, given that in our Western law, the defender's circumstances, including the traditional status of an illegal act, can still matter in sentencing.[22]

This situation renders it difficult for "progressive" or "politically correct" supporters of Aboriginal Australia to deny as thoroughly as they might want, that Aboriginal Australia has traditional violent punishments, including on the interpersonal level, because to do so runs counter to a major tool of defence for Aboriginal perpetrators. There are dangerous side-effects to this. In particular, it leaves the supporters of victims with the arduous need to claim that a particular act of violence was not traditional. The abysmal legal redress that our Western legal system has provided for Aboriginal female victims of Aboriginal male violence is testimony to the shocking winners-and-losers outcome of this cruel bargaining game, enabled by the Western legal system's compromised hold on the Enlightenment commitment to individual rights to safety in cases where "other" cultures provide mitigating circumstances for perpetrators. The history of failure to impose sentences commensurate with the brutality of the violence against Aboriginal women, because the violence was judged to have

---

21 Bolger, 1991, 50.
22 Nowra, 2007, 62-3.

a traditional association, is testimony to this. Noongar human rights lawyer, Hannah McGlade, while among those who deny the reality of customary violation of women, makes the crucial argument that whether or not violence against women is traditional, it should be "rejected outright as a matter of human rights".[23] We need to ask why our nation continues to be equivocal on this when faced with the idea of a cultural right or a cultural norm as a mitigating circumstance.

Over the past few decades, judges have become increasingly intolerant of Aboriginal male violence against women and the allowance of a customary law defence. Kimm, in an invaluable chronology,[24] has identified stages in our judicial system's trend away from allowing a customary law defence. Kimm noted that "a change is apparent between judicial attitudes of the 1970s and those of the late 1980s onwards. The courts appear to be less sympathetic to customary law being raised in litigation ... general deterrence is now held to be an equal if not more important consideration."[25] However, the obligation to account for mitigating circumstances including culture could still reduce sentence length. As Nowra observed in early 2007:

> Even though customary law can't be used as a defence in the Northern Territory, it can feature as a mitigating or aggravating circumstance in sentencing ...
>
> And the defence does work.[26]

---

23 Hannah McGlade, *Our Greatest Challenge, Aboriginal Children and Human Rights*, Aboriginal Studies Press, Canberra, 2012, 162-63. See also Kimm, 2004, Chapter 13 'Reconciling Rights in Sentencing', *passim*.

24 Kimm, 2004, Ch 9, "Different Cosmologies", *passim*.

25 Joan Kimm, *A Fatal Conjunction: Two Laws and Two Cultures: Issues of Gender, Culture and the Law (for Aboriginal women)*. Thesis for Master of Laws, Monash University (submitted 1999), 264. See Kimm, 2004, 99-101, for examples of such cases. Permission to quote from Kimm 2004 was denied by The Federation Press, hence Kimm, 1999, is quoted.

26 Nowra, 2007, 62-3. Note that Nowra's book was published months before the enactment of the NTNERA in August 2007 including its Section 91 which prevents the recognition of customary practice for sentence reduction. See also Kimm, 2004, 89. Waipuldanya in Lockwood, 1964, 140-2, provides a powerful and confronting case in point.

Australia's urban areas are not immune from the cultural defence. During field work in the mid-1990s, a lawyer told me that "cultural rights" was an effective partial defence for domestic violence:

> "Lawyers will plead with the judge to consider culture. This is used by lawyers to mitigate the sentence. For example, serious violence will get a suspended sentence instead of imprisonment. This is possible with perhaps 25 per cent of cases in Viewtown, and they will be put on bonds or similar for violence. An Aboriginal man who is more integrated, say, a professional, wouldn't be able to use such a plea. A man may be able to successfully plead 'culture' if he was, say on CDEP, been in Viewtown for two or so years, and was from a more tribal area before that."

Despite having concerns about these trends, the same lawyer adhered to the institutional principles of the legal profession within liberal-democracy – to utilise whatever legal redress is available to reduce a sentence for a client:

> "I am a professional who will act on behalf of any client, including male perpetrators ... I use whatever legal tools there are to defend my clients. That is my profession." [27]

Injustice continues in our courts against Aboriginal women victims. In 2001, Lloyd said "[t]he sentences given out to Aboriginal men committing serious offences against Aboriginal women are much, much lower than sentences given to other people in the community who commit similar offences."[28] Marcia Langton commented:

> There's a culture of unwillingness to go forward with murder charges when there's a life sentence. [There are] entire small communities where you have a violent offender who is charged with something less than murder, gets a short sentence, comes

---

27 This passage is an extract from my chapter in Johns, 2001, 108.
28 Liz Jackson, *The Shame: Assessing the Impact of Violence on Aboriginal communities*, ABC, *Four Corners*, 3 September, 2001: http://www.abc.net.au/4corners/stories/s357126.htm

back to the community and murders or rapes or sexually assaults somebody again.²⁹

In the twenty-first century, our courts have handed down abysmally short sentences for violence committed by Aboriginal men against Aboriginal women, on the basis that the violence had customary justification or purpose. These include two frequently discussed cases where middle-aged traditional men committed grievous acts, and received extremely light sentences on customary grounds associated with promised marriage.

The judgements and sentencing in a 2002 case are appalling.³⁰ For the violent rape of a 15-year-old girl, which was commuted to "unlawful sexual intercourse with a minor", the 50-year-old defendant was first sentenced by "Magistrate Luppino of the Maningrida Court" to "13 months imprisonment". The "lofty defence claim[ed] that the defendant's actions were 'entirely appropriate and morally correct within the traditional parameters of the Bururra lifeworld'."³¹ On appeal to the Northern Territory's Supreme Court, Justice Gallop found that "the Magistrate failed to give due weight to the customary practice of promised marriage, agreeing with the anthropological evidence presented to the court about promised marriage and commenting that: 'She didn't need protection [from white law] ... She knew what was expected of her. It's surprising to me [that the defendant] was charged at all'".³² Justice Gallop reduced the sentence to 24 hours. The Crown then appealed, resulting in the Court of Appeal increasing the sentence

---

29 Marcia Langton in 2006, q. in Nowra, 2007, 66.
30 McGlade provides a clear account of the inadequate sentencing regarding this case. See Hannah McGlade, "Aboriginal women, girls and sexual assault: the long road to equality within the criminal justice system", *ACSSA Newsletter No. 12*, September 2006, Australian Institute of Family Studies, 7: http://aifs.gov.au/acssa/pubs/newsletter/n12pdf/n12_4.pdf and McGlade, 2012, 143-48.
31 McGlade, 2006, 7. Note: "Burarra" is the spelling used in *Hales v Jamilmira* [2003] NTCA 9.
32 Paul Toohey, "Black, white and blurred", *The Weekend Australian*, 12-13 October 2002, 21, q. in McGlade, 2006, 7.

to 12 months "to be suspended after a period of only 1 month".[33]

In June 2004 – *The Queen v GJ* case – a 55-year-old traditional man from Yarralin committed violence and sexual assault against a 14-year-old girl he regarded as his promised bride.[34] Chief Justice Brian Martin granted a 24-month sentence suspended to one month with conditions on customary grounds that "his actions were permitted under traditional law", plus on the grounds that the offender did not know that in the Northern Territory it was "prohibited to have sexual intercourse with a person under sixteen".[35] Later, Chief Justice Martin, announcing his retirement in May 2010, "admitted he made a mistake in 2005 when he sentenced a 55-year-old Aboriginal elder to just one month's jail for the rape of his 14-year-old promised bride":

> "I got the balance wrong," he said. "I remember thinking of all the factors – the impact on the victim and the families – then trying to balance out the other side of the coin, which was an Aboriginal man who didn't know he was doing the wrong thing in the sense that it was permissible under their law and he didn't realise it was wrong in the wider law."[36]

The sentence was lengthened to three years on appeal, 18 months to be served in prison, and the High Court overturned the offender's bid to reduce the lengthened sentence. However, as Hughes notes in her analysis of this case, "the maximum allowable penalty for the crime was 16 years".[37]

---

33 McGlade, 2006, 8. The High Court rejected Pascoe Jamilmira's application to appeal against this longer sentence: *Jamilmira v Hales* [2004] HCA Trans 18 (13 February 2004).

34 *The Queen v GJ* [2005] NTCCA 20.

35 Nowra, 2006, 47. See also Hughes, 2007, 27-8; Johns, 2011, 128-29; McGlade, 2012, 148-52.

36 Lex Hall and Patricia Karvelas, "Violence to rage for years: top judge", *The Australian,* 28 May 2010: http://www.theaustralian.com.au/news/nation/violence-to-rage-for-years-top-judge/story-e6frg6nf-1225872295169

37 Hughes, 2007, 27.

Recent tougher court decisions against violent Aboriginal offenders, and the generalised longer sentences for all crime for both Aboriginal and non-Aboriginal offenders, have worked in recent years to lengthen sentences against Aboriginal perpetrators of violence. Nevertheless, shorter sentences for Aboriginal perpetrators, including for the mitigating circumstance of custom, remain all too common. The debate and the struggle for justice for Aboriginal victims of customary violence continue.

**Self-determination and difficulties in understanding white law**

One of the claimed injustices regarding Aboriginal people's interaction with white law is that the offender did not know – or understand – that his action was illegal under Western law, but knew it was permissible under customary law. There are recent cases where ignorance of white law reduced the sentence of Aboriginal perpetrators of violent acts, for instance in *The Queen v GJ*, the defendant "was ignorant of Territory law".[38] This seems surprising given that there are documentations from across Australia of traditional Aboriginal people who realised from early on that white law would punish Aboriginal people for violent acts, and so moderated their behaviour.

Perhaps self-determination has significantly reduced remote Aboriginal community understanding of Western law compared to early contact and mission times. Certainly, during the self-determination decades in remote areas, English proficiency among younger people compared to their parents has deteriorated. As Bess Price so movingly tells us:

> Education has not worked for our mob for the past 30 years. White people told us that they wanted to preserve our language so now my people can't express themselves to the rest of the world and rely on white people and city blackfellas, who know

---

38 *The Queen v GJ* [2005] NTCCA 20. Note, this is a reason that NTNERA is decried, as this cannot be used so much.

nothing about us, or who want to keep us in ignorance to do it for them. I went to school before the bilingual program started yet I speak both Warlpiri and English better than our kids and our grandkids. Our young people now need their grandparents to speak for them to the outside world. The old ones speak better English. Most of our kids now can't read and write English or their own language. They are not learning to speak their own languages properly. They are losing the best of our culture but not learning the best of the whitefella's culture. They are learning the worst instead. They are losing on both sides ... My people are linguistically talented. Many speak several Aboriginal languages. Our kids are intelligent and want to learn. Why can't whitefellas teach them English? It should be easy.[39]

Steven Etherington wrote of his decades witnessing the negative effects of poor English in remote communities. He observed that in numerous remote areas including outstations, many young people cannot speak their own languages fluently, and have not acquired English literacy:[40]

> There is a general failure to gain English literacy, learn mainstream languages and law, mathematical and other technical competencies and even knowledge of indigenous languages and culture ... [41]
>
> We have lost a generations of leaders ... the earlier generations of leadership in remote Australia had benefited from boarding experience built on what was then a sheltered and relatively intense English language primary schooling where missions protected the communities from outside pressures, and attendance was enforced.[42]

---

[39] Bess Price, *Inaugural Peter Howson Lecture*, The Bennelong Society, 3 December 2009.
[40] Steven (Steve) Etherington, pers. comm., 2010.
[41] Steven Etherington, "The most threatened people in Australia: the remote Aboriginal minority", in Johns, 2001, 97.
[42] Ibid, 99.

Decline in English proficiency is indicative, and a partial cause, of a more general decline in familiarity with Western mores and law.[43] I say "partial", because young Aboriginal people who cannot speak *any* language fluently would be, unlike older and earlier generations, poorly equipped to be taught about Western law even in an Indigenous language, nor could they adequately communicate information about Western law to anyone else in their community. Furthermore, perhaps self-determination has generated a more defiant traditional culture, at least among some communities. No doubt both trends are related, compounding the unfamiliarity with and non-conformity to Western law.

Some early observations illustrate rapid adaptation to some aspects of white law, either in preference for new less violent norms, or to avoid punishment under white law. These further highlight the enigma of incomprehension and resistance regarding white law among recent Aboriginal offenders.

### *New South Wales, Newcastle area, early 19th century*

Documenting early 19th century accounts, Gordon Bennett in 1929 wrote:

> A man was not permitted to speak to his wife's mother and could only do so through a third party. Before the advent of the whites to the district it was death for a man to speak to her, and for many years after settlement was first established the punishment was a temporary banishment from the camp.[44]

---

43 See also ARDS, *An Absence of Mutual Respect (Baynu Nayanu-Dapmaranhamirr Rom ga Norra)*, 2008, *passim*, esp. 24: http://www.ards.com.au/print/Absence_of_Mutual_Respect-FINAL.pdf

44 Gordon Bennett, *The Earliest Inhabitants: Aboriginal Tribes of Dungog, Port Stephens and Gresford*, 1929, 4, sourced from D. A. Roberts, H. M. Carey and V. Grieves, *Awaba, A Database of Historical Materials Relating to the Aborigines of the Newcastle – Lake Macquarie Region*, University of Newcastle. Link at: http://www.newcastle.edu.au/group/amrhd/awaba/bibliography/index.html

## Western Australia, Gascoyne region, 1900s-1910s

Daisy Bates related how white man's law was by the early 1900s or 1910s preventing murders for broken betrothal promises. However, sorcery appears to have been turned to instead:

> [Marriage] promises were always fulfilled, no matter how many years elapsed before the young man was ready to claim his wife, and no matter how great the distance between them. When he came he must find her waiting, or a fight would ensue. Many native so-called "murders" were brought about by a breach of promise in this respect; the girl probably grew tired of waiting, or the mother, father, or uncle, not hearing from the young man and not having received any presents from him in the interval, may have bestowed her upon a more liberal son-in-law. When the real betrothed husband turned up, however, he fought for his property, and was either killed or he killed the man who had taken the girl.
>
> Nowadays, the white man's law prevents these fights, but no white man's law can prevent magic being used as a means of revenge ...[45]

## Northern Territory, central desert region, 1950s

Meggitt observed that white law curtailed group raids, although a switch to sorcery was observed:

> [R]aids and counter-raids usually concerned only specified groups of kinsmen and could thus be kept within manageable limits; rarely would the whole community arm ...
>
> Naturally, even such restricted conflicts no longer occur, in the face of European penal sanctions ... Although the belief is still current that almost all deaths are basically "homicides",

---

45 Daisy Bates, *The Native Tribes of Western Australia (1901-1914)*, (Isobel White (ed), 1985). National Library of Australia, Canberra, 124.

men now seek to retaliate covertly through the performance of sorcery.[46]

Meggitt also observed some restraint of interpersonal violence, due to white contact. He recounts how a husband defended his wife against the molestations of another man. The woman called for her husband's help:

> [The husband's] use of his fists as weapons and his comparative restraint in this situation were explicit attempts to emulate European practices. Normally a Walbiri would never fight with his bare hands, nor would he treat a potential adulterer so casually.[47]

Another example is the experience of Justice Kriewaldt, "a judge of the Northern Territory Supreme Court from 1951 to 1960".[48] Kriewaldt observed that in his experience, Aboriginal defendants generally knew when a traditionally condoned act was breaking white law.[49] Kriewaldt was also aware that some Aboriginal people understood white law better than others. In her article about Kriewaldt, Heather Douglas documents that he imposed heavier penalties in cases where "knowledge of white law" was "sufficient":

> It is my duty [Kriewaldt said] to impose a more severe sentence than I normally impose for death resulting from fights between natives. The accused has by now sufficient knowledge of white law to know that he was acting illegally. His reputation amongst his fellow aboriginals and white community deprives him of any right to ask for leniency.[50]

---

46 Meggitt, 1962, 246.
47 Ibid, 107.
48 Heather Douglas, "Justice Kriewaldt, Aboriginal Identity and the Criminal Law", *Criminal Law Journal* Vol. 26, August 2002, 204: http://www.law.uq.edu.au/documents/kriewaldt/analysis/Justice-Kriewaldt-Aboriginal-Identity-and-the-Criminal-Law.pdf
49 Kimm, 2004, 93-4.
50 Douglas, 2002, 210.

These instances of early knowledge about and adaptations to white law highlight the anomalous situation that in the 21st century, there are dangerous Aboriginal offenders who find justification for their behaviour in Aboriginal culture, or plead ignorance of white law. White colonisation brought new triggers for violent conflict, including alcohol. But white law also led Aboriginal people to reduce the use and lethality of their violence. Self-determination and the continuing calls for the allowance of customary law in sentence mitigation threaten this gain, and continue to make legal and policy remedies difficult to implement. In his article "Should customary law be recognised by the courts?", Dave Price, white man and husband of Bess Price, quotes Baldwin Spencer, Chief Protector of Aborigines in the Northern Territory, in 1912:

> "I went to Fanny Bay ... to interview four native prisoners who have been brought in from out west. Three of them are charged with murder and one with inflicting grievous bodily harm. So far as I can tell the three former have only been carrying out their tribal customs. We have enough evidence to make a good case ..."

Sir Baldwin wasn't concerned in his role as Chief Protector to protect "lubras" or "boys" from execution under their own law. Many contemporary defence lawyers run the same line. "My client admits to killing his wife your honour but it was in conformity with Customary Law; she swore at him and prevented him from attending a ceremony so it's not really murder, it was justified under his Law". The same refrain is repeated over and over again.[51]

Later in the article Dave Price writes:

> The biggest problem with adopting old Sir Baldwin's approach is that we are no longer dealing with wild natives who know nothing of white man's law, "lubras" and "boys" whose lives

---

51 Dave Price, "Should Customary Law be recognised by the courts?", *Alice Online: Australia from the inside out*, 22 December 2009: http://aliceonline.com.au/?p=380

are expendable in the great civilising mission to tame the land and its natives. We are dealing with contemporary citizens of Australia and the world with, I would have thought, exactly the same rights as other citizens. Hasn't the achievement of that been the central aim of the struggle of the last eight decades?[52]

Dave Price then documents key "Articles" and other extracts from the Universal Declaration of Human Rights of 1948. Article Two, he urges, "makes it all pretty clear":

*Article Two*
Everyone is entitled to all the rights and freedoms set forth in this Declaration, without distinction of any kind, such as race, colour, sex, language, religion, political or other opinion, national or social origin, property, birth or other status.[53]

## Section 91 of the Northern Territory National Emergency Response Act (NTERA) 2007

In its 14 July 2006 meeting communiqué, the Council of Australian Governments (COAG) stated that

The law's response to family and community violence and sexual abuse must reflect the seriousness of such crimes. COAG agreed that no customary law or cultural practice excuses, justifies, authorises, requires or lessens the seriousness of violence or sexual abuse. All jurisdictions will reflect this, if necessary by future amendment.[54]

A ban on consideration of customary law in sentencing has been condemned by law bodies including the Law Society of South Australia, whose president Deej Eszenyi said in 2006 that South Australian lawyers are concerned that such a law would attack a central

---

52 Ibid.
53 Ibid, quoting *The Universal Human Rights of 1948*.
54 Council of Australian Governments (COAG), *Council of Australian Governments' Meeting Outcomes*, 14 July 2006: Indigenous Issues: http://www.coag.gov.au/coag_meeting_outcomes/2006-07-14/index.cfm#indigenous

principle of fair sentencing that has been available for all defendants.[55]

In the Northern Territory, the 2006 COAG statement became reflected in law in August 2007, as part of the NTER. The NTERA 2007 – Section 91 is as follows:

> **Matters to which court is to have regard when passing sentence etc.**
>
> In determining the sentence to be passed, or the order to be made, in respect of any person for an offence against a law of the Northern Territory, a court must not take into account any form of customary law or cultural practice as a reason for:
>
>> (a) excusing, justifying, requiring or lessening the seriousness of the criminal behaviour to which the offence relates; or
>>
>> (b) aggravating the seriousness of the criminal behaviour to which the offence relates.[56]

Calls for its overturn continue, with the Law Council of Australia in 2010 stating its commitment "to overturning the federal ban that prevents judges taking account of Aboriginal customary law".[57] While Section 91 is applicable to all races and cultures, there are concerns that it is discriminatory against Aboriginal people where traditional contexts and practices are part of everyday life. The North Australian Aboriginal Justice Agency (NAAJA) Submission to the NTER Review regarding Section 91 argues that these

> legislative amendments ... are discriminatory and unnecessary.

---

55 Deej Eszenyi, "Court sentence rules must be fair for all", *The Advertiser*, 3 July 2006, 18.
56 Commonwealth Consolidated Acts, *Northern Territory National Emergency Response Act 2007 – Sect 91*:
http://www.austlii.edu.au/au/legis/cth/consol_act/ntnera2007531/s91.
57 Chris Merritt, Legal Affairs Editor, "End ban on customary law in sentencing, urges law council", *The Australian*, 18 February 2010:
http://www.theaustralian.com.au/business/legal-affairs/end-ban-on-customary-law-in-sentencing-urges-law-council/story-e6frg97x-1225831554796

Prior to these amendments, there was provision for evidence about an aspect of Aboriginal customary law to be placed before a court and tested should matters be in dispute. The Court would then consider this evidence, as it considers any other material fact in reaching its decision. This decision can then be reviewed by higher courts if either party appeals the decision.[58]

There is some discussion surrounding the impact of Section 91 on sentence length of Aboriginal perpetrators of violence. As pointed out by Jenny Blokland CM, Chief Justice Martin stated, before Section 91 was enacted, that reduced moral culpability due to customary law had little effect on sentencing in cases of serious violence ranging from

> very little weight in the case of extremely serious crimes to, perhaps, quite significant weight when minor crimes are committed. It is a matter of balance.[59]

Blokland also pointed to the sentencing remarks of Chief Justice Martin for *The Queen and Roddenby*, December 2008:

> Contrary to the misleading impression conveyed by some politicians and other commentators, in recent years the Criminal court has responded to the increasing frequency of crimes of violence and to community concern. Penalties for crimes of violence have increased. In cases of violence causing serious injury, the Criminal Court rarely imposes a sentence other than a term of imprisonment ...[60]

---

58 North Australian Aboriginal Justice Agency (NAAJA), "Customary Law", *Submission by the North Australian Aboriginal Justice Agency*, NTER Review, FaHCSIA, 23 October 2008: http://www.nterreview.gov.au/subs/nter_review_report/105_naaja/105_NAAJA_5.htm See also McGlade, 2012, 162-63.
59 Jenny Blokland, Chief Magistrate, Northern Territory, "Current Legal Issues in the Northern Territory Concerning Indigenous People and the Criminal Justice System", *National Indigenous Legal Conference*, 2009, 5: nilcsa2009.com/JennyBlokland.pdf q. His Hon Chief Justice Martin (BR), Speech given 15 September 2006, SA Press Club.
60 Blokland, 2009, q. Martin CJ, *The Queen v Roddenby*, 12 December 2008.

Others are concerned that Section 91 is associated with recent reduced use of discretion in sentencing and increased sentencing penalties. The NAAJA Submission referred to the *R v Redford* case from the Maningrida area, heard in March 2007 – before Section 91 was enacted:

> the complainant (b.1990) and the defendant (b.1975) had entered into a sexual relationship when the complainant turned 14. A number of affidavits ... were tendered which established that the defendant and the complainant had entered into a tribally arranged marriage when the complainant was 13 ... This evidence was important as it led to Justice Mildren describing the offender in the following way:
>> "You are not a sexual predator. There is no suggestion that you took advantage of this child out of lust or in order to exercise control over her ... In all the circumstances, I consider there must be a period of imprisonment to deter others from offending in this way, to underline the message that offences of this nature will not be tolerated and to express the Court's disapproval of your conduct.
>>
>> However, it is clear that the community does not need to be protected from you ..."
>
> We are extremely concerned that as the law stands currently, defendants in similar positions may be prevented from raising such issues before the court and thus risk being viewed improperly as "sexual predators". Our concerns are exacerbated because in our experience, there have been trends where:
>> a. there are more defendants being charged in such situations than previously, because of changes in the way police and prosecution services have been exercising their discretion; and
>>
>> b. courts are now issuing heavier penalties for such offending than previously and in the vast majority of cases, this includes actual terms of imprisonment.[61]

---

61 NAAJA, 2008.

Nevertheless, Blokland points to Mildren J's statement prior to the NTNERA's enactment that a measure similar to Section 91 may not have effect if "applied specifically to Northern Territory law". Blokland writes:

> For example, when provocation is being utilized as a mitigating factor where provocative conduct results from an issue based in customary practice, the mitigation lessening the gravity of the offence is the provocation rather than the customary law or cultural practice ...
>
> The application of Section 91 NTNERA may prove to be less straight forward than it appears at first blush and requires analysis of motivation beyond what on the face of it is said to be the operation of customary law or practice.[62]

This suggests that customary law may in some circumstances still operate to reduce sentencing, even with the enactment of Section 91. The result brings Eames' discussion to mind, where he quotes Kearney J. in *Jabarula v. Poore* (68 ALR 26), who said that

> the ordinary person was one on the remote community where the killing occurred and was a person "who possesses such powers of self-control as everyone is entitled to expect an ordinary person of that culture and environment to have".[63]

Thus, if an "ordinary person" can be expected to be provoked to violence by certain behaviour within that cultural or environmental setting, this could be regarded as a mitigating circumstance, regardless of the factor of tradition or custom attached to the provocation. If so, even with Section 91, we may not fully escape the problem of tradition and "moral violence" while self-determination allows for the continuation of such a very different "other" ordinariness, with its high toleration of violence. Hence, the core problem is a policy issue.

---

62 Blokland, 2009, 7.
63 Eames, 1993, 156.

Despite this vulnerability, Section 91 has been applied and upheld by the Northern Territory Court, preventing customary law being used as a mitigating circumstance in a serious case of domestic violence, *The Queen v Dennis Wunungmurra* [2009].[64] The sentence could have differed greatly had Section 91 not been in place.[65] This outcome is enough to reveal the scope that the previous consideration of customary law afforded for sentence reduction. The ABC News article "Customary law no defence for accused wife-stabber", outlines this case of an Elcho Island man "who claimed he enacted traditional 'discipline' on his wife".[66] Despite the injurious nature of the assault which the man inflicted because she "had not partaken in community or family life as a traditional wife should", a legal challenge was mounted against "Commonwealth Intervention legislation that restricts the use of Aboriginal customary law ... Appearing for the defence, Rex Wild QC argued the seriousness of Wunungmurra's crime should be determined with traditional law in mind."[67]

The challenge failed. While Justice Stephen Southwood upheld Section 91, he said that "the legislation could result in disproportionate sentences, and that it distorts well-established sentencing principles of proportionality".[68] This response of Southwood's seems at odds with the statements of Martin and Blokland regarding the small impact that consideration of Indigenous customary law has had in sentencing for serious crimes of violence.

Legal fraternity discomfort about not considering customary law even in cases of violent patriarchy is telling. It illustrates that within our judiciary is a perspective that they are dealing with real,

---

64 *The Queen v Wunungmurra* [2009] NTSC 24.
65 See also McGlade, 2012, 162.
66 I am indebted to Warin for alerting me to this case, pers. comm., 2009.
67 ABC News, "Customary law no defence for accused wife-stabber", 9 June 2009: http://www.abc.net.au/news/stories/2009/06/09/2593332.htm.
68 ABC News, 9 June 2009.

not "bullshit", traditional entitlement to brutalise women. It also reveals that among key judiciary, there remain those, such as Wild and Southwood, who feel a considerable degree of righteousness with the previous situation of taking customary law into account, and great frustration with Section 91, even when that customary law was of a brutal and misogynist form, and totally incompatible with universal human rights.

Section 91 may not be strong enough, but it has demonstrably curtailed the application of the customary defence, and it increases the clarity of where the nation's law stands regarding cultural considerations and victim rights. However, the polity and the judiciary remain unsettled, divided.

### Submissions of objection and other oppositions to NTNERA

There is widespread opposition to stopping consideration of cultural practice as a mitigating circumstance in sentencing. Before the NTNERA became law, it was noted that "[s]ignificantly, of the ten publicly available submissions to the Senate Enquiry, not one supports the passage of the bill" (Crime Amendment (Bail and Sentencing) Bill 2006).[69]

Condemnations of the Bill and the NTNERA include contradictory claims that Aboriginal people have not been getting shorter sentences anyway, Eszenyi indicating that "Aboriginal offenders in the NT are not, as a general rule, receiving lower penalties than comparable offenders in NSW ... The statistics do not support claims that indigenous offenders have been treated more leniently."[70] She concludes:

> It would be disturbing if Aboriginal people were to be deprived of the same sentencing procedures as other Australians,

---

69 Frank Quinlan, "Sentencing laws will further alienate indigenous Australians", *EurekaStreet.com.au*, 16 October 2006:
http://www.eurekastreet.com.au/article.aspx?aeid=1788

70 Eszenyi, 2006.

particularly in the absence of evidence demonstrating that these cultural considerations are producing any special leniency.[71]

Adding to this contradiction, there are laments that the Aboriginal rate of imprisonment was already too high before the Act was implemented, and that Section 91 is resulting in even further increases in sentence rates and length. The Human Rights Law Resource Centre (HRLRC) submission laments the longer sentences brought about by Section 91.[72] Given claims previous to enactment that recognising customary law and cultural practice did not produce "any special leniency", the HRLRC's lack of surprise about longer jail terms should itself be "surprising". Sadly it is not, such are the twists and turns required to evade confronting the core problem – the normality of violence in traditional Aboriginal culture:

> Since the introduction of this measure, sentences have increased. This is not surprising given that Aboriginal offenders can no longer have the full context of their offending behaviour considered.[73]

There is an emphasis on Aboriginal perpetrators' status as disadvantaged people – victims themselves – rather than as criminals who have violently assaulted another (usually disadvantaged Aboriginal) person. In its submission to the Senate Legal and Constitutional Affairs

---

71 Eszenyi, 2006.

72 Human Rights Law Resource Centre (HRLRC), *Practical Implications of the Northern Territory Emergency Response*. Submission to the Northern Territory Emergency Response Review Board, 15 August 2008 (paragraphs 68 and 69), 22: http://www.hrlrc.org.au/files/YE0PPFCQTT/HRLRC%20Submission%20on%20NTER.pdf Note: the HRLRC laments NTNERA Part 6 (s90 and s91). Section 90 contains similar "Matters relating to certain bail applications": Commonwealth Consolidated Acts, *Northern Territory National Emergency Response Act 2007 – Sect 90*, http://www.austlii.edu.au/au/legis/cth/consol_act/ntnera200753 1/s90.html

73 HRLRC, 2008, (paragraph 69), 22. Their source regarding increase in sentences: *Joint Submission by the Central Australian Aboriginal Legal Aid Service and the Northern Australian Justice Agency to the Senate Select Committee on Regional and Remote Indigenous Communities*, June 2008, 7: http://www.aph.gov.au/Senate/committee/indig_ctte/submissions/sub24.pdf

Committee concerning the Crime Amendment (Bail and Sentencing) Bill 2006,[74] Catholic Social Services Australia (CSSA) wrote:

> Criminal justice is inextricably linked to social justice: Indigenous people and people from disadvantaged backgrounds are disproportionately represented in the prison population ... Evidence suggests that experience of arrest and imprisonment reduces employment prospects. So the over-representation of Indigenous people in the criminal justice system is among factors perpetuating Indigenous disadvantage ...
> Catholic Social Services Australia acknowledges the need for urgent action to address and reduce the incidence of violent crime in Indigenous communities. However, this Bill is not an effective means towards this end.[75]

Arguing that removing consideration of customary law in sentencing is futile, objectors promote the idea that Aboriginal culture did not condone sexual or domestic violence. The CSSA asks us to consider a 2000 New South Wales Law Reform Commission report "which recommended recognition of Aboriginal customary law in sentencing":

> "3.112 Any proposal to recognise Aboriginal customary law in sentencing must carry with it a caution to distinguish legitimate and authentic customary law from false assumptions and misconceptions. Specifically, there is a danger that the judiciary, and others involved in the sentencing process, will accept the claim or myth that sexual and domestic violence against women is sanctioned by Aboriginal culture, or, at least, not

---

74 This was the Bill that when enacted in August 2007, became Part 6 Sections 90 and 91 of the NTNERA.
75 Frank Quinlan, Executive Director, Catholic Social Services Australia (CSSA), *Submission to Senate Legal and Constitutional Affairs Committee: Inquiry into the Crime Amendment (Bail and Sentencing) Bill 2006*, 27 September 2006, 3: http://catholicsocialservices.org.au/system/files/Crime_Amendment_submission.pdf

regarded as seriously as it is in non-Aboriginal culture. This premise must be categorically repudiated ..."

Catholic Social Services is concerned that the motivations underlying the Bill, however well-intentioned, may be grounded in the very misconceptions of Aboriginal customary law against which the NSW Law Reform Commission warned. In particular, there appears to be an operating assumption that judges and magistrates may take account of Aboriginal customary law in such a way as to "excuse" or lessen the seriousness of offences involving violence against women. Even apart from grave doubts about whether this assumption accurately reflects Aboriginal customary law, as noted above the appeals process is the most effective means of redressing any individual inappropriate sentencing decision.[76]

CSSA then calls for "urgent need for action to address underlying causes of violence in Indigenous communities":

Catholic Social Services Australia does not believe that changing sentencing rules is an effective way of addressing the causes of violence in Indigenous communities. That requires action to address poverty, social exclusion and the deficiencies of current support arrangements for families in crisis. We endorse the following remarks by Professor Larissa Behrendt ... :

" ... the real way to start to make a difference to those levels of violence is not so much through the judiciary, because they're really at the end of the process – they're undertaking damage control – it's to get into the issues that actually compound to create the circumstances of cyclical poverty, of despondency, of despair, of substance abuse, and therefore violence and other antisocial behaviour, including sexual abuse in those communities."[77]

That the underlying causes of violence need to be addressed, and

---

[76] Ibid, 11-12.
[77] Ibid, 12, q. L. Behrendt, ABC RN, *Law Report* transcript: "Abuse in Aboriginal Communities", 30 May 2006.

that the judiciary is "the end of the process" are important and valid points. However, the CSSA submission evades two critical issues. First, an underlying cause of Aboriginal violence needing urgent action but omitted from their list is the continuing culture of violence, including the male right to beat his spouse in circumstances where she "deserves" it. Second, our judicial system is predicated on the idea of deterrence. The need to address underlying causes of violence does not negate the need for sentences commensurate with the seriousness of a crime and as deterrence. Indeed, Elizabeth Eggleston in her 1970 study of Aboriginal people and the justice system, stated that imprisonment could change customs that abused human rights.[78]

Unintentionally giving credence to the potential beneficial effectiveness of Section 91, it seems that CSSA agrees that in sentencing decisions, non-recognition of Aboriginal tradition could change cultural practices. Because CSSA has adopted a non-discerning approach to Aboriginal culture however, it is unable to see the benefits of such a change. Under the heading "Possible effect on lived experience of cultural practices", CSSA submitted its concern

> that an unintended and undesirable consequence of the proposed legislation could be an intangible but negative "chilling" effect on the maintenance of cultural practices – because a degree of legal recognition has been withdrawn.[79]

A related concern that objectors have to non-consideration of customary law and practice in sentencing is that it contradicts Aboriginal people's right to their own culture and self-determination. Under the heading "The Right to Self-Determination", the HRLRC Submission includes this grievance:

> The HRLRC recognises that rights need to be balanced against

---

78 Kimm, 2004, 138. referring to Elizabeth Eggleston, *Aborigines and the Administration of Justice*, (PhD Thesis, Monash University, 1970), 399-420.
79 Quinlan, 27 September 2006, 11.

> one another and against competing public interests. However, the blanket exclusion of customary law and consideration of cultural practices takes away a major mechanism by which Aboriginal practices and traditions were merged with the general legal system. This aspect of NTER deprives Indigenous people of a right to determine their own social and political development. It also fetters the important capacity and responsibility of the judiciary to consider all relevant factors, including as to moral culpability, in sentencing.[80]

This statement is effectively an admission that self-determination provides scope for Aboriginal perpetrators in traditional settings to have a diminished moral culpability for their violent acts. This raises a critical point, and one that challenges both sides of the debate. Self-determination has been a policy tenet for decades, and unavoidably sustains traditions with a greater capacity to tolerate violence, and more "generosity" regarding who can, and when to, carry out violent acts. It is this problem, the need to consider the environment of the perpetrator, that Eames and Eszenyi have drawn our attention to. In this light, Aboriginal perpetrators of traditionally legitimated violence become the scapegoats of self-determination in our courts. Self-determination is the main culprit here, and it is self-determination that should be brought to trial.

If there is a fundamental legal injustice against such traditional Indigenous perpetrators that Section 91 is committing here, we as a nation have a deep problem. It means that by the standard processes of Western justice, our courts should not be delivering to Indigenous perpetrators, communities and victims the full, unqualified message that brutal norms are unacceptable. And because of this, we should not be delivering the concomitant greater justice and protection for victims of traditional violence that Section 91 seeks to secure. This result is morally bankrupt.

---

80 HRLRC, 2008, (paragraph 70), 22.

Surely the nation's core obligation is to extend no consideration for violent acts knowingly, deliberately committed whatever their cultural contexts, and whatever the sense of entitlement or cultural duty that a perpetrator has to carry out those violent behaviours. When it comes to deliberate personal violence, the transgression is the act of intended aggression itself, and not to be assuaged by pleas that the perpetrator's actions comply with a different culture and law. Unless this is the bottom line, we keep confirming ourselves as a racist nation, failing to give Aboriginal victim rights to safety in law, and imprisoning Aboriginal communities within traditional, violence-based punishment regimes.

On 3 April 2009, the Rudd government "officially endorsed" the Declaration of the Rights of Indigenous Peoples. While this has "no legal impact on policy"[81] there are contradictions between the disallowance of Indigenous cultural factors in our national laws, and some Articles in this – albeit non-binding – Declaration.[82] There are aspects of the Declaration's goals with which most would agree – its condemnation of "forced assimilation", for example. However, when a culture has violent practices, including formalised violent punishment, the problem of a right to self-determination that includes freedom to practice culture becomes dangerous. The following Articles depict the problem:

**Article 3**

Indigenous peoples have the right of self-determination. By virtue of that right they freely determine their political status and freely pursue their economic, social and cultural development.

---

81 Working Group for Aboriginal Rights (Australia) (WGAR), "Australian Government supports UN Declaration on the Rights of Indigenous Peoples Friday April 3 Parliament House Canberra", 4 April 2009: http://wgar.wordpress.com/2009/04/04/ Quoting *The Age*, "Indigenous rights a step closer", 3 April 2009.

82 United Nations, *The General Assembly, United Nations Declaration on the Rights of Indigenous Peoples*. Adopted by General Assembly Resolution 61/295 on 13 September 2007: http://www.hreoc.gov.au/social_justice/declaration/assembly.html

**Article 5**

Indigenous peoples have the right to maintain and strengthen their distinct political, legal, economic, social and cultural institutions, while retaining their rights to participate fully, if they so choose, in the political, economic, social and cultural life of the State.

**Article 8**

1. Indigenous peoples and individuals have the right not to be subjected to forced assimilation or destruction of their culture.
2. States shall provide effective mechanisms for prevention of, and redress for: a. Any action which has the aim or effect of depriving them of their integrity as distinct peoples, or of their cultural values or ethnic identities ...[83]

The Declaration on the Rights of Indigenous Peoples has endowed the federal government with a high-profile contradiction, ripe for national and international attack and pressure, between its endorsement of the Declaration on the one hand, and its continuation of the NTNERA on the other. Coalition fears that the endorsement of the Declaration on the Rights of Indigenous Peoples "will elevate customary law above domestic law" have been dismissed by Megan Davis of the University of New South Wales Indigenous Law Centre.[84] Nevertheless the gravitas and wide support for the government's endorsement of this Declaration further enshrine our moral fragility and our reticence to act against Aboriginal traditional violence and to protect Aboriginal victims.

---

[83] United Nations, 2007. Note: Some other Articles in the Declaration are also problematic in this regard.

[84] WGAR, 4 April 2009, quoting *National Indigenous Times*, "UN Declaration won't elevate Aboriginal customary law: expert", 3 April 2009.

# Legitimacy of violence in Aboriginal traditional cultures

> Clearly, most of the present clamour for the restoration of "tribal law" comes from persons who have no idea of its major provisions.
> – T.G.H. Strehlow[1]

There is considerable denial that in pre-contact times, frequent inter-personal violence took place among the First Australians. This is despite observations since first contact of traditional violence particularly against women, and despite the careful collection of evidence by contemporary scholarly researchers such as Kimm, Nowra, Sutton, McKnight and Webb.[2] Here are some examples of such evasion or denial:

> While my ancestors were maintaining a harmonious relationship with each other, nature, the animal world, Europe was just involved and engulfed in huge, massive amounts of violence.[3]
>
> Family violence and abuse is about lack of respect for Indigenous culture. We need to fight it as indigenous peoples, and rebuild our proud traditions and community structures so that there is no place for fear and intimidation.[4]

---

1 T.G.H Strehlow, in K. Strehlow, *The Operation of Fear in Traditional Aboriginal Society in Central Australia*, The Strehlow Research Foundation Inc., Adelaide, 1991, 7.
2 Kimm, 2004; Nowra, 2007; Sutton, 2009: D. McKnight, 2005; and Stephen Webb, *Palaeopathology of Aboriginal Australians: Health and disease across a hunter-gatherer continent*, Cambridge University Press, Cambridge, 1995.
3 Rosemary Wanganeen, 2009, Spiritual Healer, and Adjunct Research Fellow of the University of South Australia, speaking on "Profile: Rosemary Wanganeen", ABC RN, *Bush Telegraph*, 9 March 2009.
4 Aboriginal and Torres Strait Islander Justice Commissioner, *Ending Family Violence and Abuse in Aboriginal and Torres Strait Islander Communities* Report, HREOC, Sydney, 2006, "Key challenge 7", reproduced in Tom Calma, *Social Justice Report 2007*, 20: http://www.hreoc.gov.au/social_justice/sj_report/index.html

> To reinforce that family violence in any form is unacceptable and never has been an accepted part of Indigenous culture.[5]
>
> "Spousal assault" is "learned behaviour". It was learned by Aboriginal people from the initial aggression of white occupation, and has since been transferred throughout the fabric of Aboriginal society over several generations of exposure to male-dominated colonial and paternalistic administrations. The violent and jealous behaviour of male partners, and their desperate need for dominance, has resulted in terrible mistreatment of Aboriginal women and children.[6]

Several assumptions reinforce such denial. There is a belief that a traditional culture in harmony with the natural environment and with an impressive longevity must be good for all individual members. The reality is that long-lasting cultures living sustainably with their environment can have traditional beliefs and practices that cause human suffering.[7] The US anthropologist Robert Edgerton argued that the idea that traditional cultures are "more harmonious and better adapted than larger more urbanised societies" has within "Western thought ... taken on the quality of a myth, a sacred story not to be challenged".[8] Edgerton observed that in all societies, including resilient traditional societies, "human beliefs and practices may persist even though they serve individual or social needs rather badly"[9]; that harmful practices such as deadly feuding and ill-treatment of women can coexist with long-term group survival; and that traditional practices can serve some members better than others, frequently men better than women, and adults better than children. Indeed "[t]he

---

5 White *et al*, 2006, 1.
6 Kayleen Hazlehurst, *A Healing Place: Indigenous Voices for Personal Empowerment and Community Recovery*, Central Queensland University Press, Rockhampton, 1994, 24.
7 Robert Edgerton, *Sick Societies: Challenging the Myth of Primitive Harmony*, The Free Press, New York, especially Chapter 3, "Maladaptation", 46-74.
8 Ibid, 202.
9 Ibid, 53.

presence of inequality creates the potential for the establishment of traditional beliefs and practices that serve the needs of some people at the expense of others".[10] Edgerton wrote of "the frequent occurrence of seriously harmful beliefs and practices"[11] among small traditional societies, including in Australia[12]: beliefs and practices that lead to high levels of ill-health, hunger, conflict and homicide.[13]

In his 1995 paper "Chronic problems in understanding tribal violence and warfare", Napoleon Chagnon identified a Rousseauesque romanticism that is inhibiting our understanding of traditional violence in a number of ways. The first is "professional rebuke", whereby "those anthropologists who produce ethnographic accounts of violence and warfare based on their observations are frequently criticised and accused of misanthropic malice."[14] Second is an unquestioned assumption, "warfare is introduced by Westerners", and assumed to be "something that post-dates colonialism and the undesirable effects of capitalism on native cultures".[15] Third is post-modernism and related intellectual movements, which are likely to support romantic myths about pre-contact cultures when it is "politically more correct and morally desirable" to do so.[16]

Emphasis on colonial impact is understandable. Under white colonisation, Australian Aboriginal people suffered loss of life, family, community, land and culture, and a plethora of other human rights

---

10 Ibid, 103-104.
11 Ibid, 104.
12 Ibid, 47-52, 126.
13 Ibid, 204. In the control of homicide, writes Edgerton, modern urban societies are typically better than traditional societies.
14 Napoleon Chagnon, "Chronic problems in understanding tribal violence and warfare", in G. Bock and J. Goode, *Genetics of criminal and anti-social behaviour* (1995 Ciba Symposium), Wiley, Chichester New York 1996, 207. Note: Chagnon's article includes no tilt to "genetics", apart perhaps implied shared human traits we all equally possess and tend to express given similar cultures and situations.
15 Ibid, 207
16 Ibid, 209.

abuses and oppressions. Appalling health and welfare statistics are clear indications that Aboriginal suffering still persists. There is also an understandable concern that focusing on aspects of Aboriginal traditional culture that mainstream values would find unacceptable fuels negative stereotypes, potentially hampering Aboriginal participation in the wider society.[17] Further, many Aboriginal men and women are among Australia's finest citizens, working hard, often as unsung heroes, for Aboriginal people and shunning violence with more vigour and commitment than most non-Aboriginal people. Surely these Aboriginal people might feel painfully misrepresented when the critical gaze extends beyond white contact.

Brunton, while a critic of the romantic vision – and its consequences – about traditional Aboriginal Australia, notes "the increasing celebration of indigenous cultures by the non-Aboriginal intelligentsia. For many of the people involved it has been a transforming experience."[18] The downside emerges when there is a denial of the traditional origins of today's violence, an insistent focus on white-contact-caused suffering, and a resultant misplaced optimism that traditional Aboriginal Australia contains the seeds of its own salvation. African-American economist and social commentator Thomas Sowell, while fully cognisant of the horror of racial oppression, urges caution about identifying colonialism and racism as primary causes of minority group dysfunction:

> It is difficult to survey the history of racial or ethnic relations without being appalled by the inhumanity, brutality, and viciousness of it all. There is no more humane or moral wish than the wish that this could all be set right somehow. But there

---

17 See Sutton, 2001, 125-128, on this problem. Sutton's Inaugural Berndt Foundation Biennial Lecture (2001b) is quoted by Kimm on this: Kimm, 2004, x.

18 Ron Brunton, *A Bombshell in the Centre of Perth: An Anthropologist Considers the Single Noongar Judgment*, The Bennelong Society, Occasional Paper, January 2007, 23.

are no more futile or dangerous efforts than attempts to redress the wrongs of history.[19]

Sowell also identifies the pitfall of equating "victimhood" with "virtue";[20] and observes that "no group was a tabula rasa to begin with".[21]

---

19 Thomas Sowell, *Race and Culture: A World View*, Basic Books, New York, 1994, 251.
20 Ibid, 250.
21 Ibid, 251.

# 4

# "Necessity" of violent punishment for Dreamtime sacrilege

For the first Australians, sacred life was the core, encompassing feature, as it was believed that all life depended on correct sacred ceremony. T.G.H. Strehlow in his account of the Central Australian Aranda[1] people captures the centrality of sacred life:

> ... the religious acts performed by the totemic clan members of all the inland tribes at their respective totemic centres were regarded as being essential for the continuation of all human, animal and plant life in Central Australia.[2]

There was interdependence here, with totemic clan groups being responsible for a distinct totem. For example, rain for the countryside of the Eastern Aranda Purula-Kamara local group depended on the rain ceremony of the *Ujitja*, the totemic clan responsible for making rain.[3]

The sacred and supernatural realm of Aboriginal belief and law imposed severe demands on all men, women and children: "Sacredness

---

1 "Aranda" is T.G.H. Strehlow's spelling.
2 T.G.H. Strehlow, in K. Strehlow, 1991, 80.
3 Ibid, 80.

was ... a condition of living."⁴ Ceremonial mistakes and violations were frightening events, because they could upset and trigger the wrath of the powerful ancestral creation beings, threatening the country on which life depended. In such a context, causation rather than intention was the primary consideration. Members of the tribe, particularly male elders, had the right and obligation to carry out severe punishment against those wittingly or accidentally committing sacrilegious acts, to redress such fearful rift.⁵ Under customary law, "if someone accidentally witnessed a prohibited ceremony or happened upon a sacred site, that person would be liable to punishment, regardless of motive or intention".⁶ Kathleen Strehlow writes that

> it would be no exaggeration to say that the system worked as one of sheer terror in the days before the white man came. This terror was instilled from earliest childhood and continued unabated through life until the extremity of old age seemed to guarantee some immunity from the attentions of blood avenger or scorcer [sic] alike for wrongs real or imaginary ... children were not exempted from capital punishment for persistent offences against the old tribal code.⁷

The punishment that arose from sacred Aboriginal law must have shocked early white settlers. The 1875 Irbmankara massacre "saw the killing of about 100 men, women, and children for an alleged

---

4 See Ronald M. Berndt and Catherine H. Berndt, *The World of the First Australians*, Lansdowne Press, 2nd ed. 1981, 303, where they wrote, "The Dreaming was the source of all life, and anything which touched it was, virtually by definition, sacred. Sacredness was, therefore, a condition of living."
5 K. Strehlow, 1991, 35.
6 See also Law Reform Commission of Western Australia (LRCWA), 'Traditional Aboriginal Law and Punishment', *Aboriginal Customary Laws Discussion Paper, Part V—Aboriginal Customary Law and the Criminal Justice System*, 2006, 84: http://www.lrc.justice.wa.gov.au/2publications/reports/ACL/DP/Part_05B.pdf
7 K. Strehlow, 1991, 34-35.

act of sacrilege of which most of those slain were personally quite innocent".[8] According to T.G.H. Strehlow,

> it was this readiness to kill persons who had committed sacrilege either knowingly or unwittingly (the fact alone was looked at, not any *mens rea*) that caused a great revulsion against aboriginal religion in Central Australia after the arrival of the white population.[9]

Waipuldanya, a mission-educated man and an elder of the Alawa people, Roper River, related the following:

> I remember one occasion, after particularly blatant sacrilege, when it was decided that two of the offender's relatives must die. One of the victims was a woman. The Mulunguwa dived into a billabong where she was digging lily roots, dragged her down, and broke her neck under water. Then a brother was slowly sung [sic] to death.[10]

These events, and others recorded by T.G.H. Strehlow, who spent many years observing the Aranda people's sacred life and law, illustrate the gravity with which sacred transgressions were regarded. They also illustrate key aspects of sacred law that are incompatible with human rights.

First, a sacred crime may carry a death penalty even when that crime has no direct human, animal or property victims except in the realm of Dreamtime belief. These included wrongful participation in or witnessing of certain ceremonies "from whose performances women and children and unauthorised males were excluded on pain of death".[11] Sacrilege occurred when ceremony was not performed correctly on

---
8 Hon. Mr. Justice Michael D. Kirby, "T.G.H. Strehlow and Aboriginal Customary Laws", *The Adelaide Law Review*, Vol. 7, 1980-1, 191-2.
9 T.G.H. Strehlow, "Aboriginal Customary Law", *Strehlow Research Foundation Pamphlet* No. 5, Vol. 1, August 1978, 1., q. in Kirby 1980-1, 192.
10 Waipuldanya, in Lockwood, 1964, 124.
11 T.G.H. Strehlow, in K. Strehlow, 1991, 5.

pain of severe punishment including death. Violation of sacred sites, including entering them when one's status or gender forbade entry, and violation of sacred objects (either through seeing them when one's status or gender disallowed it or damaging them even accidentally or stealing them), entailed punishment by death. In an account told in 1953 by two elderly men at Hermannsburg decades after it occurred "sometime before 1877", an uninitiated boy was caught "thieving portions of *tjauerilja*[12] meat near Manama". For this, plus the fact that he was a "hardened offender", he was drowned. Other relatives of the drowned boy later killed his mother, as "she should have kept closer watch over the boy so that he could not have thieved any *tjauerilja*".[13]

Second, causation rather than intention is central, meaning that even accidental sacrilegious acts can be subject to the death penalty. Among the Aranda, accidental dropping and breaking of sacred *tjurunga* resulted in a death sentence.[14] In one mid-19th-century example, an accidental act of grave sacrilege occurred. During the weeks-long eagle commemorative ceremonies "men were gathered together from most eagle totemic centres situated in the Lower Southern Aranda area".[15] Women and children were allowed near the festival camping ground only at night, and had to leave each morning before dawn to gather food some miles away "until well after sunset". Their morning signal to leave "was given out by a young man who climbed up the [eagle totem] pole in order to rattle the seashells suspended near its top". One morning, an accident occurred during this process:

> This accident was deemed to constitute a grave act of sacrilege against the grim eagle ancestors. There were cries of alarm

---

12 "Even the *tjauerilja* – the gift offerings of meat paid for months (even years, by young male novices who had passed through the 'man-making' ceremonies to the old men before these gave them any religious instruction) were sacrosanct", T.G.H. Strehlow, in K. Strehlow, 1991, 7.

13 T.G.H. Strehlow, in K. Strehlow, 1991, 6-7.

14 Ibid., 9; see also K. Strehlow, 1991, 35-7.

15 K. Strehlow, 1991, 75.

from the watching men and shouts of murderous anger from the ceremonial chief and his elders. The young men involved in the accident – there were either two or three of them – were immediately seized. Their necks were twisted around till the vertebrae had been dislocated, and they were probably choked to death as well ... the shock that ran through the assembled gathering which had witnessed the murderous grimness of religious power exercised so ruthlessly was so severe that no eagle *wariera* festivals were ever held again either at Uralawuraka or at Akar Intjota.[16]

Third, while acts of sacrilege were generally clearly defined and subject to predictable, obligatory punishments, deadly extension of sacred punishment took place. Some accounts point to hazardous indistinct boundaries between sacred and non-sacred misdemeanours. This provided scope for violent lawmaking, which crossed into the private, discretionary realm, which required no precedent.[17] The following example suggests this: "'Executions of younger males, especially of those who were considered disrespectful to the authority of their own elders, on charges of sacrilege were ... a feature of the accepted penal system of all ... tribes in the Centre'".[18] Sacred punishment could spiral out of control when disagreement occurred over whether a sacrilegious act had taken place. T.G.H. Strehlow noted a case where relatives objected to the execution of four young men because a sacred object they were guarding was damaged due to a bush fire:

> These relatives accordingly proceeded to avenge their dead kinsmen by killing some of the young men who had carried out the instructions of their elders. In this way a lengthy vendetta

---

16 Ibid, 76-7. T.G.H. Strehlow noted that because of taboos "against free discussion of serious acts of sacrilege", the exact nature of the accident has not been handed down.
17 LRCWA, 2006, 84, ft 7.
18 T.G.H Strehlow, 1970, q. by L. Hiatt, 1991, *Aboriginal Political Life*, Australian Institute of Aboriginal Studies, Canberra, 10, q. by Victoria Burbank, *Fighting Women, Anger and Aggression in Aboriginal Australia*, University of California Press, Berkeley, 1994, 31-2.

was started, and a number of men lost their lives because of a tragic accident.[19]

Fourth, the identity of a guilty party could be determined through sorcerous or magical means. The divination ritual, also associated with deadly vendettas,

> took place in order to divine by – to us – exceedingly haphazard means the alleged identity of murderers (by proxy or scorcery [sic]) which natives once believed provided conclusive proof necessary for the sending out of revenge expeditions.[20]

In one instance from Ellery Creek, relatives make a spindle from a murdered man's hair, and watch for when it breaks while it spins into a hair string. The distance and direction of the spindle's travel indicate the murderer:

> If it does not travel far, the [men present] know: "one of the men from his own camp killed him". If it travels a considerable distance, [they know]: "The murderer came from a distant place; and that too is the direction from which the murderer came."[21]

Fifth, sacred law discriminated on gender. Certainly, men faced restrictions on pain of death to many sacred places, objects and ceremonies, with only ceremonial chiefs and male elders allowed access to the most sacred. Women's access was particularly limited, often akin to those of young, uninitiated males and children. K. Strehlow cites numerous examples.[22] For a woman, there were more sacred objects that she could not see or touch, more sacred sites that she could not approach, and more sacred ceremonies that she must not participate in or witness, even accidentally, on pain of death. This

---

19 T.G.H. Strehlow, in K. Strehlow, 1991, 10.
20 K. Strehlow, 1991, 31.
21 T.G.H. Strehlow, in K. Strehlow, 1991, 32. For another example, see Berndt and Berndt, 1981, 354.
22 K. Strehlow, 1991, 74-5, 78.

could affect essential daily tasks such as water collection:

> Even waters open to women and children, if they were at or near a sacred site, had to be approached carefully; generally too, they had to be vacated before the rocky bottom could be seen. Thus in the Krantji area, where the dearth of other safe waters in the district made it necessary that the women be allowed to drink from the soak itself, they were permitted merely to skim the water off close to the surface: only men could plunge the vessel down to any depth.[23]

Storage places of sacred *tjurunga* were forbidden to all but "the ceremonial chief and the local group elders" and other local men were allowed "only if sent there on special errands by the ceremonial chief and his elders. Women and children were excluded at all times":[24]

> Within living memory, a thirsty Eastern Aranda woman, when walking to the Ujitja spring to fill her kangaroo-skin waterbag, cut a corner in the mile-long mountain gully on her way, and passed within sight of the trees on which the Ujitja rain *tjurunga* were stored. Her tracks were discovered soon afterward, and she was killed by a spear thrust through the side of her chest.[25]

Greater sacred realm prohibitions imposed on women featured in traditional society across the continent. W. Lloyd Warner detailed several examples of east Arnhem Land's Murnjin men and women being killed for willing or accidental totemic and ceremonial transgressions, noting that "[i]f women look at a totemic emblem they are killed by their own group". Even husbands were expected not to save their "guilty" wife, although there were brave husbands who did:

> (A)'s wife was burning a patch of brush while hunting for bandicoot. The husband had hidden the string for his totemic emblem in the bushes. The fire destroyed it. The string belonged

---

23 Ibid, 74.
24 Ibid, 78.
25 Ibid, 78.

to the Daiuror clan. They tried to kill her and would have succeeded, but she escaped to the mission with the help of her husband. He was felt to have done wrong in helping her.[26]

Gordon Bennett, drawing on records from the 1830s, noted that the Gringai people of the region surrounding today's Newcastle and Port Stephens, New South Wales, had bull-roarers or *torikotti* which were sacred initiation objects. These consisted of a piece of hardwood attached to a piece of fibre and

> on being whirled gave out a roaring drone that was the voice of the spirit. They were particularly sacred, and were never shown by the owners to anyone. If a woman heard the sound of the bull-roarer it was supposed to mean death to her.[27]

Bennett also recorded that

> among the Gringai as with other tribes, an extraordinary mystery attached to pieces of quartz crystal. They are possessed only by the "koradjis" or medicine men and were supposed to have come into their possession through the instrumentality of a spirit ... If a woman saw one by chance her brains were knocked out with a nulla. Women, therefore, were always in great dread of seeing one of them.[28]

## The debilitating terror of sorcery

From a Western-based system of thought and practice, sorcery seems the antithesis of rationality and civil society. But belief alone can render sorcery an effective, even deadly danger to believers. In Aboriginal traditional society, sorcery's victims could be controlled, made physically or mentally ill, or even die. With a few strategically arranged and placed objects, a few certain words, and a few ritual

---

26 Warner, 1958, 160. Note: Name of husband in original: fictitious initial here.
27  G. Bennett, 1929, 16.
28  Ibid, 16.

actions, men and women[29] could exercise sorcery against another with profound effect. What a powerful weapon for an aggressor, what a deadly force against a victim!

Many forms of sorcery across traditional Aboriginal Australia have been documented.[30] It included effigies, gruesome rituals, chants, "magic powder", and "magical operations".[31] The pointing bone is probably the most well known, and was "widely distributed over the Continent".[32] Sorcery was performed by experts in the rituals, primarily used against law breakers. It was also used by men and women to control or punish another. For instance,

> in Western Arnhem Land, sorcery figures are drawn on the walls of rock shelters, as well as on sheets of prepared bark. A jealous husband, not necessarily an acknowledged sorcerer, may try to punish an unfaithful wife by drawing her likeness, with an eaglehawk or Rainbow Snake head, several arms, and stingray nails protruding from her body. The conventional sequence is that she becomes ill, as the painting is retouched she becomes worse, and she finally dies.[33]

Victims' belief in its power is what made the sorcery efficacious, and "[a] person who claims to have performed magic or sorcery on another is likely to make sure that this information gets around to his intended victim".[34]

Further to this, traditional Aboriginal Australia saw death as

---

29 Phyllis Kaberry wrote that only a male could cause another to die through sorcery: Phyllis Kaberry, *Aboriginal Woman Sacred and Profane*, 1939, Routledge, London, (this edition 2004) 211-12. Note, C. Strehlow gives an account of Aranda women's sorcery that was intended to sicken or indeed kill a female rival: C. Strehlow, 1907-1920. *Die Aranda und Loritja Stamme in Zentral Australia*, Joseph Baer, Frankfurt, q. in K. Strehlow, 1991, 27-8.
30 See Berndt and Berndt, 1981, Chapter 9, "Magic and Sorcery", 304-35.
31 Ibid, 322-4.
32 Ibid, 320.
33 Ibid, 323-4.
34 Ibid, 305.

unnatural, except death of the very old.[35] Deaths that would from a Western perspective have an obvious cause including infection, accident or misadventure such as a shark attack, would be seen as unnatural: "Someone, therefore, must have been responsible."[36] The source of such convictions is belief in the supremacy of the supernatural. As Phyllis Kaberry observed,

> when an able-bodied adolescent or adult dies, the normal course of life has been subjected to interference, and the reason is sought in the abnormal or supernatural sphere ... death itself is due to the malevolent agency of the sorcerer who has misused powers from *Kaleru* and the *djua:ri*, and has directed them against individuals who have no defence at the time. This in turn entails a whole system of activities devoted to the discovery of the sorcerer.[37]

Explorer and magistrate Edward John Eyre made a similar note concerning Aboriginal people of southern Australia during the 1840s:

> as the natives do not often admit that the young or the strong can die from natural causes, they ascribe the event to the agency of sorcery, employed by individuals of neighbouring tribes. This must of course be expiated in some way when they meet ...[38]

According to Kaberry, divination and sorcery were central tools to identifying and killing the sorcerer.

> The *baramambin*, who has himself obtained his craft from the rainbow snake and the *djua:ri*, will look at the stones that have been touched by the juices fallen from the platform on

---

35 Ibid, 329.
36 Ibid, 329.
37 Kaberry, 1939, 211-12.
38 Edward. J. Eyre, *An account of the manners and customs of the Aborigines and the state of their relations with Europeans*, 1845, Chapter 2. eBooks@Adelaide 2004: http://ebooks.adelaide.edu.au/e/eyre/edward_john/e98m/complete.html (originally published with "Journals of expeditions of discovery into Central Australia, and overland from Adelaide to King George's Sound, in the years 1840-1").

> which the corpse has been placed. From these he may be able to indicate the direction from which the sorcery has come. If the guilt is established definitely, the relatives will seek to kill the murderer. If it is inconclusive, the elder relatives and *barambin* will go apart secretly about a year later, take a bone or the skull, paint it with red ochre and blood from their forearm, bury it in an ant-bed with a fire, and chant a particular spell. It is believed that the murderer will sicken and die.[39]

But sorcerous means of identifying and killing wrongdoers did not necessarily "settle accounts", and persistent feuds could result.[40]

Sorcery is still practised in remote Aboriginal Australia. In some places, reports suggest greater discontinuity with the past than in the case of violence, while in others, resort to sorcery as punishment, control or revenge has possibly increased, in adaptation to white law's restriction of more direct, physical forms of violence. David McKnight's observations on Mornington Island suggest that sorcery is now declining there. While there was a sudden, brief escalation of sorcery under contemporary pressures, the intent regarding its use remained clearly traditional:[41]

> the elders and Law men were frequently denied the right to use physical coercion by missionaries, government officials, and police, in fact by the whole legal apparatus of European Australia. The penalty for spearing or killing a wrongdoer was too harsh for the avengers or Aboriginal Law enforcers because they were apt to languish in jail for years. Hence, they turned more and more to sorcery.[42]

By the 1980s, sorcery had subsided. The old sorcerers were dying out, and Mornington Island's young people no longer believed in its efficacy, having adopted more of the white way of interpreting the

---

39 Kaberry, 1939, 212.
40 Berndt and Berndt, 1981, 330.
41 McKnight, 2005, 153
42 Ibid, 152-3.

causes of sickness and death via the mission regime and their white contact through cattle station work.[43]

Victoria Burbank conveys a discontinuity regarding contemporary sorcery's link with the past among the people of Mangrove. According to Burbank, the phenomenon of "cursing" started in 1971 as a "settlement life" phenomenon. However, the curses evoke strongly traditional references, and are used most often by men against women:

> The act of cursing appears simple. I am told that an aggressor simply says that a woman is cursed to a ceremony or to a certain sacred area in a country. By this act, the woman is removed from the world of the ordinary. She becomes sacred and by association "dangerous", as might everything that she might touch ... much like a person quarantine. She is in danger of impending death, and almost anyone who might touch her is similarly threatened.[44]

Burbank wrote that some Mangrove women appear to have little fear and perhaps no longer believe in pre-contact ideologies such as "devil-devils" and "murderers" and "supernatural aggression", due to thirty years of white teachings, both Christian and non-Christian. What surprised Burbank was that so many still believed in them.[45]

While McKnight pointed to sorcery's recent decline, Hughes has identified an opposite trend. She argues that the failure to provide people on homelands with a strong mainstream education allows a continuation of sorcerous beliefs in these communities:

> Because education has failed to introduce rules of reasoning and causal sequences, fears of malevolent spirits and sorcerers are used to strengthen the position of "Big Men".[46]

Cribb, who spent 20 years in Cape York Peninsula and developed close ties with the Wik people, wrote in 2005 that

---

43 Ibid, 209-11.
44 Burbank, 1994, 167.
45 Ibid, 175.
46 Hughes, 2007, 29.

[b]elief in magical influences in Cape York Peninsula has not lessened with increasing European contact. "Pourri pourri" is often evoked to explain physical and mental states which to clinical workers could easily be explained in other ways. Pourri pourri is frequently blamed when deaths or physical illnesses occur. This extends to mental conditions such as depression or psychosis. The fear of being accused of pourri pourri may also cause great distress and anxiety.[47]

In Central Australia, sorcerous beliefs are used to terrify young girls into having sex. The Mullighan Inquiry documents the following case of a girl in a dangerously violent relationship with an older man.

Police records show that aged 13, the girl was bashed so severely that she was admitted to hospital. This bashing breached a restraining order. Following one assault, welfare noted that "[the girl] expresses concern about her partner telling her that the evil spirits will cause her harm if she does not sleep with him".[48]

Sorcery is reported to be a potent force among today's Yolngu people, primarily as adaptation to white law's suppression of violent punishment and revenge. Burbank quotes anthropologist Nancy Williams on this:

As one clan leader put it, Yolngu had two ways to deal with people who committed serious offences: to talk to them, and to kill them. The old men ... had to face up to the problem of how to punish people who committed offences for which they should have been killed. It was better not to kill, he said, but what punishment would take its place? He implied one result was increased reliance on sorcery.[49]

The resilience and controlling power of sorcerous beliefs and their

---

47 Cribb, 2005, 6.
48 Mullighan Inquiry, 2008, 49.
49 Nancy Williams, *Two Laws: Managing Disputes in a Contemporary Aboriginal Community*, Australian Institute of Aboriginal Studies, Canberra, 1987, 151, q. in Burbank, 1994, 88-9.

continuing impact on remote communities need to be acknowledged. In particular, it seems that prioritising traditional over mainstream learning can place young Aboriginal people in peril, rendering them more subject to oppressive traditional beliefs and power, while ill-equipping them for the mainstream world.

**Scapegoats**

Perhaps not strictly "sacred", the extreme irrationality of misplaced punishments places them within a supernatural or "magical thinking" realm. One traditional punishment occurs when kin of an accused wrongdoer receive punishment. This can cause vendettas. Furthermore, in the words of Kimm,

> The concept of communal guilt is alien to Anglo-Australian law. This includes not only payback upon a family member in lieu of an offender, but the visitation of responsibility on individuals who, in the eyes of non-Aborigines, would be entirely removed from any chain of causation.[50]

Women are more vulnerable to misdirected punishments. This is particularly evident in brother-sister avoidance taboos and the associated *mirriri*. Warner, Burbank and others have noted these taboos and *mirriri* among the Yolngu and adjacent peoples of Arnhem Land. Under the heading "Legitimate male aggression: *mirriri*", Burbank writes that "the sexual asymmetry of this etiquette is one of its most striking aspects", and describes how *mirriri* operates in the Arnhem Land community of Mangrove:

> At Mangrove, women speak of mirriri as an emotion like "shame" that intensifies when etiquette associated with the brother/sister relationship is violated. When attention is called to a real or classificatory sister's sexuality, reproductive capacities, or eliminatory functions, a man's mirriri increases, and he is expected to behave aggressively toward her (Burbank 1985).

---

50 Kimm, 1999, 181.

Should a man see his sister going to one of the public toilets, for example, women say he might throw a stick or tin (can) at her. [51]

The injustice, indeed insanity of *mirriri* is that women must bear the responsibility (and punishment) for brother-sister avoidance etiquette, even if they are the innocent party. Gillian Cowlishaw describes an incident where a "brother" could not find his spears in time to punish the actual sister who innocently "broke" an avoidance taboo, so he threatened his other "sisters" instead.[52] While Western law and influence has reportedly reduced *mirriri*, it is still a force in Arnhem Land communities, particularly when alcohol further reduces inhibitions. In a 1996 case that occurred at Ngukurr, a man struck his sister over the head with a large stick, resulting in a "massive fracture of the skull" and putting her in hospital for four weeks. He did this to punish her, his right according to customary law, because her husband swore at her in the presence of her brother, the appellant. In the words of a witness, senior elder of Ngukurr, "in our ways, that – that woman who that man swore to and she get hit from the brother – it's – that's her punishment – you know. She got to take that."[53]

---

51 Burbank, 1994, 152.
52 Gillian Cowlishaw, "Infanticide in Aboriginal Australia", *Oceania*, Vol. 48 (4), June 1978, 276. This is presented with more detail in Chapter 5.
53 *Ashley v Materna* [1997]. This case is discussed by Kimm, 2004, 53, 87, and 101-2.

# 5
# Interpersonal violence in traditional times

**Violent customs against women**

It is perhaps not surprising that early white settlers were "revulsed" by some aspects of Aboriginal sacred law.[1] There was injustice, cruelty and capital punishment in Western law, with the penal settlement birth of white Australia a bleak testimony to its horrendous punishment for petty crime. However, Western law was by the late 18th century based on the principle of proven responsibility, and its Christian religion had left behind many medieval horrors and was more about redemption through repentance and forgiveness. Apart from the shared human feelings of spiritual belief, reverence, fear, anger, revenge and grief that Aboriginal sacred law gave expression to, there was little that was familiar.

It might be expected that within the everyday realm of relationships between men and women, the gap between the first Australians and white colonialists was less noteworthy. The Western world of the late 18th and 19th centuries was a misogynist one, women were not full citizens, and a woman's legal status was little more than a possession of her husband and subject to his authority. Despite this, from the first contact white men were shocked by what they saw. First Fleet officer Watkin Tench's observations of widespread brutal treatment of Aboriginal women by their menfolk, including the famed Bennelong, have been frequently noted.[2] Nowra quotes Governor Phillip's

---
1 T.G.H. Strehlow q. in Kirby 1980-1, 192.
2 For example by Kimm, 2004, 46; Nowra, 2007, 9-10.

documentation of the abusive treatment by men against women among the Eora people, and that Phillip "spent some time trying to dissuade Bennelong from killing a woman".[3] Early accounts from other colonial settlements sadly provide a similar portrayal, indicating that subjugation of women in pre-contact Australia was similar across the continent and included wife beatings, rape, promised marriage from birth, marriage of adolescent girls to much older men, woman stealing, wife swapping, wife lending including to appease would-be executioners, and polygamy. As noted by Nowra,

> Despite local variations, there is a consistent pattern of Aboriginal men's treatment of women that was harsh, sexually aggressive (gang-rape, for instance) and, in our term, misogynist. Given its pervasive nature across the whole of Australia, we can say that it was ancient and long-lasting.[4]

Eyre wrote about the tribes of the Adelaide Plains and the Murray River in South Australia, including the treatment of women. His knowledge comes primarily from years of getting to know the Aboriginal people of South Australia, including three years as Resident Magistrate of the Murray District during the early 1840s.[5] He documented his observations because he found that Aboriginal people were "misjudged and misrepresented" as fierce and dangerous, whereas he found them to be helpful and friendly even while he "stood singly amongst them in the remote and trackless wilds". Eyre wrote critically of the white occupation of Australia, which he called aggression.

> To sanction this aggression, we have not, in the abstract, the slightest shadow of either right or justice – we have not even the extenuation of endeavouring to compensate those we have

---

3 Nowra, 2007, 10.
4 Ibid, 24.
5 Eyre acknowledges M. Moorhouse, Esq., Protector of Aborigines in Adelaide, for his contribution to this account, particularly in relation to the Aboriginal people of the Adelaide Plains: Eyre, 1845, Chapter 1.

injured, or the merit of attempting to mitigate the sufferings our presence inflicts.⁶

Eyre's ability to see colonial injustice and aggression did not compromise his depiction of Aboriginal women's subjugated status in the region:

> In their domestic relations with one another polygamy is practised in its fullest extent. An old man having usually from one to four wives, or as many as he can procure.
>
> The females, and especially the young ones are kept principally among the old men, who barter away their daughters, sisters, or nieces, in exchange for wives for themselves or their sons. Wives are considered the absolute property of the husband, and can be given away, or exchanged, or lent, according to his caprice ... Female children are usually betrothed from early infancy ...
>
> Women are often sadly ill-treated by their husbands or friends, in addition to the dreadful life of drudgery, and privation, and hardship they always have to undergo; they are frequently beaten about the head, with waddies, in the most dreadful manner, or speared in the limbs for the most trivial offences. No one takes the part of the weak or the injured, or ever attempts to interfere with the infliction of such severe punishments.
>
> Few women will be found, upon examination, to be free from frightful scars upon the head, or the marks of spear wounds about the body. I have seen a young woman, who, from the number of these marks, appeared to have been almost riddled with spear wounds.⁷

Evidence from other regions indicates that women had little choice but to comply with their lot, although some did resist. Kimm writes that "young girls were taught through legends that they should go

---

6 Eyre, 1845, Chapter 1.
7 Ibid, Chapter 4.

obediently to marriage.⁸ This was necessary as many young girls rebelled against arranged marriages, and strongly disliked the promised husband.⁹ Indeed, one attraction of the missions was that they provided refuge for young Aboriginal girls fleeing promised husbands.¹⁰ In some regions, girls were beaten or killed for refusing to comply.¹¹ In others, a girl's persistent refusal could work. Regarding a Kimberley region, Kaberry writes that she "was told about girls… who had run away from their husbands because the latter were too old or had frightened them. They were generally sent back, but a few persisted and finally the project was abandoned."¹²

Women's subjugation and violent treatment reflected troubled gender relations in traditional Aboriginal society, as evident in Eyre's writings. Referring to Stanner's study of the Daly River tribes, Kaberry wrote that

> [T]he entire psychic relationship of the sexes is one of great social significance: there is much distrust, hostility, and insinuation of misconduct between them; jealousy, suspicion of infidelity and endless quarrelling with and over women strike a constant note in the *Dirawur* life; and the working of social mechanisms

---

8 Kimm, 1999, 135, referring to J. Isaacs (ed), *Australian Dreaming: 40,000 Years of Aboriginal History*, Landsdowne Press, 1980, 160-9.

9 Kimm, 1999, 135, referring to Kaberry, 1939, 100-101 and 103; and Annette Hamilton, "The role of women in Aboriginal marriage arrangements", in Fay Gale (ed), *Women's Role in Aboriginal Society*, Australian Institute of Aboriginal Studies, Canberra, 1978, 34.

10 Bishop Francois Xavier Gsell, who established a mission at Nguiu in 1911, is a famous example. When a young girl, speared in the leg for refusing an arranged marriage, sought refuge at the mission, Gsell realised that the only way to protect such girls was to "buy" them. Over the years, Gsell "bought 150 girls, all considered under tribal law as his wives". Thus freed from elders' harems, young women were able to marry young men in a "free Christian marriage": James Franklin, "The Missionary with 150 Wives", *Quadrant* Vol. LIV, No. 7-8, July-August 2012, 30-2.

11 Kimm, 2004, 68, referring to J. Lingard, *A Narrative of the Journey to and from New South Wales*, (J. Taylor, Chapel-en-le Frith, England), 33; and S. Davis, *Above Capricorn*, Angus and Robertson, Sydney, 1994, 30.

12 Kaberry, 1939, 100.

which function to subordinate women socially...tend to induce psychic unrest.[13]

Eyre observed that while men of southern Australia typically had a strong, healthy appearance, the women appeared physically deprived. This was probably, Eyre thought, due to the "hardship, privation and ill-treatment" the women must endure:

> To her belongs the duty of collecting and preparing the daily food, of making the camp or hut for the night, of gathering and bringing in firewood, and of procuring water. She must also attend to the children; and in travelling carry all the moveable property and frequently the weapons of her husband. In wet weather she attends to all the outside work, whilst her lord and master is snugly seated at the fire. If there is a scarcity of food she has to endure the pangs of hunger, often, perhaps, in addition to ill-treatment or abuse.[14]

In reference to palaeopathologist Stephen Webb's 1995 study of thousands of pre-historic post-cranial and cranial samples from sites across mainland Australia, Sutton wrote:

> If people are in any doubt as to whether or not serious armed assaults on women and men took place in Australia over thousands of years prior to conquest, the archaeological record of prehistoric human remains settles the question decisively.[15]

Along with widespread reports of violence-enforced authority that husbands had over wives,[16] are frequent reports of violent force surrounding the process of marriage, particularly if a woman showed

---

13 Ibid, 152, referring to W.E.H. Stanner, "The Daly River Tribes", *Oceania*, vols. iii and iv, 1932-4. Note that Kimm, 2004, 57, stated that Kaberry was applying this observation to a Kimberley people. Kaberry was referring to Stanner's Daly River findings, emphasising that it could be applied only partially to the Kimberley as it reflected only Kimberley men's and not Kimberley women's attitudes. See Kaberry, 1939, 153.
14 Eyre, 1845, Chapter 2.
15 Sutton, 2001, 152, referring to Webb, 1995.
16 For example, Eyre 1845; Warner, 1958; and Meggitt, 1962.

resistance. In 1830, R. Dawson observed that the Port Stephens tribes north of Newcastle,

> generally took their wives from other tribes if they could find opportunities to steal them. The consent of the female was never made a question of the transaction. When the tribes appeared to be in a state of peace with each other, friendly visits were exchanged, at which times the unmarried females were carried off by either party. The friends of the girl never interfered, and in the event of her making any resistance, which was frequently the case, her abductor silenced it by a severe blow on the head with his club while carrying her off.[17]

Polygamy was widespread across the continent, contributing further to the harshness and conflict in the lives of both men and women, although Meggitt in his "Walbiri" study, recorded that "most of the people believe that polygyny benefits the wives as much as the husbands".[18] There was frequent violent conflict and rivalry between co-wives; polygamy unavoidably created a shortage of women, thus increased competition and violence between men for women, it "necessitated" the practice of making girls marry very young to increase the supply of available women; and it increased social pressures to reduce the number of men, such as the killing of young men in war. Warner documents these facets among the Murngin.[19] J.W. Fawcett, in 1898, reported that among the Wannah-Ruah tribe, Hunter River region, New South Wales, "a large number of men were unable to obtain a wife", due to "the law of consanguinity", "the paucity in female children reared" and polygamy among older men.[20]

---

17 G. Bennett, 1929, 4-5.
18 Meggitt, 1962, 113.
19 See Mary Bennett, "evidence to Moseley Royal Commission, 19 March 1934", transcript pp. 215-16, q. in Keith Windschuttle, *The Fabrication of Aboriginal History, Volume Three: The Stolen Generations 1881-2008*, Macleay Press, Sydney, 2009, 464-5; Burbank, 1994, 111-12, 116; and Warner, 1958, 155-6; 158-9.
20 J.W. Fawcett, "Customs of the Wannah-Ruah Tribe and Their Dialect or Vocabulary", in *Science*, 21 September 1898, 180, sourced from D. A. Roberts *et al.*

Fawcett's account adds poignancy, because amidst the harshness of woman shortage, great affection flourished between spouses, and some women maintained considerable standing and influence:

> Sometimes a strong minded woman left her husband and married the man she liked ... Some of the women had great influence with their husbands, and demanded and secured undivided attention. Most of the married aborigines showed great affection for each other.[21]

Of less favourable aspects, Fawcett wrote:

> As soon as a girl was born she was given by her father, or allotted by the council of her tribe (which consisted of the older men) to be the wife of one of the men who could either marry her or dispose of her to someone else. In either case she became a wife at about twelve or thirteen years of age, and a mother often before she was fifteen or sixteen ...
>
> If a young man possessed any sisters or female relatives, he often exchanged one of them for someone else's sister. Sometimes a young man bought a wife from a previous husband; at others a man stole a wife from some other tribe. This latter mode of securing a wife often led to fatal results, for at times the thief had to fight the men of his wife's tribe in order to get safely away with her, and ran a good chance of being killed in the event. Men renowned as warriors frequently attacked their inferiors and took their wives from them.[22]

## Customary rape of young women and sexual abuse of children

Perhaps most difficult to fathom is the prevalence and "normality" of rape against women in traditional Aboriginal society. In a speech to the Sydney Institute in 2006, Co-chair of Reconciliation Australia Mark Leibler argued that "to suggest that rape and paedophilia are part of Aboriginal culture is defamation ... It is slanderous and it is

---

21 Ibid, 180.
22 Ibid.

wrong".[23] Brunton wrote the following response:

> Intimidating words from a prominent lawyer but ... it is he who is wrong. Classic works from distinguished anthropologists such as Mervyn Meggitt, W.E.H. Stanner, W. Lloyd Warner, and Ronald and Catherine Berndt show that traditionally, in many Aboriginal communities, practices that contemporary Australians would unequivocally define as rape and paedophilia were culturally legitimate and commonplace. The ethnographies contain accounts of adult men taking girls as young as eight or nine as wives and sexual partners, gang rape as socially sanctioned punishment for certain transgressions, and a number of other indefensible customs. Nevertheless, Mr Leibler's assertions went unchallenged.[24]

Nowra's documentation of early accounts regarding customary gang rape of newly pubescent girls for marriage consummation, which in some districts included large sticks "for the purpose of tearing the hymen and posterior vaginal wall'[25], leaves no doubt regarding the force, violence, terror and brutality of it all. These accounts of customary rape are more than enough to counter any claim that Aboriginal Australia has "no cultural traditions based on humiliation, degradation, and violation".[26] Here Nowra draws upon the anthropological work of A.W. Howitt's *The Native Tribes of South-East Australia* of 1904:

> For example, girls from the Dieri tribe would be kidnapped by their intended husbands and friends, who would then drag her away, she screaming and biting as much as she was able. If she put up too much resistance, other men were called in to help constrain the struggling girl. Then all of the men took turns to

---

23 Brunton, January 2007, 25-6.
24 Ibid, 25-6.
25 Nowra, 2007, 16, including his quotation from A.W. Howitt, *The Native Tribes of South-East Australia*, 1904.
26 Mick Dodson, "Violence Dysfunction Aboriginality", Address to the National Press Club, 11 June 2003: http://law.anu.edu.au/anuiia/dodson.pdf

have sex with her over a one- or two-day period, which was regarded as consummation of the marriage. After this, the group, with the resigned girl in tow, would return to camp where there were "several days of ceremonial dancing during which time there was between her and the men of the camp a period of unrestricted licence, not even excluding her father".[27]

In some districts in traditional times, young boys did not escape the sexual exploitations of older men. Nowra documents customs of "boy-wife arrangements", which included penile sexual acts between a young unmarried man and a "boy-wife" who may be as young as five. A measure of how much these boy-wife relationships were an accepted custom is that it was rule-governed, so that in boy-wife relationships, the man was expected "to take as a boy-lover a member of the prescribed kinship section from which he must later obtain his wife".[28]

Despite this harsh, unrelenting evidence from a range of early sources and regions, there are still denials regarding pre-contact sexual abuse of children.[29] Indeed, girls before puberty were protected in many districts, as indicated by Bates' observation regarding Western Australia that "it was against Aboriginal law to tamper with a girl child until her first menstrual period had passed, and her young breasts had begun to swell. This law held throughout the State".[30] This concurs with McGlade's statement that "the sexual violence and abuse of children that is occurring today is not part of our [Noongar] culture".[31]

Furthermore, early observers also witnessed the gentler side of family life. Aboriginal parents showed love and tenderness for their children, and both sons and daughters were considered important.[32]

---

27 Nowra, 2007, 17.
28 A.R. Radcliffe-Brown (1881-1955), q. in Nowra, 2007, 21.
29 McGlade, 2012, 55-64; see also McGlade, 2006, 7-9.
30 Bates, 1901-14, 127.
31 McGlade, 2012, 64.
32 Warner, 1958, 69.

Fawcett wrote that the Wannah-Ruah people "were a very affectionate and emotional people and they showed great attachment to their children. Their offspring, especially when little, were always well cared for ... by both the father and mother".[33] Warner, writing of the Murngin, "recorded several instances of a woman's going through the most difficult privations and risking probable death to return to her children after she had been stolen by a man from another tribe".[34] Within the birth family, traditional Aboriginal societies expected young children to be cared for and protected from dangers. However, this could be hazardous for women. Mothers could be subject to violence if the father thought her neglectful of the children, even when they suffered a mishap that was not the mother's fault. In his Murngin study, Warner wrote that "[s]hould a mother neglect her child, or through some misadventure allow it to be harmed, most fathers would become angry and beat her, and in some cases try to kill her".[35]

There were other hazards for women in traditional family obligations. Families continued to have responsibilities to their children and siblings even after they married, including protecting them from violent husbands. Warner observed that a younger brother, or *yukiyuko*,

> always accompanies yeppa (older sister) when she first goes to her husband's clan to live after their marriage. The brother is usually pre-adolescent, but sometimes he may be older. He is supposed to look out for his sister, seeing that she does not commit adultery, preventing older men from seducing her, and by his presence protecting her from ill treatment by her husband.[36]

---

33 J.W. Fawcett, "Notes on the Customs and Dialect of the Wonnah-Ruah Tribe", *Science*, 22 August 1898, 153, sourced from D. A. Roberts *et al.*
34 Warner, 1958, 77.
35 Ibid, 71. See also Meggitt's account of a wife-beating for assumed child neglect, 90.
36 Ibid, 65. In brackets my addition.

However, fathers and brothers were expected to enforce the law with physical punishment onto errant daughters and sisters who did not comply with the marriage obligations:

> A brother is like a second father to a sister. If she is caught in adultery he gives her a beating and, if not stopped, tries to kill her.[37]

Another factor that makes denial of traditional Aboriginal child sexual abuse understandable is that it now occurs in a different context to classical times. The sexual abuse against children in traditional times was confined to specific, predictable, rule-governed contexts. Today, child sexual abuse is frequently not limited by rules or law, is terrifying in its chaotic and unpredictable nature, and is often made worse by the presence of petrol sniffing, alcohol and other drug abuses, gambling and pornography. Hughes reports that white paedophiles also prey on children in remote Aboriginal communities.[38]

Traditional, rule-governed sexual abuses, however, were also terrifying and injurious, and by universal human rights standards, dreadful. Anglican lay missionary Mary Bennett, while "scathing" of Chief Protector A.O. Neville's Aboriginal administration in Western Australia,[39] also strongly objected to Aboriginal customs that abused women and girls, including child-marriage, "little mothers" too physically immature to give birth to viable babies,[40] and female incision:

> Girls are made to suffer incision at puberty at the hands of one of the old men, but if they get wind of it they come to the mission till the danger is passed ... I remember hearing my old

---

37  Ibid, 65.
38  Hughes, 2007, Chapter 4.
39  Windschuttle, 2009, 462.
40  Ibid, 463, referring to Mary Bennett, evidence to Moseley Royal Commission 19 March 1934, transcript p.220.

Aboriginal nurse speak with horror of the suffering which she had been made to undergo."[41]

Even in districts with less cruel practices, the traditional Aboriginal notion regarding the age of female readiness for marriage and child-bearing is of human rights concern. Regarding a Kimberley region, Kaberry wrote of a transition time before puberty, in which a girl has a "gradual introduction into married life". During this time, "she has no full sexual intercourse with him: and she is gradually accustomed to his presence ... By the time she reached puberty she would be fitted to ... fulfil her role as his economic and sexual partner."[42] While Bates wrote of the Aboriginal law against tampering with a pre-pubescent girl, she also noted that some girls began menstruation at nine years of age, particularly in northern districts, and hence considered ready for marriage:

> sometimes they begin to bear children when very young. In these cases the labour is both prolonged and severe, and many a young mother, who ... would scarcely be thought out of childhood, has endured days of agonising labour only to succumb at the end. Baby and mother are then buried together whether the baby be dead or alive.[43]

Hence, there is a background of traditional legitimacy extended to sexual relations between adults and children, and to rape including gang rape against young girls barely out of puberty. Until acknowledged and challenged, traditional legitimacy of such behaviours would compromise the capacity of too many remote Aboriginal people to realise, with deep enough conviction, that such abusive behaviours against children and young teens are just plain wrong.

---

41 Mary Bennett, evidence to Moseley Royal Commission 19 March 1994, transcript p.220, 20 March 1934, p. 299, q. in Windschuttle, 2009, 464
42 Kaberry, 1939, 96.
43 Bates, 1901-14, 127. Also quoted in Windschuttle, 2009, 464.

## Women's sadness, women's protest: infanticide

Cowlishaw wrote that in traditional Aboriginal Australia, infanticide "has been reported for most of the areas of Australia for which information was available"[44] and women from most areas "would raise two or three infants".[45] Eyre reported infanticide among the Aboriginal people of Adelaide in the 1840s to be "very common", with women generally bearing five children but rearing an average of two. The first three or four were often killed. Eyre also wrote that "half-castes appear to be always destroyed".[46]

Cowlishaw notes that the usual theories for infanticide focus on the child, such as deformity, pre-maturity, or twins; or on environmental or economic factors such as the demands of breastfeeding plus caring for older children plus the workload of wife and food gatherer. She argues that this does not explain why it is frequently the first-born who are killed, by very young, just pubescent mothers, "and that there is an element of rejection of motherhood that is significant in tracing the source of the mother's motivation".[47] Cowlishaw's point concurs with Eyre's that the first three or four children are the most likely to be killed:

> Infanticide is very common, and appears to be practised solely to get rid of the trouble of rearing children, and to enable the woman to follow her husband about in his wanderings, which she frequently could not do if encumbered with a child.[48]

However, Cowlishaw sheds a more compassionate light. From her 1970s study of the Goinjimbe people of southern Arnhem Land, Cowlishaw argues that young mothers' rejection of motherhood by

---

44 Cowlishaw, 1978, 263.
45 Ibid, 263.
46 Eyre, 1845, Chapter 4.
47 Cowlishaw, 1978, 267.
48 Eyre, 1845, Chapter 4.

committing infanticide is a tragic protest against the relentless, unfair workload and exacting, rule-bound, misogynist oppressions and violences she must endure:[49]

> Resentment leads girls and women to deny their male kin, especially husbands and brothers, their infants.[50]

Cowlishaw's seminal article makes for harrowing reading. First, women's workload from childhood was much greater than men's. Women's role was defined by "self-sacrificing behaviour". This included sacrificing food prepared for themselves, to men who happenstance came across the women and demanded the food. Second, women's daily lives were steeped in the fearful, impossible, punishing demands of brother-sister avoidance.

> It is brother or "brother" who must not suspect that a girl or woman is going to relieve herself. A sister must avoid sitting or walking too close to her brother; she has to avoid anything that would cause anyone to shout or swear at her; she cannot touch anything her brother has handled. To a young girl who has a brother a few years older, avoidance must be first impressed dramatically ...
>
> One girl of ten was sitting on the toilet when her "brother" (25 years) opened the door. He at once ran to get his spears but could not find any. He then threatened his little "sisters" of three and five years old. The older one disappeared ...
>
> Actual attacks must be made with spears because a brother cannot touch his sister with his hand. Women cannot retaliate but only run away.[51]

Third is the oppression that young girls endured by being promised from before or at birth to be the wife to a much older man, often as old as her father: "The high rate of elopements which is evident despite

---

49 Cowlishaw, 1978, 273-281.
50 Ibid, 281.
51 Ibid, 276-7.

violent even fatal punishments, is evidence of the dissatisfaction with marriage which many women feel."[52] Cowlishaw notes that "[t]he relaxation and lightheartedness apparent when women are away from camp on fishing expeditions and during the women's ceremony, is direct evidence of the pressure they are usually under".[53]

Bates' conjectures regarding a young Western Australian girl's reasons for infanticide have echoes of Cowlishaw's analysis: "[O]ne very young girl gave birth to a baby after days of prolonged labour, and whether it was fear of the young life to which she had given birth, or revenge for the pain it had caused her, whatever the reason" she immediately killed the infant.[54]

Not disputing Cowlishaw's insights, infanticide for population control is also likely. Historian William Rubinstein wrote that in Australia, infanticide was practised on a massive scale before white contact, with perhaps 30% of babies killed, and was a form of population control, given the imperative to survive within the tight limitations of their economy and environment. It remained widespread on remote communities until a few decades ago.[55] Rubinstein wrote:

> The anthropologist Aram A. Yengoyan, who carried out field work among the Pitjantjatjara people in 1966-67, found that infanticide there "may have varied from 18 per cent to 20 per cent of all births" ... Yengoyan states that "Presently infanticide is no longer openly practised on missions and government stations".[56]

---

52 Ibid, 277.
53 Ibid, 278.
54 Bates, 1901-14, 127.
55 William D. Rubinstein, "The Biases of Genocide Studies", *Quadrant Online*, Volume LIII, No. 3, March 2009:
http://www.quadrant.org.au/magazine/issue/2009/3/the-biases-of-genocide-studies
56 Ibid, referring to Aram A. Yengoyan, 1972, "Biological and Demographic Components in Aboriginal Australian Socio-Economic Organisation", *Oceania*, 43, 1972, 88.

Kimm noted that Julius Brockman's diaries of 1880s Kimberley life record the occurrence of infanticide during dry seasons.[57] Writing in the 1880s about the Aboriginal people of New South Wales, John Fraser observed:

> If the season has been hard and there is a scarcity of food, or if the mother is already burdened with many children or with heavy labour for her lord, the little one is left to perish.[58]

Eyre's and Fraser's above accounts both suggest women were expected to prioritise their role of wife, and caring for another child could clash unacceptably with that. In addition, decisions about a newborn's survival were based on food availability for the group, suggesting that a mother may have had little say. Fawcett reported that in the Hunter River district there were older women designated to undertake infanticide, perhaps indicating that it was not a mother's decision alone.

## Traditional clan conflict and warfare: the slaying of young men

In traditional Aboriginal societies, violence, conflict and warfare were inevitable, at times "necessary" aspects of clan and tribal relations, with significant impacts in some regions on age and gender demographics. Early colonial officials, explorers and anthropologists reported these conflicts. The following examples convey the similarity across time and place, one from the north in the 1920s, the other from southern Australia in the 1840s. These accounts evoke great sadness in the "utility" of injury and death of warrior men. The hesitation to ritually injure a neighbouring warrior to expiate his tribe's possible sorcerous guilt, and the victim's call, "Spear [me]!" evokes its own

---

57 Kimm, 2004, 171, q. J. Brockman (ed), *He Rode Alone*, Artlook Books, Perth, 1987, 131-2, 146.
58 John Fraser, "The Aborigines of New South Wales", 200, *Journal and Proceedings of the Royal Society of NSW for the year 1882*, 16. Sydney: Thomas Richards, 1883, 193-233, sourced from Roberts *et al*.

poignant sadness. Also in both accounts can be seen an enmeshment of conflict and war into social life, custom and law as expected, almost seasonal events.

Inter-clan and inter-tribal conflict frequently involved two main spheres: factors regarding women; and avenging misdemeanours committed by another clan or tribe against one's own group. Warner wrote that warfare among the Murngin helped maintain polygamy for older men. The Murngin population was about 3000, and each married man averaged three or four wives. The resultant "excess" of men was partly solved by men marrying mainly at middle age, while women married before puberty (with sexual relations occurring after puberty):

> The killing of young men below the age of twenty-five, because of the ever-present blood feuds, makes up the balance.
>
> The one important effect of warfare on Murngin society is the seasonal slaying of a small proportion of young men who have passed adolescence and are potential or eligible mates ...
>
> Warfare, then, is one of the mechanisms on which polygyny is based. If war were abolished, the percentage of men would increase, and the pressure on the social structure created by seeking mates would probably be too strong for the present form of polygyny ... to survive.[59]

Warner estimated that about 200 young Murngin men were killed in warfare over 20 years, meaning that 700 less women were needed for marriage partners.

Warner also illustrates the enmeshment of inter-clan battle killings with the stealing of women, sacrilege, and the need to settle scores:

> Of seventy-two recorded battles of the last twenty years in which members of Murngin factions were killed, fifty were for blood revenge ...Ten killings were due to stealing or obtaining by illegal means a woman who belonged to another clan. Five supposedly guilty magicians were killed by the clan members

---
59 Warner, 1958, 158.

of victims of black magic. Five men were slain for looking at a totemic emblem under improper circumstances and thereby insulting the owning clan and endangering the clan's spiritual strength.

The idea underlying most Murngin warfare is that the same injury should be inflicted upon the enemy group that one's own group has suffered. This accomplished, a clan feels satisfied; otherwise, there is a constant compulsion towards vengeance.[60]

Eyre's description of spearings and warfare among the peoples of southern Australia bears general similarities to Warner's account. In the Murray district, Eyre witnessed a large meeting between the Nar-wij-jerooks and the Moorunde peoples, where restrained, controlled spearings played a crucial role in settling blame over those "unnatural" deaths that inevitably took place between infrequent meetings:

> If the tribes have been long apart, many deaths may have occurred in the interim; and as the natives do not often admit that the young or the strong can die from natural causes, they ascribe the event to the agency of sorcery, employed by individuals of neighbouring tribes. This must of course be expiated in some way when they meet, but the satisfaction required is regulated by the desire of the injured tribe to preserve amicable relations with the other, or the reverse ...[61]

> In advancing, the Nar-wij-jerooks again commenced the death wail, and one of the men, who had probably sustained the greatest loss since the tribes last met, occasionally in alternations of anger and sorrow addressed his own people. When near the Moorunde tribe a few words were addressed to them, and they at once rose simultaneously, with a suppressed shout. The opposite party then raised their spears, and closing upon the line of the other tribe, speared about fifteen or sixteen of them in the left arm, a little below the shoulder. This is the generally understood order of revenge; for the persons who

---

60 Ibid, 159.
61 Eyre, 1845, Chapter 2.

were to receive the wounds, as soon as they saw the weapons of their assailants poised, at once put out their left foot, to steady themselves, and presented the left shoulder for the blow, frequently uttering the word "Leipa" (spear), as the others appeared to hesitate.[62]

Eyre observed that tribes also met "for the purpose of war", with both sides fully armed, and formal battle lines, place, time of day agreed upon, and usually lasting three or four hours. These could involve many injuries, some serious, "but it rarely happens that more than one or two are killed, though hundreds may have been engaged".[63]

Nevertheless, inter-tribal conflict also broke out of controlled dimensions, as chaotic, dangerous fights or cold-blooded slayings. Eyre reported that "the most dangerous and fatal affrays" were those that occurred spontaneously between tribes "encamped near one another on amicable terms", when a conflict suddenly erupted:

> probably in relation to their females, or some recent death, which it is imagined the sorcerers have been instrumental in producing. In the former case a kind of melee sometimes takes place at night, when fire-brands are thrown about, spears launched and bwirris ("A short, heavy wooden stick, with a knob at one end"[64]) brandished in indescribable confusion. In the latter case the affray usually occurs immediately after the body is buried, and is more of a hand-to-hand fight, in which bwirris are used rather than spears, and in which tremendous blows are struck and frightful wounds inflicted.
>
> In wars males are always obliged to join their relatives by blood and their own tribe. Women frequently incite the men to engage in these affrays to revenge injuries or deaths, and sometimes they assist themselves by carrying spears or other weapons for their husbands. I am not aware that women or children are ever

---

62  Ibid, Chapter 2.
63  Ibid, Chapter 2.
64  Eyre's note.

butchered after a battle is over, and I believe such is never the case. Single camps are sometimes treacherously surprised when the parties are asleep, and the males barbarously killed in cold blood.[65]

---

[65] Eyre, 1845, Chapter 2.

# Continuity of traditional violence

Many details of Dreamtime myths, ceremonies and sacred law of Aboriginal tradition have been lost or are no longer practised. Even the more traditionally intact communities have lost significant amounts of sacred traditions, and where it remains strong, the context for its practice has greatly altered. Nevertheless, Aboriginal culture and beliefs display resilience, Aboriginal tradition has had little more than 200 years of colonial interception, and where practice is no longer extant, calls for a restoration of tribal law and the right to practise Aboriginal culture can reach into living memory. Tradition's resilience and calls to recognise Aboriginal law as a subset within Australian law, mean that traditional beliefs and practices have implications for the well-being and rights of present-day Aboriginal people.

Sadly, thousands of examples of "legitimised" injurious violence, debilitating beliefs and misogyny of traditional origin continue to give power to some and hurt many others in Australia's remote Aboriginal communities. While violent behaviours may be shaped by modern impacts, they point to continuing stark differences between traditional belief systems, power relations and customary law, versus mainstream norms and law based on individual human rights. Furthermore, cultural and geographical distance attenuates mainstream influence. This protects perpetrators, and increases the vulnerability of victims and whistleblowers. By providing scope for other cultural norms, our culturally respectful legal and policy systems render remote communities as places where authoritarian, misogynist men can continue to maintain their rule. However, while cities are safer places for Aboriginal people, the chronic gap between non-Aboriginal and

Aboriginal levels of violence in the cities, and the stress this places on race relations causing additional harm to Aboriginal people, are enough to cause alarm.

# 6
# Dangerous lands

> In the course of teaching I discussed with two Aboriginal students issues of domestic violence, an area in which I had some experience as a solicitor, although only with non-Aborigines. The two students were intelligent, self possessed and mature young women who were leading independent lives in an urban environment. Each said that while they would not tolerate violence from men in an urban setting they would do so if they were living a traditional lifestyle, that this was expected and would be part of their life under customary law.
>
> – Joan Kimm, 1999[1]

**Where violence is normal**

The above quotation from Kimm shows how Aboriginal communities remain caught in tradition. The passage is both hopeful and disturbing. It is hopeful because it suggests that today's violence among Aboriginal people has meaning only in certain contexts. In particular, it indicates that the norm of violence is not readily transported out of traditional contexts by Aboriginal people who, when not in their traditional community, lead integrated lives in mainstream society. Also, these Aboriginal women have a level of choice, or at least objectivity, about when and where they will tolerate violence. To that extent, they have more control and freedom than if only the traditional context were available to them.

But the quotation is also disturbing because it means that even among urban, educated Aboriginal women, there is a respect for, and a

---
[1] Kimm, 1999, Preface p. iv.

willingness to be subjugated by, the violence of Aboriginal custom and law. It means that visits to traditional communities can be dangerous for women. The following incident depicts the peril experienced by one young Aboriginal woman. What she learnt was not what she sought, and to call her naïve is to excuse too lightly the purveyors of the traditional as idyllic.

> A young woman of some aboriginal blood came from the south to one of the communities. She was looking for her "tribal family" and to learn traditional ways. She was a reasonably well-adjusted and successful singer. She was married off to a young full blood. He locked her in the house, denied her contraceptives and when she did not fall pregnant blamed her and beat her dreadfully. She was in fear of her life. But how to escape? He took her money, made her into a slave and when the light plane came, as it did regularly, there was no way she could escape from such remoteness. She did, with help eventually. She was destroyed.[2]

McKnight relates the phenomenon of white women whose romantic ideas about traditional life placed them in peril:

> There have been a few cases of young White women forming relationships with Mornington Island youths and expecting to live an idyllic life close to nature. They soon discovered that their boyfriend's behaviour changed when they were on Mornington. They usually departed after the first "proper good hiding" and invariably by the second.[3]

These men knew when and where it was acceptable to be violent. It is an indicator that the violence is not caused by Aboriginal men's loss or brokenness due to colonisation, such as separation from their spiritual lands or being part of the stolen generation; or the need for anger management or cultural healing; or even the curse of alcohol or other violence-promoting substance abuse.

---

2 Pers. comm. from nurse, 2008.
3 McKnight, 2002, 225, Note 59.

No doubt these realities can be contributing factors. Nevertheless, traditional expectations, mores and permissions to be violent remain central. No matter how unfair they, their family, or their community have been or continue to be treated by mainstream Australia, it is – in seeming irony – the mainstream context where Aboriginal violence is more effectively suppressed and less tolerated by Aboriginal people themselves. It is in traditional contexts, on lands of dreams and ideals hard-won after years of political battles with white conquerors, where violence is a legitimised tool to uphold law and male dominance.[4] This chart shows that the higher "normality" of violence in remote Australia still has lethal consequences.

**Homicide rate per 100,000 persons, by remoteness, 1999-2000 to 2004-05**

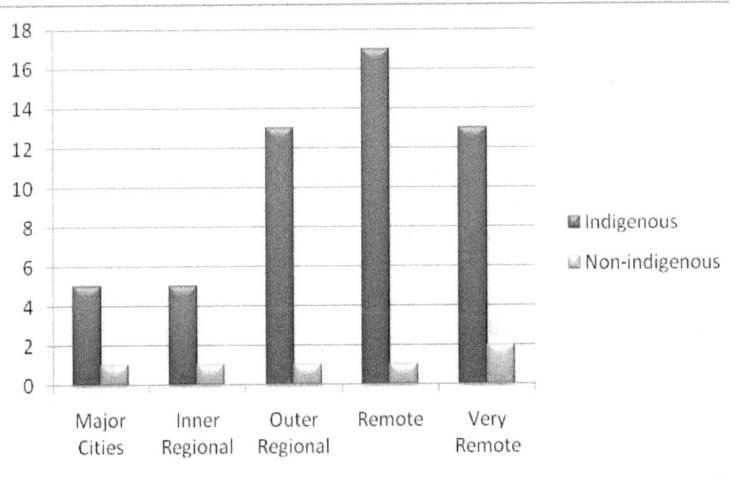

Source: Productivity Commission, *Overcoming Indigenous Disadvantage: Headline Indicators 2007*, 3.100. *Note:* Indigenous homicides are where both victims and offenders of homicide are Aborigines or Torres Strait Islanders. Non-Indigenous homicides are where neither the victim nor the offender is Aboriginal.

---

4 For further on the danger of these lands, see Jenness Warin with James Franklin, "Remote Aboriginal Communities: Why the trade in girls and other human rights abuses remains hidden", *The Bennelong Society Occasional Papers*, October 2007.

## Observations in dangerous places

### *Mangrove: Victoria Burbank*

In her examination of women and violence in Mangrove, Burbank describes a fight between a woman named Lily and several other women, because Lily thought that they broke her son's arm. The fight ends in minor injuries and apologies when Lily realises that her son's injuries were superficial. Burbank remarks that "the manner in which Lily and her opponents fought was, for the most part, rule-governed behaviour". She describes the woman's eucalyptus fighting stick of 3 to 4 feet long, and that limbs, not the head, were to be hit. Nevertheless, the women attempted to hit Lily on the head, which Lily blocked with her fighting stick, and that in attempting to hit Lily's head, "her opponents were not acting in a completely lawless manner; it is recognised that someone who is very angry may well attempt such a blow". Burbank quotes some community comments:

> "You shouldn't hit someone on the head, but you do if you get wild for something like food or about your children ... You have to be careful of the other women when you fight. Watch her eyes [to see where she is going to strike]."[5]

Burbank writes, "a part of learning how to fight with a stick is learning how to protect the forehead". She describes rules governing non-combatant intervention to reduce serious injury. While these might reassure some, Burbank depicts a world where violence is a feature of everyday culture, where physical aggression is quickly resorted to, and everyone has a familiarity with fighting sticks, beatings and blood. By mainstream standards, traditional rules for fighting should carry little reassurance.

---

5 Burbank, 1994, 74 (Burbank's brackets).

## *Mornington Island: David McKnight*

McKnight's analysis of violence on Mornington Island depicts continuity with the past:

> Even before the advent of Europeans there was much violence among the Kaiadilt and other Wellesley Islanders. This was particularly so for the Kaiadilt, where most of the violence appears to have been about women.[6]

Over the years, differing white impacts affected its rate and expression. In the pre-Mission era before they were co-located on Mornington Island, the various tribes were warrior peoples where competition over resources included fighting and killing between clans and tribes for women and food. On the Wellesley Islands, "the incidence of polygyny was high and the competition for wives was intense and sometimes lethal, especially among the Kaiadilt".[7] This became more intense in times of "population pressure and poor hunting conditions", as witnessed among the Kaiadilt during 1944-47,[8] when fights over women and food increased, with more killings between warriors and more abductions of women.

In 1948, the killings stopped. From 1948 to 1978 "when the Kaiadilt were under Mission hegemony, there were no more killings".[9] Nevertheless, fighting remained normality during Mission years, with fighting rules shaped by kinship lines, "self-help", payback, and "square-up":

> Everybody, boys and girls, men and women, young and old, stand up for themselves. Although women are disadvantaged nevertheless they, as persons, participate in the fights. Even though a woman knows she may be beaten, and in the pre-Mission period risked being killed (although the risk was greater

---

6 McKnight, 2005, xix.
7 Ibid, 25.
8 Ibid, 47.
9 Ibid, 55.

for men), nevertheless as a person she evidently feels compelled to give voice to her opinions and fight just as earnestly as men, otherwise people would regard her as a coward ...

The lot of women had improved because they had recourse to *kantha* Belcher when their domestic situation became particularly dangerous. Women felt safe under the missionaries.[10]

With the departure of the Mission, lethal violence rose again. Mornington Island presents a tragic and telling lesson. The Mission era offered women protection, but suppressed rather than ended the norm of violence, which remained strong. The Mission era undermined, probably irreversibly, traditional beliefs such as sorcery, Dreamtime cosmology and law, while the post-Mission era brought dependence on white administrators, welfare dependence, alcohol, and inadequate authority. McKnight depicts a situation where the past is gone and the limited mainstream engagement demands minimal responsibility or effort. McKnight's depiction of the post-Mission era on Mornington Island evokes the "fork-in-the-road" heartbreak facing many remote Aboriginal communities, and a part-explanation for the attraction of cultural restoration. Facing alcohol abuse, meaninglessness of life and associated suicide,[11] and the epidemic of violence, options for escape are integration, or restoration of the past, where Dreamtime cosmology and its powerful, fierce law gave shape and pride to the old law makers and the brave young warriors.

While the latter has strong romantic or ideological appeal, as McKnight has pointed out, "post-Cartesian" thought is now too strong amongst the people of Mornington Island, rendering restoration of

---

10 Ibid, 140. Rev. ("*kantha*" or "father") Belcher was Mission Superintendent on Mornington Island from 1952 to 1972.

11 See Colin Tatz, *Aboriginal suicide is different: Aboriginal youth suicide in New South Wales, the Australian Capital Territory and New Zealand: Towards a model of explanation and alleviation*, CRC funded reports, Criminology Research Council, 14 July 1999. In the Executive summary, Tatz writes that suicide was "a phenomenon virtually unknown in Aboriginal societies until 30 years ago": http://www.criminologyresearchcouncil.gov.au/reports/tatz/tatz.pdf

traditional belief systems patchy or superficial. What is more, the path to more tradition is a path back to sanctions and norms that are violent, vengeful and misogynist. Above all, there is a tendency to identify the violence on communities as manifestations of despair. Instead, the causal relationship may well be the reverse. The cruel juxtaposition of communities' atavistic norm of violence with the anti-violent norms of mainstream Australia is a probable cause of despair, with any "legitimate" reason for an act of violence quickly followed by an aftermath of grief and self-blame that would be experienced by any young Australian man.[12]

### *Ngukurr: Kate Senior*

Kate Senior's valuable study of the "aspirations and expectations of a group of young Aboriginal women" in the south-east Arnhem Land community of Ngukurr indicates that traditional attitudes about the male right to authority and violence continue to oppress young women's lives there.[13] As on Mornington Island, the years of Mission intervention brought benefits for Ngukurr women:

> Prior to the arrival of the Christian Missionary Society (in 1908), girls had lives that were tightly prescribed by adults. Adolescence in the sense that it is a period between being a child and being an adult did not exist, as females were promised and married prior to the onset of puberty ...
>
> Cole (1985) in his history of the Christian Missionary Society described the marriage arrangements made for young girls of the Mission as a "great and enduring problem". The solution in Ngukurr was the establishment of a dormitory system which separated young men and women from their families. As one older woman from the community recalled:
>
> > "The dormitory was really strict, nobody was allowed to see men, only at school time, not even in the village.

---

12 Youth suicide is discussed again in Chapter 8.
13 Kate Senior, *Boyfriends, Babies and Basketball: Present Lives and Future Aspirations of Young Women in Ngukurr*, 2004: http://naru.anu.edu.au/files/58_Senior.rtf

> You were not allowed to go home and sleep in the house with your mum and daddy. We used to just play in that dormitory. There was a big fence around that dormitory."[14]

This no doubt sounds unacceptable to modern ears, an example of a harsh stolen generation regime.[15] However, while strict and possibly resented, the Christian Missionary Society offered to young women an escape from the oppressive marriage system, while also increasing their skills and aspirations:

> Older women look back at the Mission as a time when young girls were controlled and disciplined and contrast this with the situation today:
>
> "Our time was good, single girls didn't have children, didn't have a family. We learnt about work side, didn't think about boyfriends, there was plenty of time for that, do your work first. Young girls today make me feel worried, feel no good inside. It didn't happen like that when I was young. They don't have time to learn anything, just busy nursing the baby."
>
> Enforced segregation of young men and women, in terms of the dormitory system, ceased when the Mission withdrew in 1968.[16]

Senior describes how the girls in Ngukurr today, at least until a baby comes along, might appear to have more freedom than the earlier Mission time. Certainly, they resist adult control, and much focus is on hanging out with girlfriends, including "'walking about at night' in

---

14 Ibid, 2.
15 However, a 2010 news item reported that "Parents say they have been forced to pull their children out of Darwin's Kormilda College because of rampant problems at its boarding houses ... [My daughter] said 'I can't sleep because the boys jump the wall' ... They crawl across the roof, climb down the palm trees into the girls' dorms". Alyssa Betts, "Parents tug kids out of lawless school", *Northern Territory News*, 14 May 2010: http://www.ntnews.com.au/article/2010/05/14/147561_ntnews.html
16 Senior, 2004, 2-3.

groups when the adults have gone to bed", in order to form a sexual relationship with a boy. Promised marriage and right skin marriage are still a pressure, though most girls are said to "choose their own". However, adolescence for many girls is short, with first pregnancy at or before age 16 for most, and aspirations are limited. They expect to get married, and that marriage will involve subjection to men's authority. In the words of a 15-year-old girl,

> Boys don't help in the house, they are big bosses. He'd kill you if you didn't wash his clothes, he'd bash you up.[17]

Senior adds:

> Most of the young women also considered that violence towards women was part of marriage. Although women stated that violence that was a result of drinking, drug abuse or bad temper should not be tolerated (and could be reported to the police), they did describe situations where male violence against women was accepted as being appropriate behaviour ...
>
> > "Sometimes their wives are lazy and don't know how to cook or clean around the house. And they answer back their husbands when their husband is saying the right thing. When they answer back their husband gets cross and starts hitting them. I think it's their own fault because they should listen to their husband and what they say to them." (Age 14)[18]

Other girls spoke of greater freedom for boys, and implied that girls have little choice regarding whom they marry:

> Boys have more freedom, boys can find their own wife. They can go and live somewhere else. They can go away from their family.
>
> Girls have lots of hard times. Girls stay at home all the time.[19]

---

17  Ibid, 12.
18  Ibid.
19  Ibid, 15.

For these young Ngukurr women, violence in their sexual relationships was certain and unavoidable, indeed one young woman "suggested that the only way to avoid violence in relationships was 'to go to Melbourne and have a sex change to become a boy'".[20]

## *Helen Hughes*

Hughes documents some of the cruelty and depravity of violence and sexual abuse against Aboriginal women and children on remote communities. It is devastating reading. She indicates that even among key activists, there is a view that the human rights of remote Aboriginal girls, while important, should sometimes be secondary to protecting the culture:

> Sharon Payne, the prominent director of the North Australian Aboriginal Legal Aid Service that strongly supports "customary exceptionalism" ... claim[ed] that "there was usually nothing wrong with promised marriages as such. Promised brides are really about keeping kinship systems here, making sure the story continues as it should." She concedes that "the issue of forcing somebody to have sex against their will is a different matter altogether."[21]

As Hughes points out, this "concession" is far from enough:

> But Indigenous girls, like all other Australian girls, must have the right to follow primary school with secondary education so that they can go on to work or further studies as they choose. To marry or not to marry, and whom and when to marry, must be their choice. The practice of children bearing children is unconscionable.[22]

Continuity of indigenous promised marriage means that in Australia, a girl's right of freedom to choose if, when and whom she marries can be secondary to securing traditional kinship ties. With its

---

20  Ibid, 15.
21  Hughes, 2007, 31.
22  Ibid, 31.

prioritisation of culture, and the promise made at a young age, as a marriage system it lacks even the saving grace of parents choosing a partner for their children based on personal compatibility (although no doubt some parents include this consideration).

Many of us love the idea of a living ancient culture, the idea of "continuing the story". We need to know that young girls must endure the reality of our romantic notions, and that these ideas are trapping and limiting young and innocent lives.

**The fear of mentioning anything**

The ferocity with which remote community perpetrators and their supporters attack those who speak out against violence is testimony to the high value placed on the male "right" to practise violence. This "other" country is a dangerous country. Under-reporting of violence and abuse on communities is a major recognised problem mentioned in several reports.[23] A nurse who worked for years in remote communities related the devastating readiness of communities, including "tiny little communities", to use violence to silence nurses and other health workers.[24] On some communities, the culture of protecting perpetrators was so strong that it could be dangerous for nurses to perform their vocation of care and advocacy for patients who are victims of violence. Speaking out for these patients could result in the nurse receiving threats or actual violence from the perpetrator or the perpetrator's family.[25] Furthermore, while improvements in nurses' housing security and clinic security took place, in the health services there seemed to be compliance with this norm of protecting the perpetrator. Hence, when nurses and other health professionals spoke out about violence in the community including against staff,

---

23 For example, the Mullighan Inquiry, 2008.
24 As communicated to the author by a nurse who spent years working in remote communities, 2008-09.
25 Ibid, 2008-09.

they could receive either no support or worse, might lose their job or be blacklisted.[26] This situation reflects *The Australian* journalist Nicolas Rothwell's quote from "a respected council clerk in a remote community":

> There's no control and no responsibility. It's a beautiful system designed by the Aboriginal men to protect Aboriginal men. They've got the white people sorted out; if you mention anything, you're fired instantly and will never get another job in the Aboriginal industry again.[27]

The following witness observations reflect years of experience:

> When violence was addressed in the communities, one was either attacked directly, or down the track later on when it did not seem connected to the reporting, or someone in the person's family was injured. The police spoke to me very strongly one time about a knife attack on me, asking that I lay charges. The youth's uncle asked me not to do it and that they would deal with it in ceremony. I laid charges. One of the nurses in a neighbouring community was raped while beaten in the head with a rock …
>
> I am sad that some events out bush caused dreadful anguish for some staff and has affected their lives. There really were some terrible events. I recall some of the Aboriginal people did try to shield staff at times, probably placing themselves in danger also.[28]

Other actions against nurses for speaking out against community violence include being threatened that they or others were going to be killed; being threatened with weapons including guns, axes, sticks, rocks or star pickets; and being shot at, or beaten, or molested or raped. They include their homes or vehicles being broken into and items stolen or smashed or despicable things done to personal items. Nurses have also been publicly defamed, called dreadful adjectives

---

26  Ibid, 2008-09.
27  Nicolas Rothwell, quoted in Nowra, 2007, 67.
28  Pers. comm. from nurse, 2008.

in public, derided at professional remote area health organisations, or had their careers stopped if they didn't toe the line by keeping silent.[29] These witness accounts point to a ferocity in defence of perpetrators that suggests a different, pre-contact norm. The nurses found that when they did speak out, until recently no one believed them, neither about the violence in the community, nor about the threats that the nurses themselves received.[30] Given that these are experiences from a just few communities, how great must be the extent of cover-up across remote Aboriginal Australia?

With such threats, it is little wonder that few service providers, victims or their families speak out. In her article "Secrets in the shadows", journalist Natasha Robinson writes of the "terrifyingly dangerous" situation of whistleblowers:

> This is the real story behind the emergency intervention in remote Aboriginal communities, where vigilante justice is aimed not at perpetrators but at whistleblowers, and reporting child abuse is so terrifyingly dangerous that even the secret codes of the nation's top crime commission cannot encourage those who know to speak up ... *Inquirer* was told of a case in [a] central Australian community of a child witnessing the rape of a toddler. The alleged perpetrator was a 12 year old boy. After a child witness confided to an adult about the incident, it was reported to authorities. The whistleblower was hunted for weeks by members of one of the community's powerful families.[31]

## The Mullighan Inquiry into child sexual abuse

Even with likely under-reporting of child abuse among Aboriginal communities, statistics signal that the level of child abuse is much higher among Aboriginal children than non-Aboriginal children.

---

29 Ibid, 2008.
30 Ibid, 2008.
31 Natasha Robinson, "Secrets in the Shadows", *The Weekend Australian Inquirer,* 21-22 June 2008, 22.

Australian Institute of Health and Welfare (AIHW) statistics are indicative here:[32]

## Children (aged 0–16 years) who were the subject of a substantiation 2007-08: Rate per 1000 children[33]

### Type of abuse or neglect

#### Indigenous Children

|                | NSW  | Vic  | Qld  | WA   | SA   | Tas  | ACT  | NT   | Aust |
|----------------|------|------|------|------|------|------|------|------|------|
| Physical abuse | 10.3 | 19.5 | 8.1  | 2.4  | 3.6  | 0.5  | 1.6  | 5.2  | 7.7  |
| Sexual abuse   | 4.9  | 1.7  | 1.3  | 2.3  | 1.2  | 0.1  | 1.1  | 3.3  | 2.7  |
| Emotional abuse| 18.3 | 26.8 | 8.0  | 3.8  | 23.7 | 1.8  | 22.9 | 6.5  | 12.2 |
| Neglect        | 19.5 | 6.9  | 9.7  | 9.1  | 19.8 | 2.6  | 22.3 | 8.8  | 12.7 |
| Total          | 53.0 | 55.0 | 27.1 | 17.7 | 48.4 | 5.0  | 47.9 | 23.7 | 35.3 |

#### Non-Indigenous Children

|                | NSW | Vic | Qld | WA  | SA  | Tas | ACT | NT  | Aust |
|----------------|-----|-----|-----|-----|-----|-----|-----|-----|------|
| Physical abuse | 1.4 | 2.0 | 1.7 | 0.4 | 0.6 | 1.6 | 0.9 | 0.9 | 1.4  |
| Sexual abuse   | 1.1 | 0.3 | 0.5 | 0.4 | 0.2 | 0.7 | 0.4 | 0.8 | 0.7  |
| Emotional abuse| 2.4 | 2.1 | 2.4 | 0.4 | 1.8 | 3.1 | 3.0 | 1.3 | 2.1  |
| Neglect        | 1.8 | 0.5 | 1.6 | 0.7 | 1.4 | 3.2 | 2.1 | 1.1 | 1.3  |
| Total          | 6.8 | 4.9 | 6.2 | 1.9 | 4.0 | 8.6 | 6.3 | 4.0 | 5.5  |

Perhaps the most heart-breaking silences are depicted in the 2008 Mullighan Inquiry into child sexual abuse on the Anangu Pitjantjatjara

---

32 For further tragic statistics on child sexual abuse, see Nowra, 2007, 48-51.
33 Productivity Commission, 2009, Attachment Tables, Table 4A10.2.

Yankunytjatjara (APY) Lands.[34] The Inquiry emphasised the serious under-reporting of child abuse, with fear of dangerous consequences, lack of a sense among victims of a right to say no, young age and language barriers among causes of this under-reporting. Eight years earlier, under-reporting of child sexual abuse was observed by Jane Lloyd, who worked for years with the NPYWC Domestic Violence Service Project:

> *Jane Lloyd:* We really don't know the rates or figures. I think largely they're detected through health clinics, picked up by children having STDs.
>
> Occasionally a report is made. A child will, you know, disclose or report something, but they're very difficult – and it's difficult when you're talking about small, kin-based communities again, because – you know 95, 99 per cent of the times it will be a family member who has probably committed the assault.
>
> *Liz Jackson:* Which means the chances of it being reported are ... ?
>
> *Jane Lloyd:* Are really really low.[35]

The Mullighan Inquiry concluded that "the incidence of sexual abuse of children on the Lands is widespread",[36] and some of the sexual abuse involved children well under the age of 10 years. Many children were probably repeatedly abused over some years.[37] The cases were placed into the following categories:

---

34 Mullighan Inquiry, 2008. See also Johns, 2011, 188-192; and McGlade, 2012, 96-103. As stated in the Mullighan Inquiry, the APY lands (the Lands) in South Australia "are part of the Western Desert in central Australia and cover 102,360 square kilometres in the far north-west of South Australia in and around the Musgrave Ranges. The population of the Lands varies from time to time but there are about 2,700 Anangu, including about 1,000 children, living in small communities and many homelands", xi. The entire Western Desert "cultural bloc" is "a region covering some 600,000 square kilometres within South Australia, Western Australia and the Northern Territory", 8.

35 Jane Lloyd, extract of interview by Liz Jackson: Jackson, 2001.

36 Mullighan Inquiry, 2008, xiii.

37 Ibid, xiii.

extra-familial men abusing girls, extra-familial men abusing boys, extra-familial children abusing children and intra-familial abuse. An abused child rarely fell into only one of these categories.[38]

Teachers spoke of widespread sexualised behaviour among children, including rape of young girls by young boys. The school is seen as a place of safety for children, and teachers try to equip girls with the idea that they can say "no" to sex. In the words of one principal:

> The majority of our boys and the majority of our girls I have no doubt, when they're not in our care are sexually active, and I have no doubt that the great majority of that activity that takes place is without consent in our terms ... the girls very clearly say "Well, we can't say no, and if we say no, they're going to drag us off anyway, so we do", and that happens.[39]

One "silence" story is of a teacher's suspicion

> about a young Aboriginal girl who had otherwise been a bright, happy child. One day the girl came to school and "just laid her head on my lap and sobbed. Like, heartbreaking, wrenching sobs. There was snot and tears dripping down my legs and she sobbed, probably for about 20 minutes."[40]

While she did not feel the girl had been sexually abused at the time, from then on she "just kept an eye on her". Later when the girl's and her siblings' behaviour changed too, she notified the Department, but the teacher left the school and "doesn't know what happened to the children".[41]

---

38 Ibid, xiii.
39 Ibid, 211.
40 Ibid, 211. See also p. 196, "Of particular concern for education professionals was the high proportion of children who arrived at school without food having suffered sexual, physical or emotional abuse."
41 Ibid, 211.

Just as heart-breaking is a "double silencing" – lack of English *plus* fear to speak in the presence of an Aboriginal worker. Illiteracy and inability to speak English are a theme in many instances of child abuse investigated by the Inquiry.[42] For example, one mandatory notifier told the Child Abuse Report Line (CARL) that a girl aged 14 years

> is having difficulty explaining how she is feeling because of language and cultural issues, but [the girl] refuses to have an Aboriginal worker present when she talks to notifier and other non-Aboriginal people.[43]

Fear of speaking out because of the consequences is well-justified:

> You can be violent and destructive to get your own way ... and anybody who stands up to you gets hounded, sometimes having to leave communities and always being talked about and sniggered about by ... often powerful men in communities, so, not surprisingly, people don't want to testify.[44]

The Inquiry is also permeated with reference to customary demands and practices, such as boys being away from school for initiation ceremony and when back at school, no communication must occur with the girl students or with the younger boys.[45] There is wrong-way marriage, promised marriage, trouble communicating in English among some of the children, the threat of sorcery to force a girl to have sex. One health professional became aware of elderly men and middle-aged men sexually abusing girls, the girls telling their stories in the sand.

> Girls were in her home nearly every night and "they sit outside and they sit and talk the story with the wire and they tell stories in the sand". Sometimes they mentioned the names of some of the men.[46]

---

42 Ibid, 201.
43 Ibid, 201.
44 Ibid, 46.
45 Ibid, 202.
46 Ibid, 29.

The Inquiry believes that forced sex and sex outside marriage are not traditional,[47] even though perpetrators themselves are said by one health professional to see it as "their kind of cultural initiation ... as regards consent ... I think very, very few men would see it as an issue".[48] The Inquiry comments:

> These observations are contrary to views expressed by traditional men and women to the Inquiry. Sexual contact between young persons should not occur outside "marriage".[49]

Perhaps sex outside marriage was not allowed in traditional times on the APY Lands. However, as Jane Lloyd pointed out, family- and kin-based structures make it difficult for remote Aboriginal children to seek outside help.[50] Furthermore, across much of traditional Aboriginal Australia in former times, forced, promised marriage of young girls to much older men was a customary practice, with young girls having no option on pain of severe violence, even death, for refusal. Such tradition warrants consideration as a likely key source of male, including older male, prerogative over young women on the APY Lands.

## More than just the drink

Cultural legitimation of violence across remote Aboriginal Australia makes the addition of risky alcohol consumption particularly dangerous. However, long-term reduction of alcohol consumption to well below mainstream levels – and that is the level needed – across remote Aboriginal Australia is probably unachievable. Moreover, recent statistics suggest that the link between reducing alcohol consumption and reducing violence is weak.[51]

---

47 See also McGlade, 2012, 98.
48 Mullighan Inquiry, 2008, 64.
49 Ibid, 64.
50 Lloyd, in extract of interview by Liz Jackson: Jackson, 2001.
51 These statistics are examined below in this chapter.

Severe and life-threatening violence has a much higher association with risky drinking among Aboriginal than non-Aboriginal Australians. Jack Dearden and Jason Payne of the Australian Institute of Criminology (AIC) calculate that "the odds of alcohol involvement [are] nearly five times higher for homicides involving an Indigenous offender".[52] The difference becomes even more marked for intimate partner homicide, with Indigenous-on-Indigenous intimate partner homicide incidents being "more than 13 times as likely to be classified as alcohol related" than non-Indigenous cases or in cases involving different races.[53] The Productivity Commission refers to the 2008 Snowball and Weatherburn statistical study's finding that among Aboriginal Australians, "[t]he impact of high-risk alcohol consumption on violence behaviour far exceeded that of any other variable examined".[54]

These figures suggest that there should be great scope for reducing Aboriginal life-threatening violence and homicide by reducing alcohol consumption. Indeed, there are communities where reduced local alcohol sales have resulted in significant declines in violence. "Alcohol limits in Fitzroy Crossing (WA)", "The Groote Eylandt Liquor Management System (NT)", and "Alcohol Management Plans in Cape York, Queensland" are highlighted by the Productivity Commission as schemes that have reduced violence and led to other important improvements in community function.[55] However, we need to know whether model projects indicate not just reductions in violence, but *sustained* reductions, and trending well towards

---

52 2000-06 figures. Jack Dearden and Jason Payne, "Alcohol and homicide in Australia", *Trends and Issues in Crime and Justice* No. 372 July 2009, AIC, 4-5. Source: http://www.aic.gov.au
53 2000-06 figures. Ibid, 4-5.
54 Productivity Commission, 2009, 10.14, referring to Snowball and Weatherburn, 2008, 216-235.
55 Productivity Commission, 2009, 10.16.

mainstream levels. Also, to be considered "models", there should be confidence in their widespread applicability to reduce violence across many self-determined communities. In this light, north-east Arnhem Land's Groote Eylandt experience is instructive.

### *The Groote Eylandt and Bickerton Island Alcohol Management System*

After 25 years of various attempts at alcohol restrictions with limited success, the Groote Eylandt and Bickerton Island Alcohol Management System, which "requires every person in the region, Aboriginal or non-Aboriginal, to hold a permit to buy or consume takeaway alcohol" was introduced on 1 July 2005.[56] Community groups, businesses and services including police were involved in its design and implementation. The July 2007 *Evaluation of the Groote Eylandt and Bickerton Island Alcohol Management System* indicates impressive success, with marked reductions in violence and other crime and improved social indicators such as CDEP and school attendance since its introduction.[57]

Nevertheless, police figures in the *Evaluation* depict a decline both mixed and uncertain in several ways. First, "Assaults" as "Incidents coming to the attention of police" record a dramatic decline of around 70% from about 55 in 2004-05 to about 17 in 2005-06.[58] However, "Assaults" as "Recorded offences" fell by a smaller 22%, from 76 in 2004-05 to 59 in 2005-06.[59] Also, the half year 1 July-31 December

---

56 Kate Conigrave, Elizabeth Proude and Peter d'Abbs, *Evaluation of the Groote Eylandt and Bickerton Island Alcohol Management System*, A Report for the Department of Justice, Northern Territory Government, 31 July 2007, 4:
http://www.nt.gov.au/justice/licenreg/documents/reports/Groote%20Eylandt%20Alcohol%20Management%20Evaluation%20Report.pdf

57 Ibid, 33-44.

58 Ibid, Figure 3, 33. (For purposes of simplicity here, I have aggregated Figure 3.'s "assaults" + "aggravated assaults" = "assaults").

59 Ibid, Table 4, 37. Note that Table 4 does not specify if the category "Assaults" includes "aggravated assaults".

2006 had 36 assaults as "Recorded offences", which is close to the *per annum* rate for 2004-05.[60]

Second, despite these declines, when compared with overall Northern Territory figures, assault rates on Groote Eylandt still appear high in the year following implementation of the Alcohol Management System. Only cautionary comment is possible, as police figures in the *Evaluation* do not categorise for Indigenous and non-Indigenous incidents.[61] Also, comparing rates across sources is risky, given differences in collecting and categorising data. However, Groote Eylandt's Indigenous population continued to have much higher imprisonment numbers than its larger non-Indigenous population. Prison statistics (all crimes) confirm that imprisoned Groote Eylandters were nearly all Indigenous. In 2005-06, 40 Groote Eylandt Indigenous people were "received by prison" and no non-Indigenous people, with only minor fluctuations in these figures between 2003-04 and 2007-08.[62] This rate differs little from other troubled communities such as Hermannsburg with a similar Indigenous population of 505[63] and 33 Indigenous prisoners received in 2007-08.[64]

Regarding assault rates, with a Groote Eylandt total population of

---

60 Ibid, Table 4, 37.

61 My calculations are likely to be conservative, given the high Groote Eylandt Indigenous vs. non-Indigenous imprisonment rate, plus if my calculations here could be based on Groote Eylandt's Indigenous population of 656 only, + if the police figures provided Indigenous identity, + if they were calculated for the population of 10+ years as are the ABS NT offender figures, the results for Groote Eylandt Indigenous assault rates would probably be worse than my calculations suggest.

62 Northern Territory Department of Justice (NTDJ), *Correctional Services Annual Statistics* (CSAS), (for the years 2003-2004, 2004-2005, 2005-2006, 2006-2007, 2007-2008), Northern Territory Government. Eg. 2006-07: http://www.nt.gov.au/justice/policycoord/documents/statistics/ntcsannualstatistics2006-07_EBook.pdf

63 ABS, 2006 *Census Quickstats*: Hermannsburg (L) (Urban Centre/locality).

64 NTDJ, *CSAS 2007-08*.

1,539[65] the 2005-06 assault number of 59 as a "Recorded offence" approaches a high one assault per 26, or 3833 per 100,000. For 2005-06, 17 assaults as "violent incident coming to the attention of police", is approximately 1,100 per 100,000. For comparison, for "Acts intended to cause injury", the Northern Territory offender rate per 100,000 (age 10+) in 2007-08 for Indigenous = 3,395.4; for non-Indigenous = 283.5; and for Northern Territory's total (10+) population = 1,126.6 per 100,000.[66]

Third, the *Evaluation* notes the following regarding domestic violence on Groote Eylandt:

> In contrast to the consistent reports of decreased violence from Indigenous female community members, those agencies dealing with domestic violence (clinic, police and domestic violence officers) reported that incidents of domestic violence coming to their attention had not reduced greatly. But while alcohol was previously the most common reason for violence, now cannabis (sometimes paranoia related to its use, but more often attempts to get money for cannabis or resulting from cannabis itself) or other reasons were the commonest factors. Alcohol was now only a sporadic cause. One interviewee from Angurugu estimated that alcohol was now a factor in perhaps one in ten cases.[67]

Indeed after one year of reduced alcohol consumption on Groote Eylandt, there were marked differences in declines across crime categories. For recorded property offences, there was a 52% decline, for recorded

---

65 Northern Territory Government, *Regional Socio-economic Snapshots, Groote Eylandt Region,* 2006: http://www.nt.gov.au/dbe/documents/general/Groote_Snapshot_2008. pdf Note that the 2006 Indigenous population of Groote Eylandt is 656 (42%). Original source: 2006 ABS Census of Population and Housing.

66 ABS, *Recorded Crime – Offenders, Selected States and Territories, 2007-08, 4519.0,* 2009: http://www.abs.com.au/ausstats/abs@nsf/mf/4519.0?OpenDocument. This is the first time the ABS has released a publication which focuses on "recorded crime- *offenders*", which is why 2005-06 figures are not presented here. There are earlier NT assault statistics, but they tend to focus on *victim* rates.

67 Conigrave, Proude and d'Abbs, 31.

offences against the person, a 24% decline,[68] and for domestic violence, apparently no decline. Police figures indicated that "[i]n contrast to the decrease in incidents involving assault and property crimes, there was no reduction in reported domestic disturbances" as follows: 2002-03 = 90; 2003-04 = 123; 2004-05 = 100; 2005-06 = 117.[69] While increase in reporting rather than in actual incidents is a possible factor,[70] with a total population of 1,539 including an Indigenous population of 656, these are high rates of domestic disturbances. On Groote Eylandt, it seems that property offences are the most responsive to changes in alcohol consumption, while domestic violence and disturbance are least responsive.

The *Evaluation* also observes that "[t]he relative isolation has made controlling the supply of alcohol easier than might be possible on some mainland communities".[71] Other model schemes provide evidence of even poorer outcomes. In Fitzroy Crossing, the hospital and the police report reductions in assaults since the introduction of take-away alcohol bans. However in September 2009, "Fitzroy Crossing businessmen say the town's population has more than halved since a ban on take-away alcohol was introduced in 2007". One businessman, Bob Lyons, said that "it is no wonder" shops such as his have experienced an 80% decline in trade. "There's no population left here, we're down to about 400 people I think, out of about 1,200."[72] Further to this, while violent incidents have decreased, the level of

---

68 Ibid, Table 4, 37.
69 "[W]hich includes both violent and non-violent incidents", Ibid, 35.
70 Ibid, 36.
71 Ibid, 58.
72 ABC News, "Liquor bans blamed for Fitzroy Crossing Decline", 11 September 2009: http://www.abc.net.au/news/stories/2009/09/11/2683110.htm

violence in Fitzroy Crossing remains alarmingly high.[73]

*Alcohol and violence trends*

While decades of alcohol reduction initiatives have demonstrated promise within the self-determination framework, broad scale, sustainable reductions in both alcohol *and* violence remain elusive. Accounts of attempts to enforce Dry Area or sanctioned limits on canteen sales can read like low-level war between enforcement agents and insurgents, such is the commitment to the grog among too many hardened drinkers, and among those, including non-Aboriginal opportunists, intent on providing liquor at inflated prices to remote communities.[74] Further, statistics regarding the impact of alcohol restrictions on violence look unpromising. Despite the Queensland government's Alcohol Management Plan effective from 2002-03,[75] which sought to restrict alcohol sales in 19 remote communities, recent years have experienced increases in Aboriginal assault offences and minimal change to Queensland's Aboriginal hospital admission rates for assault.[76]

---

73 Paige Taylor, "Violence reports surge after grog ban in Fitzroy Crossing", *The Australian*, 22 January 2009: http://www.theaustralian.com.au/news/nation/violence-reports-surge-after-grog-ban/story-e6frg6pf-1111118629326

74 For examples of difficulties facing alcohol restrictions and Dry Area strategies, see
– Paul Toohey, "No end to drug and grog runners", *The Australian*, 16 May 2009. Available at: http://www.theaustralian.com.au/news/no-end-to-drug-and-grog-runners/story-e6frg6po-1225712735544
– Skelton, 2007.
– Rebekah Cavanagh, "Grog runners use kids to hide booze", *NT News*, 9 September 2009: http://www.ntnews.com.au/article/2009/09/09/83011_ntnews.html
– Larine Statham, "Alcohol, drugs hidden in dead animals", *Adelaide Now*, 24 November 2009: http://www.adelaidenow.com.au/national/alcohol-drugs-hidden-in-dead-animals/story-e6frea8c-1225803421275
– Jane Bardon, "Dry areas just send grog elsewhere: study", ABC News, 13 December 2010: http://www.abc.net.au/news/stories/2010/12/13/3091747.htm

75 Tanya Chikritzhs, Dennis Gray, Zaza Lyons and Sherry Saggers, *Restrictions on the Sale and Supply of Alcohol: Evidence and Outcomes*, National Drug Research Institute, Curtin University of Technology, WA, 2007, 72-84: http://ndri.curtin.edu.au/local/docs/pdf/publications/R207.pdf

76 Johns, 2011, 169-170.

ABS figures indicate that variations in drinking rates between Indigenous and non-Indigenous Australians, and between remote and non-remote areas, fall far short of explaining the much higher presence of alcohol in cases of Aboriginal violence in remote areas. Aboriginal rates of violence including homicide in the more remote regions are much greater than non-Aboriginal homicide rates, while figures indicate that risky drinking among Aboriginal people in remote regions is at a lower rate than among non-Aboriginal people in remote regions.[77] Moreover as seen in the following Productivity Commission table, the Aboriginal rate of risky drinking is on the decline and is now nearing non-Aboriginal levels.

**"Alcohol consumption by short-term and long-term risk status, people aged 14 years and over, Australia"[78] (%)**

|  | Abstainer/ ex-drinker | Short-term risk | | Long-term risk | |
|---|---|---|---|---|---|
|  |  | Low risk | Risky or high risk | Low risk | Risky or high risk |
| **2007** |  |  |  |  |  |
| Indigenous | 23.4 | 49.2 | 27.4 | 64.2 | 12.5 |
| Non-Indigenous | 16.8 | 63.1 | 20.1 | 73.0 | 10.2 |
| **2004** |  |  |  |  |  |
| Indigenous | 21.3 | 40.0 | 38.7 | 56.0 | 22.7 |
| Non-Indigenous | 16.1 | 63.3 | 20.5 | 74.1 | 9.7 |
| **2001** |  |  |  |  |  |
| Indigenous | 20.6 | 30.7 | 48.7 | 59.5 | 19.9 |
| Non-Indigenous | 17.3 | 48.4 | 34.3 | 73.0 | 9.7 |

There is also a fairly steady decline in association between Indigenous "offender under the influence of alcohol", from 85% of

---

77 Productivity Commission, 2009, Table 10A.3.9, 117.
78 Ibid, Table 10A.3.1, 75.

Indigenous homicides in 1999-2000, to 71% in 2006-07.[79] This means a steady increase in the percentage of Aboriginal homicides where the offender was not under the influence of alcohol. In some contrast, since the early 2000s, most measures for hospitalised Aboriginal victims of violence have registered little change, remaining well above non-Aboriginal rates[80] and for hospitalised sexual assault, this appears to be increasing, although lower numbers for this form of violence reduce certainty.[81] For homicide, while lower numbers entail uncertainty regarding trends, there appears to be a promising, slight downward trend in overall Indigenous homicide rates. However, such a trend is barely detectable – if at all – for the more remote regions, while "major city" and "inner regional" Aboriginal homicide rates appear to be in steady decline.[82] Also, while the reported drinking patterns between major city and remote Indigenous Australians differ very little,[83] the homicide rates differ markedly, being much higher in remote locations. Indeed in some recent years, "major cities" experienced Aboriginal homicide rates of less than double non-Aboriginal rates.[84]

This lack of positive correlation between risky alcohol consumption and assault trends indicates that alcohol, while undeniably an exacerbator of violence, is not the primary cause of the high rates of violence in remote Aboriginal Australia. There is a consistent and widespread view among authoritative researchers that risky alcohol consumption is not a sufficient factor in itself to trigger violent behaviour. Dearden and Payne note that

> alcohol may indeed increase the probability of violence among those with violent dispositions. However, because the majority

---

79 Ibid, Table 4A.11.22, 612-13.
80 Ibid, Tables 4A.11.3-11, 566-92.
81 Ibid, Tables 4A.11.3-11, 566-92.
82 Ibid, Table 4A.11.15, 596-9.
83 Ibid, Table 10A.3.9, 117.
84 Ibid, Table 4A11.15, 596-9.

of persons who drink alcohol do not become violent, it suggests alternative factors mediate the alcohol-violence relationship. It is for this reason that many of the dominant explanations for the alcohol-violence relationship focus on other factors, such as personality, environmental and social cues.[85]

Maggie Brady's work on the nexus between alcohol, violence and traditional norms provides a clear illustration of why alcohol is such a dangerous drug in remote Aboriginal Australia.

### An ancient practice in modern times: women's head injuries[86]

*Maggie Brady's study of alcohol impacts on Aboriginal women*

In her article, "Alcohol use and its effects upon Aboriginal women",[87] Brady writes that

> social scientists studying the social organisation of alcohol use ... argue persuasively that the behaviours that occur after drinking has taken place are determined by what that society defines as permissible drunken comportment. They provide evidence that even the inebriated observe limits and rules.[88]

Brady's own study suggests that culture is a strong "mediating" factor in the "alcohol-violence relationship" among remote Aboriginal Australians. Her 1982 and 1987 research among a Pitjantjatjara community found marked differences in alcohol-fuelled violence injuries received by men and women. In 1982, "head injuries constituted 25 per cent of all female injuries, and only 7 per cent of all male injuries ... Men on the other hand, presented at the clinic most frequently with thigh lacerations. No woman sustained a thigh injury

---

85 Dearden and Payne, 2009, 1, drawing on work by B. Felson, B. Teasdale and K.B. Burchfield, "The influence of being under the influence: alcohol effects on adolescent violence", *Journal of Research in Crime and Delinquency*, 45(2), 2008:119-41.
86 See also Jamieson, Harrison and Berry, 2008, 576-9.
87 Maggie Brady, "Alcohol use and its effects upon Aboriginal women", AIC, 1990.
88 Ibid, 7.

over a six-month period." In 1987, while there were more female victims of alcohol-fuelled violence, up from 38% to 50%, the gender pattern in injury type remained the same. Brady added that "the high number of head injuries sustained by women in this community, meant that they frequently suffered life-threatening injury". "Women also sustained more arm fractures than men ... Over a seven-year period, 17 women received treatment for arm fractures and only 3 men." Moreover:

> The differentiation between male and female injuries to parts of the body is significant for two reasons. Firstly, spearing in the thigh (in men) and arm-breaking (in women) are documented in the anthropological literature as being the two areas of the body subjected customarily to blows of punishment. Secondly, the fact that the inebriated (in at least some instances) were able to place their blows to specific parts of the body, suggests that strong cultural factors were at work. It also suggests that even the apparently inebriated were capable of a degree of controlled action.[89]

In particular, the kinds of violence inflicted onto men and women by a drunken offender could still draw upon strong cultural roots and justifications:

> Spearing in the thigh of a man is still used as a form of social control as a punishment for serious misdemeanour in several regions in Australia ... arm-breaking of women (by both male and female assailants) is noted by Sansom (1980) and Bell and Ditton (1980). Bell and Ditton note an incident in which an Aboriginal man hit his wife's arm with a boomerang for not preparing his dinner (1980). He claimed he was justified under customary law.[90]

---

89 Ibid, 6. Note: Brady's article has important content on court cases and customary law.
90 Ibid, 6.

## Conclusion

Perspectives on the role of resilient traditional violence norms, as opposed to reactive violence due to contemporary factors, have critical implications for those trying to combat Aboriginal social and economic malaise. In his review of McKnight's *From Hunting to Drinking* and *Of Marriage, Sorcery and Violence*, James Franklin pointed out that focus on post-contact causes falls short even as an explanation let alone as a basis for strategy:

> The facts of violence are clear but the causes and cure are not. Or rather, some of the causes are clear enough but the full story of why things are so bad remains baffling. Obviously alcohol and welfare dependency are important parts of the causes, but those factors are operative in many communities, white and black, and it is far from clear why the effects in remote communities are so far beyond anything found elsewhere, in their extreme levels of violence, ill-health and atrocious education.[91]

There are harsh realities here. The idea that violence was not part of tradition has allowed policy rhetoric about Aboriginal violence to appear relatively non-threatening to Aboriginal culture and power structures. Indeed, emphasis on the white invasion and the effects of alcohol could enhance the palatability of programs addressing Aboriginal violence. While providing scope for progress here and there, overall this approach has not worked because the premise is wrong. Change has to occur on the deeper level of traditional beliefs, laws, tolerances and measures of "normality". The prevailing traditional toleration of violence as a normal and useful phenomenon, plus the idea that individual rights and needs are secondary to keeping culture alive, are key reasons why violence has a tenacious hold over remote Aboriginal communities, and why reducing that violence is so difficult, even when it is clearly destroying Aboriginal lives.

---

91 Franklin, 2008.

# 7
# Outstations

I love coming to these outstations. We generally find that people living on the homelands are much healthier. They're not exposed to all the junk food that you can buy in the stores and they rely much more on hunting and fishing bush tucker. And they love having us out here as well.
— Vicki, health clinic nurse, north-east Arnhem Land.[1]

This man had a violent history. In fact, he'd been acquitted of murder in the late 1990s. The offences occurred at outstations, which are often highly dangerous places to be for women and children, because they are often unable to escape any of the violence.
— Nanette Rogers, Crown Prosecutor in Alice Springs for 12 years, 2006.[2]

## Return to Country

The homelands movement across Australia is primarily an Aboriginal initiative. It commenced in the 1970s, and arose from the "desire of Aboriginal people to move out of the settlements, reserves and missions and back to traditional country".[3] The large, colonially created settlements

Characteristically contained many people living as "guests"

---

[1] Anna Daniels, "The Outstation of Balma: Gapuwiyak Day Four", ABC Darwin, 17 November 2007: http://www.abc.net.au/local/stories/2007/11/17/2095948.htm?site=darwin&microsite=gapuwiyak&section=latest

[2] Tony Jones, "Prosecutor Speaks Out About Abuse in Central Australia." *ABC Lateline* 15 June, 2006. Transcript available at: http://www.abc.net.au/lateline/content/2006/s1639127.htm

[3] House of Representatives Standing Committee on Aboriginal Affairs (HRSCAA), *Return to Country: the Aboriginal Homelands Movement in Australia*, Australian Government Publishing Service (AGPS), Canberra, March 1987, 13.

on land, which traditionally did not belong to them, alongside the traditional owners. For Aboriginal people the perceptions of these communities were as "no good", "too much trouble", "people fightin'", too much worry", "sad place", and "too much sick there". By contrast, outstation life offered a return to "a healthy social and physical environment", away from the tensions and trouble associated with large communities and mixed groups.[4]

"Homelands" fulfilled prevailing policy ideas about how governments should respond to Aboriginal aspirations such as self-determination, cultural revival and traditional lands. The RCADC affirmed this policy direction, arguing that access to traditional or historically significant lands, including homelands, is an essential part of counteracting the harm done to Aboriginal family and community by colonisation. Meeting "land needs" was seen as crucial in reducing the high Aboriginal arrest rate.[5]

### Key "solutions" as key problems: continuity of violence on outstations

The two quotations opening this chapter capture the excruciating dilemma confronting policy makers regarding funding support for outstations. Nanette Rogers' 2006 interview on *Lateline* exposed to the nation the reality that in outback Australia, there is no safe place "category" for Aboriginal women and children. Even outstations are too often dangerous places. The 2007 *Little Children Are Sacred* report drew attention to prevalent child neglect and abuse across remote Australia. The NTER was the Howard government's response. A

---

4 Ibid, 14, including quotes from Transcript of Evidence pp. S79-80, and from P. Nathan and D. Leichleitner Japanangka, *Settle Down Country*, Central Aboriginal Conference, Kibble Books, Malmsbury, 1983, 91-2.
5 The RCADC prefers the term "land needs" rather than "land rights", to capture the sense that Aboriginal people need land to restore their individual, family, and community well-being. See Elliott Johnston QC, *Royal Commission into Aboriginal Deaths in Custody*, AGPS, Canberra.1991, Chapter 19 in Vol. 2, 467.

central strategy of the NTER is to focus funding for services, including health, housing, education and police, onto twenty selected growth towns, and to reduce government funding for smaller communities including the approximately 500 Northern Territory outstations.[6] The well-serviced town centres should thereby attract larger populations and businesses. With home ownership, no permit system, and openness to white residents as well, it is the government's hope that these towns will increase access to the positives of mainstream life for outback Aboriginal people, thereby helping to break chronic community dysfunction.[7]

However, studies and commentaries about the benefits of outstation life write of the harmony, safety and healthy living that characterise daily life for outstation communities. Typically located beyond easy commuter distance from the alcohol canteens and other damaging "attractions" of town life, they are places where older people can extend enough traditional authority to restrict access to alcohol, illicit drugs and petrol sniffing, and uphold traditional prohibitions regarding

---

6 – Northern Territory Government, "Territory Growth Towns", *Working Future, A Territory Government Initiative*: http://www.workingfuture.nt.gov.au/download/working_future_growth_towns.pdf
– Northern Territory Government, "Homelands", *Working Future, A Territory Government Initiative*: http://www.workingfuture.nt.gov.au/Homelands/outstations.html
– Northern Territory Government, "Outstations/homelands policy: Headline Policy Statement", *Working Future, A Territory Government Initiative*. Northern Territory Government, May 2009: http://www.workingfuture.nt.gov.au/Homelands/docs/Headline_Policy_Statement.pdf
7 Paul Toohey, "A new lease of life", *The Australian Weekend Magazine*, 10-11 January 2009, 14-18.

violence and abuse against women and children.[8] Studies indicate that outstation dwellers are typically healthier. Outstations provide better access to employment than other remote localities, particularly through small enterprise development. Submissions objecting to funding cuts for outstations point to reduced violence and child abuse on outstations, compared to larger Aboriginal settlements. Such benefits suggest that the outstation model can fulfil Coombs' idea that a resumption of traditional life by self-determined small communities is both possible and can improve Aboriginal social and physical health, including safety for women and children. Thus the defenders of outstations have an ostensibly credible challenge to the idea that integration, rather than separation, is the necessary policy direction for securing Aboriginal well-being.

The idea of starving small, safer, healthier outstation settlements of funding, while boosting funds for the larger Aboriginal townships, some of which such as Wadeye epitomise the stricken Indigenous community, does seem unfair and unjustified. Nevertheless, scepticism about outstations is warranted. Too few people, particularly young people, want to live on them; and outstations facilitate the continuation of traditions that are dangerous to women, children and young people, and regularly fail to protect them from violence.

---

8 For examples, see:
– Sarah Marland, "Healthy homelands", Amnesty International Australia, 11 March 2010: http://www. amnesty.org.au/poverty/comments/22681/
– Lindsay Murdoch, "Living in fear of losing everything", *The Age*, 17 October 2009: http://www.theage.com.au/national/living-in-fear-of-losing-everything-20091016-h17l.html
– Socom and DodsonLane, *Our home, our homeland, Community Engagement Report*, Northern Territory Government: Outstations Policy, January 2009: http://www.workingfuture.nt.gov.au/Homelands/docs/Community_Engagement_Report.pdf
– Frances Morphy, *The Future of Homelands in North-East Arnhem Land*, CAEPR, ANU, Canberra, 5 December 2005: http://caepr.anu.edu.au/system/files/cck_misc_documents/2010/06/Homelands_future_FMorphy.pdf

## Some scholars' observations

It is difficult to have a well-informed debate about violence on outstations, because of the scarcity of data and research with that focus. Key sources do not provide statistical data on Australia's 500 outstations as a separate category. Police and hospital data, AIHW, Productivity Commission, AIC, and NATSISS, have only larger location categories of "major cities", "inner regional", "outer regional", "remote", and sometimes "very remote". "Remote" and "very remote" include large town centres such as Nhulunbuy, smaller hub townships such as Maningrida, small communities too large to be called outstations such as Ski Beach, and outstations. To date, most scholars with critical, rigorous insight about Aboriginal interpersonal violence have paid scant analytical attention to violence on outstations. The observations they do make signal that outstations are limited solutions at best to the harshness and danger of remote Aboriginal life.

### *Steven Etherington*

Steven Etherington stands out as a rare scholar who has analysed and spoken with great compassion about the failures of outstations. Etherington is an Anglican minister and expert in Aboriginal education practice. Over many years of living in Northern Territory Aboriginal communities, Etherington witnessed the "living hell" suffered by outstation residents, even when those outstations are well-funded and well-serviced. Etherington observed that from their beginnings in the 1970s, outstations held promise as places where with some level of protective assistance, Aboriginal people could establish a healthier lifestyle away from the hazards of bigger towns, with a degree of independence and self-sufficiency. However, any chance of these developing into self-determined places based on Aboriginal people's own decision-making and hard work was pushed aside by the intrusion of federal funding, white decision-makers and experts, and welfare:

> By the mid eighties whites drove the whole thing from grant harvesting to imposing an utterly dependent and non accountable lifestyle. I have been eyewitness to event[s] like white people arriving in expensive four wheel drive vehicles to mow grass at outstations ...
>
> As for life on the outstations, the essential corruption of having everything supplied free of accountability or cost was just one step in the spiral downhill. The atmosphere across Australia in the eighties was insistent on Aboriginal difference and there was very serious underreporting of crimes (including murder) and a willingness to interpret pathological behaviours as acceptable because cultural. Meanwhile those of us living on the outstations or in the communities were seeing a small hell being made. The moral collapse of a group of people was accelerated and made guilt free by whites who brought their own spiritual emptiness to the task ... [9]

Etherington details the impact this lack of accountability had on outstation education, crippled further by the rule, "always to avoid confrontation or reporting". In one area, the outstation schools were well-funded and well-resourced, with "good classrooms" and sports facilities. On one or two days per week, white teachers were flown in. Local teaching aides were expected to teach on the other days.

> I was often in the outstations when there were no teachers present. No, the local teaching aides didn't keep things running; the school was used for other purposes especially at night, there was no pretence of ongoing school work. Kids played or hung around their parents, who waited on the shop plane, the medical plane and the other fly in services, whilst playing cards or watching video ... The education outcomes were of course wretched ... [10]

A few years earlier, Etherington made the following bleak observation:

---

9 Etherington, pers. comm., 2010.
10 Ibid.

We have intentionally created a group of people who are allowed or required to be on permanent holiday at these centres without any meaningful employment. In a typical outstation there will be anywhere between half a dozen and fifty or, rarely, a hundred or more people, depending on the time of year, mainly from one family or clan. Houses and other buildings are new. Water supply, power supply, aircraft access to medical services, microwave ovens, phones and TV, schooling are all provided. There has been no attempt to provide an appropriate, lesser, level of infrastructure ...

More significantly ... [t]here is built-in protection (through isolation) for sexual abuse and neglect of women and children. There is little evidence of systematic cultural learning or practices, except exploitative magic or the usual recreational hunting of any group of humans with spare time in a remote environment. Most people spend a great part of the day playing cards or driving back and forth between the outstation and the nearest shop or alcohol outlet. This kind of publicly supported pseudo-traditional lifestyle bears only the most superficial resemblance to pre-contact way of life. It is producing unemployable people capable only of living in an artificial economic environment.[11]

For Etherington, the most destructive, violence-producing aspects of recent policy for remote Aboriginal people – dependency, unemployment and unemployability – have also occurred where they were not expected: the outstations.[12] A decade ago, Etherington's writing was hopeful that the abysmal situation on remote communities could be turned around, as evidenced in his recommendations.[13] This hope has faded. The Indigenous Literacy Foundation emphasises the centrality of English literacy to Indigenous young people's opportunities:

the development of English literacy skills is important for the life opportunities of Indigenous children and youth. Literacy

---

11 Etherington, 2001, 90.
12 Ibid, 90.
13 Ibid, 90-101.

"provides them with the necessary skills to interact within mainstream society and avail themselves of the broadest range of civic, social, educational and employment possibilities."[14]

While it is modern, mainstream life that young, remote Aboriginal people aspire to, Etherington now considers that small remote communities including outstations are too small, isolated and dysfunctional to provide the wide-ranging education needed. Many remote-area young people including those on outstations cannot speak their own languages fluently, nor have they acquired English literacy.[15] Many speak Kriol as their first language.[16] This is a severe impediment to independence and employment.

## *Peter Sutton*

In his 2009 book, Sutton noted the waning pull of outstations in the Aurukun region. From the 1970s until the 1990s:

> outstation development proliferated until up to 300 Aurukun people were spending at least the dry season time out in their countries. That era had come gradually to a close by the 1990s when only small numbers of diehards abandoned the allurements of town to spend time in the bush beyond daily commuting distance from Aurukun. During my visits to Aurukun in the dry seasons of 2006 and 2007 and, ... 2008, not a single outstation of Aurukun was occupied. Funding for outstation development was by then far more substantial than it had been at the height of the re-occupation of traditional countries in the 1970s and 1980s.[17]

Early in his book, Sutton recounts the heartbreaking tragedy of too

---

14 Indigenous Literacy Foundation, "Indigenous Literacy", (including quote from S. Mellor and M. Corrigan, "The case for change: a review of contemporary research on Indigenous education outcomes", *Australian Education Review*, ACER, 2004, p. 39): http://www.indigenousliteracyfoundation.org.au/about/indigenousliteracy
15 Etherington, 2001, 97; Etherington, pers. comm., 2010.
16 Etherington, pers. comm., 2010.
17 Sutton, 2009, 24-5.

many violent deaths, including people who grew up on the Watha-nhiin outstation:

> The cemetery at Aurukun reminds me of the Australian war graves at Villers-Bretonneux in France. In my time with the Wik people up to 2001, out of a population of less than 1000, eight people known to me died by their own hand, two of them women, six of them men. Five of them were young people. From the same community in the same period, thirteen people known to me had been victims of homicide, eight of them women, five of them men. Twelve others had committed homicide, nine of them men and three of them women ...
>
> The most wrenching suicide was Marjorie's daughter Ursula Yunkaporta, my "full niece". At Watha-nhiin in the 1970s she had been one of a number of lively, sassy, school-age kids. In the 1990s she presented at Aurukun Hospital scores of times over a two-year period of heavy drinking, repeatedly bashed by her boyfriend and others with whom she also fought. She was treated for being savaged by dogs at night, and was twice examined after giving details of how she was pack-raped by local boys. In the end she took her own life by hanging, at twenty-seven, also in 1998.[18]

It seems that neither a seemingly happy childhood spent on a homeland outstation, nor the continued presence of Wik outstations during their adult life, was enough to save these young people's lives.

### *Victoria Burbank*

In a footnote in her 1994 book, Burbank describes the unpopularity of outstation life, perhaps particularly among young people, compared to town life:

> In 1977, groups of Aboriginal people were leaving Mangrove to set up small communities on their clan lands. By 1981, eleven outstations had been established. In 1988, the outstations seemed

---

18  Ibid, 2-3.

to hold little attraction for most of the people I knew.[19]

By 1988, some were nearly deserted. Burbank notes that "there are many possible reasons that the outstations have not provided more of a long-term alternative to settlement residence."[20] There were disincentives to go to outstations, including off-putting talk of fining parents for taking children away from schooling to visit outstations. Other factors were pulling people from outstations:

> Though outstations can be seen as a means of regaining autonomy and preserving Aboriginal practices (Altman 1987; Burbank 1988), their residents, nevertheless, continued to depend on many of the goods and services provided through Mangrove. Trips to the settlement were made, for example, to obtain foodstuffs from the shop and medicine from the health clinic. In 1988, the people I knew expressed much more interest in visiting "town" or other settlements to attend such events as Bible meetings, dance festival, or rock concerts. Alcohol may also be a factor affecting outstation residence ... Aboriginal people who want to drink, as a number do, are more likely to visit towns or settlements where alcohol is available than an outstation where it is not. The use of outstations as "punishment" for adolescents who misbehave may also reduce the desire of young people to visit them voluntarily (Burbank 1988).[21]

Burbank does not say how "punishment" might cause young people to shun outstations. Were they mild but boring places of "home detention", safe away from risky town attractions, or were they places where specific, perhaps traditional punishments, were undertaken? Northern Territory court records suggest that the use of outstations as places of "home detention" are common sentence strategies for errant, at-risk young Indigenous people who have access to a family

---

19 Burbank, 1994, 196.
20 Ibid, 196.
21 Ibid, 196-7.

outstation. Northern Territory courts also record at-risk Indigenous young people breaking outstation detention orders to get back to risky town life and access to dangerous substances.

## *My field work*

My field work revealed to me the critical issue of homelands in one southern community.[22] The Aboriginal residents of the mainstream regional centre of Viewtown spoke of their dreams and anxieties due to the chance of having a family outstation, or "homeland" as they called them. In the mid 1990s there were several homeland applications in Viewtown, all made by prominent Aboriginal Viewtown families. Two families already had homelands in an adjacent town's hinterland. Potentially this meant that more than 100 Aboriginal Viewtowners might access homeland properties. Much as is claimed in *Return to Country* and by the RCADC, Aboriginal Viewtowners commonly visualised their future homeland as a kind of Arcadia where present worries are left behind, and a harmonious family life is restored:

> *Woman elder*
> I'm all for Homelands because for me it means getting away from all these problems – I'm tired of working and struggling to get the right things to happen and now I just want to rest. Our family has a beautiful homeland we're working to get – a little north from here. I just want to relax and sit in the sun and put all these problems behind me.

There were attempts on existing homelands to implement strategies to benefit the social health of residents, such as limits on alcohol imports and visitor numbers. These were contested, however, with one elder, a Viewtown resident, railing against such "stupid"

---

22 Field work for PhD thesis, Stephanie Jarrett, *"We Have Left it in Their Hands": A Critical Assessment of Legal and Policy Responses to Aboriginal Domestic Violence: A Location Study*, Dept. of Geography and Dept. of Politics, University of Adelaide, 1997. These issues were also discussed in Jarrett, 2001, 118-22.

rules because they mean that "We can't do what we like on our own land!" Homelands appeared unlikely to eliminate family conflicts; rather they were introducing additional conflicts, rendering domestic violence even more prevalent. With no clear traditional guidelines or other precedents regarding rights to homeland economic opportunities in this semi-integrated context, family and domestic contests over who had authority emerged:

> *Woman*
>
> My family has a claim in but it causes lots of arguments. See, my sister is married to a white man, and he wants to put pigs on the homeland. But we don't want pigs on it. And anyway, what right does he have to say what is going on the homeland? He's a Whitey! So he can't have a say over what happens on the homelands of his wife's family!
>
> *Male elder*
>
> It's no good for me and my own direct line at the moment and there's bad feeling between me and my two brothers over this, plenty of bad feeling over there! ... My two brothers' children, they think they can make all the rules because they live on the homeland permanently. But the elders, and there are 10 of us, should be equal bosses; with equal rights to pass on the land's houses to our own direct bloodlines. None of this sideways takeover which is happening now. Because we don't live there permanently, my own children and grandchildren haven't got right of access anymore to the houses there!

A white service provider reported that homeland-associated community, family and couple tensions were widespread in Viewtown.

> "Homelands" is already having a big effect on family conflict here. It is causing a huge volume of conflict between families over which families have rights to funding and which don't. It's also creating a huge volume of dispute within families. This occurs in some families around the fact that husbands and wives

come from different families with planned or present homelands in very different locations ... There is one family that I know of where the husband and wife have actually split. The woman wanted to shift to her family's homeland, and the man didn't want to and the arguments between them included a lot of physical violence by the man against the woman ...

[In some cases] only one of the partners wants to actually shift to the homeland and the other wants to stay in Viewtown for work or education or just prefers city life.

*But Aboriginal people that are for the homelands talk about it as getting back family unity, for healing.*

Oh yes! of course that's what's said! That's the ideal, the dream about homelands. But the reality of homelands is very different from that dream.

So even within families, there existed racial issues, conflicting aspirations to stay or to leave mainstream society, and little consensus on basic economic and social guidelines for the family homeland. They seemed to lack enough shared vision or cultural purpose to avoid chronic conflict and to establish a reasonably harmonious group life. Indeed, the addition of a chance for homelands onto an already troubled and divided urban Aboriginal community was proving to be a source of further anguish and division, and likely to increase the dysfunction of Aboriginal "community" as a basis of service provision. One prominent Aboriginal Viewtown man, despite his involvement in homeland funding negotiations and his own family's bid for homeland funding, expressed his concerns about homeland implications for "community" and Aboriginal services:

> Homelands tend to emphasise family rather than community, with each homeland family attempting to get funds for services on their own homeland ... Homelands will tend to draw funding away from centralised services to the point that centralised services established for all the community become starved of funds and threatened thus with contraction or collapse ... This may result in families languishing away from the towns on their

own property, underserviced and in squalor perhaps like in times past, just the sort of thing we want to avoid, that we've been working to move away from.

The experience of one "non-local" Viewtown family portrays how homelands can emphasise family over community in another way:

> My father came to Viewtown 16 years ago. He was a good worker in mainstream Viewtown, and was the main driving force behind the setting up of the Aboriginal Housing Unit here. But he was the first to acquire homelands money in Viewtown too. This upset the other Aboriginal families very much as we weren't considered local, being here for only 16 years. And Viewtown Aboriginal Association actually voted us out of the community, voted that we were non-members of the community!

An observation of a young Aboriginal mother of relatively recent arrival to Viewtown provides a glimpse of how homelands can reduce the safety of Aboriginal victims. While the rate of Viewtown Aboriginal domestic violence appeared much higher than the white rate, the presence of homelands could render it even worse:

> There's less domestic and other violence among the Aboriginals of Viewtown than in other places I've lived before, because there's no nearby mission or outstation that they can escape to here. Here they have to try to get along with each other and with whites as there's not much escape from each other. They can't just storm into town and out again like they do in Darwin, Alice Springs and Port Augusta.

This provides a key insight: outstations impact on life in main towns. The scholars' observations indicate that outstations struggle to be ideal "worlds of their own". Nearby towns and the mainstream world beckon, as outstations are too small to provide today's needs and attractions. Furthermore, as signalled by the young mother, outstations in a town's hinterland could increase violence in hub town communities.

## Sad documentations: court records

The Northern Territory Supreme and Coroner's courts note "outstation" when it is relevant to a case. With no police or hospital data that systematically records injuries or deaths by assault for the geographic category "outstation" or "homeland", these court documents are a critical source of information regarding outstations and the geography of Aboriginal violence. In Northern Territory court cases, "outstation" arises for several reasons: as an offender's or victim's place of upbringing, residence, employment, where a crime was committed, or a place for home detention. Given considerable search result fluctuations, hence the risk of providing a misleading picture, on my search of the Supreme Court website there were 862 results for "Aboriginal assault", 662 for "Aboriginal assault community", 163 for "Aboriginal assault town", 75 for "Aboriginal assault town camp", and 99 for "Aboriginal assault outstation/out-station/homeland". Excluding "Aboriginal assault outstation" results that were duplications or speeches and similar, in about half the remaining 40 or so results, the outstation was a place where the offence was committed, or where the offender either grew up, presently resided, or had a very strong connection, for instance worked for an outstation organisation.[23] Given the small size of the total Northern Territory outstation population compared to the other categories, this "first take" on distribution signals, if nothing more, that outstations show no obvious exemption from violent events. Indeed, outstations seem to feature prominently as places where Northern Territory's most heinous, notorious acts of violence against Aboriginal women and children committed in the first decade of the 21st century occurred.

Nevertheless, a search through court proceedings risks being a "cherry-picking" task. Searching awful crimes from other groups

---

23 Source: Northern Territory Supreme Court http://www.supremecourt.nt.gov.au Search date: 10 May 2010.

such as white or city-based-Aboriginal violence and homicide, could also create a terrible litany. Perhaps, but it is important to recall that the Aboriginal violence and homicide rate is much higher than the non-Aboriginal rate, and that homicide and injury hospitalisation rates are particularly high for remote and very remote Aboriginal people. Court cases give us a rare window into the cultural, social and geographic contexts of these violent events among remote and very remote Indigenous Australians. In particular, court cases confirm that outstations regularly fail to provide safety to vulnerable Aboriginal people.

Taken together, the cases reveal a picture of a resilient, continuing Aboriginal culture and law, with terms such as "traditional man", "promised marriage", and "payback" appearing regularly. Self-determination and everyday life on separate lands and outstations away from the mainstream seem to be safeguarding a distinct Aboriginal law and culture. The cases also illustrate that an outstation upbringing or residence is far from a reliable protection against a life of violence, victimhood, alcohol abuse, petrol sniffing and suicide. They also concur with Burbank's observations that young people tend not to like staying on outstations. And as places of detention for men who have assaulted their wives, I wonder about the safety of women who ask that their husband be released from a prison sentence to stay with them on an outstation, because "he only hits me when he's drunk", and there is no alcohol on the outstation. Extracts from some cases are presented here.[24]

### *Gamurru-Gayurra outstation near Maningrida, 2002*

This is the high-profile crime covered in the media and by a number of writers.[25] It occurred on Gamurru-Gayurra outstation near

---

[24] For a contemporary picture, I have included crimes committed after January 2000 only. I have selected cases for their illustrative power.
[25] These include Kimm, 2004, esp. 69, 72-4; and McGlade, 2006, 7-8 and 2012, 143-8.

Maningrida in 2002, and extracts give a sense of its traditional, geographic and other life influences. The defendant was born and lived on an outstation. It seems that he had a strong cultural life, as well as good education and employment within the mainstream world. This did not prevent binge drinking and violence earlier in his life. It appears that he no longer had a drinking problem when this 2002 crime was committed.

> [The defendant] was a resident of an outstation, Gamurru-Gayurra, which is located approximately 120 kilometres east of Maningrida by road. He is a 50 year old male ... on the evening of Monday 20 August, the defendant approached the victim, A, whose date of birth was 19 May '86, making her 15 I think at the relevant time, who he states is his promised wife.[26]

The defendant had under-age sex with her while at the outstation. The next day, the girl tried to leave the outstation:

> the defendant became upset when his stated promised wife, the victim, A, tried to leave the outstation to return to Maningrida in the vehicle ... driven by friends.
>
> The defendant got a single-barrel 12-gauge shotgun ... After telling the victim not to leave, the defendant fired the weapon once into the air. The victim returned to the defendant's side and remained with him as she feared for the safety of her friends and herself if she didn't comply ...
>
> It will be noted from the Crown that when the respondent was asked if he was aware that it was an offence to have sex with a 15 year old girl, he replied, "Yes I know; it's called carnal knowledge, but it's Aboriginal custom – my culture. She is my promised wife."[27]

"A" was promised to him since shortly after her birth, "in accordance with traditional culture". This includes mutual obligations whereby he

---

26 *Hales v Jamilmira* [2003] NTCA 9.
27 Ibid.

gave a "significant proportion of his money" to her family from the time she was promised. According to the "sworn evidence" of another Maningrida man, while the promised marriage custom was "slowly being lost" through marriage for love, nevertheless "[i]f the promised bride does not want to go to the man there is 'big trouble'".[28] The pre-sentence report concerning the offender includes the following:

> he was born at an outstation 25 kilometres west of Millingimbi, an Aboriginal man with strong cultural ties to his homeland, being fully initiated into tribal customs, and he was considered by many to be a custodian of traditional knowledge. He achieved a good standard of education and ... maintained employment for most of his life. ... His marriage of 1979 was "culturally arranged", but ... was marred by frequent episodes of binge drinking by both partners and associated domestic violence leading to a fight between them in 1994, as a consequence of which the respondent was convicted of manslaughter ...
>
> The Report indicates that he has rehabilitated himself from his pattern of binge drinking, now drinking infrequently and only moderately, and the substance abuse did not appear to have been a factor in contributing to the commission of present offences.[29]

McGlade noted that:

> The 15 year old's police statement was revealed in a national newspaper, in which it was stated that the defendant had forced her to his outstation whereupon she was subjected to violent beating and sexual assault ... The lofty defence claim that the defender's actions were "entirely appropriate and correct within the traditional parameters of the Bururra world ..." (Bryant, 2002, p.20)[30]

---

28 Ibid.
29 Ibid.
30 McGlade, 2006, 8; see also *Hales v. Jamilmira*.

## *Spring Park outstation near Jabiru, 2000*

The *Alderson v The Queen* case of "aggravated unlawful assault" occurred at an outstation on 16 November 2000.[31] One reason for the appeal against the sentence was "whether the sentencing Judge erred by not taking into account the special impact of imprisonment upon Aboriginal people who live largely a traditional life – sentence on the face of it manifestly excessive". Since 1980, this offender had accumulated convictions for serious assaults, including "12 years imprisonment for manslaughter":

> the accused ... drove with his brother-in-law and others, including the victim, his de facto of some weeks ... from Spring Park Outstation into Jabiru town centre. On the return journey a carton of VB beer was purchased ... Upon arrival at Spring Park the group proceeded to the home of the accused's mother where they continued consuming alcohol on the verandah.
>
> After a short time the brother in law of the accused returned to his own home ...
>
> An argument developed between the accused and his de facto. ... the accused walked behind her with a stick and struck her on the back of the head causing a lump on the back of her head ...
>
> The victim said that "her head was swollen; that she felt sick; and that she suffered a headache as a consequence of the assault. After that assault ... she left you because she was frightened of you".[32]

The Spring Park outstation afforded this young woman no protection from the dangers of alcohol, nor protection from that violence with deep traditional precedent against women, the injurious impact of a stick to the head. When our courts are asked to consider extending leniency to the perpetrator of this tradition due to "the special impact of imprisonment upon Aboriginal people who live largely a traditional life",[33] surely the cruel irony is obvious.

---
31 *Alderson v The Queen* [2002] NTCCA 10.
32 Ibid.
33 Ibid.

### Outstation near Yarralin, 2004

This is a notorious case of physical and sexual violence by a middle-aged man against a young teenage girl,[34] which has also been widely examined.[35] It is presented here because the offender took the victim to an outstation where the crimes occurred. It shows that outstations can indeed safeguard culture, but this can include practices that abuse the rights and safety of children. Indeed, her own family – her grandmother – assisted this brutal man, even participating in the violence against her own granddaughter. Further, this case illustrates cultural continuity, with pre-contact precedents to draw upon, and is repulsive to mainstream values. On June 2004, a crime against a young girl was committed by a 55-year-old "traditional Aboriginal man" who

> was brought up in the traditional way and grew up at Yarralin, a remote Aboriginal community located 382 km southwest of Katherine ... He had a strong ceremonial life across a number of communities and is regarded by the Yarralin community as an important person in the ceremonial life of the community. He is responsible for teaching young men traditional ways ... The respondent has a good relationship with his wife.[36]

His victim was 14 years old, and when she was about four, "the child's family promised her as a wife to the respondent in accordance with traditional Aboriginal law". She was staying at her grandmother's at Yarralin during school holidays from a Darwin college. During these holidays, she "formed a friendship with a young male":

> On about Friday 18 June 2004, the child stayed in the home of a mutual friend with whom the boy also stayed. Word spread

---

34 *The Queen v GJ* [2005].
35 Jones, 15 June 2006; Nowra, 2007, 47-8; Hughes 2007, 27-8, 40; Johns, 2011, 127-9; and McGlade, 2012, 148-52.
36 *The Queen v GJ* [2005].

about this and the respondent believed that a sexual relationship had occurred between the young boy and the child.

On Saturday 19 June 2004, the respondent and the child's grandmother went to the house where the child and boy had stayed... The grandmother took the child outside. The respondent had gone to the house armed with two boomerangs.[37]

With a boomerang, he struck the child on her shoulders and back with some force, and her grandmother also "struck the child with a big stick". The grandmother insisted that the child go with the offender to an outstation, and the child was forced into the car, to sit next to his "wife and two small children". The offender drove the child to the outstation, and "the child was taken into the house with the respondent and his wife and two small children".[38] It was accepted by the sentencing judge that

> according to traditional law the striking of the child was justified as a means of punishing the child for having a sexual relationship with the young boy when the child was already promised to the respondent. However ... there was nothing in the respondent's traditional law which required him to either strike the child or to have sexual intercourse with her in the circumstances.[39] The learned sentencing judge ... was satisfied that the respondent was asserting his rights as he believed them to be and that he was doing so forcefully to give the child the message that she had to do what the respondent told her to do ... his Honour accepted that the respondent's beliefs meant that the respondent's moral culpability was less than those who know that this type of thing is wrong.[40]

Tony Jones interviewed Nanette Rogers about this awful case:

---

37  *The Queen v GJ* [2005].
38  Ibid.
39  That is, "he was entitled to act as he had done according to traditional law, [he] was not obliged to do so, and was not under any pressure to do so": *The Queen v GJ* [2005].
40  *The Queen v GJ* [2005].

*Tony Jones:* She gave some quite heartbreaking evidence. She said, "I told that old man I'm too young for sex, but he didn't listen".... Are these cases common?

*Nanette Rogers:* They are common in the anecdotal sense. They're not common in terms of us getting prosecution ... All child sexual assault is happening at much higher rates than are currently reported to police, as is violence on Aboriginal women and children ...

Aboriginal society here tends to be very punitive. So if a witness goes into court and tells ... they're liable to get physically punished by the offender's family for telling the story and getting the offender into trouble ... it's a punitive culture, you know, at every turn.[41]

### *Araru outstation, Cobourg Peninsula, 2005*[42]

On 25 May 2005, a 27-year-old Aboriginal woman was killed by her Aboriginal husband at Araru outstation, Cobourg Peninsula. The cause of death was "intracranial haemorrhage with associated blunt head, chest and abdominal trauma". This case demonstrates Jane Lloyd's point regarding the danger of outstations for women with violent husbands. Alcohol was said not to be a feature of this murder. The deadly danger this man posed for his wife was known and recorded. A 2003 psychologist's report had predicted that "if the relationship continues" the consequences "might well be" fatal.

The victim and her husband, who was two years younger than her, were, "from a very young age ... 'promised' to each other in accordance with Aboriginal tradition and law". They commenced their relationship when they were teenagers. It was harmonious until they had children. He then became violent towards her including while she was pregnant. In 2000, he tried to kill her.

He murdered her while he was on parole, despite parole conditions

---

41 Jones, 15 June 2006.

42 *Inquest into the death of JP\** [2006] NTMC 083 (\*full name in source: initials only used here)

"designed to prevent the deceased from suffering further injury at her husband's hands while he was on parole for the crime of pouring boiling water over her during a domestic argument". While in prison, the offender "undertook courses in anger management and Aboriginal family violence". Community Corrections notes of October 2003 recorded that he decided to separate from his wife, and that "[h]e has the support of his family and a desire to return to a more traditional lifestyle, which enhance his prospects of completing a period of parole supervision". Among his parole conditions were that he "proceed to Araru outstation; ... not contact or approach the victim ..." However, his parole officers did not check on his stay at the outstation as often as required: "Should those parole orders have been enforced or obeyed, the tragedy of [her] death, in every likelihood, could have been avoided."[43]

The offender stayed out of contact with the victim for 12 months. Then "evidence of his father suggests that he had been residing at Araru with the deceased prior to Christmas 2004", even though he was still on parole:

> The deceased's mother ... told the Inquest that although she tried to dissuade her daughter from resuming the relationship with [the offender], the deceased travelled to Araru with her children for a "bush holiday" ...
> 
> Precisely what happened in the hours that led to the death of [the victim] on 25 May is unknown ...
> 
> The evidence before Justice Thomas was that over the evening of 24 and the morning of 25 May ... [he] continually assaulted the deceased by kicking and punching her to her head, limbs and torso. During the assault he said to the deceased: "You don't do anything for me and I'm going to kill you".[44]

It was confirmed to police by a relative "that neither the deceased nor [he] had been drinking or smoking marijuana while at the outstation".

---

43 Ibid.
44 Ibid.

## Conclusion

Homelands or outstations can offer, to some, a haven from the worst aspects of mainstream life, and a chance to maintain some good and cherished aspects of Aboriginal social and spiritual life. However for the young and vulnerable, the isolation of outstations can make them perilously boring places where abuses including traditionally justified, dangerous practices occur, far from scrutiny, far from help. For the victims of these crimes, and for the people who love and care for these victims, outstations offered false hope, and a haven for the continuation of brutal beliefs and practices.

# 8

# The Yolngu of north-east Arnhem Land

> The homelands movement is now under threat from the Federal government. The one development in north-eastern Arnhem Land that has produced good social outcomes is now threatened with annihilation by a government that wants good social outcomes. Go figure.
> 
> – Eddie Mulholland, CEO, Miwatj Health Aboriginal Corporation[1]

When I started this book, I did not know that the Yolngu would be the focus of a chapter. It was their impressive campaign against homeland funding cuts[2] that demanded this attention. Campaigners plead that north-east Arnhem Land's homelands must be saved because the Yolngu living culture and law, nurtured on their homelands, is keeping many Yolngu safe from alcohol-fuelled community breakdown and violence. If so, the Yolngu experience provides a challenge, or at least an important exception, to the core argument of this book, because it suggests major reductions in violence without the need for solutions based on integration.

## Homeland pioneers

The Yolngu Yirrkala community of north-east Arnhem Land "was one of the earliest to articulate to government their desire to decentralise to homeland centres":

---

[1] Eddie Mulholland, "Improving Health in East Arnhem Land", in *Issues,* Volume 83, June 2008: http://issues.control.com.au/issues2008/bi83.shtml

[2] For a detailed look at Australian Government policy of Aboriginal community funding consolidation, see Johns, 2011, 254-62.

Dr Coombs has described the proposal to decentralise submitted by the Yirrkala Community Council to the Council of Aboriginal Affairs in the early 1970s:

> They plan a return of many of the clan members to their traditional lands to resume a way of life more closely geared to the pattern of the past. At the same time they see the traditional economic practices of hunting and gathering being supplemented by European-style production both for their own use and for sale ...
>
> They envisage a number of "decentralised" villages surrounding and linked with the Mission centre at Yirrkala which would serve the villages as an administrative, educational, commercial and, to a modest degree, industrial centre for the whole complex.[3]

Nearly forty years later, the Laynhapuy Homelands Association Inc. (LHA), which represents the 19 Yolngu homelands (outstations) of the Yirrkala hinterland, is among the strongest decriers of outstation funding cuts by the Australian government. Along with other Laynhapuy clan elders, Barayuwa Mununggurr, chairman of LHA, expressed alarm at what they see as a flawed and unjust policy:

> Most homelands are ancestral estates near a sacred site, which senior elders look after. During a visit to Gurrumuru and two other homeland communities, Garrthalala and Yilpara, clan elders told the *Herald* how the respect and authority in which senior Yolngu lawmen and women are held has helped keep their children from Western vices and safe from abuse.
>
> Traditional kinship structures and culture, still intact in the homelands, have many prohibitions and processes for dealing with the care and protection of children, they said ... They warned that if services were cut, many of the 800 people in the Laynhapuy homelands would have to move to towns like Yirrkala on the Gove Peninsula, creating law and order problems,

---

3  RHRSCA, 1987, 13-14.

while those who remain where they were would be significantly disadvantaged.⁴

Police records indicate that child sexual abuse rarely occurs on Yolngu outstations. Trudgen says that Gawirrin Gumana, who has an Order of Australia and is "the most senior traditional leader in Arnhem Land",

> is sending an important message to white politicians and bureaucrats, and English-speaking Aboriginal people who influence them, that they will destroy the Yolngu culture if they depopulate ancestral lands. "It is quite clear. If you bring a whole lot of clan groups into a central hub – on somebody else's land – you destroy everything that is good about Yolngu culture," Mr Trudgen says. "The traditional lawmen have no authority on other people's land. People learn a new culture ... white man's culture which revolves around grog, drugs, prostitution and social disorder. Violence erupts between clans."⁵

Michael Christie and John Greatorex note regarding Yolngu homelands, that

> where a minimum level of infrastructure is provided, and where the residents are determined to succeed, the social outcomes at Homeland Centres represent a huge improvement over those of the centralised former mission communities.
>
> Clues to the connection between these good outcomes and the land-based knowledge inherent in life at Homeland Centres can be found in research pointing to the presence of strong traditional authority over land and law (e.g. Altman 1987) and the good availability of traditional foods (e.g. Altman and Taylor 1989) as being key factors in the viability of homeland centres.⁶

---

4  Lindsay Murdoch, "Wrong side of the great divide", *The Sydney Morning Herald*, 27 September 2008: http://www.smh.com.au/article/2008/09/26/1222217517616.html
5  Murdoch, 17 October 2009.
6  Michael Christie and John Greatorex, "Yolngu Life in the Northern Territory of Australia: The Significance of Community and Social Capital, Inter-Networking-Communities", *ICT and Remote Capacity Building*, School of Australian Indigenous Knowledge Systems, Charles Darwin University, 2006, 6-7: www.cdu.edu.au/centres/inc/pdf/Yolngulife.pdf

These authors also point out that

> It is commonly observed that Homeland Centres have been more successful in the Top End of the Northern Territory, where food and other resources are relatively plentiful, than in Central Australia, where the desert landscape means day-to-day life is harder. A number of Homeland Centres in Central Australia have been abandoned, probably for this reason.[7]

Even Yolngu homeland defenders, however, point to serious lost opportunities. Trudgen described the failure during the self-determination era to equip Yolngu with essential education and skills for engagement with the *balanda* or mainstream world, and for an economically viable life on their homelands. For example, government bureaucracies favoured faster house building techniques, imported from outside along with white workers, pushing aside skilled Aboriginal tradespeople. Welfare was introduced even though the older people pleaded for this not to happen.[8] Everywhere across north-east Arnhem Land, people became dependent and broken.[9] This usurpation of self-determination by white outsider "help" and free money did not undermine Yolngu culture so much as put it in an increasingly negative social setting. Dangerously low self-esteem, boredom and disillusionment exacerbated alcohol abuse, petrol-sniffing and other substance abuse, violence and suicide.[10]

There seems a level of consensus that under a different self-determination model, one based on earlier missions of the more enlightened kind (such as the mission at Yirrkala) a slower paced,

---

7 Ibid, 6. Note: Burbank, 1994, 196, McKnight, 2002, 168-75, and Sutton, 2009, 24-5 have observed that many northern, high rainfall outstations have been abandoned, or are now occupied by few, or just part-time, or just seasonally.

8 Trudgen, 2000, 160-1.

9 Ibid, Chapters 2 and 10. Etherington, 2001, and McKnight, 2002, have observed similar failures regarding self-determination and welfare in other northern regions.

10 Ibid, 173-4.

more "protective", self-determination process that included homelands might have worked. Such missions learnt Indigenous languages and culture, to better communicate with and understand traditional Aboriginal people. This was seen as essential to equipping Aboriginal people with the skills necessary for the mainstream world. Not only did enlightened missions keep drink at bay and suppress violence, they also constructed a tolerated path to integration without harsh separation from culture or land. Self-determination based on this model may have provided engagement with the mainstream wherein traditional Aboriginal people had some control, and mediated by highly skilled and committed non-Aboriginal people whom they could trust.[11] However as the 1970s ended and the homelands movement – in some places with mission encouragement – and self-determination policies gathered momentum, the Arnhem Land missions bowed to outside political pressure and withdrew:

> A Yolngu elder put it bluntly, "It is too early to do this ... We are pretty sure we still need someone to work with us, to teach us and train us for many things we do not know."[12]

Despite debilitating "self-determination" circumstances in the post-mission years, homelands have provided some benefit for Yolngu. Homeland centres are distant from town supply of alcohol so there is less violence; hunting and gathering of bush food result in better health compared with town residents; there are overall better employment opportunities than in town centres; separation from other clans reduces inter-clan conflict; and it assists the practice of traditional Yolngu culture and traditional authority. Hence, the federal government decision to withdraw service, housing,

---

11 See Trudgen, 2000, 43-4; Etherington, 2001, 89; McKnight, 2002, Chs. 7 and 8, esp. 94-5; Sutton 2009, 16-17; Johns, 2011, 30.
12 Trudgen, 2000, 45.

infrastructure and other funding from homeland centres is seen by Yolngu spokespeople and their supporters as a calamity.[13]

## Justifying the Yolngu homelands

Are claims about the beneficial impacts of Yolngu culture, particularly in terms of personal safety, justified? Are their homelands deserving of the nation's support because they are vital to maintaining culture? Do the Yolngu warrant special consideration because, unlike many other Aboriginal communities, the social benefits of their resilient culture negate the need to consider solutions based on some form of voluntary integration and cultural change?

The available qualitative and quantitative evidence that might answer these questions is either patchy or seemingly paradoxical. The Yolngu present us with some enigmas. Classical Yolngu culture was extremely violent. Yet in response to white rule and law, Yolngu seem more successful than other Aboriginal communities in suppressing traditional murderous laws, violent punishments and inter-clan warfare, while still keeping Yolngu culture and law, or *rom*, alive, as evident in their still vibrant ceremonial life and complex clan relations and obligations. Yolngu seem particularly skilled at communicating their culture to the non-Aboriginal world through popular cultural outreach programs. For example, they have constructed a written form of some of their Yolngu law, available in English and Yolngu language as a website.[14] Yothu Yindi, the Garma Festival, Women Weaving,

---

13 Lindsay Murdoch, "We want to live on our homelands", *The Age*, 28 September 2009: http://www.theage.com.au/national/we-want-to-live-on-our-homelands20090927-g7py.html

14 Melŋurr Gapu Dhularrpa Gawiya Raypirri ŋärra'ŋur Romgurr Mägayakurr, 3 September 2005. The website includes this note: "The information contained in this document is offered as a glimpse into the complex cultural material provided in educational introductions to traditional law. It is brief and incomplete in both depth and scope. The publication of this information is authorized by the ?aymil Gampurrtji, ?aymil Bulkmana, ?aymil Dätiwuy and ?aymil Gondarra clan nations." Sourced at ARDS: http://www.ards.com.au/www.ards.com.au/yolngu_law.htm

the Chooky Dancers, and Mawu Rom are further examples of their cultural outreach skills, popularity and high standing in the wider Australian community.

Regarding Yolngu social health, recent discussion puts more emphasis on the positive, with a shift away from earlier more probing presentations. Trudgen, for example, presented the vivid portrayal of failed "self-determination", and contains tragic passages:

> self-mutilation, attempted suicide, and suicides are all on the rise. Domestic violence, alcoholism, drug abuse and homicide are also increasing. Where the Yolngu once enjoyed full employment and were highly interested in contemporary education, chronic unemployment and disillusionment with education are now typical, as high truancy rates in school indicate ...
> All this impacts on the people's physical well-being. People who were comparatively healthy twenty years ago now have high levels of sickness and death ... Where once elderly people with walking sticks were a common sight, now almost no old people exist. Many are dying in their late 30s or early 40s.[15]

In his recent defence of homelands, however, Trudgen paints Yolngu homeland life in a more favourable light. It is doubtful that conditions have improved markedly over the past ten years, particularly given comments made by other observers such as John Cook and Banambi Wunungmurra.[16]

It is difficult to discern with precision north-east Arnhem Land's quantitative level of violence in relation to other regions of the Northern Territory or Australia, because publicly available regional data is sketchy, inconsistent and unclear regarding factors being measured. Further, not all population centres of north-east Arnhem Land have permanent police presence. Although this would be true

---

15 Trudgen, 2000, 59; also q. in Nowra, 2007, 38-39.
16 John Cook and Banambi Wunungmurra, "Communities in Action for Crime Prevention, East Arnhem Harmony Mawaya Mala, c.2006-7: http://www.sitebuilder. yodelaustralia.com.au/sites/5530/John%20Cook%20and%20Banambi%20 Wunungmurra.doc

for other regions too, even the Elcho Island town of Galiwinku, population over 2000 and "one of the largest indigenous communities in the Territory" did not get permanent police presence until March 2009, despite constant requests from community elders. The Galiwinku community and its elders wanted the police station "to work in conjunction with indigenous law", and saw that a permanent police presence "was critical for community safety".[17] An absence of police presence mean more crime occurring unknown to police, thereby distorting crime statistics. Also a 2002 article, "Nurses warned of working risks in East Arnhem Land", reported that two nurses were evacuated after rocks were thrown at the nurses' station at Milingimbi.[18] With similar incidents happening for two years, a warning was issued by the Australian Nurses' Federation Northern Territory branch "in the union's national journal". Paul Niewenhoven of the federation said:

> We don't know what it is, why there is an incidence of violence in East Arnhem way above the rest of the Territory ... I mean from time to time other communities will have an incident but not in the proportion that we are seeing in East Arnhem Land at the moment.[19]

Nevertheless, quantitative data supports claims that Yolngu are having greater success than most other communities of the Northern Territory in reducing interpersonal violence, or at least the reporting of it.[20]

---

17 Kate Humphris, "Police finally on the beat in Galiwinku", *105.7 ABC Darwin*, 10 March 2009: http://www.abc.net.au/local/photos/2009/03/10/2512466.htm

18 ABC, "Nurses warned of working risks in East Arnhem Land", *ABC NewsOnLine*, 19 January 2002: http://www.abc.net.au/news/newsitems/200201/s461982.htm

19 Ibid.

20 The following results are illustrative only, because of the patchiness of the regional data, especially the lack of Indigenous status for assault data. Some data from outside the Northern Territory is included to provide a further indication of north-east Arnhem Land's level of violence, but this too needs to be read with caution.

## Police Recorded Assaults

The (very remote) town of **Nhulunbuy**, 6.4% Indigenous population, total population 2009 = 5007

Total number of assaults Sept 2008- Sept 2009 = 114, or **2.3 per 100 total population.**

The (remote) town of **Katherine**, 27.3% Indigenous population, total population 2009 = 10,107

Total number of assaults Sept 2008- Sept 2009 = 695, or **6.9 per 100 total population.**

All of **Northern Territory**, 31.6% Indigenous population, total population 2009 = 226,207

Total number of assaults Sept 2008- Sept 2009 = 6072, or **2.7 per 100 total population.**[21]

There is a much lower rate of recorded assaults committed by non-Indigenous people in the Northern Territory.[22] Hence, given the low Indigenous population of Nhulunbuy, these Nhulunbuy figures could mean the rate of assaults there per Indigenous person is on the high side. This tends to support Yolngu supporters such as Christie, Greatorex and Trudgen, that Nhulunbuy with its alcohol outlets and opportunities for clan clashes is a focal point for Yolngu violence.[23] When assault data shifts away from just Nhulunbuy to include all east Arnhem Land, we get data indicating a significantly lower rate of assault occurring in east Arnhem Land than in the rest of the Northern

---

21 *NT Quarterly Crime and Justice Statistics, Issue 29 September Quarter, 2009 – Facts Sheets*, pages 4, 21, and 29: http://www.nt.gov.au/justice/policycoord/documents/statistics/29/Issue-29_Fact%20Sheets.pdf For population statistics, ABS 3218.0, *Regional Population Growth, Australia*, 31 March 2011.
22 ABS, *Recorded Crime – Offenders, Selected States and Territories 2007-08*, 2009, 19.
23 Murdoch, 17 October 2009; Christie and Greatorex, 2006, 6-8.

Territory.[24] This lower rate becomes even more significant given that north-east Arnhem Land has an Indigenous population percentage of about twice that of all Northern Territory.[25]

## Northern Territory Magistrates Court 2007: acts intended to cause injury

**East Arnhem Land**, 61% Indigenous population, total population 2007 = 15,258

Total number of acts intended to cause injury = 112, or about **0.73 per 100 total population.**

The town of **Katherine**, 27.3% Indigenous population, total population 2007 = 9846

Total number of acts intended to cause injury = 503, or about **5.1 per 100 total population.**

**Northern Territory**, 31.6% Indigenous population, total population 2007 = 214,804

Total number of acts intended to cause injury = 2897, or about **1.3 per 100 total population.**[26]

## Domestic Violence Applications

**East Arnhem Land** (very remote), 61% Indigenous population

Total dva rate (lowest for NT, 2007) = **68 per 10,000**, (83% undertaken by police)

---

24 The ABS and The NT Magistrates Court 2007 have figures for East Arnhem Land. "North-east" and "East" Arnhem Land, in the various data drawn upon here, often seems to mean the same region going by the population figures, but the different identifier still raises a note of caution when comparing figures.

25 A further comparative illustration here: the 2005 rate of NT assault victims recorded by police was 3.8 per 100 for Indigenous, and 0.9 per 100 for non-Indigenous people. Source: Productivity Commission, 2007, 3.119.

26 For NT Magistrates Court 2007 crime statistics, ABS, *Regional Statistics, Northern Territory*, 1362.7, 2008 Reissue, 63; for population statistics, ABS 3218.0, *Regional Population Growth, Australia*, 31 March 2011.

**Barkly** (very remote), 60% Indigenous population
Total dva rate (highest for NT, 2007) = **449 per 10,000**, (83% undertaken by police)

**Darwin** (outer regional), 10.3 % Indigenous population
Total dva rate (second lowest for NT, 2007) = **94 per 10,000**, (62% undertaken by police)

**Northern Territory** Total 31% Indigenous population
Total dva rate **145 per 10,000**, (63% undertaken by police)[27]

Domestic violence application (dva) rates further support claims that Yolngu experience less domestic assaults than other regions. The figures indicate that north-east Arnhem Land has nothing like the distress levels of the people of the Barkly region, which includes the town of Tennant Creek. New South Wales provides another useful comparison. In 2007, New South Wales experienced a rate of apprehended domestic violence orders (advos) of 32 per 10,000.[28] East Arnhem Land's 2007 dva rate of 68 per 10,000, low in the Northern Territory context, is still more than double this New South Wales rate. However, direct comparisons of Northern Territory "dva" and New South Wales "advo" are possibly unfair due to different state procedures governing their implementation.

### *Hospitalisations 2006-07 for injuries, poisonings and toxic effects of drugs*

**East Arnhem Land** Indigenous = 98 = about **1.0 per 100** Indigenous population

East Arnhem Land non-Indigenous = 33 = about 0.45 per 100 non-Indigenous population

---

27 ABS, 1362.7, *Regional Statistics, NT 2008 Reissue, Summary*, October 2008.
28 ABS, 1338.1, *NSW State and Regional Indicators Summary.* September 2009.

**Barkly** Indigenous = 147 = about **4.0 per 100** Indigenous population
Barkly non-Indigenous = 23 = about 0.9 per 100 non-Indigenous population

**Total NT** Indigenous = 1477 = about **2.5 per 100** Indigenous population
Total NT non-Indigenous = 1006 = about 0.7 per 100 non-Indigenous population[29]

### *Hospitalisations 2006-07 for burns*

East Arnhem Land Indigenous = 10 = about 0.1 per 100 Indigenous population

East Arnhem Land non-Indigenous = 7 = about 0.1 per 100 non-Indigenous population

**Barkly** Indigenous = 6 = about **0.15 per 100** Indigenous population
Barkly non-Indigenous = 1 = about 0.05 per 100 non-Indigenous population

**Total NT** Indigenous = 145 = about **0.25 per 100** Indigenous population
Total NT non-Indigenous = 127 = about 0.1 per 100 non-Indigenous population[30]

Hospitalisations for factors that would include cases associated with assault are lower for east Arnhem Land than for other regions of the Northern Territory. These data provide Indigenous status, rendering them more valuable.

### *Suicide*

Northern Territory has a higher suicide rate than the rest of Australia, among both Indigenous and non-Indigenous residents. For the period 2004-08, Northern Territory's overall suicide rate per 100,000 of

---

[29] ABS, *Regional Statistics NT 2008*, 67, 68.
[30] Ibid, 67, 68.

22.0 is more than double the overall rate for Australia of 9.8.[31] In the Northern Territory, suicide among both Aboriginal and non-Aboriginal people has been rising since the 1980s, but more so among the Aboriginal population, particularly young men. While the year-to-year rates fluctuate considerably, suicide deaths per 100,000 Northern Territory Indigenous people was 6.1 in 1981 and 50.4 in 2002; and among Northern Territory non-Indigenous people it was 8.9 in 1981 and 22.8 in 2002.[32] This illustrates the differing but rising trend for both groups since the early 1980s. For 2008 in the Northern Territory, the ABS documents 20 Indigenous suicides (15 male, 5 female) and 21 non-Indigenous suicides (18 male, 3 female).[33] Expressed as rates per 100,000, this is 28.4 for Indigenous and 14.1 for non-Indigenous Northern Territorians in 2008.[34]

East Arnhem Land is one of Australia's Indigenous regions that experiences "cluster" suicides, where a suicide is followed by several more suicides in the same community.[35] This tragic pattern can greatly increase the rate of suicide in a small population. Between 1992 and 2002, the "Mental Health Inpatient hospital separation data (HSD) for

---

31 ABS, 3303.0_12 *Causes of Death, Australia, 2008. Excel Data Cube Suicide (Australia)*. See also Department of Health and Ageing, and Hunter Institute of Mental Health, "Overview of Suicide in Australia". *Response Ability*, an initiative of the Australian Government Department of Health and Ageing, 2009: http://www.responseability.org/site/index.cfm?display=134569

32 Mary-Anne L. Measey, Shu Qin Li, Robert Parker and Zhiqiang Wang, "Suicide in the Northern Territory, 1981–2002", *Medical Journal of Australia*, 185(6), 2006, 315-19: http://www.mja.com.au/public/issues/185_06_180906/mea10056_fm.html

33 ABS, 3303.0_13 *Causes of Death*, Australia, 2008. Excel Data Cube "Deaths of Aboriginal and Torres Strait Islander Australians" 2008.

34 This is based on the 2008 NT total population of 219,800: see ABS 3235.0 *Population by Age and Sex, Regions of Australia 2008*, 2009. See also ABS 4713.0, *Population Characteristics, Aboriginal and Torres Strait Islanders Australians, 2006*, (2010 Reissue) which states that 32% of NT's population is Indigenous (= 70,336 in 2008).

35 Leonore Hanssens and Peter Hanssens, "Research into the clustering effect of suicide within Indigenous communities, Northern Territory, Australia", *Paper Presented at Postvention Conference May 24-26th Sydney*, 2007, 8: http://www.whatsworking.com.au/WomenforWik/pdfs/Cluster_suicides.pdf

attempted suicide or deliberate self-harm" measure for east Arnhem Land was 150 per 100,000 pa.[36] Among Yolngu, "[b]etween January 2007 and December 2008 there were 143 attempted, threatened or completed suicides among 9500 people."[37] In the Yolngu community of Ski Beach, "[s]ix Yolngu took their lives in a population of only 400" which is a suicide death rate of 750 per 100,000 pa.[38]

*Prisoner numbers*[39]

East Arnhem Land has a lower than average rate of Northern Territory Correctional Services prisoners. However, in 2009, all prisoners from east Arnhem Land were Indigenous. This signals that social distress among Yolngu is significantly higher than for east Arnhem Land's non-Indigenous population.

In 2009, there were 26 "Nhulunbuy"[40] Indigenous adults (and no non-Indigenous) in prison in the Northern Territory: meaning that about 0.25% of east Arnhem Land's Indigenous people were in prison in 2009. Also, during 2008-09, 58 Indigenous "distinct adults" from "Nhulunbuy" were "received by prison" (and no non-Indigenous). This means that about 0.6% of north-east Arnhem Land's Indigenous people was "received by prison" during 2008-09.

---

36 Leonore Hanssens, "'Echo Clusters' – are they a unique phenomenon of Indigenous attempted and completed suicide?", *Paper presented at the 2nd Postvention Conference May 2009*, Melbourne, 3. Forming part of her *Submission to the Senate Community Affairs Committee Inquiry into Suicide in Australia 2009*, referring to R. Parker's Presentation at the "Suicide Is Everyone's Business" Forum, Darwin, May 2005. Hanssen's paper at: http://www.aph.gov.au/Senate/committee/clac_ctte/suicide/submissions/sub83a.pdf

37 Lindsay Murdoch, "Saving the Yolngu people", *The Age*, 7 November 2009: http://www.theage.com.au/national/saving-the-yolngu-people.20091106-i28q.html

38 I am assuming here that the 6 lives lost occurred over 2 years as well, between January 2007 and December 2008.

39 Statistics in this section are from: *Northern Territory Department of Justice: Correctional Services Annual Statistics 2008-2009*, Tables 10 and 19 on pages 16 and 23.

40 "Nhulunbuy" here includes all of mainland east Arnhem Land plus Elcho Island.

For the whole of the Northern Territory, 860 or about 1.25% of the Indigenous population were in prison in 2009. For Northern Territory's non-Indigenous people, 191 or about 0.13%, were in prison in 2009. Regarding total Northern Territory "distinct adults" "received by prison" in 2008-09, there were 2045 Indigenous, or about 2.9% of the total Northern Territory Indigenous population; and 332 non-Indigenous, or about 0.2% of the total Northern Territory non-Indigenous population.

Hence the imprisonment rate of the Indigenous people of north-east Arnhem Land in 2009, in terms of being "in prison" or "received by prison", was about two to three times the overall Northern Territory non-Indigenous rate, but about one fifth the overall Northern Territory Indigenous rate.

## *Summary*

The high suicide numbers for north-east Arnhem Land are tragic. Nevertheless, other north-east Arnhem Land statistics warrant a pause for thought among those of us raising alarm about traditional revival as a solution to Aboriginal malaise. What basis is there to make critical comment in the light of these favourable claims and favourable data? The basis resides in substantive misgivings about Yolngu culture and law unless a substantial, modifying presence of liberal democratic principles is maintained. Resilient homelands assure the continuation of Yolngu custom and law, which include principles far removed from Western notions of equality and liberty. In the light of Yolngu calls for self-government, with their isolation and permit system, can the nation know how safe their homelands really are?

## **Clan conflict among Yolngu, then and now**

In his article on the positive impacts of homelands, Eddie Mulholland writes of the good health of Yolngu in classical times:

> The first white man to walk across Arnhem Land, Donald

> Thomson, noted in the 1930s the general, robust good health of the Aboriginal people there. Photos taken by Thomson at the time show breastfed babies with rolls of happy fat! They show lean and muscular adults with white teeth and healthy, gleaming skin. Anyone comparing them to photos of Aboriginal people from that region today can see the difference.[41]

Mulholland writes that inadequate access to health services is only a partial explanation for the poor social and physical health of today's Yolngu. The primary reason, he argues, is the white disruption to Yolngu people's attachment and care for country, epitomised by the moonscape mine at Nhulunbuy. Homelands provide a tangible buffer against this:

> Today there are 20 or 30 homeland centres out from Yirrkala, all of them happy and healthy places, where there is no alcohol or drugs, where people live on their own clan country, kids go to school, bush tucker is a significant part of the diet, kinship is maintained and where people dance and sing to their ancestral spirits, which created the land ...
>
> *Yolngu* living at homelands – where social relationships are correct, where kinship is strong and country is cared for – are generally healthier than *Yolngu* at the centralised settlements and ex-missions such as Yirrkala.[42]

Mulholland evokes the Yolngu good health of classical times to emphasise the modern source of their present social and physical ill-health, and hence the corollary restoration of Yolngu good health brought about by homeland life based on traditional culture, law and caring for country. If we are to evoke the traditional past as a guide to understanding the Yolngu present, this is "only the half" of it. What Mulholland and other homeland supporters do not draw attention to is the lethality of traditional Yolngu clan warfare in previous times, as documented by a contemporary of Donald Thomson, anthropologist

---

41 Mulholland, 2008, 1.
42 Ibid, 4.

W. Lloyd Warner. Healthy the (surviving) Yolngu warriors may have been in times of old, but many healthy young warriors died in the fierce inter-clan battles that frequently gripped north-east Arnhem Land. Then as now, many Yolngu died as young men, never to reach middle or old age.[43]

In the light of this traditional inter-clan violence, so lethal less than a century ago, the present low level of Yolngu violence has an inherent fragility, seen in its dependence upon living within small clans on discrete homelands where daily interaction is within the bounds of traditionally non-violent[44] intra-clan relations. Beyond that, correct procedure regarding inter-clan relations to avoid their traditional potential for ready conflict and violence, and the continuing imposition of white law that forbids violent excesses of Yolngu traditional punishment regimes, are essential, because the use of violence in response to perceived wrongs still has legitimacy there. The importance of homelands to maintaining this delicate state of low violence is one reason why Yolngu homeland dwellers and their supporters are worried about federal withdrawal of homeland funding.[45]

Hence, the "necessity" of the homeland structure is an expression and continuation of traditional, inter-clan rivalry. Homelands are justified by their supporters as essential to prevent clan violence. They avoid stating this in the negative: that homelands are repositories of traditional, dangerous clan conflict. While defenders of today's Yolngu homeland centres point to their necessity because they keep conflicting clans separate, they fail to argue that it is clan conflict that

---

43 Warner, 1958, 155-9.
44 Ibid, 155.
45 Lindsay Murdoch, "All-in communities will be death of the Yolngu, elder says", *The Sydney Morning Herald*, 17 October 2009: http://www.smh.com.au/national/allin-communities-will-be-the-death-of-the-yolngu-elder-says-20091016-h14x.html See also Cook and Wunungmurra, 2; Christie and Greatorex, 2006, 5, although they write that this "did not present an unmanageable situation in the mission days".

should be challenged and overcome. The need to live in tiny isolated clan-based settlements to avoid clan violence is an atavism that causes considerable harm to Yolngu. In particular, it limits the ability of Yolngu to live peacefully with each other beyond the homeland, beyond clan size, with unavoidably stifling effects on participation in mainstream life.

Warner studied the "Murngin" (now Yolngu)[46] during the 1920s, before more than minimal contact with white Australia, and when traditional life was fully practised. He wrote of the Murngin need to live in small clans because the clan was the largest unit within which people did not fight each other[47] (although intra-clan violent punishments including of husbands against wives, and brothers against sisters, were features of Murngin life).[48] Conflict readily became warfare:

> The clan, the largest group unit without internal armed conflict, is usually the war-making group. The causes leading to warfare are the killing of a clansman by a member of another clan, and inter-clan rivalry over women. The latter is the usual cause of a killing. Blood vengeance forces further killings ...
>
> An isolated killing, owing to the strength of the kinship structure, usually results in the whole of north-eastern Arnhem Land becoming a battle ground at fairly frequent intervals.[49]

Warner also wrote that "warfare is one of the most important social activities of the Murngin and surrounding tribes.[50] As well as being "one of the mechanisms on which polygyny is based", warfare helped "to prevent the breaking of tribal laws by the threat of retaliation from other social groups".[51]

---

46  Sutton, 2009, 168.
47  Warner, 1958, 155.
48  Ibid: see below, this chapter.
49  Ibid, 155-6.
50  Ibid, 155.
51  Ibid, 158-9.

Murngin deadly warfare, as described by Warner, places it among the world's most lethal societies.[52] The classical Murngin annual homicide rate of 330 per 100,000[53] was 15 times the 2006-07 national very remote Indigenous homicide rate of 22 per 100,000, and 300 times the 2006-07 national (all areas) non-Indigenous homicide rate.[54] In the 21st century, only the most dangerous societies have rates near Murngin levels. Mexico's Ciudad Juarez, among the world's deadliest cities, has an annual homicide rate of 300 per 100,000.[55] On the United Nations list of national homicide rates, Honduras is highest at 82.1 per 100,000.[56] Surely no aspect of Murngin culture, such as polygamy, was worth the lives of the many young men sacrificed in war to maintain it. Surely such lethality equates with a dysfunctional society of the kind Edgerton refers to.[57]

Rarely if ever do defenders of Yolngu culture and homelands refer to the chronic deadly warfare of their classical past. Instead, in reference to today's violence, we get this statement from Trudgen:

---

52 Warner, 1958, 158.
53 Chagnon, 1996, 216. This figure is probably conservative. Chagnon's figures (from Knauft 1987) seem based on Warner's estimates of young men's deaths in Murngin warfare. That is, about 10 per annum out of a total male plus female population of about 3000. This figure does not include homicides involving female victims, nor non-war homicides involving male victims. If these were also included, the figure would be higher, and could be much higher. In Chagnon's chart of homicide rates, the range for traditional societies is wide, e.g.,, !Kung = 41.9, Yanomamo – 165.9, Murngin = 330, and Hawa = 778, per 100,000 pa.
54 These comparisons are calculated using figures in the Productivity Commission, 2009, Table 4A.11.15.
55 Charles Bowden, interviewed by Kirsten Garrett in "Murderous Mexico", ABC RN, *Background Briefing,* 7 August 2011: http://www.abc.net.au/radionational/programs/backgroundbriefing/murderous-mexico/2934362 See also Geoffrey Blainey, *Triumph of the Nomads: A History of Ancient Australia,* Sun Books, South Melbourne, 1976 (first published 1975), 106-112.
56 On the same UN data series, homicide per 100,000 in Australia = 1.2 (2009); and USA = 4.6 (2010): http://www.unodc.org/documents/data-and-analysis/statistics/Homicide/Homicide_data_series.xls
57 Edgerton, 1992, 103-4.

> I must stress that this violence is not due to the nature of the Aboriginal people or their communities. I lived for eleven years in north-central Arnhem Land among kind, gentle people who looked after each other. There were occasional individuals who were aggressive, as in any community. It was only when alcohol came into the communities in the middle to late 1970s that we saw the first real act of violence. So this is not a traditional condition.[58]

The violence now is much less than in former times observed by Warner, a testimony both to a positive outcome of white contact, and to the Yolngu adaptation to white law. Nevertheless inter-clan tensions continue and can still threaten to become large-scale revenge violence among Yolngu.

### *Recent Yolngu clan and community clashes*

Clan conflict and violence are reported to be a chronic problem in the towns, particularly on pay days when people from homelands and other small communities gather in Nhulunbuy with townspeople to shop and drink.[59] Some serious criminal incidents also have clan underpinnings.

In late 2000, prominent, well-respected Yolngu leaders became embroiled in a tense inter-clan conflict surrounding two killings committed by two members of the "powerful Gumatj clan".[60] One member killed his sister-in-law, a Djapu clanswoman, by a single kick to the head in August 2000, at Ski Beach.[61] Clan tensions deepened when his uncle "allegedly speared a Djupa [sic] tribesman to death at Ski Beach three months later".[62] The aggrieved clans of the victims

---

58 Trudgen, 2000, 174.
59 Cook and Wunungmurra, 2.
60 There was also a third murder, the victim a petrol sniffer, a few months earlier in June 2000, committed by another Yunupingu family member, on Elcho Island. See Paul Toohey, "Murder, sorcery and tribal law spill bad blood between native leaders", *The Weekend Australian*, 25-26 November 2000, 1-2.
61 *The Age*, June 24, 2002: http://www.theage.com.au/articles/2002/06/24/1023864547058.html
62 Ibid.

were upset with the white justice procedures, which appeared to them to be too lenient. Paul Toohey wrote:

> Aboriginal law allows little for the white legal concept of presumption of innocence and the principles of criminal law. It requires that both deaths be avenged. People are threatening to raise arms against Yunupingu and the Gumatj ...
>
> Payback arguably affects anyone who belongs to the Yunupingus' Dumatj clan which means hundreds of people are living with the thought that their own life might be required to set the world back on track ...
>
> They are outraged that Makuma was granted bail, allowing him to live with relatives on an outstation in Central Australia ... [63]

There were strong arguments over which clan should hold the funeral of the Djapu woman, and on whose land it should take place, because she was married to a Gumatj man. Galarrwuy Yunupingu won this argument, preventing a "huge loss of face". Nonetheless, "rocks were thrown at the Gumatj, and people began producing spears. Many were flung and certain white invitees took flight."[64] At the same funeral, a high-profile leader of the Wangurri clan tried to stab a Gumatj dancer, in response to a perceived threat:

> The former ATSIC chairman is better known as a conciliator in a suit and tie. It is easy to forget he is also a tribal man who does tribal things ...
>
> Gatjil Djerrkura says he was standing next to the dead woman's grave when "the Gumatj mob came dancing by, too close to me, with killing spears, and I was offended by it.
>
> "They were doing a stingray dance. ... If you're a leader, and some dance is done close to you appears to be a threat, you show your opposition. And that's what I did.
>
> "The young bloke who was dancing close to me, I broke his

---

63 Toohey, 2000.
64 Ibid.

spear. I had the shovel nose [sharp] end. I grabbed it and went for his guts."

Were you really going to stab him? "Yes," Gatjil says, "but he grabbed the spear."[65]

While details of the murder are not available,[66] one wonders what drove his lethal behaviour, whether or not alcohol was involved. The judge dismissed deprivation as a factor:

> Justice Brian Martin noted that his father was the long-time leader of the NLC [Northern Land Council] and his uncle was Mandawuy Yunupingu, who fronts the internationally renowned band Yothu Yindi. Both are former Australians of the Year.
>
> But Justice Martin told [the defendant], who spent two years at Sydney's prestigious Scots College, he would not receive special treatment because of his well-known and influential family.
>
> "It cannot be said you came from a deprived background," the judge said.
>
> [The defendant] played a corrections officer in the movie *Yolngu Boy* – his role calling for him to warn three Aboriginal youths they were heading for Darwin's Berrimah jail.
>
> He is also a songwriter and a musician who toured the world with Yothu Yindi.[67]

In his studies of the kinship-based Yanomamo people, Chagnon found that greater resources were associated with more, not less, conflict and fighting.[68] Violence in traditional Yolngu times was a tool of power, control, punishment and conquest. Could violence wielded by high-status Yolngu be a sign of power and status, of a resilient culture still in operation? As a further measure of the resilience of non-liberal notions of justice among Yolngu, "a relative, Sidney Yunupingu, accepted a spear in the thigh on Makuma's behalf as payback for the

---

65 Ibid.
66 Stated in Ibid.
67 *The Age*, June 24, 2002.
68 Chagnon, 1996, 228.

death of Sidney's aunt".[69] This was a brave and selfless act undertaken by Sidney Yunupingu. I just lament the cultural belief of "deferred guilt" requiring such sacrifice from an innocent clan member for the restoration of peace between clans.

There are recent Yolngu violent conflicts involving large numbers, as in the following examples. At least two of these have a pattern, noted by Chagnon, to be typical among "kinship-organised" (rather than state-based) peoples, whereby a dispute between individuals escalates, with "larger conflicts grow[ing] out of a sequence of previous conflicts of interest among smaller groups of individuals, often traceable back to single conflicts between specific individuals".[70]

At 6pm on 20 April 2008, Ramingining police were called to an outstation in east Arnhem Land:[71]

> Approximately 300 people were observed yelling near the clinic and surrounding area and a number of persons were armed with assorted weapons.[72]

It seemed to arise from an incident earlier that day where "a group of people were drinking and two men aged 34 and 44 began to fight", with the younger man producing a knife and

> cutting (the older man's) hands and arms before embedding it a short way into the victim's back as he tried to get away.
>
> The 34-year-old and another aged 23 allegedly struck a 46-year-

---

69 *The Age*, June 24, 2002.
70 Chagnon, 1996, 203, 219.
71 Ramingining is a Yolngu town within the western boundary of Yolngu lands. *Ten Canoes* was filmed on Ramingining land: Rolf de Heer, Director, *Ten Canoes,* 2006.
72 Northern Territory Police, Fire and Emergency Services (NTPFES) Media Release "Disturbance – Ramingining", 21 April 2008: http://www.nt.gov.au/pfes/index.cfm?fuseaction=viewMediaRelease&pID=8248&y=2008&mo=4 See also a 2010 incident also near clinic, at: NTPFES Media Release "Disturbance – Ramingining", 12 July 2010: http://www.nt.gov.au/pfes/index.cfm?fuseaction=viewMediaRelease&pID=10994&y=2010&mo=7

old man in the head a number of times after he attempted to intervene.

During the fight, a 46-year-old woman was also struck in the head.

The victims attended the clinic for treatment and a large number of community members formed outside the clinic creating a disturbance.[73]

A couple of months earlier on 28 February 2008, police report that they "had to use force to control a dispute involving 400 people" in the town of Galiwinku on Elcho Island.[74] Late in 2010, at 12.30am police attended a disturbance in Galiwinku of "500 people involved in an altercation at the Council Offices":

It is alleged the disturbance broke out after a 15-year-old girl was assaulted by an unknown person and as a result family members became involved in a loud argument on the street.[75]

If every person participating in these clashes involving hundreds were itemised separately, how would that affect violent incident statistics among the Yolngu?

**Strong clans, subjugated women**

While today's homelands may offer some respite from the alcohol-fuelled and clan violence of the towns, gender-based abuses and injustices are inherent aspects of the traditional law and clan structures which homelands are said to protect and uphold. Warner wrote of the more restricted access that Murngin women had to sacred sites,

---

73 NTPFES, 21 April 2008.
74 ABC News, "Man dies following riots on Elcho Island", 11 February 2008 (note: the man does not die of violence-associated causes):
http://www.abc.net.au/news/stories/2008/02/11/2159634.htm
75 NTPFES Media Release "Disturbance – Galiwinku", 22 December 2010:
http://www.gov.au/nfes/index.cfm?fuseaction=viewMediaRelease&pID=11544&y=2010&mo=12

ceremonies and objects, and if they breached these restrictions even accidentally, punishment could be death.[76] Western law has curtailed punishment by death, and the Yolngu *rom* document includes law against murder.[77] However, more restrictions against women are still part of Yolngu *rom* (law). This law concerns the "child" status of women within the traditional, sacred realm:

> 29. Neither women nor children nor the uninitiated (in respect to that law) shall enter into or any way be familiar with the chamber or restricted surrounds of the ŋärra' parliament. If you do this you will incur the wrath of the elders and political leaders and bear the associated consequences. In addition you will be required to make recompense concerning your legal ability by the payment of valuable items.[78]

The domestic realm was also hazardous for Yolngu women in traditional times. Warner depicts husbands' punishment of their wives as a normal part of life. Indeed, if a husband chastised his wife, her father and brother would help him rather than come to her aid. This was unless the husband was too brutal or "for no just cause" killed her (meaning there were causes that *justified* his killing her?), and then her clan or more commonly his clan would interfere against his brutality.[79] A husband considered it his duty to beat his wife if she had extra-marital affairs.[80] As extra-marital affairs were common, so were the resultant beatings of errant wives, and continuing unfaithfulness might mean a wife is killed by a magician.[81] It was frequent for a Murngin girl to have intercourse with other men before living with her husband, and this "usually results in a beating for the girl and

---

76  Warner, 1958, 6, 131-3, 157, 160.
77  Melŋurr Gapu Dhularrpa Gawiya Raypirri ŋärra'ŋur Romgurr Mägayakurr, 3 September 2005.
78  Ibid.
79  Warner, 1958, 110.
80  Ibid, 82.
81  Ibid, 81.

a heated quarrel between the husband and the lover".[82] There were also serious, injurious fights with weapons between a man's wife and his mistress.[83] Liaisons between taboo relatives were risky for both the man and the woman, but Warner suggests more dangerous for the woman who would be either severely beaten or even killed.[84] Warner also wrote that most fathers would beat a mother if she neglected their child, sometimes even killing her.[85]

As Warner describes it, fathers and brothers had significant control over a woman, because it was through a family's daughters and sisters that clan solidarity was reinforced, and proper kinship ties were created through correct marriage. Murngin fathers and brothers beat their daughter or sister for misdemeanours. Fathers and brothers had the power and responsibility to force a woman into a favourable marriage. After marriage, a woman was still considered to belong to her original family's clan more than her husband's clan. This seems to have offered her some protection in that a brutal husband, or a husband that killed his wife, might face the wrath of her original clan. However, a brother could even *kill* his sister, and their clan would not act against him, because the solidarity of the clan was considered more important.[86]

Brother behaviour surrounding *mirriri* is a clear demonstration of how women's rights were traditionally secondary to clan safety. *Mirriri* occurs when a brother hears someone swear at his sister, an event not meant to happen. The brother feels compelled to take action. However, clan solidarity is too important to throw spears at the member of his clan who swore at her. If her husband was the one who swore at her in her brother's hearing – and her husband, writes Warner, is the person

---

82  Ibid, 79.
83  Ibid, 81.
84  Ibid, 83.
85  Ibid, 71.
86  Ibid, 110.

who most often swears at a man's sister[87] – it is too dangerous to throw spears at her husband, because this would enrage the husband's clan, triggering an inter-clan fight and possible forceful re-exchange of women. So he throws spears at his sister, the victim of the swearing herself, and all his other sisters. Warner emphasises that this is not because of a belief that his sister deserved the swearing, because it occurs in cases where the sister clearly committed no misdemeanour. It is more that his sister, already victim of the swearing, becomes a proxy for her husband (or others who swore at her) and so takes yet more punishment by having spears thrown at her, in order to avoid damaging clan relations.[88] The brother throws spears not just at her, but at all his sisters, because of the intensity of his feeling, because he is meant to treat all sisters equally, and to express its ritualised nature.[89] *Mirriri* is still a requirement today among Yolngu and adjacent peoples of Arnhem Land, and is discussed by Cowlishaw[90], Burbank[91], Kimm[92], and others. The injustice and irrationality of punishing innocent sisters in this manner causes bafflement for Western courts.[93] Yolngu *rom* still includes the *mirriri*:

> 13. You will not speak in the hearing of the brother things which pertain to his sister, which are of a sacred or intimate nature (that will cause him to feel angry, or ashamed), or else you will

---

87 Ibid, 67.
88 Ibid, 112.
89 Ibid, 112-13.
90 Cowlishaw, 1978, 275-7.
91 Burbank, 1994, 151-5, 198.
92 Kimm, 2004, 52-3.
93 For example, *Ashley v Materna*, [1997], ("Appeal – Aboriginal Customary law") where one of the paragraphs of "extempore reasons for sentence" of a man for hitting his sister's head with a stick when he heard her husband swear at her, includes: "I regret to have to say this to you in the presence of elders, but it is, in my view, of such a nature that people in many countries would hold it to be discriminatory and I believe the Discrimination Boards of this country and missions and whatever would call it discriminatory."

desecrate the law of the ŋärra' Parliament, and the foundational Madayin Law, established from the creation of the world.[94]

Kimm observed that the Yolngu prefer that domestic violence remains under the purview of community and customary law, rather than white law intervention.[95] Isolation from Anglo-Australian law would prevent many cases of violence against Yolngu women from reaching our courts. Indeed, given the permit system, isolation of homelands and other small communities, and Yolngu control over domestic affairs, female victims may remain invisible to outsiders, beyond the knowledge and help of outside intervention. Nevertheless, there are cases that have reached our courts. Here are some sad examples.

### *The "duty" of Dennis Wunungmurra*

The traditional victimisation of "Murngin" women, particularly their subjection to violence in order that law, kin and clan structures were upheld, needs to be considered, not dismissed, as a potent factor in today's domestic violence against Yolngu women. This is particularly so when Yolngu people themselves claim its traditional justifications. The assault by Dennis Wunungmurra on his wife is a telling case. On 8 September 2008, an assault occurred in the Yolngu town of Galiwinku, Elcho Island. Dennis Wunungmurra stabbed his wife "multiple times with a steak knife":[96]

> Wunungmurra's wife had left the community for a number of years, and on her return had not partaken in community or family life as a traditional wife should ...
>
> An expert in Yolngu traditional law, Rosa Laymba Laymba, testified that Wunungmurra was the equivalent of a law enforcer or magistrate within his community and that under Yolngu law,

---

94 Melŋurr Gapu Dhularrpa Gawiya Raypirri ŋärra'ŋur Romgurr Mägayakurr, 3 September 2005.
95 Kimm, 2004, 107-8.
96 "Customary law no defence...", ABC News, 2009.

husbands were allowed to punish errant wives as they saw fit, leaving scars, but not killing them ...[97]

The court record of this affidavit portrays enduring, detailed traditional knowledge and expectations of Yolngu clan structure, inherited status, male rights and wife subservience. Ms Laymba Laymba stated that as a "Dalkaramirri", the defendant "has a role similar to a judge or magistrate", "sings ceremonial songs", is a leader, and an enforcer of traditional law. Here is an extract:

> Ms Laymba Laymba is a senior member of three Aboriginal clan groups at Milingimbi. She is one of nine Jungaya for the Gamaalanga, Malarra and Gorryindi clan groups. She is knowledgeable about customary law and cultural practices of the Yolngu people who live at Milingimbi. She is a distant relative of the defendant ...
>
> The defendant comes from the Yidditja and Dhalwangu clan groups at Milingimbi. He is a Dalkaramirri.
>
> In her affidavit Ms Laymba Laymba deposes to certain traditional Aboriginal laws that apply to women who are married to Yidditja men and the circumstances when according to traditional Aboriginal law a man who comes from the Yidditja and Dhalwangu clan groups may inflict severe corporal punishment on his wife with the use of a weapon. It is her opinion that the defendant acted in accordance with traditional Aboriginal law when he engaged in behaviour which is the subject of the counts charged on the indictment. Ms Laymba Laymba states that the defendant was carrying out his duty as a responsible husband and father and he was acting

---

97 Ibid.

in accordance with his duty as a Dalkarra man.⁹⁸

Warner observed that a Murngin husband was meant to be less than brutal when he disciplined his wife.⁹⁹ However, Warner described circumstances where it was the norm and duty for husbands to beat their wives, and it is unclear where traditionally a Murngin husband's acceptable level of beating stopped and where brutality by modern Western standards started.¹⁰⁰ Dennis Wunungmurra's assault on his wife was brutal, but Ms Laymba Laymba maintained his assault was within a traditionally acceptable limit of "leaving scars, but not killing".¹⁰¹

I share the outrage expressed by Adrian Howe in his article "R v Wunungmurra: 'Culture' as Usual in the Courts", that courts have considered cultural defences for Aboriginal husbands who have assaulted their wives. Such defence has in some instances delivered appallingly short sentences for deliberate, brutal acts.¹⁰² Howe expresses justified alarm that while Southwood quashed the short sentence originally handed down to Wunungmurra,

> Southwood J's reading of the restrictions placed on the use of customary Aboriginal law in criminal cases still leaves the

---

98 *The Queen v Wunungmurra* [2009] NTSC 24. See also discussion of this case in Chapter 3, where the NTERA ensured that this customary defence appeal failed. See also, Tara Ravens, "Aboriginal justice group calls for federal government to allow customary law", *National Indigenous Times*, 12 June 2009. This article, focusing on this case, writes that the "North Australian Justice Agency (NAAJA) is calling on the Commonwealth to repeal the [legislation that restricts the use of Aboriginal customary law], introduced by the Howard Government as part of the federal intervention, following the case of a Yolngu man who allegedly stabbed his wife with a steak knife ... [Rosa Laymba Laymba] said the Yolngu man, who was allowed to inflict severe corporal punishment but not to kill, had a role in society similar to that of a judge or magistrate, and was required to act as a role model": http://www.nit.com.au/story.aspx?id=17927

99 Warner, 1958, 110.

100 Ibid, 79, 81, 82, 90. See also 110.

101 "Customary law no defence ...", ABC News, 2009.

102 Adrian Howe, "R. v Wunungmurra: 'Culture' as usual in the courts', *The Australian Feminist Law Journal*, June 2009: http://findarticles.com/p/articles/mi_7466/is_200906/ai_n39235223/ See also McGlade, 2012, 162-3.

door wide open for a consideration of exculpatory evidence in sentencing decisions ... The judge's decision therefore betrays a profound, well-drilled ignorance of Aboriginal women's scathing criticism of the use made of such evidence in criminal courts. Second and related, it is extraordinary that Southwell [sic] J could have forgotten the "precise mischief that S 91 was intended to remedy ... [and forgotten that] ... the Council of Australian Governments agreed "that no customary law or cultural practice excuses, justifies, authorises, requires or lessens the seriousness of violence or sexual abuse".[103]

The shortcoming of Howe's argument is that he tries to strengthen his valid case by denying that pre-contact Aboriginal men abused women, and he reiterates some Aboriginal women's claims that the idea of Aboriginal women as subordinate "was actually something imposed by Western culture". He writes:

[Southwood] might have had occasion to listen to what Aboriginal women had to say about [Nanette] Rogers' allegations and other reports about violence against women and children within Aboriginal communities. For example, Larissa Behrendt, speaking on Tateline [sic] about how customary law had been used in sexual assault cases involving Aboriginal men, offered a different understanding of Aboriginal culture than that presented by the defence in the Wunungmurra case. There was, she said, "nothing" in Aboriginal culture or values that suggested it was "appropriate to treat Aboriginal women and children with disrespect" and "nothing in those cultural values that actually permitted people to abuse" them. Indeed, those cultural values were "very much the antithesis of that".[104]

Given the overwhelming evidence that in traditional culture women and children suffered violence and abuse and disrespect for their human rights, to engage with Howe's and Behrendt's argument must surely be a debate about semantics, values and evasions rather

---

103 Howe, 2009. Section 91 is discussed in Chapter 3 of this book.
104 Howe, 2009.

than facts. Certainly, aspects of Yolngu culture can be highlighted that counter the idea of Yolngu women's traditional subordination and punishment. Warner observed affection and solidarity between husbands and wives,[105] that Murngin women were not badly treated, stood up for their rights, were quite independent, and would punish husbands such as by not giving them food.[106] Murngin women were also physically aggressive. Brawls between women were "fairly frequent", usually because a husband was seduced by a younger woman, involved women's ironwood digging sticks as weapons, and fought with "such intensity that bloodshed always results".[107] Warner noted that a wife "can attack and abuse her husband's mistress".[108]

Women's assertiveness and readiness to fight physically were observed by Burbank in "Mangrove",[109] which she interprets to mean that subordination is not an aspect of these women's experience of male violence.[110] However, women can be assertive and willing to fight but still suffer subordination. What the West brings is a liberal-democratic revulsion against the threat and reality of physical violence as first resort means to control and exploit, whether or not one's victim also uses physical aggression. Murngin women may have been brave and resilient, but violence and control by men permeated their lives, and they developed tolerances and coping mechanisms to survive.

Many Western women are acquainted with domestic and public oppression, but may still be assertive, stand up for their rights, and venture out at night, despite the fears and restrictions felt by some of us. I am well aware of women's vulnerability in the realm of domestic

---

105 Warner, 1958, 89-90, although he observed that conjugal love was rare, 89.
106 Ibid, 91.
107 Ibid, 176.
108 Ibid, 81.
109 "Mangrove" is an Arnhem Land community south of Caledon Bay. Burbank has disguised its exact location and identity.
110 See Burbank, 1994, 176-7. Note though her discussion that women's subordination still occurs but through other means. See also Burbank, 1994, on *mirriri*, 149-58.

relations, and the danger of being out alone after dark – "she asked for it" (a similarly insane oppression to the *mirriri* perhaps?[111]) – even in 21st century liberal democratic Australia. Please do not tell me that classical north-east Arnhem Land's *mirriri* is not a severe abuse of women and a sign of their subordination[112]; that fathers', brothers' and husbands' power and duty to inflict physical punishment onto daughters, sisters and wives who committed misdemeanours is not abusive; that a brother could kill his sister and not be punished is not abusive; that forced, promised marriages, polygamy and wife-stealing, all part of classical Yolngu tradition, some of them still practised today, are not abusive to women and acts of extreme disrespect against women.

They are frightening abuses of women's universal human rights. If you deny that aspects of Yolngu traditional culture are abusive to women, maybe you are unfamiliar with these features. Or you find it too difficult to acknowledge the harsh aspects of their traditional culture. Or you are so aware and outraged at the injustices and harm of white colonialism that it seems unfair, another act of racism, to heap criticism onto such a victimised and suffering people. Better to keep to a "Rousseauesque view" of hunter-gatherer harmony.[113] Perhaps you focus on oral accounts based on living memory of the calmer, intervening mission years. You may have a different, more lenient interpretation of terms such as "abuse" when they are in the context of Aboriginal culture. Maybe you hold back your caring when Aboriginal women are abused because you care so much about preserving their ancient culture.[114] Or perhaps you worry that by acknowledging the

---

111 Not an exact analogy I know. But blaming a woman for being a victim of violent male attack or rape because of the way she dressed, or because she was alone at night? – deferred blame, deferred punishment, universal.

112 See Cowlishaw, 1978, 273-81, and Burbank, 1994, 152.

113 See Chagnon, 1996, 206-9.

114 See Rev. Steve Etherington PhD, "Coming Ready or Not! Aborigines are heading for town", *Occasional Paper*, The Bennelong Society, October 2007, for our reasons for wanting to keep Aboriginal culture alive, even while Aboriginal people, including children, suffer to meet our needs for their culture.

traditional, pre-contact violence against Aboriginal women, you weaken Aboriginal women's protection in our courts. There are examples of all these positions, and they are all ultimately disabling, even the last, most understandable, forgivable of these reasons.

Howe is outraged that cultural considerations in sentencing Aboriginal men who have assaulted Aboriginal women may still be interpreted, as by Justice Southwood, as a possibility even under Section 91. Nevertheless, Howe and Behrendt have obscured the path to their very goals by weakening their argument against cultural defence, by making it partially dependent upon whether traditional violence against women exists. "Bullshit" tradition occurs, but sadly in the case of Dennis Wunungmurra, there is plenty of real Yolngu tradition of abuse against women to "consider" in sentencing. It is on the *reality* of traditionally justified violence that we must focus the task of protecting Yolngu and Aboriginal women generally, in and out of the courts.

### *"Honeymoon helicopters" and polygamy*

In her article about the impact of polygamy on women, Vanessa von Struensee writes:

> Although civil law has banned polygamy in many nations, customary law in many places still allows it. In many countries with multiple legal systems, the customary law on polygamy ... prohibits a current wife from objecting to her husband's marriage to a new woman ... Conflicts erupt among the families because several wives and children are competing for small and finite amount of resources. Although polygamy itself is not a prohibited practice under international human rights law, it reaches [sic] other fundamental rights such as the right to dignity, the right to equality within the family and the right to equal protection under the law. It also tends to perpetuate women's low social and economic status by forcing women to share valuable resources with their husband's other wives and children.[115]

---

115 Vanessa von Struensee, "The Contribution of Polygamy to Women's Oppression and Impoverishment: An Argument for its Prohibition", *Murdoch University Electronic Journal of Law*, 2005: http://www.austlii.edu.au/au/journals/MurUEJL/2005/2.html

Polygamy was practised across Aboriginal Australia in classical times. The Aboriginal people of north-east Arnhem Land are noteworthy because men tended to have more wives there than men of other regions. As summarised in 1964 (1977) by the Berndts:

> The number of women a man actually has at any given time, in a polygamous marriage, varies a great deal. In most desert regions the maximum is about six, with two or three much more usual; this is so in western Arnhem Land too ... In north-eastern Arnhem Land the figure is higher: anything up to ten or twelve is not regarded as odd, although actually most men have fewer than this ...
>
> In north-eastern Arnhem Land the men with the most wives were originally those with a reputation as fighters, or with access to special trading monopolies ... Because of his reputation, and because he has goods which can be used as gifts in betrothal arrangements, fathers of eligible girls are ready to negotiate. They may even promise their daughters to several men more or less simultaneously ... with the strongest taking the initiative and claiming the girl.[116]

Polygamy is still practised in north-east Arnhem Land, reportedly "as high as 90 per cent" just 30 years ago, and "[t]oday, about half of the marriages in the region involve multiple wives".[117] While today more of these marriages are said to be based "on the heart" than on family negotiations and promised brides, conflict and violence both of

---

116 Berndt and Berndt, 1981, 202-3.
117 Jennifer Sexton and Ashleigh Wilson, "Fallout over four wives", *The Australian*, 12 July 2006. This article includes important commentary from Kimm, and Howard Morphy: http://www.kooriweb.org/foley/news/2006/july/aust12jul06.html See also Hughes, 2007, 31, where Hughes documents that polygamy, although illegal in Australia, is nevertheless "condoned by legal practice in the Northern Territory, Queensland, Western Australia and South Australia and by the welfare system which grants spouse allowances for several wives. Welfare staff argue disingenuously that this saves taxpayers' money". See also Australian Law Reform Commission, *Recognition of Aboriginal Customary Laws* (ALRC Report 31), 1986: "12. Aboriginal Marriages and Family Structures: Marriages in Aboriginal Societies Today": http://www.alrc.gov.au/publications/12.%20Aboriginal%20Marriages%20 and%20Family%20Structures/marriages-aboriginal-societies-today

the husband against his wives, and between the man's wives,[118] remain prone to occur. As with Yolngu clan conflict and violence, having high status and wealth offers no immunity from the conflict and violence associated with polygamy. Galarrwuy Yunupingu has exemplary status in both the Yolngu world and mainstream Australia. He was Australian of the Year in 1978. In 2006 Yunupingu, at age 58, made headlines when accused of violent behaviour. Yunupingu has four wives. In their article "Fallout over four wives", Jennifer Sexton and Ashleigh Wilson report that Yunupingu's fourth and youngest wife, at the age of 29, "took out an interim domestic order against him", claiming he

> grabbed her by the neck ... pushed her to the ground, kicked her in the back and pulled her hair ... threatened to kill her ... [and] tried to strangle her with an electric cord.[119]

Yunupingu denied her claims, maintaining that his actions were to stop her from killing herself.

Yunupingu's older wife did not "welcome" her husband's youngest wife, so he kept them many miles apart. He would spend weekdays at Ski Beach with his older wife, and fly a helicopter bought with Gumatj Association funds, dubbed "Honeymoon Taxi", to be with his youngest wife on weekends at Yinyikay outstation.[120] In similar fashion to keeping potentially conflicting clans separate, here the homeland (outstation) separates women in conflict, but it would surely be mocking or tragic to justify homelands on these grounds. Tension and violence between Yunupingu's wives and their families has been documented:

> [The older wife's] status as dominant wife sometimes boiled over into trouble for the families. One of [the youngest wife's]

---

118 The missionary, Mary Bennett, recorded severe violence between co-wives in polygamous marriages among Western Australian tribes in the 1930s: Windschuttle, 2009, 464. See also Burbank, 1994, 111-13.
119 Sexton and Wilson, 2006.
120 Ibid.

sisters was once mistaken for her in the supermarket and was punched by a member of [the older wife's] family.[121]

Echoing von Struensee's observations about polygamy in other countries, disputes over property between Yunupingu's wives and children have occurred, although in this case the dispute over royalties paid to the Gumatj Association arises more from resource abundance, not scarcity:

> The royalties ... distributed by Yunupingu have also been the centre of rivalry between the offspring. The children of [the youngest wife's] sisters have argued ... that [the older wife's] family have had preferential treatment ...[122]

Galarrwuy Yunupingu's attitude to traditional Yolngu marriage is a defensive one. In his 2003 objection to new Northern Territory laws "that removed traditional marriage as defence against having sex with underage children", Yunupingu argued

> Our traditional systems of promised marriage have nothing to do with abuse in any form ... Marriage systems which have existed for thousands of years must be dealt with separately to serious issues like child abuse or violence.[123]

One strategy to compensate for the shortage of women which is an outcome of polygyny is to lower the female marriageable age to early teens or younger, while increasing the male age for marrying. It should be no surprise that polygamy and child brides occur simultaneously.[124] Bride price is another associated feature, and while its extent is uncertain, it is still practised in some Aboriginal

---

121 Ibid.
122 Ibid.
123 However regarding "his succession line," Galarrwuy Yunupingu "is training his daughter ... to follow in his footsteps": Nicolas Rothwell, "Going Home – Line in the Sand – End of the Dream", *The Weekend Australian Magazine*, 6-7 December 2008, 20.
124 See Mary Bennett's observations in Windschuttle, 2009, 463-4.

communities, today as a money payment.¹²⁵

Sexton and Wilson question Yunupingu's defence of traditional Yolngu marriage systems by drawing our attention to the 1969 northeast Arnhem Land case. Polygamy, forced marriage, an older man and a child bride are all here, plus shocking violence and ostracism. A 42 year old man seriously assaulted a 14 year old Yirrkala girl for refusing to become his third wife. While the magistrate's court accepted his cultural rights defence, the victimised girl "knew that to resist the marriage and to press charges meant she would no longer be welcome to live with her family. She had to leave the area."[126] This girl had no say, no rights. By speaking out, as well as the violence she received, she became an exile. Her powerlessness against male right and customary obligations gives an indication of the hidden oppression and violence endured by Yolngu women.

While some observers have attempted to make Aboriginal polygamy appear economically rational[127], their argument is weakened by the oppression, violence and economic rivalry that polygamy imposes on women and on the men who miss out on getting wives.[128] Polygamy is

---

125 See Kimm, 2004, 66. Also, the Lajamanu Submission in 1981 to the ALRC contained the following proposed codified customary law: "5. Promise systems must be fulfilled. If broken, compensation must be paid to the man who the parents promised their daughter (for the straight one)": in ALRC Report 31, 1986, "19. Aboriginal Customary Law Offences: Aboriginal Customary Law as a Ground of Criminal Liability":  http://www.alrc.gov.au/publications/19.Aboriginal%20Customary%20Law%20Offences/Aboriginal-customary-law-ground-criminal-liability. See also von Struensee, 2005, her footnote 120. Bride price is a serious problem in some African countries, and she has references regarding the harm to African women's rights caused by bride price. She writes, "The payment of bride price to the wife's family at the time of their marriage makes it difficult for women to leave abusive husbands, unless their families of origin are willing to return the amount paid."

126 Sexton and Wilson, 2006. Their source, Kimm 2004, 69-70.

127 For example, Dominic McCormack, "The Substance of Australia's First Men", *A Presentation to the National Mental Health and Homelessness Advisory Committee of St. Vincent de Paul Society*, Darwin, 20 July 2006, 4: http://www.bowden-mccormack.com.au/uploads/articles-papers/substance-first-men.pdf

128 See Mary Bennett (1934) q. in Windschuttle, 2009, 463.

about competitive male power, and what some men gain, others lose. Polygamy leads to scarcity of marriageable women, particularly for younger men with fewer resources in relatively closed communities. One outcome of this could be heightened predatory and controlling behaviour, not only among the powerful men with multiple wives, but also by young men struggling to obtain and retain one wife in competition against older men with more resources. However, there is scant scholarship which explores whether female scarcity and polygamy are a factor in today's high rate of controlling, violent behaviour by Aboriginal men towards women in remote communities. In her article, "Remote Aboriginal Communities: why the trade in girls and other human rights abuses remain hidden", Warin with Franklin made rare observations regarding this issue in remote Aboriginal Australia:

> Under-age and non-consenting marriages continue to occur. Many marriages under age are not registered and polygamy is still practised ... Females are designated marriage partners from birth, marrying within, it is said, the kinship systems. Those having a relationship outside of the kinship system are frowned upon by community members and, anecdotally, are at risk of payback ...
>
> Young men, as noted decades ago in Hardy's *Unlucky Australians*, find it difficult to marry as the younger women are taken by the older men as second, third or fourth wives. There are, however, other acts of violence by young men against marriage partners who try to escape.[129]

## Yolngu and suicide: a search for causes

Yolngu law might be strong, and their homelands their pride, but Yolngu young people have a high suicide rate, which has risen further recently, causing the Yolngu people deep anguish and concern. Lindsay Murdoch wrote in 2009:

---
129 Warin with Franklin, 2007, 2.

> The deaths were inexplicable in the ancient Yolngu culture, where there is no word to describe suicide. Families in small communities were being destroyed at a rate never seen before. Police started counting how many times they had to investigate the deaths of mostly young Aboriginal men and women.
>
> Between January 2007 and December 2008 there were 143 attempted, threatened or completed suicides among 9500 people.[130]

The Yolngu community of Ski Beach "became known for having one of the world's highest suicide rates. Six Yolngu took their lives in a population of only 400." Murdoch concludes that there are "promising signs. Police have not been called to investigate a suicide in the Ski Beach area for almost 12 months".[131] Let us hope this continues, but such vulnerability to suicide among Yolngu is a national tragedy. As Tatz reminds us:

> That so many young Aboriginal people prefer death to life implies a rejection of what we, as a society, have to offer. It reflects our failure, as a nation, to offer sufficient incentives for remaining in life.[132]

Our nation has failed them. And their culture has failed them. Strong in culture they may be, but the high suicide rate is a cry that something is deeply amiss, and indicates a perilous vulnerability among its young people when stress or change press upon them. If strong culture and resilient homelands are meant to be beneficial and protective of young people, this is a puzzle. The Yolngu have sacred, clan-based lands. They have the longest-running outstation movement, and these outstations are blessed with an ecology richer in bush food than many other Northern Territory regions. Their culture, language and *rom* are strong and alive.

---

130 Murdoch, 7 November 2009.
131 Ibid.
132 Tatz, 1999, 9

Tatz noted that "[a]s late as 1988, Harry Eastwell confirmed the 'low risk of suicide among the Yolngu of the Northern Territory'".[133] Suicide among the Northern Territory's Indigenous young people started its disturbing rise during the 1990s. Since the mid 1990s Yolngu young people have become among the most vulnerable of Northern Territory's Indigenous young people to suicide, particularly in an "echo cluster" or "copycat" pattern, which experts consider to be the most preventable form (if only).[134]

A range of factors associated with the high Yolngu suicide rate have been identified. Police note that alcohol is "the obvious common factor".[135] The NTER is considered by some to be a recent factor.[136] The NTER and the withdrawal of homeland funding are causing anguish and uncertainty about the future among Yolngu. Yothu Yindi Foundation's Nathan Evans, who conducted a study into Gove Peninsula suicides for Anglicare Northern Territory, said that the federal intervention "has made many Yolngu people feel 'denigrated' ...":

> this continued disenfranchising and alienation from the mainstream community and economy contributed to people's low sense of self-worth and sense of belonging.[137]

This is similar to earlier observations about suicide clusters during the years of the RCADC. Neill noted a North Queensland report's statement that the RCADC may itself "have unwittingly fuelled

---

133 Tatz 1999, 23, referring to H. D. Eastwell, "The low risk of suicide among the Yolngu of the NT: The traditional Aboriginal pattern", *MJA* 148 (7), 1988, 338-40.
134 See Leonore Hanssens and Peter Hanssens, 2007 *passim*, esp. 3, 7, 8. Across the NT, the main rise among Aboriginal people commenced during the 1990s. For trends up to 2002, see Measey, Shu Qin Li, Parker and Zhiqiang Wang, 2006. For NT 2008 level, see ABS, 3303.0_13 *Causes of Death*, Australia, 2008. *Excel Data Cube "Deaths of Aboriginal and Torres Strait Islander Australians"* 2008.
135 Murdoch, 7 November 2009.
136 For example, see John Greatorex, *Submission on Regional and Remote Indigenous Communities*, 2008: http://www.aph.gov.au/Senate/Committee/indig_ctte/submissions/sub79.pdf
137 Murdoch, 7 November 2009, quoting Evans.

a rash of indigenous suicides outside custody", by "bringing the additional distress of media scrutiny, sensational coverage, substantial misrepresentations, shame and an even greater sense of loss of control over events and community problems".[138] Neill also wrote that

> indigenous people are about seven or eight times more likely to commit suicide outside jail than in ... Australians have yet to confront the reality of indigenous communities so alienated that teenagers conceive of their own funerals as status symbols, or see jail as a rite of passage to manhood.[139]

Referring to the same North Queensland report, Neill observed:

> Suicide has become increasingly common among indigenous peoples around the world, as they struggle to reconcile two cultures ... It offered a typical profile of an indigenous Australian at risk of suicide: a male in his twenties, who has a relative who recently suicided. He is unemployed with CDEP ... doing manual labour. He has a history of binge drinking and is heavily drunk at the time of his death. He has threatened his life before ... the incident that triggers his death – an argument with a relative or partner – is seemingly trivial.[140]

Among the Yolngu, traditional belief systems appear to add to the family and community pain surrounding suicide. Some Yolngu people blame suicide deaths on sorcery, and there is

> fear of blame or payback for Yolngu who are with or near a person who commits suicide. Evans says many partners have also been blamed for the death of a spouse. "This ongoing ostracising and alienation of people further compounds the trauma of losing someone ..."[141]

---

138 Neill, 2002, 217-18, including q. from a report titled "An Analysis of Suicide in Indigenous Communities of North Queensland: the Historical, Cultural and Symbolic Landscape".
139 Ibid, 217.
140 Ibid, 219.
141 Murdoch, 7 November 2009, quoting Evans. See also Greatorex 2008, 2.

Sutton noted the particular adaptivity of Yolngu culture to outside pressures, compared with most other Australian Indigenous cultures.[142] One of the pressures it has adapted to is white law insistence that revenge killing and execution as punishment must end. A result of this is a shift to sorcery. Has this partial adaptivity spawned sorcery and social ostracism so debilitating to the individual that they lead to violence directed against oneself, including suicide?

Alcohol in the context of traditional beliefs has further, particular dangers. Referring to Aboriginal suicides in general, while Joseph Reser emphasises the role of history and acculturation, he notes that "the importance of traditionally oriented beliefs and their relationship to the meaning and consequences of 'being drunk' cannot ... be simply dismissed ..."[143] Reser includes a statement, collected by Ernest Hunter, of an Aboriginal respondent from Broome speaking of a dangerous fear state while in custody:

> After heavy drinking you know, you get paralytic drunk and get the shakes, you can hear voices, voices saying, "I'll kill you". I've been through that, you can hear voices and things. It makes you feel you want to commit suicide. Makes you think that before they get you you'll kill yourself, commit suicide ... When you're locked up and going through that thing you need people around, you should have the lights on. In the light you're safe but in the darkness you think that person's going to come and kill you.[144]

Nathan Evans noted that

> many Yolngu have spoken about the dilemma they face when family members return home intoxicated. [Evans] says being

---
142 Sutton, 2009, 156.
143 Joseph Reser, "Aboriginal Mental Health", in Janice Reid and Peggy Trompf, (eds), *The Health of Aboriginal Australia*, Harcourt Brace Jovanovich, 1991, 275.
144 Words of an Aboriginal respondent in Broome lock-up, 1987, in Reser, 1991, 275. q. E.M. Hunter, "Aboriginal Suicides in the Kimberley", *Australian and New Zealand Journal of Psychiatry* 22, 1988, 279.

refused entry into a home could be taken as the equivalent of "galka", or sorcery, and could create feelings of "hopelessness, aloneness and disempowerment that are magnified and could contribute to the person's sense of not belonging, particularly when people are not thinking straight whilst drunk".[145]

In the same article, Murdoch reported, "Northern Territory deputy coroner Celia Kemp acknowledged during a recent enquiry into the death of a 19-year-old Yolngu man that family members often believe suicide deaths are the result of sorcery or black magic".[146] It thus appears that punishment is now carried more within the mind, and is a powerful creator of fear and blame in the Yolngu community. We do not know the victims' state of mind just before suicide, but did they feel that some transgression, minor or major, made them susceptible to sorcery as punishment, and when affected by too much alcohol, this was experienced as sheer terror, dangerously intensified by feeling cut off from their community?

Tatz has written, "suicide research is quintessentially guesswork ... Aboriginal suicides rarely leave notes."[147] Tatz and Neill have remarked on the scarcity of data regarding Indigenous suicide outside of custody. Some factors such as alcohol have been clearly linked to Yolngu suicide, while others such as sorcery are possibilities to consider. However, neither these chronic factors, nor correlations of increased suicides with acute stressors such as the RCADC or the Intervention, help our understanding of why young Yolngu people in particular, and only since the 1990s, are one of the most highly vulnerable of Australia's Indigenous populations to suicide.

Is it possibly that young Indigenous people in the more resilient, intact Indigenous cultures such as Yolngu, find the task of reconciling two cultures more difficult, more painful? Perhaps the outside world is

---

145 Murdoch, 7 November 2009.
146 Ibid.
147 Tatz, 1999, 35.

experienced as more beckoning but beyond reach, or more threatening, or more irreconcilable with their own beliefs and practices, by those in relatively intact cultures? Do young Indigenous people in such societies feel a terrible burden of guilt when their culture, so rich and beloved to them, is nevertheless unable to fulfil their personal needs and dreams, such as living a life beyond the boundaries of the Yolngu homelands and Yolngu culture? And do they experience a terrible ostracism when they need to defy the ancient Yolngu law to follow their heart and dreams, and experience pain that is too great to bear?

### *Beloved lands, beloved culture, but are they no longer enough?*

Marcia Langton outlines research identifying a link between cultural continuity and reduced suicide among young indigenous Canadians. She writes, however, that

> Chandler and La Londe use the expression – and I emphasise it – "*healthy* cultural continuity", and tackle problems that we too must acknowledge and bring into the policy debate. They identify two key issues in the North American context that also apply here: isolation and privilege.
>
> They write that the isolation of community members from the outside world is a serious problem. Too many young people conclude that the only place they can live is on the reserve.[148]

Christie and Greatorex argue that in the homeland centres (outstations), Yolngu social capital has remained strong.[149] These authors suggest that governments' and ATSIC's centralising of funds onto Yolngu's ex-mission settlements rather than homeland centres portrays little understanding of Yolngu culture and society, and of where Yolngu strength lies. They also note:

---

148 Marcia Langton, "The end of 'big men' politics", Griffith Review Edition 22 *MoneySexPower*, 16 September 2008: https://griffithreview.com/edition-22-moneysexpower/the-end-of-big-men-politics referring to M.J. Chandler and C.E. Lalonde, "Cultural continuity as a moderator of suicide risk among Canada's First Nations", *Transcultural Psychiatry*, 35(2), 1998, 191-219.

149 Christie and Greatorex, 2006, 6-7.

> The co-location of a spectrum of clan groups, each with its own language and estates, did not present an unmanageable situation in mission days, but with the demise of the missions and the rise of government and council bureaucracies, the powerful authority of collaborating Yolngu elders has eroded. The number of Yolngu estranged from their ancestral land is accelerating. Increasing numbers of young people are looking westward, as the grasp of community life weakens. Today, as is frequently reported, "the youth control the elders". These tensions have led to distress, concentrated in the former mission settlements. Incidents of suicide, substance abuse, and widespread fear of sorcery have been documented for the former mission settlements ...[150]

Tatz, Hunter and others, writing about the once low, and now high, Aboriginal suicide rate, also point to the dysfunctional "communities" that emerged when the old protectionist institutions and mission regimes ended. Tatz writes:

> the old authoritarian laws and regulations ... together with mission evangelism, gave these institutions a viability of a kind. The struts and pillars of these institutions began to be removed only in the 1970s ... Lacking structure, many "communities" lacked order, and have become *disordered*. These much respected Aboriginal values of affection, reverence for family and kin, reciprocity, care of the young and aged, veneration for law, lore and religion, are floundering or have been displaced.[151]

There is a time gap between the end of the missions and the beginning of ready access to alcohol during the 1970s, and young people starting to suicide at high rates during the 1990s. Why this time gap of about one generation? Perhaps by the mid 1990s the generational shift away from those brought up with mission education and the application of skills and hard work had occurred, and self-determination's harm to young people, as described by Trudgen, was reaching its full expression.

---

150 Ibid, 7-8.
151 Tatz, 1999, 30 (Tatz's italics).

Today's defenders of homelands see a solution there. They assume that young Yolngu people would regain robustness if they resided or spent more time in the homeland centres. They also assume that focus of funding onto homeland centres and not the towns could make all the difference to where most Yolngu young people would choose to reside. Is this akin to trying to keep young people from leaving tiny towns anywhere in Australia, to protect them from the attractions and risks of big town or city life? Local festivals celebrating one's ancestral culture and history are enriching for many of us from time to time. However, I do not expect myself – let alone a younger generation – to live within a past tradition every day. Perhaps the comparison is unfair, but it may also be too difficult for young Yolngu to live within the bounds of Yolngu tradition, even for those raised on a homeland. The ubiquitous mainstream world and its attractions, and the difficulty of keeping within older modes of relationship, thought and practice once modernity is experienced or even just known about, would render this very difficult.

In his 1993 book *Aboriginal Health and History*, Ernest Hunter dedicates a chapter to suicide. He refers to studies that point to a traditionally derived vulnerability to heightened individual distress in situations of social isolation. Decades earlier, Warner noted this among traditional Arnhem Land people.[152] Hunter writes:

> These [social] networks of interpersonal relationships necessary for the construction and maintenance of personal identity are of particular importance in Aboriginal societies. Reid made this point with respect to the Yolngu of Arnhem Land, for whom "it is rather like being in the centre of a series of concentric circles" (1983: 86). Myers identified a similar dynamic in the Central Desert ... threats to relatedness – if significant, widespread, or persistent – may represent an assault on the very fabric of identity and self.[153]

---
152 Note that Warner's "Murngin" are the Yolngu.
153 Ernest Hunter, *Aboriginal Health and History: Power and Prejudice in Remote Australia*, Cambridge University Press, Cambridge, 1993, 161.

Demanding and often lethal the old Yolngu culture may have been, but it had high compliance because in the old hunter-gatherer economy, it was seen as necessary for survival. Thus, debilitating isolation (as a consequence of non-compliance) was probably less commonplace in former times. The pressures of their culture on today's Yolngu people, including its traditional relationships and social expectations, and the fears and consequences surrounding culturally wrong action are still extant, and when mixed with drink, very hazardous. Perhaps this disjuncture – a weakening belief in, and necessity for, their ancient, clan-based culture, but remaining fears, superstitions and threats of isolation if one commits a relational or other traditional wrong – help explain why young Yolngu are so vulnerable in the context of a still *strong* Yolngu culture, particularly given its violent punishment, sorcery, clan rivalry, payback and oppressive marriage systems. For young Yolngu people, it could be the *strength* of their traditional culture that makes reconciling the two cultures that they move between so very distressing for them.

### *Yolngu suicide, right marriage and polygamy?*

Warner observed years ago, "[i]f war were abolished, the percentage of young men would increase and the pressure on the social structure created by seeking mates would probably be too strong for the present form of polygyny ..."[154] In the 1930s, Mary Bennett observed the harmful effects of polygamy on young women in particular, but also on young men: "One result in a settled district that I know is that there are at least fifty young men unmarried, and with no prospect of marrying for many years ..."[155] What pressure does polygamy place on the social structure of today's Yolngu? Does polygamy increase the vulnerability of young Yolngu men to suicide? The traditional marriage system of polygamy as a recent suicide factor might seem

---

154 Warner, 1958, 158.
155 Mary Bennett (1934) q. in Windschuttle, 2009, 462.

curious, given that high suicide rates did not emerge until the mid 1990s.[156] Nevertheless, polygamy as an additional stressor for today's young Yolngu men warrants consideration.

The resilience of Yolngu culture means that its young people are shaped by that culture. These young people are members of a still relatively closed community with cultural demands and practices that set them apart from mainstream life. Even young Yolngu who receive acclaim as performers on the world stage need interpreters to communicate with non-Yolngu, and when they do, they tell us about a continuing very "other" culture. In 2010, a Yolngu performer in his early twenties spoke through an interpreter of the correctness of "right skin", and "looks dimly on his peers who hook up with lovers of the 'wrong skin'":

> "When people go with wrong skin, it can be the cause of some really major fights and dysfunctions within the community", he says. "For myself, I'll stand within my culture and stick to my law, which decides who is the right skin for me." As this young man talks he looks sideways, avoiding eye contact, yet he speaks about his culture with a fierce, even angry conviction.[157]

How do young Yolngu men cope with the limits on marriageable partners, with exacting Yolngu partner restrictions and community condemnation if you fall in love with the wrong skin, along with female scarcity due to Yolngu polygamy? Young Yolngu men with a worldview and language so different from the mainstream would face considerable difficulties if they seek a partner outside Yolngu

---

156 If by the mid 1990s, self-determination's harm was reaching a peak (as described by Trudgen) in terms of a new generation of young people less able to function within the mainstream, less in command of English, etc, unlike their mission-trained parents: this generation would have less alternative other than keeping their lives within the boundaries of their own culture. Polygamy could then increasingly become a stressor, as these young men might have less success in marrying out.

157 Rosemary Neill, "From Elcho, an affair to remember", *The Australian*, 5 March 2010: http://www.theaustralian.com.au/news/arts/from-elcho-an-affair-to-remember/story-e6frg8n6-1225837098543

community and culture.[158] Are today's Yolngu young men less able to find non-Yolngu partners – Indigenous or non-Indigenous – compared with other more integrated Aboriginal men? Further, does polygamy and the resultant shortage of women increase the stress of insecurity even within marriage?[159]

As Neill observed, "[s]uicide has become increasingly common among indigenous peoples around the world, as they struggle to reconcile two cultures".[160] For Yolngu, love and marriage are proving to be difficult sites in this cultural struggle. Certainly, some modernisation is occurring. Young Yolngu people are turning away from polygamy. Promised and arranged marriage is declining, but still part of cultural practice. Choosing a partner on the basis of love is more frequent, but such marriages, especially if they are of "wrong skin" or entail the breaking of a "promised" marriage, can evoke opposition from one's family and community. What a choice. The modernity and cultural liberty of the mainstream is beckoning Yolngu young people, but too often they lack the education, skills and even enough English to venture forth. But are the demands and restrictions of their beloved ancient, clan-based culture, perhaps felt most painfully in the realm of the heart, at times too much to bear?

---

158 For some measure of the poor understanding of English language among Yolngu, see *An Absence of Mutual Respect* (ARDS, 2008). Although problems across age groups were found, "we found it much easier to explain Balanda legal concepts to this (pre-1965 born) group compared to the younger group" (p. 24).

159 I ask this question because Leonore and Peter Hanssens argue that unlike in mainstream society, marriage is no protector against suicide among young NT Indigenous men, based on the fact that in the NT, in percentage terms there were slightly more married (including de facto) than single Indigenous men who committed suicide. However, the Hanssens' article provides no rate comparison, rendering the impact of marriage difficult to discern. See Leonore Hanssens and Peter Hanssens, 2007, 5. Also, Sutton notes that in contrast to the very high Aboriginal out-marriage rates (marrying a non-Indigenous partner) for most of Australia in 2006 (over 80% in Sydney), remote Indigenous rates are low. The lowest out-marriage rates were for NT Indigenous people outside Darwin, particularly for males: 8.5% for females, and 4.2% for males: Sutton 2009, 159.

160 Neill, 2002, 219.

## *"Ngurrumilmarrmiriyu (Wrong Skin)"*

Since writing the above section, I have seen *Ngurrumilmarrmiriyu (Wrong Skin)*,[161] a performance by Elcho Island's Chooky Dancers about a Yolngu wrong-moiety romance. I wanted to weep at the enormity of what these young Yolngu performers were revealing, and that they did so with such creativity and courage as well as a good deal of humour. A few days prior, I read Rosemary Neill's preview article, "From Elcho, an affair to remember", and was mightily impressed. There was the courage of one young Chooky Dancer sharing his perspective on the conflict-ridden matter of wrong-moiety love. When I quoted this performer earlier, I did not mention that he was a Chooky Dancer, because it seemed insensitive to overtly extend his insights about "wrong" love and community conflict into the terrible issue of youth suicide.

That was until I saw the Chooky Dancers themselves portraying lethal male-on-male violence and suicidal youth as potential outcomes of ancient moiety rules clashing with wrong-skin love. Clearly, these young Yolngu people see the connection. With a heart-broken young man weeping in the arms of a loving male elder, the play seems to conclude that Yolngu can find peace and healing in the ancient ways. However, the rest of the play is telling us that young Yolngu are subjected to an irreconcilable clash of cultures, one celebrating personal liberty, the other demanding cultural submission. The words of Neill, Tatz and Hunter on Indigenous youth suicide come to mind, "they struggle to reconcile two cultures" ... "people floundering" ... "threats to relatedness" ... "an assault on the very fabric of identity and self".

The pain and despair visited upon the young by this clash between an ancient culture's demands and modern freedoms are perilous. But this is only part of the story. Yolngu forbidden love has always occurred, and in the days of old, Yolngu could face execution for following their erroneous heart. Today, the young realise that the old

---

161 Nigel Jamieson, Director, *Wrong Skin*, 2010.

Yolngu rules are no longer "necessarily so", but that realisation still leaves them more likely to be victims than winners.

### *Why these talented young men?*

The most talented and traditional of young Yolngu men are among those who have committed suicide. These young men bore their status in a very different but equally perilous world from the young Murngin warriors' world of yesteryear. Like the young Ramingining visitors to Singapore who on returning home became petrol sniffers,[162] an intensity of contrasting cultural experience seems somehow linked to consequent self-harm and suicide among vulnerable Yolngu.

iDIDJ Australia, a Melbourne-based business set up to improve life for Arnhem Land communities, including a focus on supporting yidaki[163] players, expresses grief over the suicides of outstanding young Yolngu performers. iDIDJ has been "working with and living alongside" Arnhem Land people for 16 years.[164] Unlike others' recent emphasis on the benefits of Yolngu homeland centres, iDIDJ depicts an Arnhem Land that is experiencing an equivalent level of community disadvantage and dysfunction to other regions of the Northern Territory. iDIDJ argues that

> figures under-represent the grim reality in Arnhem Land communities which are among the most remote and under-serviced places in Australia. Some would say these communities resemble Third World living conditions ...
>
> At iDIDJ Australia, we don't need statistics to know that there is suffering and devastation in Aboriginal Australia. Four of our star YouTube yidaki players ... have passed away from suicide. [The y]oung actor ... shown in our Ten Canoes trailer, also took his own life ... We know of many more deaths, assaults,

---

162 Trudgen, 2000, 240-243.
163 "Yidaki" is the Yolngu term for "didjeridoo".
164 iDIDJ Australia, "iDIDJ Philanthropy": http://www.ididj.com.au/ididjphilanthropy.html

injuries and illnesses that have afflicted our Aboriginal friends and families.[165]

All of these men are Yolngu, most of them young, and had exceptional talent and commitment to share their culture with the wider world, including through YouTube and many successful overseas performances. On the iDIDJ and Yirrkala Yidaki websites,[166] the moiety, clan and homeland names of yidaki artists including these men are given, indicating their connection to tradition and access to homeland life. While most were in their twenties, one was a mature man of 40 – still far too young – when he took his own life. He was an original Yothu Yindi member, and a brilliant yidaki player who produced an instructional CD on the art of yidaki playing.[167]

*The Age* outlined the situation surrounding the suicide of one young man. On 23 July 2008 a young man, a yidaki player with Yothu Yindi, danced with other Yolngu men for Prime Minister Kevin Rudd at festivities after Federal Cabinet was held in Yirrkala. After the performance, it was reported that the young man "had argued with his wife". Later that evening at the dry community of Ski Beach, drinking continued, and there, he argued with a young woman friend, and stabbed her 14 times. "Apparently believing her to be dead, (the young man) then committed suicide." He was 26 years of age. His victim was hospitalised and a week later was in a stable condition. Murdoch, reporting this tragedy, writes:

> Only the most trusted of Mr Yunupingu's Gumatj warriors were chosen to perform the dance, which few white people have seen.[168]

---

165 iDIDJ Australia, "iDIDJ Philanthropy".
166 – iDIDj Australia, "Education – profiles": http://www.ididj.com.au/education/profiles.html
  – Yirrkala Yidaki, "Artists": http://www.yirrkala.com/yidaki/artists/index.html
167 iDIDJ Australia, "iDIDJ Philanthropy".
168 Lindsay Murdoch, "Celebration spirals into tragedy", *The Age*, 30 July 2008, 1.

Just a few months later in October, another young Yolngu man, aged 19 years, took his own life, shattering his father's hopes for a leadership future for his son. His suicide was queried as a death in custody because he was conveyed to his Yirrkala home in the back of a police van. He was moderately drunk that evening, and both he and police were keen to get him home, away from a disturbance outside a Nhulunbuy hotel at closing time. He hung himself after arriving home. His wife on her way home found him hanging from a tree near their house. At the Nhulunbuy disturbance, the young man had been "angry, frustrated and emotional", arguing with his wife and others, including "an argument with his cousin ... about cultural issues". It "looked like he was about to hit one of the aunts" but a security officer "grabbed him to stop it".[169]

At the Nhulunbuy Coroner's Court, Professor Robert Parker contributed his expert understanding regarding suicide in Aboriginal communities:

> [Parker] said that the circumstances of his death, that is a hanging in the context of two previous episodes of self-harm, alcohol intoxication and a significant argument with his wife and another man *are very consistent with other Aboriginal people who have killed themselves.* He considered the two previous attempted suicides to be particularly significant ... the fact that [his] grandfather had died in the weeks before his death as also a risk factor for suicide.[170]

The young man was a regular drinker, commencing from age 16. His father said that when he did not drink he was a "very, very good young man, but on the grog it was *no good*". However he never harmed anyone while drinking. Also,

> [h]e had no previous dealings with the police at all: In a

---

[169] NTMC 044, No. D199/08, Coroner's Court, Nhulunbuy, Northern Territory of Australia 2009.
[170] NTMC 044, No. D199/08, 2009, 24 (italics in court transcript).

community where there is a relatively high rate of interactions with police, this is an impressive testament to his character and behaviour.[171]

He grew up on the east Arnhem Land homeland (outstation) of Gan Gan, recently depicted as "one of the notable success stories of the homelands movement":[172]

> He learned the traditional ways of his family and ancestors. Gan Gan is a very important place to [his] family and it is a place for creation and symbolism. [He] would eventually have gone on to be a traditional leader at Gan Gan ...
>
> [He] upheld the traditional culture of his area and was a tribal dancer. He had been employed as a contractor at the Laynhapuy Homelands Association ... They [he and his wife] had been living at Yirrkala, where his wife's family were located, for some months prior to his death. Previously they had lived at Gan Gan.[173]

## Conclusion: Yolngu homelands: clouded havens

In recent decades the Yolngu people have embarked on a diligent project of keeping their traditional culture and law alive, while limiting its violent excesses so it complies with Western law. In this project, the Yolngu have provided for the nation a glimpse at solutions to Aboriginal suffering and violence based on "successful" separatism and traditional culture. Since the retreat of the missions, the return to homelands, and the decades of self-determination, strong Yolngu leadership and cultural resilience have resulted in a level of behavioural restraint and orderliness that has evoked praiseworthy comment. Just as supporters of a return to culture and homelands have argued, the strong homeland life of Yolngu has facilitated a solid base for maintaining traditional law, order and practice, a haven from the

---

171 Ibid, 5.
172 Murdoch, *The Age*, 17 October 2009.
173 NTMC 044, No. D199/08, 2009, 4.

contaminating influence of ready grog, easy money, and "wrong" love of mainstream life in the towns.

And yet north-east Arnhem Land is an enigma. The recent Yolngu clan clashes and domestic violence belie the subdued statistics, and evoke Kimm's concern that among the Yolngu, there is a strong wish to control domestic matters and to minimise outside exposure and intervention.[174] There is a continuing culture of violence and volatility among Yolngu, with violence a normal response in too many circumstances. This is because the traditional culture and law still contain aspects that are violent, as well as other oppressive practices so incompatible with mainstream liberty that they cause great anguish, both to those who uphold these features, and to those who resist them.

The Yolngu experience shows that while successful implementation of traditional law and social structures can, at least among some groups, secure a kind of peace, order and reduced violence among 21st century remote Indigenous Australians, it does so at huge cost to other critical, universal values such as equality and liberty, and freedom from violence. This is evident in the cases of "justified" violence against Yolngu women who flout Yolngu's traditional, patriarchal requirements; the outrageous *mirriri*; the continuation of traditional polygamy, promised marriage, and early teen marriage for girls; the ancient, exacting, clan-based "wrong skin" marriage rules and the rupture, violence and ostracism triggered by their transgressions; the readiness of even the most respected Yolngu leaders to commit violence when traditionally aggravated; the need to live in isolated tiny homeland settlements to prevent traditional clan (and co-wife) clashes, limiting participation in mainstream life; the poison of sorcery; and perhaps above all, the tragedy of so many talented and beloved young Yolngu men killing themselves.

Are these costs not testimony enough to the danger and futility

---

174 Kimm, 2004, 106-7.

of enforcing ancient traditions on ancient homelands, rendered even harder to bear in face of the mainstream's irresistible attractions and individual liberties? Homelands are a temporary haven at best. In their present form and usage, homelands strengthen the continuation of ancient, oppressive, hunter-gatherer law, authority and culture, playing havoc with the lives of their young people. If the Yolngu homelands are to be supported, they need to be part of a compassionate process of adjustment to the universal values, rights, responsibilities and opportunities of mainstream life. In our insistent, relativist respect for Indigenous culture, how much more suffering do we demand of the Yolngu?

# 9
# Towns and cities

> The man would be out all day at work or CDEP, then come home, start drinking and bashes her – and why would he bash her? She must have given him some reason to do it!
>
> – older Aboriginal woman, resident of regional city[1]

> NEVER go on the street at night by yourself, just don't do it! ... I've had plenty of friends who have been bashed up on the street at night while going to the shop, by Aboriginals demanding cigarettes or $5 or whatever off you ...
>
> – young white mother, resident of regional city[2]

Most Aboriginal people live in mainstream towns and cities. Cities offer greater access to social and economic opportunities, thus reducing some of the more obvious explanations for Aboriginal community dysfunction such as remoteness from essential services. Cities are also where the majority of Aboriginal and non-Aboriginal people encounter and develop favourable or negative attitudes about each other.

## Statistics: cities, safer for some

Assault and homicide statistics show that cities and rural towns are safer than remote places for Aboriginal people. Aboriginal violence in urban areas, however, is greater than the non-Aboriginal rate. Here are some of these telling statistics.

---

1 Field work, mid 1990s.
2 Ibid.

For the years 2002-03 to 2006-07, the average rates per 100,000 per annum for homicide victims are:

| Homicide victims | Indigenous | Non-Indigenous |
|---|---|---|
| Major cities | 3.0 | 1.2 |
| Inner regional | 3.9 | 1.3 |
| Outer regional | 8.9 | 0.8 |
| Remote | 13.7 | 1.0 |
| Very remote | 16.3 | 1.4[3] |

For 1999-2005, hospitalisation for head injury rates per 100,000 over the six-year period are:

| Head injury hospitalisation | Indigenous | Non-Indigenous |
|---|---|---|
| Metropolitan areas | 214.8 | 23.9 |
| Rural + remote areas | 1499.7 | 163.2[4] |

The 2002 NATSISS results for interviewees reporting, to a survey interviewer, neighbourhood/community conflict and assault, are included for illustrative purposes:[5]

**Indigenous Neighbourhood/Community problems (%)**

| | NT(remote) | NT(non-remote) | ACT |
|---|---|---|---|
| Family violence | 36.2 | 16.9 | 7.5 |
| Assault | 42.4 | 11.7 | 9.1 |
| Sexual assault | 9.5 | 3.1 | 2.6 |
| Neighbourhood conflict | 30.7 | 10.5 | 9.0 [6] |

Overwhelmingly, interpersonal violence is intra-racial in all regional categories, with most victims of Aboriginal violence being

---

3 Productivity Commission, 2009, Table 4A.11.15.
4 Jamieson, Harrison and Berry, 2008 (Q, WA, SA and NT hospital data).
5 For reasons presented in Chapter 1, I have presented these statistics with some hesitation. In particular, these results are of *reporting* experience to an interviewer, often in less than optimal levels of privacy.
6 NATSISS 2002, "revised_4714_0 tables_nt", and "revised_4714_0 tables_act".

Aboriginal, and most victims of non-Aboriginal violence being non-Aboriginal. By bringing populations together, however, cities provide greater opportunities for inter-racial interaction. Hence in the city, while Aboriginal victimisation to Aboriginal violence declines, inter-racial violence tends to increase. In the city, while by far most Aboriginal violence is directed against Aboriginal people, white victimisation to Aboriginal violence is a significant enough problem to counteract any argument for reluctant intervention based on the (albeit morally bankrupt) position that Aboriginal violence is an Aboriginal problem, for Aboriginal people to solve. The AIC depicts the greater danger that Aboriginal violence poses to Aboriginal people in remote areas, while non-Aboriginal people in the cities become vulnerable targets:

> Discussions of violence in Indigenous communities tend to focus on spatially separate remote or semi-remote communities. In these situations, the impact of violence is likely to be particularly damaging because both the perpetrators and victims of such behaviour generally come from within the community and are often related through complex kin networks. However, the situation may be quite different in the major cities where:
>
>> there are often a number of different Indigenous groups or social networks, defined according to the part of the state from which the members originated or the kinship groups to which they belong;
>>
>> the members of these networks are likely to be scattered across the suburbs, thereby reducing the intensity and frequency of interaction between them; and
>>
>> the "pool" of potential victims is larger, with Indigenous victims having a greater opportunity to offend against non-Indigenous people because of the co-location of the two groups.[7]

When inter-racial violence does occur, it is much more likely

---

[7] Joy Wundersitz, *Indigenous Perpetrators of Violence: Prevalence and Risk Factors for Offending: Appendix B: Key Concepts.* Australian Institute of Criminology, Research and Public Policy Series no. 105, 31 March, 2010: www.aic.gov.au/publications/current%20series/rpp/100-120/rpp105/10.aspx

to be an Aboriginal perpetrator and a non-Aboriginal victim. The AIC documents earlier 1993 data indicating that 22% of assaults in Western Australia for that year were inter-racial. Further, of these 852 inter-racial assaults, "over 9 in 10 (n = 794) comprised an Indigenous perpetrator and a non-Indigenous victim". The AIC further comments that while these figures are dated and in a large percentage of cases the identities were unknown, "these findings point to a higher level of inter-racial offending by Indigenous offenders than is generally acknowledged".[8]

More recent, national figures also demonstrate a higher Indigenous perpetrator rate for inter-racial homicide. In 2006-07 out of a total of 247 homicides 14 had an Indigenous perpetrator and a non-Indigenous victim, while only one had a non-Indigenous perpetrator and an Indigenous victim. While no remote–urban distribution of inter-racial homicide was provided, no inter-racial homicides occurred in the Northern Territory that year, even though the Northern Territory registered by far the highest Indigenous homicides by number and rate. Furthermore, New South Wales, with its more urbanised Aboriginal population, had the highest Indigenous-non-Indigenous homicide rate, and all seven involved an Indigenous perpetrator and a non-Indigenous victim.[9] A group of non-Indigenous men murdered an Indigenous man in Alice Springs in 2009.[10]

## "Gangs", dog patrols, and frightening public violence

The AIC has classed violence in Aboriginal communities into five categories: one-on-one adult fighting; inter-group violence; cyclic or inter-generational violence; dysfunctional community syndrome; and

---

8 J. Wundersitz, *Indigenous Perpetrators of Violence: Prevalence and Risk Factors for Offending: The prevalence and nature of Indigenous violent offending*, AIC Research and Policy Series no. 105, 7 April 2010: www.aic.gov.au/publications/current%20series/rpp/100-120/rpp105/05.aspx

9 Productivity Commission, 2009, Table 4A.11.16.

10 "Five men charged over Alice Springs murder", *National Indigenous Times*, 6 August 2009: http://www.nit.com.au/news/story.aspx?id=18381

sequential (retaliatory or payback) violence. It describes inter-group violence thus:

> this ranges from violence between different kin groups in remote areas to forms of gang violence involving predominantly young Indigenous males in urban settings.[11]

This "range" may exist beyond just passive verbal categorisation. That is, the "violence between different kin groups in remote areas" and traditional norms about violence might be contributing factors to the "gang violence involving predominantly young Indigenous males in urban settings". In South Australia, towns and cities with significant Aboriginal populations, including Adelaide, have experienced in recent years a disturbing level of public disorder and threatening, criminal behaviour committed by some, mainly young, mainly Aboriginal people, often in gangs. A couple of separate phenomena signal that this dysfunctional public behaviour might be traceable, at least partially, to traditional patterns of conflict.

The most well-known of these phenomena is the so-called "Gang of 49". Not really a gang, it refers to groups waging a chronic crime wave, frequently robberies with the threat or use of weapons, in Adelaide for over five years.[12] Most members are young Aboriginal men and boys, some as young as ten. In 2010, journalist Bryan Littlely pointed to the presence of at least six Aboriginal street fighting gangs in Adelaide whose main inspiration is non-traditional, being "American street-gang inspired clans" and these are somehow "feeding in to"

---

11 AIC, 31 March 2010.
12 "Tackling the gangs of Adelaide", Editorial, *The Advertiser*, 9 April 2010, 20. See also Greg Kelton, "Put culprits behind bars for as long as we can", *The Advertiser*, 13 October 2009, 7.

or "driving" the "Gang of 49".[13] Littlely refers to Laura Swanson of James Cook University who in 2009 undertook four weeks of research among "Gang of 49" members. She found that they adopt "the image, music, clothing and language" of American gangs. Nevertheless, she found that "while the Gang of 49 is a group largely consisting of indigenous males who are connected by kinship ties, it does not have an organised structure, actively recruit members or have an identifiable leadership".[14] Littlely writes that in most of the gang's attacks,

> weapons are whatever is easy to get hold of – knives, screwdrivers, iron bars and bats are most common.
>
> Guns, particularly hunting-style rifles, are now being used more regularly in hold-ups. Guns are common in the country communities the Aboriginal members originate from. Often a simple show of force, standover tactics and committing crimes in twos and threes, means weapons are not even needed.[15]

In one attack on a cafe,

> three men "terroris[ed] 30 staff and customers with a gun.
>
> One man, believed to be a chef, was allegedly struck across his face with the weapon when he ignored the gang's orders not to look at their faces.[16]

---

13 Bryan Littlely, "Crime Club: Inside the Gang of 49", Special Investigation, *The Advertiser*, 9 April 2010, 1. These well-organised street fighting gangs have names including "Black Scorpions, West Side Bloods, Crazy After Dark, and RBM (Real Black Nungas)": "Members of the street gangs, primarily formed for street fighting, have a formal initiation, which generally involves bashing someone or 'taking a hiding' themselves, and actively recruit new members." Unlike the criminal activities of the "Gang of 49", there are official doubts that these Aboriginal street-fighting gangs are linked to criminal activity (apart from street fighting?): Littlely, "Crime Club ...", 2010, 4.

14 Littlely, "Crime Club ...", 2010, 4.

15 Bryan Littlely, "Gangs crime and bloodshed", Special Investigation, *The Advertiser*, 9 April 2010, 4.

16 Sean Fewster, Jordanna Schriever, Ken McGregor, "Spirit of Gang of 49 on show outside court", *The Advertiser*, 13 October 2009, 6.

One reason why the crime wave of the "Gang of 49" is difficult to control is that the offenders are not concentrated as they might be in a remote community, but live dispersed, across the city's suburbs, and undertake their crimes in small groups requiring little organisation.[17] One would have hoped that such dispersal across the mainstream suburbs of Adelaide would have a beneficial impact on behaviour, but not with these young offenders. Rather, there are signs of increasing menace:

> Police have Operation Mandrake at the ready for the next wave of offending, but now face a much more sinister, dangerous and unpredictable enemy than first thought. Police cannot be sure when they will strike, who will initiate the assault, because of the scattering of this loosely linked network of criminals.
>
> There is no Gang of 49 ringleader to monitor and shut down. There is no pattern to their crimes. There are many young Aborigines eager to join the ranks of their jailed heroes who terrorised shop keepers, bar staff, bakers and bankers with their brash, reckless onslaught which has logged 1000 offences over six years.[18]

The "Gang of 49" is not only, perhaps not even primarily, a metropolitan-generated problem. Adelaide is attracting a number of young Aboriginal people for no good purpose from South Australian towns and communities, but what is *pushing* them? For the "Gang of 49", there is no need for active recruitment, with some members being drawn "to the city from regional centres and Aboriginal communities with excitement, quick cash, drugs and alcohol in mind ... Members can be traced to a number of country communities."[19] Some of these communities such as Port Augusta have hinterlands with connections to tradition.

> Most of the lads, as young as ten, have ventured to the city from country Aboriginal communities from places like Port Augusta,

---

17 Littlely, "Crime Club ...", 2010, 4.
18 Ibid.
19 Ibid.

Port Lincoln, the West Coast, Raukkan on the Coorong and Point Pearce on Yorke Peninsula.[20]

One web comment posted in response to Littlely's story, "Behind the door of gang central", included this:

> The Aboriginal offenders who were involved in recent crimes all seem to have ties to the West Coast (Eyre Peninsula). They steal cars and drive down to Adelaide where they commit break and enters before scoring drugs and taking them back to their homes. Their friends and family from the West Coast who live in Adelaide provide protection and support for them and benefit from the proceeds of crimes.[21]

Murray Bridge, about 80 kilometres from Adelaide, is another town that has a link. A key "Gang of 49" leader was arrested and tried in the Murray Bridge Court.[22]

In the regional towns from which these young Aboriginal people are venturing to commit crime in Adelaide, there is despair over lack of safety on the streets. Four of South Australia's regional centres have debated using dog patrols as a solution. In the public debates surrounding plans for dog patrols, two of these towns – west coast's Ceduna[23] and the Spencer Gulf city of Port Augusta[24] – made clear

---

20 Bryan Littlely, "Elders plea to be involved in curbing gang crime", *The Advertiser*, 10 April 2010: http://www.adelaidenow.com.au/news/south-australia/elders-plea-to-be-involved-in-curbing-gang-crime/story-e6frea83-1225852031542

21 "Power to the people of Croydon", one of the Comments on the story: Bryan Littlely, "Behind the door of gang central", *The Advertiser*, 12 April 2010: http://www.adelaidenow.com.au/news/south-australia/behind-the-door-of-gang-central/story-e6frea83-1225852460424

22 Fewster, Schriever and McGregor, 2009, 1 and 6.

23 "Security in Ceduna", *The Nomad*, 11 July 2008: http://www.thegreynomads.com.au; Neil Gillespie, ALRM CEO, in *Your Legal Rights*, Information about the Aboriginal Legal Rights Movement Inc for the Indigenous community of South Australia, Edition 14, June 2008, 2: http://www.alrm.org.au/newsletter/SD.YLR.June%202008.pdf

24 ABC News, "Port Augusta pushes ahead with dog patrols trial", 26 November 2008: http://www.abc.net.au/news/stories/2008/11/26/2430255.htm

that the main problem is Aboriginal public anti-social behaviour and violence. Indeed, Ceduna and Port Augusta have implemented dog patrols to curb public anti-social and violent behaviour.

Whatever we may think of dog patrols, we need to acknowledge the justified fear that triggered such a response. For decades, these mainstream towns have had well-developed Aboriginal services, projects and programs to improve the lives and opportunities of their Aboriginal residents. Some of these programs are outcomes of major reforms, such as self-determination, the RCADC recommendations and the Decade for Reconciliation. Clearly, these well-intended programs have not been effective enough, and too many young Aboriginal residents of these towns remain at serious risk. In Ceduna and Port Augusta, comments from organisations, residents and travellers about dog patrols give a sense of crisis.

Ceduna was the first town to implement the dog patrols. Neil Gillespie, CEO of the Aboriginal Legal Rights Movement, expressed concern that the dogs were unmuzzled:

> Our issues in relation to human rights and social justice are very real. I note the Ceduna Council has unmuzzled security dogs patrolling the foreshores of Ceduna. Whilst I met with the Mayor of Ceduna Council where he assured me the dogs are muzzled, I simply refer the reader to the recent article in the *Advertiser* Newspaper clearly showing the dogs were not muzzled. It appears that we in South Australia are introducing the practices of the former Apartheid regime of South Africa to our fair shores.[25]

In November 2008, the Port Augusta Council approved trial dog patrols for the summer:

> They will coincide with Aboriginal families travelling down from the APY lands in the far north over the school holidays and have been labelled racist.

---
25 Gillespie, 2008.

> [The mayor, Joy Baluch] says the patrols are only a three month trial to see whether there will be a reduction in vandalism and other crime.[26]

When the trial was due to end, a petition to maintain the dog patrols, which seemed to be curbing the numbers of loiterers, collected 700 signatures.[27] By September 2009, the situation in Port Augusta appeared to have become worse, with community leaders warning that "Port Augusta is heading for an 'explosion' because local police are failing to control rampaging gangs of young people".[28] Note that Aboriginal people are among the innocent victims. Aboriginal elder, Aaron Stuart, a former policeman, contacted *The Advertiser* and said he

> was disgusted that police twice hung up on his mother when she had rocks thrown through the front window ...
>
> Four youths were heard threatening to "murder" whoever was inside the house before using rocks to smash the window just before 2 am.
>
> "My mother is nearly 70 and she was shaking, hysterical and frightened and rang the police and they hung up on her twice so she rang me," Mr Stuart said.
>
> Mr Stuart, 41, said he went to the Port Augusta police station, where it took him some time and a "full-on discussion" to convince officers to attend his mother's home.
>
> "The policing service is the worst in the world. It should be a service to our community but the police here are too gutless to do anything," he said.
>
> Mr Stuart said groups of youths – mainly Aboriginal – were targeting elderly people and using mobile phones to set up all-in brawls in the town.

---

26 ABC News, 26 November 2008.
27 Nicola Gage, "Petition to save dog patrols", *The Transcontinental*, 25 March 2009: http://www.transcontinental.com.au/article.aspx?id=1469570
28 Andrew Dowdell, "Port Augusta elder warns of explosion of gang violence", *The Advertiser*, 4 September 2009: http://www.adelaidenow.com.au/news/in-depth/port-augusta-elder-warns-of-explosion-of-gang-violence/story-fn31yuc0-1225769553231

"What they do is send one carload to a house, start a fight, then send a text or ring their friends who are in two other cars around the corner and they also join in," he said.[29]

Port Augusta's mayor, Joy Baluch, also expressed alarm over police inaction:

> "People being hassled in their homes are sick and tired of ringing the coppers and saying this is happening and the first question they ask is 'Are they black?'," she said ...
>
> Mrs Baluch said the violence had been going on for several years but had reached "boiling point" in recent months, adding that much of the conflict came between rival tribes, of which there are 28 living in Port Augusta ...
>
> Mrs Baluch said Mrs Stuart was a "good-living" member of the community who kept to herself and would have done nothing to incur the wrath of street gangs.[30]

The "Gang of 49" has received high-level attention for years now, including the South Australian Police Operation Mandrake and South Australia's 2006-11 Commissioner for Social Inclusion, Monsignor David Cappo. In his 2007 report, *To Break the Cycle*, Cappo made 46 recommendations, including a set that "focuses specifically on addressing the offending by young people identified through Operation Mandrake and the communities in which they live."[31] In 2010, while the South Australian government said it had implemented 42 of the recommendations, Cappo was disillusioned with the government's response:

> "We're not seeing the real engagement, particularly with young kids coming out of institutional care. We haven't got the right supports in place for them, the right joined-up support services

---

29 Ibid.
30 Ibid.
31 Monsignor David Cappo AO, *To Break the Cycle: Prevention and rehabilitation responses to serious repeat offending by young people*, Report, 2007: http://www.socialinclusion.sa.gov.au/files/breakthecycle2007.pdf

and so I don't think we're seeing any real change in behaviours," he said.

"We know we have a very hardcore group of young offenders whose behaviour, violent behaviour, is escalating.

"I don't want in six months' time to have to ... report that we've had the death of someone, a bystander, someone involved in one of those crimes."[32]

Cappo's report emphasises that the difficulty in engaging with these young offenders resides in their highly disaffected backgrounds, including violence in the family home:

> It was evident through the consultation process that young people were aware that these family experiences helped shape their behaviour. Many young people spoke of escaping the chaos of the family home – chaos shaped by substance abuse, gambling, overcrowding and violence. They spoke of being unsupervised from a very young age and of siblings "growing each other up". This can often produce, from a very young age, an independence of spirit and physicality in interacting with other children ... When escaping the chaos of home, some young people spoke of taking younger siblings with them to protect them. This often resulted in very young children becoming involved in petty crime with older siblings and other relations ... [33]
>
> Simply put, many young people who go on to become serious repeat offenders have come from circumstances that have involved neglect and abuse. This experience has not gone unnoticed by our child protection systems, but the child protection systems have not been able to intervene effectively to bring about its cessation. Consequently, the lives of these young people have continued on a trajectory toward hopelessness, criminality, violence, endangering the lives of others and, sometimes, self-destruction.[34]

---

32 ABC News, "SA scores '1 out of 10' on youth crime fight", 4 June 2010: http://www.abc.net.au/news/stories/2010/06/03/2916932.htm *For more recent reports of gang and other violence, see Australian Database of Indigenous Violence: http://indigenousviolence.org

33 Cappo, 2007, 13.

34 Ibid, 15.

"Child protection systems have not been able to intervene effectively" is a tragic indicator that something is deeply, systemically amiss with policy. The implementation of dog patrols by regional towns is an outcome of decades of policy and program failure to address Aboriginal anti-social and violent behaviour. Field work in Viewtown gave me an opportunity to examine why such well-intentioned and hopeful policies of self-determination could result in such disaster.

**Violence: Attitudes and experiences in Viewtown**

During the mid 1990s, I undertook field work in a small regional city with a minority Aboriginal population. I call this place Viewtown. Comprehensive service surveys that I conducted found that Viewtown's human services, including police, came into contact with about 10 times the rate of Aboriginal people, compared to white people, associated with violence and domestic violence: as victims, perpetrators, or as a member of a family where violence is occurring. Non-Aboriginal residents more readily sought preventive help such as counselling and support groups, while Aboriginal violence cases were over-represented in the emergency services such as medical services and police.

As in other mainstream towns and cities, there are many places for segregation in Viewtown including separate Aboriginal community centre, health centre, women's centre, pre-school centre, employment program, education program, housing program, recreation and sporting facilities including a separate football team and clubrooms, and programs for young people. Gathered together away from the mainstream, women would gossip about violence – a confronting phenomenon to observe. Gillian Cowlishaw's insight in her Mount Druitt study is poignantly relevant:

> if we bypass the spokespersons or representatives, who are the ones listened to because they speak the language of governments, and get close to these marginal people, their conditions become

more complex and baffling ... The ability to live with violence, to ignore contempt and to laugh at insult, or to display aggression towards elusive sources of injury, are disturbing to outsiders. But further, these problematic qualities that we want to explain as consequences of subordination, and therefore remediable, may be valued as elements of a normal environment, a familiar homely style of interaction, a *habitus*.[35]

Violence among people they knew seemed to elicit women's amusement more than disapproval or sympathy. Even among women concerned about violence, it could be tempered by other priorities. One woman related her concern about Aboriginal domestic violence, and the lack of appropriate responses. Nevertheless her attitude emerged that male violence against a female partner is justifiable:

> The man would be out all day at work or CDEP, then come home, start drinking and bashes her – and why would he bash her? She must have given him some reason to do it!

Such "blaming the victim" was more forthcoming than sympathy. "If he hit her, she must have done something wrong", "she wasn't a good mother", "she didn't keep the house clean", "she couldn't handle the household money" are some excuses Viewtown Aboriginal women make for male violence against a partner. While female victims are seen as "deserving" of domestic violence, such violence does not give positive status to the men who commit it. Rather, they are to be protected from such accusation. The process results in Aboriginal women being further victimised. A woman "bringing shame" onto an Aboriginal man by publicly declaring that he beat her, for instance by going to the women's shelter, can engender sympathy for the man even from professional Aboriginal women, and condemnation of the woman for sullying his good name. Aboriginal community anger is thus focused onto the female victim, and the need for the man to feel

---

[35] Gillian Cowlishaw, *The City's Outback*, University of New South Wales Press, Sydney, 2009, 214.

"shame" is thereby reduced. Perhaps this arises more in mainstream towns, where one's public status depends upon mainstream opinions too. Preventing Viewtown victims from causing shame to offenders may thus be a public attempt to hold at bay the mainstream principle that domestic violence is unethical. For to admit that would be to threaten the traditional acceptability of male control of women through violence.

Regarding the extent to which life in Viewtown leads to a reduction in traditional forms of violence against women, a white professional's positive note is qualified:

> In my conversations with the traditional Aboriginal prison inmates, I have discovered that the Aboriginal traditional community in the [nearby hinterland] is very male-dominant. I have heard talk of men's right to crack women's skulls if they as much as utter certain male-only terms, especially when they are drunk. That is, when the men are sober other conditioners are able to work in preventing the violence, but when they are drunk these other barriers are reduced and there's an increase in the traditional rights as the main determinant of the action. The result is that terrible violence against women occurs …
>
> I don't think that such traditional justification of violence has survived with such specificity in Viewtown. However, male domination in the Viewtown Aboriginal community has survived in more general terms. I have never heard of women having equivalent rights versus men regarding men transgressing women's language and space, in either the urban or traditional context.

Continued approval or practice of various forms of traditional violence were observed in Viewtown, including violence against adults for family transgressions. The following tale received nods and words of approval from some women, while others listened in silence:

> GM's done something "wrong way" to the family. He's got it coming to him from his people! So he's not going back there,

he's staying away from "Sandytown" for sure. Because he knows that when he goes there he faces a beating from his family. But it's not right, he should go to "Sandytown", because he must take what is due to him.

There is payback too. Viewtown demonstrates that escalation of violence through payback can persist into urban life. In the words of a young Aboriginal woman,

> The police are often too frightened to intervene, because in an Aboriginal domestic violence incident, you're not only dealing with a couple, but you're dealing with the whole families of both persons. Payback is really big here.
> 
> *What do you mean by "whole families" and "payback"?*
> 
> Families come in to take one side of the fight against the other, so whole families become involved in the dispute, and the paybacks can spread on and on, go on and on, for a long time. This makes it hard for the police, with so many people involved like this in a fight. But the police can also become victims directly in this payback, and so they are quite often too scared to act.

Amidst these accounts of violence, I became aware of a malaise, based on fear, in Viewtown's race relations. A white resident related it thus:

> Aboriginal people in this town live in a deep and freezing fear of one another. They are not really afraid of whites. Rather, the shoe is on the other foot: whites live in fear of Aboriginals.

Fear of Aboriginal violence was commonplace among Viewtown's white residents. This fear was heightened by a greater prevalence among Aboriginal Viewtowners to respond violently to even trivial social upsets. Their fear arose from several sources: witnessing Aboriginal fights; a relative or friend being physically assaulted by an Aboriginal person; being personally "menaced" by an Aboriginal person; or by being aware of Aboriginal violence through friendships and family ties with Aboriginal people. Men and women, young and old, the wealthy, working people, welfare recipients, white people who befriend, partner with, and sympathise through to those who resent and avoid Aboriginal people, and professional people working with Aboriginal clients, are among those who hold these fears.

Aboriginal violence, more than any other factor, strained non-Aboriginal Viewtowners' genuine attempts to be non-racist. A common non-Aboriginal response to Aboriginal violence was retreat from contact with Aboriginal people: to spend money on increasing home security, to shift locations within Viewtown, to change their children's schools, to avoid befriending Aboriginal people, to limit their use of time, space and services within Viewtown, or to shift out of Viewtown altogether, in a bid to secure physical safety by separating themselves from Aboriginal people. At the same time, many of these non-Aboriginal Viewtowners identified Aboriginal separate services and spaces as exacerbating Aboriginal violence, and called for more shared public services and facilities. A Viewtown woman who is committed to social justice and abhors racism illustrates the harm of violence to good race relations:

> I'm very concerned about how racist my daughter has become. She even calls them "boongs" now. I had to transfer my daughter out of the public high school because of the behaviour of the Aboriginal students ... When she was alone in the toilets a group of Aboriginal girls ambushed and bashed her up. Now my daughter hates Aboriginal people.

Indeed, non-Aboriginal women in Viewtown were not infrequent victims of domestic violence committed by Aboriginal partners. One professional explained a particular vulnerability:

> The only reason that he has gone for a white girlfriend is that he is well known as an exceptionally violent man even among the local Aboriginal women, and so they won't have him. The local Aboriginal girls are "street-wise" to the worst of the violent

men among them, but the white girls are not. She has tried to get away from him but he has always found her and she's gone back to him out of fear.

## City life and self-determination: no solution

Viewtown is an exemplar of the self-determination model in an ideal setting. If the basic premise of self-determination were correct, the Aboriginal people of Viewtown should be thriving. Viewtown has a strong mainstream economy, a well-intentioned white population that would like more Aboriginal participation in mainstream life, and its Aboriginal population has a comprehensive array of well-funded separate services and programs meant to assist Aboriginal people to be healthy, well-educated, well-housed and employed.

Rather than a solution, self-determination is a chief culprit. Its fostering of separation and difference has resulted in Aboriginal family and community life in Viewtown becoming conflict-ridden along the lines of "local"–"outsider" competition, male rights, extended family expectations, and an anti-white, "you owe us" sentiment. These are incompatible with participation in mainstream economy and social life. Furthermore, a traditionally-derived norm of violence means that these lines of conflict are triggers for violence. Compounding this conflict and violence, the separate, unemployed lifestyle of too many Aboriginal Viewtowners has fuelled despair, drunkenness, drug abuse, gambling and child neglect.

While cities are safer than remote communities, reducing urban Aboriginal violence and upholding victim safety entails a shift away from separate urban services and places, and more emphasis on integration. For the sake of urban victims of Aboriginal violence, for the sake of the disaffected, out-of-control young Aboriginal people in our towns and cities, and for the sake of healthy race relations, we have no other option.

# Shedding tradition's violent shackles

> Let me ask you this – it's an almost impossible question to ask a prosecutor and I appreciate that before I start – but how do you actually deal with this without pulling apart the traditional culture which is sustaining it?
>
> – Tony Jones, interviewing Nanette Rogers[1]

Our insistence that white colonisation is the key culprit in today's Aboriginal violence has hindered the nation from reacting with due distress to the "normality" of violence in traditional Aboriginal Australia. Programs shaped by the premise that Aboriginal violence is caused mainly by white colonisation include cultural restoration, incorporation of customary law into judicial procedures, community and women's empowerment, and perpetrator healing, within the self-determination framework.[2] Night patrols and women's shelters are often essential adjuncts to these programs.[3] As an example, the Aboriginal Family Violence Strategy incorporates some of these principles and "emphasises that solutions to family violence must":

- Come from within the community.
- Build on customary and contemporary structures and practices.

---

1 Jones, 15 June 2006.
2 See Sutton, 2001, 149-50, regarding the limits of "healing programs" for Aboriginal alcohol dependence, quoting M. Brady "Introducing brief interventions for indigenous alcohol misuse: can doctors make a difference?", Paper presented at Australian Institute of Aboriginal and Torres Strait Islander Studies seminar, 18 September 2000.
3 See Calma, 2007, Part 2 (f), "Safe Houses: a tool against family violence" (i) Yuendumu 2007, 151. See also T. Calma, *Ending family violence and abuse in Aboriginal and Torres Strait Islander communities – Key issues: An overview paper of research by the Human Rights and Equal Opportunity Commission*, 2001-2006, June 2006, 7-8: http://www.humanrights.gov.au/social_justice/familyviolence

- Further strengthen the skills and competence of individuals/families, and the capacity of communities to respond to this and other issues.
- Adopt whole-of-community planning and integrate women's and men's voices in decision making.
- money paid by the government for the benefit of children is directed to the priority needs of children.[4]

Also included are major measures such as the NTER and the South Australian Mullighan Inquiry,[5] which aim to modify Aboriginal violent and other dysfunctional behaviours in remote, traditional contexts on the premise (or hope) that effective intervention is compatible with the *in situ* traditional culture. Some of these programs may be worth undertaking, but we need to be aware of their limits and what they leave untouched and unchallenged.

Aboriginal traditional culture includes customary aspects – particularly its condoning of the individual resort to violence – that are maladaptive to the modern world that Aboriginal people, like all of us, have no choice but to adapt to. Self-determination thus thwarts and delays Aboriginal people's ability to make essential adaptive changes. While self-determination helps keep alive the many praiseworthy, unique aspects of Australia's first culture, it also perpetuates the culture's high acceptability of violence as a means to uphold traditional law, control others, and settle conflicts. Worsening this, competition for sought-after mainstream goods such as jobs, money, housing and land can generate additional conflict and violence in poorly integrated Aboriginal communities, where access to such things is too often based on contested, traditionally or historically derived

---

4 Al-Yaman *et al*, 2006, 12. See also SuccessWorks, Courage Partners, and Morgan Disney Associates, "Appendix 3: Literature Review", *Evaluation of the Family Violence Activities Program (FVRAP) Final Report*, Appendices, 2005, esp. 17-21: http://www.fahcsia.gov.au/sa/indigenous/pubs/families/fvrap/Documents/FRVAP_Final_Report_Appendices.pdf

5 Mullighan Inquiry, 2008.

entitlements rather than individual merit. Given mainstream culture's high requirement for non-violent behaviour, this conflict-ridden approach to accessing things is maladaptive. Self-determination also helps perpetuate a sense of being "other" from mainstream society, and thus a candidate for special consideration as "first peoples", and a victim of white invasion. This can intensify the sense of entitlement to things without personal endeavour, which is corrosive to mental health, personal responsibility and race relations. The principle of self-determination also inhibits effective policy, judicial and service intervention into Aboriginal violence. Indeed, our legal systems have at times accommodated, even condoned some forms of Aboriginal violence. It seems that Aboriginal self-determination entails a national obligation to care less about Aboriginal victims of Aboriginal violence. What a travesty.

The Australian nation is profoundly concerned about the level of Aboriginal violence. There is a consensus that violence in Aboriginal communities, particularly by men against women, and the level of child abuse, are at catastrophic levels. At the same time, Aboriginal culture must not be criticised. This logic necessitates a consensus that the violence sits outside the culture, and a pretence that the violence can be extracted without fundamental alterations to Aboriginal culture. As Hirsi Ali has so powerfully signalled, the West's commitment to unrestrained multiculturalism renders it difficult to address irreconcilable cultural *clash*.[6] For the sake of everyone's well-being – in the majority, indigenous and minority migrant populations – it is imperative that liberal democracies welcome diversity without accommodating to customs that are maladaptive and which violate human rights. Regarding Aboriginal violence, policy-making based on the premise that Aboriginal traditional culture contains maladaptive violence norms and practices would be a significant advance. At the very least, the nation could then develop

---

6 Hirsi Ali, 2010.

a more accurate understanding of the tasks and challenges required to reduce Aboriginal violence.

Reducing Aboriginal violence is not primarily about advocating for more or better women's shelters, night patrols, police stations, anti-violence education programs, alcohol and drug programs and restrictions, or longer sentences for Aboriginal perpetrators of violence. While such measures may have crucial roles in securing victim safety, they have been unable to address the ability of separate Aboriginal communities, either in remote, discrete locations, or in the cities, to expunge norms of violence. If we keep to a self-determination model, we will keep needing crisis responses, major enquiries and interventions, and decades more of assaulted Aboriginal women facing the terrible dilemma of abandoning their country and their community, to get some safety. We will keep having to endure the painful dilemma of leaving Aboriginal children in households and communities of chronic neglect and abuse, or taking them away to a place of safety to live their lives with the indelible pain of being removed from their families.

Writing this book has confirmed for me the conclusion that mainstreaming or integration is the necessary path if we are to overcome the traditional acceptability of Aboriginal violence. Both Sutton and Hirsi Ali have brought my attention to a reverse way of looking at this: that maladaptive traditional practices inhibit integration,[7] because they are major inhibitors to establishing successful pathways into the mainstream and its many social, physical and economic benefits. While integration is needed to overcome the traditional acceptability of violence, conversely, the violence itself impedes this necessary integration. The other important way of interpreting the continuity of traditional violence is as a sign of the failure to integrate. The nation's policies of encouraging separatism, self-determination and cultural

---

7  Sutton, 2009; and Hirsi Ali, 2010.

continuity, rather than equipping Aboriginal people with a benign or empowering self-sufficiency, have trapped them in an oppressive, violent, non-Enlightenment culture. The only way to counter this is to develop effective pathways to the mainstream.

# 10
# Aboriginal men's apology for violence

A positive, unexpected outcome of the NTER is the Central Australian Aboriginal Congress (CAAC) Aboriginal men's public apology for violence against women and children. This apology – the Inteyerrkwe Statement – was made in 2008 at a Central Australian Aboriginal male health summit attended by nearly 400 men:

> We the Aboriginal males from Central Australia and our visitor brothers from around Australia gathered at Inteyerrkwe in July 2008 to develop strategies to ensure our future roles as husbands, grandfathers, fathers, uncles, nephews, brothers, grandsons and sons in caring for our children in a safe family environment that will lead to a happier, longer life that reflects opportunities experienced by the wider community.
>
> We acknowledge and say sorry for the hurt, pain and suffering caused by Aboriginal males to our wives, to our children, to our mothers, to our grandmothers, to our granddaughters, to our aunties, to our nieces and to our sisters.[1]

The Inteyerrkwe Statement was delivered by John Liddle, manager of the (CAAC) Aboriginal Male Health Summit 2008, and was signed by Summit participants. The Summit, which was "organised as a response to the Federal intervention",[2] includes practical

---

1 Central Australian Aboriginal Congress Inc. (CAAC), *Aboriginal Male Health Summit 2008, Taking care of our children, taking the next steps*: http://www.caac.org.au/malehealthinfo
2 Alice Brennan, "Indigenous men apologise for violence", ABC, *Lateline*, 3 July 2008, transcript: http://www.abc.net.au/lateline/content/2008/s2293873.htm

measures and goals to improve men's behaviour and their chances to "reach their true potential and take their place alongside the wider community". Proposed outcomes of the Summit include that "200-300 Indigenous males attend a summit that increases their knowledge of the responsibilities required of a parent or community member in providing for their children"; and, "delegates have an enhanced understanding of changes required under the NT Intervention to support children and their families".[3] The process is an ongoing one.[4]

The Summit goals' emphasis on personal responsibility, reaching one's potential, and lining up with the goals of the Intervention, is inspiring and deserves support, because it recognises that Aboriginal men need to be active participants in improving their own lives, and the lives of their families and communities. Joe Hayes, who lives on an outstation near Alice Springs, said he "walked away from the gathering a proud Aborigine", and said, "We have got to try to be responsible parents and our attitudes have got to change ... saying sorry is the best part of healing."[5]

It is therefore with a heavy heart that I write about obstacles facing the Inteyerrkwe Statement's goal of reducing Aboriginal male violence. Indeed, there are barriers evident in the reasons for organising the Aboriginal Male Health Summit, in the core of the Summit goals, and in reported responses to the Inteyerrkwe apology. Moreover, these barriers arise from the problematic context of Aboriginal self-determination, which downplays pre-contact violence and emphasises colonial causes of Aboriginal men's violence against women.

On the CAAC website, *Aboriginal Male Health Summit 2008*, under the heading "Why an Aboriginal male health summit", three

---

[3] CAAC, 2008.
[4] For example, CAAC, *Stop the Violence, Inteyerrkwe Journey of Family Violence Prevention Workshop*, 10-14 May 2010: http://www.caac.org.au/stoptheviolence/
[5] Tara Ravens, "Aboriginal men say sorry to women", *Herald Sun*, 4 July 2008: http://www.heraldsun.com.au/news/national/aboriginal-men-say-sorry-to-women/story-e6frf7l6-1111116814778

points are featured. The first is to "Better understand issues being faced by children in communities". The second is to "Address the stereo type casting [*sic*] 'labels' (drunk, unemployed, paedophiles just to name a few) that have been placed on all Aboriginal men since the release of the *Little Children are Sacred* report and the subsequent NT intervention." The third point is to address a range of issues that make it difficult for men to make good lifestyle choices, such as never having "experienced a stable family life themselves", childhood abuse and neglect, and "stolen generation issues".[6] While these all have validity, the issues in points two and three have been canvassed for years in an attempt to take the heat off Aboriginal men for their violence against women. Wife-murderer Alwyn Peter got a reduced sentence and much public sympathy through such emphasis in the 1991 film *State of Shock*.[7] In the 1990s in Adelaide, I saw a conference workshop's attempt to discuss Aboriginal women's victimisation to violence collapse under the weight of this concern for Aboriginal men's standing. Is the problem that some Aboriginal men might be unfairly blamed seen as a greater issue than the appalling rate of Aboriginal women suffering violence? The Summit points' focus on factors that assuage men's personal responsibility can also be disabling, because even while it seeks to engage men as active, responsible agents in reducing family violence, it depicts Aboriginal men as victims rather than masters of their own actions.

At the same time, it is understandably a keenly-felt injustice to be stereotyped as violent when one is not. We all need to state clearly that many Aboriginal men are not violent, and many Aboriginal men such as Liddle work to reduce violence in their communities. It is the *higher rate of violence* among Aboriginal men that is the issue.

While under the heading "Goals of Summit" are exemplary aims, the same website continues this concern about unfair male shaming, as

---

6 CAAC, 2008.
7 David Bradbury, *State of Shock*, 1991.

well as denying traditional origins of the violence, as seen in Goal 1:

> Acknowledge the hurt caused by a proportion of the male community against family and community members through violent acts, which are not historical cultural practices, which is shaming many Indigenous males who are not violent.[8]

Responses from some delegates to the Inteyerrkwe apology suggest that the barriers to addressing Aboriginal male violence might prove too great in a self-determination context. Under the heading, "Apologetic Indigenous men not accepting total blame" ABC Radio's *PM* reported a view among Summit attendees that the Intervention "has damaged how men are seen by their families, and also how they see themselves". Also, not all the men "accept responsibility for the violence that led to the emergency response". Philip Wilika, an elder from Titjikala community, Central Australia, expressed his concerns:

> (*speaks in Aboriginal language*) So what I'm saying is about, you know our grandfathers haven't taught us to live what we are living now and now, with bureaucrats pointing fingers and blaming Aboriginal people for the wrong that they've been doing against their own family which isn't true.
>
> (*sound of applause*) ...
>
> I hope you politicians have a time out with us here because the main issues we been talking about, that people, bureaucrats always put the blame on black, Aboriginal men ...
>
> We are all proud men and we're cultural men and we are loving fathers, uncles and nephews. So to say a word to the bureaucrats who are blaming Aboriginal people are stupid and bastards, but we are not![9]

While clearly concerned to address the violence, Liddle was also concerned about the misrepresentation of Aboriginal men:

---

8 CAAC, 2008.

9 Eric Tlozek, "Apologetic Indigenous men not accepting total blame", ABC, *PM*, 3 July 2008, transcript: http://www.abc.net.au/pm/content/2008/s2294058.htm

> After the intervention, and before the intervention a lot of men felt like they were mistreated and misunderstood ...
>
> I actually had guys come into our men's health service, who told us that they feel guilty to walk down the street, to stand in a line at the shopping centre, because they can feel people are looking at them, and almost accusing them of being paedophiles and wife bashers and those types of things.[10]

Rex Wild QC, one of the authors of the *Little Children Are Sacred* report, was in the audience when the Inteyerrkwe apology was delivered. He commented that

> child abuse was not just an Aboriginal problem and it had been unfair of governments to single them out. "They are not acknowledging that there is a higher rate," he said. "They are acknowledging that there is a rate – that there is a level of domestic violence they have now said sorry for."[11]

ABC's *Lateline* pointed to further troubling aspects of the Summit:

> While the men present their resolutions to politicians and bureaucrats, there's still one group we are yet to hear from, and that's the women who are so often the silent victims of domestic violence and abuse.
>
> And some issues were difficult to resolve.
>
> (*To John Liddle*): No resolutions made about when yes means yes and no means no?
>
> *John Liddle:* No.
>
> *Alice Brennan:* Why not, it seems to be a big issue?
>
> *John Liddle:* It is a big issue, but there wasn't a resolution.
>
> *Alice Brennan:* Why not?
>
> *John Liddle:* That's a good question.[12]

---

10 Tlozek, 2008.
11 Ravens, 2008.
12 Tlozek, 2008.

Two years later, in May 2010, CAAC held the Inteyerrkwe Journey of Family Violence Prevention Workshop. In the media release before the event, Liddle gave categoric emphasis to the greater severity of violence in the Aboriginal population, and on the need for zero tolerance, "to not just reduce the violence but actually stop the violence":

> Like most Aboriginal males in Central Australia I am sick of going to funerals and seeing our courts, jails, health clinics and hospital filled with brothers and sisters who have been involved in family violence.
>
> It is time Aboriginal males stood up both morally and culturally, taking positive action and a zero tolerance approach to stop excessive violence in families, communities and towns, a crisis that is having a devastating effect on community members of all ages and genders, especially the children ...
>
> In the past our ancestors walked together with mutual respect, where legitimate authority was culturally sanctioned and leadership earned ...
>
> Government at all levels, Federal, Territory, and local, have for years funded libraries of research, developed hundreds of strategies, plans and media campaigns but not enough will be achieved unless the majority of Aboriginal males become part of the grass roots solution taking action every time violence occurs.[13]

These are powerful, heartfelt words, indicating that strong Aboriginal men such as Liddle are critically objectifying the violence in their communities, close to the process of "rethinking culture" that Sutton writes "might prove beneficial".[14] While Liddle's words state the problem, however, they do not indicate an imminent solution, and beg questions regarding the dearth of Aboriginal community action against violence. In particular, if "most Aboriginal males in Central

---

13 CAAC, 2010.
14 Sutton, 2001, 156.

Australia" are "sick of going to funerals and seeing our courts, jails, health clinics and hospital filled with brothers and sisters who have been involved in family violence", why has there not been an effective movement among Aboriginal men in Central Australia against family violence before now? If the Intervention's shaming of men and hence their concern for men's public standing was the catalyst, rather than any previously held grief at the suffering of Aboriginal women victims, how confident can we be in the long-term impact of the Inteyerrkwe apology?

Also, Liddle does not make a critical assessment of traditional culture itself. How confident can we be in yet another program which evokes a traditional past based on "mutual respect" but makes no mention of the harsh pre-contact violence, and which attributes all causes for Aboriginal violence to post-contact injustices? Nevertheless, breakthroughs can happen in unexpected ways, and perhaps the Inteyerrkwe Statement signals that the Intervention's painful mass shaming of Aboriginal men is a catalyst for improving behaviour. The Intervention's unfair labelling of Aboriginal men who are not violent may even increase its beneficial impact by mobilising non-violent Aboriginal men to be positive mentors, and to work on improving the behaviour of others in their communities.[15]

We are, however, dependent on the premise that the Aboriginal men who are violent can be persuaded that there is more value in giving up violent behaviour than in maintaining it. In non-integrated community settings where traditional gender and family power relations and norms about violence remain intact, the need to choose non-violence may not be so obvious. We should also remember that many women in these communities are violent. Gender relations can be very conflicted, jealousy-ridden in these communities, presenting a particularly challenging setting for change. Also, shaming is a complex state of mind. Shame is a sign that the person cares about

---

15 I am indebted to Irene Franklin for this important insight.

their standing in a community. That Aboriginal men care about how they are perceived by mainstream people in the supermarkets of Alice Springs is a positive, adaptive response. Nevertheless for years before the Intervention, Aboriginal people have experienced the discomfort of white condemnation and public shaming of male perpetrators. Unfortunately, one community response is to rally around the perpetrator and condemn the woman who by seeking help sullied his name.

Like multitudinous government reports, CAAC Inteyerrkwe Aboriginal men's anti-violence summits display an apparent "wilful blindness"[16] to traditional causes of violence, preferring to focus on white causes. Such a restrictive agenda is likely to limit any attempts to reduce male violence. Organisers and participants at such anti-violence programs do want to reduce violence, and their programs may well have beneficial impacts. There are, however, resilient, traditional forces which allow, even require, the settlement of transgressions and conflict through violent means. It is these traditional forces that must be overcome, but at this cultural level, too few seem willing to admit to, let alone tackle, the problem. It is a lot to expect a community to change its core cultural practices. Perhaps the denial responses to the Inteyerrkwe Apology, and CAAC insistence that the causes of the violence are post-contact are (along with all such denials across the country) attempts to evade the confronting reality that to give up violence is to threaten core aspects of traditional culture including its law, gender hierarchy and kinship obligations. Sowell has identified a critical dilemma in cultural choices such as these:

> The values of a culture are revealed by the choices actually made – and sacrifices endured – in pursuing some desired goals at the expense of other desired goals. The fact that many different groups may regard many of the same things as desirable does not mean that they will all exhibit the same patterns of trade-offs

---

16 Sutton's term, see above.

when actually confronted with the inevitable sacrifices of the real world, as distinguished from the costless choices of attitude surveys. Education and personal safety may be valued by a wide range of human beings in a great variety of cultures, but what they are prepared to do – to sacrifice – in pursuit of those goals varies enormously.[17]

Perhaps this is a partial explanation for the discordance between the men's distress at going to too many funerals, jails and hospital visits due to violent injury and death, and the high rate of Aboriginal male violence that continues around them. Sowell's confronting observation is central to the difficulty of expunging Aboriginal violence. Violence may indeed be a shameful thing in the contemporary world, but without the threat or use of the instrument of violence, can traditionally-deemed transgressions be punished and settled, traditional male authority be maintained, and traditional kinship obligations such as promised marriage be upheld?

Robinson's 2008 article, "Secrets in the shadows", suggests that the Intervention is a fundamental challenge to aspects of traditional culture. While referring to "perverted" traditional law, Robinson's article portrays the strength of customary law in remote cultures, and its continuing utility as a source of power and intimidation. Some of the opposition to the Intervention emanates from its threat to expose and eliminate violent and corrupt community power structures, steeped in traditional forms and expressed in contemporary contexts. Robinson writes of a tragic incident near Papunya, central Australia:

> Months ago, a 14-year-old boy dropped dead after a footy match in Mount Liebig, about 70 km down the road to the west. Senior men have been on the warpath ever since. The boy's death was nobody's fault, but this is a world where payback, retribution, spearings and mob violence are ever-present. Since the boy's death in February, clan clashes have rocked Papunya and Mount

---

17 Sowell, 1994, 10.

Liebig. The perpetrators from powerful families call it payback. Rather, it is traditional law perverted to maintain the power and status of the men who are fighting to maintain an iron grip on their homelands in the face of the biggest intervention in indigenous affairs in recent history.[18]

The profound and violent community upset that ensues when traditional violent punishment practices are forbidden by Western law is another illustration of how difficult it can be to change a culture's very different, utilitarian attitudes to violence. In November 2009, it was reported that

> senior Indigenous people in the Northern Territory have called on the Prime Minister to officially recognise their customary laws including traditional punishments such as spearing ...
>
> They argue that traditional punishment is not against human rights and in fact, they say it helps promote peace in communities. It helps reduce violence in their view and brings down the number of Indigenous people going to jail.[19]

In 2009, the documentary film *Bush Law* was made about this call for customary law recognition. An extract from the ABC's report on this film conveys the support and justification for such a recognition:

> Billy Bunter from the remote community of Lajamanu ... wants the Government to officially recognise customary law, including the system of traditional punishment often known as payback.
>
> He wants the courts to grant bail to Indigenous offenders so they can face traditional punishment before going to jail.
>
> He says the failure to carry out payback means the matter is never settled according to Aboriginal law. As a result, revenge attacks between the families of the victim and the accused ensue ...
>
> The punishments Billy Bunter and others in the film want

---

18 Robinson, 2008.
19 ABC News, "Indigenous leaders urge recognition of traditional punishments", 28 November 2009: http://www.abc.net.au/news/stories/2009/11/28/2756266.htm

recognised range from public shaming to spearing in the leg for the most serious crimes.
He says the intention of spearing someone is not to kill them. He says the payback is controlled to make sure the injury is not worse than intended.[20]

The film's producer, lawyer Danielle Loy, while at first "not convinced", expressed her support. Is such support a sign of her (and other lawyers') pessimism that non-violent solutions are at times impossible in traditional Aboriginal culture?

> "Hearing over and over stories of when traditional punishment had taken place and the peace that had come to the community and hearing stories over and over of when traditional punishment couldn't take place and joining the dots as to why two families had been warring for 20 years," she said.
>
> "I don't believe it is [the state condoning violence]. Who am I to say that it is violent to do that when if it is not done, 30, 40 ... 100 people are hurt and they are not hurt properly?
>
> "It is not done in a regulated manner. It is done in random drunken stabbings or catching someone in the bushes or at a football match ...
>
> "Let's codify it. Let's do the same we do with our legislation. What is our alternative? We are just going to go up and up and up and up in crime. No one wants that. Everyone wants peace."[21]

Our Western legal system has already experienced a period of allowing traditional punishment under controlled circumstances. Although this was officially abandoned in the mid 1990s,[22] traditional, controlled punishments witnessed by Western officials have occurred since then. A Northern Territory Supreme Court hearing of a man from Utopia accused of murdering his customary law wife in 2002 documents his witnessed payback thus:

---

20 Ibid.
21 Ibid.
22 Northern Territory police officer, pers. comm., 2010.

> Whilst on bail ... the accused underwent payback whilst at Ti Tree ... The payback took place in the presence of a registered nurse ... as well as a police officer ... who were requested to attend by the elders. The payback took the form of the accused being hit with nulla nullas by various members of both his family and the family of the deceased. Quite a number of blows were delivered to the accused's body, particularly on the arms and legs. There were no blows administered above the shoulders. The accused ... said that he was also hit by a boomerang on his back. The blows were delivered over a period of between 15 to 20 minutes; people in groups of three or four came forward, hit the accused a few times, then retreated and, after some discussion, others would come and repeat the punishment. On two occasions, the accused had to be assisted to his feet after he had fallen down as a result of the blows.
>
> When the punishment was completed, he was assisted onto a stretcher, placed in an ambulance and driven back to the Ti Tree clinic for full assessment ... the accused was able to walk from the ambulance into the examination room.[23]

Do we really want to condone such practice as routine procedure, even as some kind of *solution*? What is more, this physically punished man had only been accused, not convicted.

In reference to controlled physical punishment, Loy asks, "Who am I to say that it is violent ... ?" and "What is our alternative?" Her stand may be reluctant and pragmatic, but it remains disappointing that highly educated Western observers such as Loy seem unwilling or unable to keep a sustained, critical focus on the core problem in traditional culture – another case of "wilful blindness" perhaps. It is unacceptable that when a culture is barred from carrying out traditional violent punishment against an offender, it enacts its irrational compulsion to commit devastating, ongoing violence against innocent kin or other innocent proxies. This inherent catastrophic potential

---

23 *R v Ronnie Pangate Nelson*, NTSC 64 [2003].

should be overcome, not appeased. Who is Loy to say that measured physical punishment to prevent long-term retribution is violent? She is a privileged member of an Enlightenment polity, with a professional, moral obligation to uphold the universal human rights value of non-violence. Not to do so betrays Aboriginal people, and betrays human rights. Loy, and many others like her, have accommodated to a maladaptive Aboriginal practice, thereby prolonging, not alleviating, the suffering.[24] Rather, she should act on the knowledge that change is desperately needed among Aboriginal people for the fundamental reason that violence is universally harmful and wrong, by being there with them to assist in the change process. As Bess Price has so poignantly urged:

> The Racial Discrimination Act was there to protect us from white racism and we needed that protection. But it has not protected our people from ourselves. We need an act, we need laws that recognise that the problem now is blackfellas killing blackfellas and killing themselves. If a law like the Racial Discrimination Act gets in the way of doing that then it must be changed. We are different, we are special, we have special needs. We are caught in a trap. They want us to be citizens with the same rights but then they want us to keep our culture with no changes. How can we do both? We need to do some special things to solve our problems. Now we know that and can do something about it. Let's roll forward instead of backwards.[25]

Dave Price has also written powerfully on this issue:

> It seems to me that the recently renewed support for the legal recognition of Traditional Law has been at least partly prompted by an incident that recently occurred at Lajamanu ... A police woman had driven onto the men's ceremonial grounds while young men were being initiated ... I was very impressed with the dignified way in which the old men of Lajamanu made their protest at the time. I was a lot more concerned with the lack of

---

24  See Hirsi Ali, 2010, xviii.
25  Bess Price, 2009.

reaction to what Lyndsay Bookie, Chairman of the Central Land Council, had to say on ABC TV evening news ... in an interview with Eric Tlozec in response to that incident:

> *"It's against our law for people like that breaking the law, they shouldn't be there. Aboriginal ladies, they're not allowed to go anywhere near that. If they had been caught, a woman, aboriginal lady got caught she [would] be killed. Simple as that."*

I could not see Lyndsay actually killing anyone. He's not that kind of bloke. In fact, it could be said that he was extremely brave to make a statement like this. He only stated in public what all of us who have had anything to do with traditionally minded Aboriginal people in the NT, or anybody who has read the classical anthropological accounts, and all Aboriginal people keeping their languages and traditions, have always known but not wanted to talk about. Both men and women are threatened with execution and grievous bodily harm for offences against the Law. Rape was added to possible punishments in the case of women ... This is a fact of life. Lyndsay didn't invent this Law, it is unchanging, it comes from the Jukurrpa, the Dreaming.

It wasn't Lyndsay's statement that disturbed me so much. It was the deafening silence of the human rights activists, the opponents of capital punishment, of the feminists and domestic violence activists, of that army of righteous whitefellas inflamed by any public expression of what they deem to be racism or sexism that happens to pop up in the public domain, from any other quarter ... So I can only assume that threatening to execute women is OK in Australia as long as it is done by someone who is male and indigenous, it is done for cultural reasons and the women threatened are also indigenous. It's OK. It's their culture. They know the rules. They have to cop it sweet.[26]

While Liddle and CAAC are committed to ending violence in Aboriginal communities, it is reasonable to ask how, in the face of profound, traditional causes. Do CAAC solutions include allowing

---

26 Dave Price, 2009. (Price's emphasis in quote.)

violent traditional punishment? If so, that is surrender to a violent traditional regime. If not, what scope is being envisaged for traditional culture and community, given that in traditional Aboriginal culture, communities can become war-like and dysfunctional when traditional punishments against transgressors are not implemented?

Traditional punishment, moreover, does not always prevent ongoing vendettas. As described by T.G.H. Strehlow, revenge attacks and vendettas occurred when the punished culprit was believed to be falsely identified, or when the punishment was resented by the culprit's relatives even when correctly identified. Given that sorcery (still in use) was a frequent method of identifying a guilty party, questionable and wrongful accusations and ensuing violent dispute and vendetta were inevitable hazards in classical times.[27] There is also the problem, almost certainly more pronounced in the post-contact era, of wrongdoers not voluntarily submitting to traditional physical punishment. Even in times past, there were families who helped alleged wrongdoers flee from punishment, such as the case recorded by Warner of the husband helping his wife flee to the mission to escape execution for her accidental sacred transgression. This case raises yet another issue: the traditional punishment of people for actions (or for being innocent proxies) that on universal human rights grounds are not crimes. "Wrong way" love relationships and marriage, refusal to be a promised bride, accidental sacrilegious acts, and *mirriri* are examples. Non-Aboriginal people can be unwitting victims of traditional punishment as well, such as by unknowingly but wrongly entering a sacred site or ceremony.

Even if Australian governments on grounds of harm minimisation allow traditional physical punishment, there are some settings – wrong or disputed accusation, a person's refusal to submit to traditional punishment, and traditional punishment for non-crimes – where such appeasement is either unworkable or particularly immoral.

---

27 See Chapters 4 and 5.

There are fundamental human rights dangers. On the one hand, there is a minority group's assertive sense of cultural right to implement traditional law, including the right to define what is a crime, the method of judgement, and the method of punishment. On the other, the nation is having great difficulty in facing the reality that to address Aboriginal violence, change is needed in Aboriginal culture itself. The Inteyerrkwe Statement is a positive event. The Intervention generated a response among Aboriginal men against violence on a level not seen before, and some reduction in violence is likely. However, the familiar evasion in the Inteyerrkwe Statement's associated commentaries and programs regarding the traditional generators of violence suggest that cultural reform remains a "no-go" area. As violence has a central role within Aboriginal traditional culture, traditional violence norms are probably too powerful for the Inteyerrkwe Statement to have a major impact in many remote communities.

## 11

# Income Management as a pathway to the mainstream?

The NTER targets a deeper, cultural level for reform than previous attempts to address Aboriginal violence, reflected in: its Income Management (IM) strategy; commitment to increase police presence in townships and smaller communities; diligent pursuit of perpetrators of child sexual abuse; tougher penalties for violence against women; and as catalyst for the CAAC men's apology for violence. Another federal initiative launched in July 2010, the Indigenous Family Safety Program (IFSP), also holds promise. Along with a major study into foetal alcohol spectrum disorder, and more and tougher alcohol restrictions, the IFSP includes "community safety plans ... in 29 remote priority locations" with a focus on "community attitudes to family violence".[1]

Nevertheless, these strategies must still guard against being just more tinkering. For instance, the IFSP draws some inspiration from the CAAC anti-violence summit of 2010 following the men's apology. Such inspiration is good, but this summit romanticises traditional culture as a source of strength against violence, rather than a core source of violence.[2] The federal government's Closing the Gap

---
1 Patricia Karvelas, "Fetal alcohol study set up", *The Weekend Australian*, 17-18 July 2010, 2.
2 FaHCSIA, *Indigenous Family Safety Agenda*, July 2010: http://www.fahcsia.gov.au/sa/indigenous/pubs/families/Documents/indig_family_safety_agenda.pdf

initiative also focuses on changing deeper levels of behaviour,[1] and for this it has attracted criticism. I do not share in Jon Altman's attack on this necessary focus. Nevertheless, his point on the intrusiveness of interventions when cultural contexts resist change has validity. Also, while my answers would differ from Altman's, his questions go to the heart of the problem with trying to achieve essential changes in behaviour and attitude in remote small communities. Altman writes:

> The overarching Closing the Gap framework is driven by a policy imperative "to rebuild the positive social norms that underpin daily routines like going to work and school". But what if work is not available and schooling is either substandard or irrelevant to local opportunity? Or what if people have other priorities and aspirations?
>
> It seems that the Rudd government's notion of social democracy is about enhanced and targeted state intervention, but beneficiaries must ascribe to just one limited set of western values. Where is there room for diversity and difference in pluralistic liberal democratic Australia?
>
> The choice is stark: embrace mainstream values or miss out; the Australian state is not enabling, despite the rhetoric about community-led solutions, but insisting on top-down paternalistic directives ...
>
> The framework's statistical targets are unrealistic given current demographic pressures and historical experience, but the government has persisted with them despite warnings ...
>
> Might Indigenous Australians be entitled to ask for a backflip too from the hegemonic Closing the Gap framework to one that is more pluralistic, realistic, community-driven and of lower risk both for them and the nation?[2]

---

1 Hon. Jenny Macklin, "Closing the Gap, Building Momentum", Statement by FaHCSIA Minister, 11 May 2010: http://www.aph.gov.au/budget/2010-11/content/ministerial_statements/indigenous/download/ms_indigenous.pdf
2 Jon Altman, "Closing the gap between rhetoric and reality", ABC, *The Drum Unleashed*, 17 May 2010: http://www.abc.net.au/unleashed/34484.html

At the risk of misinterpreting Altman here, if a "realistic" framework for Aboriginal remote community people is one that does *not* seek acquisition of the full attainment of "social norms that underpin daily routines like going to work and school", Altman shares in the general pessimism about what can be achieved by most Aboriginal people while they continue to live on remote communities. He seems to have accommodated to, even embraced, low expectations.

A major problem with recent government responses such as the NTER is that they can be experienced as heavy-handed crisis management. Yet the argument that these desperate communities need crisis intervention is also valid. Indeed in August 2010, Top End child protection workers, in a submission to the Northern Territory's child protection inquiry, said "a foreign aid-type program was needed to deliver essential food supplies to children who are failing to thrive" in Top End remote communities. In their criticism of the Northern Territory Department for Families and Children (NTFC),

> The workers claim that children identified as failing to thrive in communities were "victimised" under current child protection practices. They demanded an immediate response that "stops victimising the children who are subjected to starvation".
> This could simply be a foreign aid (Red Cross, Oxfam, etc) type feeding program that does nothing more than deliver essential food to starving children whilst other programs address the underlying issues of poor parenting, poverty, overcrowding, violence, drug abuse, alcoholism, gambling, etc.[3]

The stream of emergency policies and programs for Aboriginal communities, while critically necessary, nevertheless bring to mind an indefinite occupation force constantly managing but never solving

---

[3] Natasha Robinson, "Children in remote centres 'starving'", *The Australian*, 3 August 2010: http://www.theaustralian.com.au/in-depth/aboriginal-australia/indigenous-children-in-remote-centres-starving/story-e6frgd9f-1225900257221

an inherently violent, perilous situation. How long can the "occupied" populations tolerate such interventions? It must be demoralising to be so heavily focused upon with critical gaze and charity-type aid; badgered to modify behaviour by outside forces even while still immersed in a cultural setting full of signals not to change; especially painful that Aboriginal people are being singled out for such treatment. And can the "troops" ever come home? Surely we all, Aboriginal and non-Aboriginal people alike, want Aboriginal people to be able to live their own lives, in good physical and mental health, individual freedom, economic independence and safety? How do we get to this better place?

In the search for effective solutions to traditionally-generated Aboriginal violence, major contextual problems become evident. Few communities have more than limited capacity to change deep cultural norms. Decades of self-determination have consolidated the idea that separate Aboriginal identity and culture must be protected, committing the state to providing the special services and income support that such separateness unavoidably requires. In the main, these are artificially maintained communities, and so receive inadequate market signals that cultural adaptation is necessary, even in urban locations. Belated programs to change behaviour and reduce violence are likely to have minor impact without the support of strong economic or market signals to move towards the mainstream society and economy.

**Welfare: compatible with maladaptive traditions, blocks market signals to go mainstream, but such suffering in the stopping ...**

Welfare income, while an essential feature of a humanitarian society, can be a serious impediment to adaptive behavioural change. A difficulty with liberal democracy's welfare state is its compatibility with unhelpful traditional Aboriginal practices. In addition, welfare facilitates new maladaptive behaviours like substance abuse and gambling, while weakening market messages on the need for positive adaptation to a new social and economic world. Noel Pearson has consistently drawn our attention to the deleterious impact of welfarism on Aboriginal individuals and communities, robbing Aboriginal people of the incentive to get employment that builds their skills and self-esteem. Welfare thereby contributes to community and individual breakdown and violence.[4] Furthermore, welfare payments undermine the need to leave small remote communities to find mainstream work, thereby depriving community people of the opportunity to participate in mainstream society and acquire its stronger anti-violence norms. Reducing welfare dependency and increasing attachment to employment is thus one way to change attitudes to violence.

The need for welfare not to reduce the incentive to find work is presented in a compassionate manner by Ken Henry.[5] Drawing on the Household, Income and Labour Dynamics in Australia (HILDA) survey, Henry writes that most people in Australia who experience poverty do so for only short periods. However, a small number of households "are at risk of long-term income poverty".[6] Regarding determinants of long-term poverty and inter-generational disadvantage, Henry writes that, along with the need for "human capital investment strategy",

> The evidence points toward the need to design income support programs and policies in a way that encourages, or at least does not discourage, active labour market participation ... [7]

Referring to Amartya Sen's concept of "capability deprivation",

---

4 For example, Noel Pearson, *Up from the Mission: Selected writings*, Black Inc, Melbourne, 2009, 282-91.
5 Ken Henry, "Addressing extreme disadvantage through investment in capability development", Keynote Address to the *Australian Institute of Health and Welfare Conference on Australia's Welfare 2007*, Canberra, 6 December 2007: http://www.treasury.gov.au/documents/1327/PDF/Health_and_Welfare_Conference.pdf
6 Ibid, 4.
7 Ibid.

Henry emphasises the centrality of education, and that "people who are educated have greater freedom to choose lives of real meaning and value".[8] Henry writes that Australian public service leaders have "come to the view that enhanced Indigenous educational attainment is unlikely to be achieved without seven developmental platforms being in place". Non-violence, supportive home environment, and real employment feature significantly:

> First and fundamentally, there must be basic protective security from violence for Indigenous parents and children ...
>
> Second, ... early childhood development interventions, coupled with parental support to develop at-home learning environments ...
>
> Third, the home environment needs to be conducive to regular patterns of sleep and study, free from overcrowding and distraction.
>
> Fourth, there needs to be access to suitable primary health service infrastructure ...
>
> Fifth, particularly in an environment where real jobs are not currently the norm, incentives in the welfare system cannot be allowed to work against the promotion of investment in human capital, particularly of children through the provision of safe and healthy living environments and their attendance at school ...
>
> Sixth, there must be a realistic prospect of an educated Indigenous person securing a real job, with the support of appropriate employment services ... Where remote locations cannot produce sufficient job opportunities for local people, there is no point in relying on miracles. A better strategy is to ensure that people have the opportunity to move to take up work if that is what they want to do.
>
> Seventh, governance systems have to support the "political freedom" and "social opportunities" of local Indigenous people (both men and women) to be engaged in policy development.[9]

---

8  Ibid, 8.
9  Ibid, 8-9.

Confirming Sutton's and Hirsi Ali's concerns about the way tradition prevents integration, the tangled web is that while education is a critical pathway out of unemployment and violence, families and communities rife with unemployment and violence can seriously inhibit a child's access to education.[10] Regarding employment opportunities, Henry points out that "almost three-quarters of Indigenous Australians live in cities and regional centres, the vast bulk of which have thriving labour markets". However,

> In some remote areas, not one of the seven platforms exists. In the cities, if we look hard enough, we see pockets of disadvantage; several of the seven platforms may be in place, with others less developed. There is disadvantage nonetheless.[11]

Welfare dependency in remote communities is difficult to solve for numerous reasons, with two reasons perhaps most resistant but most necessary to address. First, while it is easy to argue for tough unemployment benefit ("Newstart") eligibility for healthy, young people,[12] more lenient criteria are appropriate for the Aged Pension, Disability Support Pension (DSP), and Parenting Payment for families with young children. The second reason is that traditional "humbugging" makes it hard to stop welfare dependency among young unemployed, even if Newstart is subject more stringent work tests. One of the more robust, less work-test-dependent welfare payments is the Parenting Payment (PP) for families with young children. Welfare-to-work criteria since 2006 have connected this payment to work-test

---

10 Policy changes needed to address factors preventing Aboriginal children's success in education in remote areas are discussed by Gary Johns in his *Aboriginal Education: Remote Schools and the Real Economy*, Menzies Research Centre, May 2006.

11 Henry, 2007, 9.

12 For unemployed Aboriginal people, main welfare incomes are the work-test dependent Newstart, and "work for the dole" through the Community Development Employment Program (CDEP). The CDEP, still available in remote communities, is less subject to work-test pressure.

requirements once the youngest child turns six.[13] Nevertheless, the PP still provides a degree of income security for even very young unemployed sole parents, and enables them to postpone for years the need for work. It is also a "mobile" payment, available in locations with high or low employment prospects. Given that about 30% of Indigenous families are sole parent families compared with 10% of non-Indigenous families[14], this is a major source of stable income in remote Aboriginal communities.[15]

It is difficult to introduce PP work tests for single mothers with very young children without directly impacting on children's welfare and rights. Mothers need to feed, clothe and house their children whether or not they are willing or able to work, and wherever they live. Furthermore, the PP is given in recognition that caring and raising young children particularly on one's own requires a great deal of a parent's time and energy, and is not always compatible with employment. The trouble is, the PP sends a market signal to young single women with low attachment to the workforce to have babies, hence it is likely to be picked up strongly by remote area young Aboriginal women.[16] Elcho Island is an example of how welfare payments associated with having babies have big impacts on Aboriginal community birthrates, as observed by Rothwell:

---

13 Centrelink, *Parenting Payment – Eligibility.* (Update of 16 November 2009): http://www.centrelink.gov.au/internet/internet.nsf/payments/parenting_eligible.htm See also Human Rights and Equal Opportunity Commission, *Welfare to Work Submission,* c. 2005: http://www.hreoc.gov.au/disability_rights/employment_inquiry/w2wsub.htm

14 Australian Human Rights Commission, "Appendix 2: A statistical overview of Aboriginal and Torres Strait Islander peoples in Australia" Section 3, *Social Justice Report,* 2008: http://www.hreoc.gov.au/social_justice/sj_report/sjreport08/downloads/appendix2.pdf

15 Couples with children can also receive Parenting Payment, eligible when one of them receives Newstart or other welfare payment or low income: Centrelink, *Parenting Payment – Eligibility,* 2009.

16 There are other forces at work here too, but PP would be an additional factor.

> More than 1000 people at Galiwinku are under 15; 600 of them are under six: the policies of the past few years, with extensive family payments and baby bonuses looming large in the subsistence economy, have helped spawn this state of affairs: Elcho is a child-dominated world.[17]

The Mullighan Inquiry has troubling evidence of baby bonus money leading to increased pregnancies among young people of the APY lands:

> Several health workers told the Inquiry that the desire to get pregnant was also being influenced by the availability of the Commonwealth Government's baby bonus. Nganampa reported it had observed from its family planning education in schools that more of the older girls wanted to get pregnant than did not want to get pregnant. Further, it is concerned that partners and families are pressuring teenage girls to become pregnant in order to access the grant, which will be $5,000 from 1 July 2008.
>
>> "Once the child is born, the mother or the family gets the grant but then the kid is dumped on normally grandparents, who don't see any of the money."
>
> The expression "baby cars" also has been coined to describe the practice of young fathers using the Baby Bonus to purchase a car.[18]

In addition, the (albeit appropriate) robustness of the PP when children are young can undermine market signals – such as tougher Newstart work tests – to unemployed Aboriginal community men, because the PP can make Aboriginal mothers comparatively lucrative targets for traditional "humbugging". This can both reduce the need to become "work-ready" among unemployed Aboriginal men, and increase their violence against women. Referring to observations made by Ernest Hunter, Partington described these serious hazards thus:

> Hunter noted that the greater availability of welfare payments for

---

17 Nicolas Rothwell, "And they call it failure to thrive", *The Australian*, 8 May 2010: http://www.theaustralian.com.au/news/opinion/and-they-call-it-the-failure-to-thrive/story-e6frg6zo-1225863617761

18 Mullighan Inquiry, 2008, 173.

women with children encouraged high rates of teenage pregnancy, reaching in Western Australia eight and a half times the rate for non-Aboriginal teenagers by 1987. He also argued that for many a man an "exploitative relationship" with a woman with children "offered his only chance of obtaining regular money". There is evidence of considerable Aboriginal male resentment at dependency on women, which results not in expressions of gratitude but in increased violence towards them.[19]

The NTER's IM strategy is an acknowledgement of the clash between indispensable welfare income for vulnerable people including children, and "humbugging" of this essential income by relatives. Centrelink outlines IM for the Northern Territory thus:

> If you are on Income Management, part of your regular fortnightly payments and all of any advance or lump sum payments will be income managed. Your income managed money can be used for priority items such as food, rent, utilities and clothing.
>
> The rest of your regular fortnightly payments will be paid to you in the usual way.
>
> You can spend your income managed money by using the BasicsCard, or by organising direct payments to organisations such as stores, landlords, or utility providers.[20]

A Closing the Gap report found that

> Children, women and the elderly reported feeling safer, better fed and clothed, getting more sleep and being subjected to less humbugging for money for alcohol, gambling and drugs. These outcomes were attributed to income management, alcohol restrictions, community store licensing and an increased police presence.[21]

---

19 Partington, 1996, 138.
20 Centrelink, *Income Management in the Northern Territory*, 16 August 2010: http://www.centrelink.gov.au/internet/internet.nsf/individuals/income_mgt_nt.htm
21 FaHCSIA, *Closing the Gap in the Northern Territory Monitoring Report, July – December 2009, Part One*, 17: http://www.fahcsia.gov.au/sa/indigenous/pubs/nter_reports/closing_gap_NT_jul_dec_2009/Documents/closing_gap_NT_part_1.pdf

In 2009, Bess Price made an impassioned plea that IM was essential, and that those who protested against the Intervention, often outsiders, were failing to listen to the plight of those at Yuendumu who desperately needed it:

> I know plenty of Aboriginal women here who want the Intervention because they can feed their kids now. The protestors treat them like enemies as well ... They took the side of the violent men and the corrupt ones in our communities and refused to support the women worried about their kids, sick of being beaten up by drunks. They have never even tried to talk to us. We are very grateful to the government for keeping income management going.
>
> My people don't use money the way white people do. They don't save, they don't budget, they can't say "no" to relatives even when they are drunks and addicted to gambling and drugs. They need help in spending their money wisely. We are very happy that the government has decided to extend income management to everybody. That is what we have always asked for. Don't stop doing it for us, do it to everybody who needs it if you are worried about racism. Even Warren Snowdon, our ALP Federal member admits now that it is working. That is a big change for Warren.[22]

That the elderly, women and children are reported to be better fed, clothed and feeling safer because of IM is a confirmation that the problem existed, and IM was needed. The children might also become healthy enough to regularly attend school. The Federal Department of Families, Housing, Community Services and Indigenous Affairs (FaHCSIA) points to the travesty that more cash in these communities is a harm in itself, irrespective of whether enough money goes to children's needs. That is, more cash too often means more money spent on items that harm communities. As FaHCSIA stated, IM ensures that

- money paid by the government for the benefit of children is directed to the priority needs of children

---

22 Bess Price, 2009.

- money paid by the government for the benefit of children is directed to the priority needs of children
- the amount of cash in communities is reduced to help counter substance abuse, gambling and other anti-social behaviours that can lead to child abuse and community dysfunction.
- Income-managed funds must be directed towards agreed priority needs and services such as food, rent and utilities. This process assists families to meet essential household needs and expenses.
- Income-managed funds cannot be used to purchase prohibited items such as alcohol, tobacco, pornography or gambling products.[23]

While these are real gains, time will tell if IM's reduction of "demand-share" cash is market signal enough to encourage many remote area Aboriginal people to become work-ready, keen to be skilled, educated, employed people for their local and mainstream economy and society. Early signs are not good. Forces still operate in remote areas against the need for employment in the real economy. These include remote area CDEP, and indeed, trading or humbugging Centrelink vouchers meant to reduce humbugging in the first place.[24] Furthermore, while the NTER was followed by a shift away from Newstart, this was only partially – it seems not even primarily – due to mainstream employment. Figures suggest that larger numbers shifted to welfare payments without work-readiness requirement, namely the DSP and Carer Payment.

National Welfare Rights Network (NWRN) documented the federal government's finding of these shifts. From June 2008 to June 2009, "in prescribed areas subject to the NTER", a 30% increase

---

23 FaHCSIA, *Income Management in the Northern Territory Emergency Response, Commonwealth of Australia 2009*, (from last modified 13 April 2010): http://www.fahcsia.gov.au/SA/INDIGENOUS/PROGSERV/NTRESPONSE/Pages/default.aspx

24 National Welfare Rights Network (NWRN), "NT intervention shows claims for some Centrelink payments up 30%", Media Release, 1 November 2009: http://www.welfarerights.org.au

occurred in DSP and Carer Payment recipients; Newstart and Youth Allowance recipients fell by 20%; and PP Partnered and PP Single recipients fell by 7% and 8% respectively. Overall, "there were 20,090 on payments at June 2009, with numbers down by 700 (4%) between June 2008 and June 2009".[25] NWRN argues that this increase in DSP and Carer Payment recipients is because of an improved Centrelink engagement with remote communities subject to the Intervention. As Kate Beaumont, President of NWRN, stated,

> The increased numbers receiving Social Security payments who cannot look for [work] comes as no surprise. NWRN has been telling the Government for years that many people in Indigenous communities were on the wrong type of payments and forced to undertake inappropriate activity requirements ...
>
> The most significant reason behind the changed profile of income support recipients in the locations subject to the intervention has been the new way that Centrelink has actively engaged with local Indigenous communities. This is the first time that Centrelink has made a concerted effort to regularly service many of these remote Indigenous communities.[26]

There is no doubting the validity of Beaumont's observation. Chronic illness and disability are tragically high across these communities. The result has exposed another tragedy: an unexpectedly high number of people in these communities are essentially beyond the reach of market signals to join real employment. Those on DSP would include parents of young children. Unless solutions can be found, another generation of children will receive scant work culture from their parents and other community members.

The DSP has become – comparatively speaking – an even more attractive payment. In July 2010 major reform to IM took place, extending the scheme from beyond the prescribed remote communities

---

25 Ibid.
26 Ibid.

to cover all Northern Territory, including many non-Aboriginal people. Under this reform, IM becomes voluntary for some, including short-term recipients and those not subject to income management relating to child protection orders.[27] DSP becomes exempt from IM. In her commentary on the extension of IM to non-Aboriginal people, Centre for Independent Studies (CIS) policy analyst Jessica Brown, while supporting the concept, alerts us to potential pitfalls of IM, for both Aboriginal and non-Aboriginal people. Her concern is that IM may inadvertently render welfare recipients more, not less dependent, arguing that "the reforms will fail if people become more reliant on government to manage their budget, instead of taking up the responsibility themselves".[28] Also, by exempting DSP from IM, this pension becomes more attractive, and once on the DSP it becomes even more difficult to get "marginally disabled" people who can work off welfare. Brown writes:

> It is politically difficult for the government to extend income quarantining to DSP recipients, many of whom have severe physical and mental disabilities and would see income management as an unfairly punitive measure. But this difficulty simply highlights the need for reform of this payment. Perhaps it is time for a two-track system where severely disabled people are exempt from measures such as income management but those with a greater capacity to work are not.[29]

This point further underlines the possibility that a shift of marginally disabled Aboriginal people from Newstart to DSP on remote communities could harm rather than benefit these individual welfare recipients and their communities.

It is doubtful that IM enriches the life choices of young Aboriginal

---

[27] See Centrelink, *Income Management in the Northern Territory*, 16 August 2010.
[28] Jessica Brown, "Antidote to welfare dependency", *The Australian*, 19 January 2010: http://www.theaustralian.com.au/news/opinion/antidote-to-welfare-dependency/story-e6frg6zo-1225820989453 Note: Brown refers favorably to Noel Pearson's Family Responsibilities Commission in Cape York.
[29] Brown, 2010.

mothers receiving PP. For some mothers, IM works just as intended: a welcome benefit that helps them keep humbuggers at bay and meet their children's needs.[30] For others not subject to much humbugging, or who already fend off humbuggers without IM help and manage their finances well, it can be experienced as a paternalist, racist intrusion, and a sense of unfair shame at the supermarket.[31] Indeed, there is both support and opposition for IM emanating from women of Northern Territory communities. Ironically, some mothers who experience IM as an overall benefit might feel even less inclined to break out of their welfare dependence on a remote community: Sutton's term "tinkering" comes to mind.

For some young women, the independent income of a mainstream job in a town or city might start to look more attractive than the upsetting aspects of Centrelink IM. However, given that the negative consequences of humbugging – actual harm to their children's health and welfare – were not enough to cause many mothers of affected young children to leave these communities, I am not confident. I do not wish to be too critical of this choice to stay: it would be hard to leave the people and country one loves. Moreover, if there is domestic violence, attempting to leave a violent partner can be dangerous, even more so if there is no ready access to safe transport, and no clear, safe place to go. Indeed, the Northern Territory Council of Social Service has stated that "a lack of public transport in remote communities means people are not always able to escape domestic violence".[32]

Another item for "humbugging" is housing. A prominent perspective on overcrowding is government negligence in not

---

30 FaHCSIA, *Closing the Gap,* July-December 2009.
31 For example, see Stephen Lunn, "Shame of 'susso' to spread: ACOSS", *The Australian*, 11 March 2010: http://www.theaustralian.com.au/news/nation/shame-of-susso-to-spread-acoss/story-e6frg6nf-1225839328237
32 Alison Middleton, "Domestic violence escape route lacks transport", *ABC News*, 18 April 2011: http://www.abc.net.au/news/stories/2011/04/18/3194517.htm I am indebted to James Franklin for this link.

providing enough houses for remote Aboriginal communities. Certainly across Australia, decline in public housing supply for both Aboriginal and non-Aboriginal people means that not even being a family on welfare with young children warrants priority housing,[33] which is now available only for people deemed in particular high need including homelessness, fleeing domestic violence, or with a disability.[34] However, there is a high tolerance for overcrowding among Aboriginal people plus an obligation to provide shelter to "humbugging" kin. This makes overcrowding an intractable, conflict-ridden problem even in places of adequate housing supply, for instance "humbugging" on a relative's home to avoid paying rent or electricity;[35] or where low-cost opportunities to build one's own home are not pursued.[36]

I am afraid this examination does not lead me to a place of optimism regarding the scope for market signals to enter the mainstream, especially for people in remote communities. Additional barriers

---

[33] For example, the non-priority waiting time for public housing in NT is typically several years, from about 2 years in Katherine, up to nearly 8 years in Nhulunbuy, as at January 2011. See Department of Housing, Local Government and Regional Services, "Wait Times", Northern Territory Government: http://www.territoryhousing.nt.gov.au/public_housing/new_tenants/wait

[34] Department of Local Government and Housing, *Priority Public Housing*, NT Government, Fact Sheet December 2009: http://www.territoryhousing.nt.gov.au/_data/assets/pdf_file/0007/7099/priority_housing_web.pdf

[35] Field work, mid 1990s.

[36] We need more understanding about what is preventing remote area, unemployed, able-bodied young Aboriginal people from building their own homes, especially in the face of terrible overcrowding. They have time, and plenty of land with building materials: clay for bricks, fire or sun to bake them, in some areas lots of timber, and money (especially if drinking money and other wasted money was pooled). Certainly, building our own homes is beyond most of us, but I am sure there are young remote Aboriginal people able to, so what is preventing them? – no doubt a range of factors: despair, substance abuse, a soul-destroying "victim" mentality and the "learned helplessness" of welfare dependency. Fear of humbugging for a stay in the house they built for their nuclear family, and community land title would also be disincentives. A reason for government seeking long-term lease of Aboriginal community land is to provide individual Aboriginal families control over a private housing block through a long-term lease-back arrangement. See Sutton, 2009, 126-33.

against mainstream entry have been triggered by the NTER itself, such as increased uptake of welfare payments less subject to work tests, especially the DSP. What seems to be the underlying, stubborn issue causing such resistance to market forces is the high tolerance for poverty, illness, overcrowding, violence and indeed, intervention, among many Aboriginal people. Staying in remote, barren, dangerous places without work prospects, crowding into terrible houses, enduring shocking health, shocking relationships, child neglect and abuse, where ready cash can cause more harm than good, is testimony to a toleration for situations that most Australians would not endure. Even prison can be safer and more comfortable than life on many of these communities.[37]

---

[37] For example, see ABC Online News, "Jail a 'rite of passage' for Indigenous youth", 23 September 2009: Youth Affairs Network Queensland: http://www.yanq.org.au/our-work/projects/mynq/2065-jail-a-rite-of-passage-for-indigenous-youth

# 12

# From cultural compliance to personal choice

> She did not want to go. She – you know, it's that kind of new breed of young women hopefully coming through who see the choices that they've got and also, importantly, see the choices that non-Indigenous women have in the broader society.
> – Nanette Rogers[1]

> It is a myth to think that people's minds will be opened by their government or some higher authority; even teachers in school are not as effective as peers. Classmates ... ask each other questions in the school yard. Colleagues confront each other on the work floor, neighbours in each other's kitchens.
> – Ayaan Hirsi Ali[2]

**From traditional compliance to individual freedom: the necessary journey**

Adjustment to the mainstream is not about taking anything from Aboriginal people, but about equipping Aboriginal citizens for full participation in contemporary Australia and all its health, education and economic benefits, and their full universal rights. Aboriginal lands won back after years of hard political struggle are precious ancestral lands, including for Aboriginal people living mainstream lives. The problem is the maintaining of oppressive and violent traditions. We need to reverse policies and programs that have encouraged Aboriginal people to remain separate, particularly geographically separate, from

---
1 Rogers on *Lateline*, 15 June 2006.
2 Hirsi Ali, 2010, 209.

mainstream culture, and have allowed their subjugation to traditional practices that are incompatible with principles of human rights. Before colonial times, traditional Aboriginal culture's violent practices would have been hard to abide, even when no alternatives were known. Today, with mainstream alternatives available, the harsh demands of tradition must be even harder to bear.

The chasm between "traditional culture" and Enlightenment's "individual freedom" needs to be bridged. About twenty years ago, a young Malaysian woman and I, strangers, started chatting at a city bus stop. She said she loved being in Australia because Australians have no culture. I was taken aback a little and asked what she meant. She said that in her country, her life is dominated by the demands of her culture, making it hard to be one's own person, while here, we are free to live our own lives, to be our individual self. She wished that her own life could be so free.

It is likely that young Aboriginal people's yearning (not necessarily conscious) for mainstream's freedom *from* culture, and the generational clash this engenders, is both contributing to Aboriginal violence, and pointing to young people's successful entry into the mainstream as a solution to this violence. Older Aboriginal people are filled with grief and despair at the social breakdown of their young people, particularly when the young commit violent crime against family, end up in prison, or die through drink or suicide. These older people look to former times, recent and vivid as their own parents and their own childhood, as a time of more traditional discipline. The mainstream world was pressing upon them, but there was enough youthful respect for the traditional authority of elders, enabling elders to guide children to a life of belonging and accomplishment in both worlds. This included wise parents voluntarily sending their children to mission or town schools, indeed insisting that their children attend. It seems that remote young Aboriginal people of one and two generations ago could comply with the heavy demands of both the Aboriginal world's respected, traditional authority of older people which taught, implemented and so handed down the culture, and of the Western world's disciplined mission schools, facilitating traditional young students' adaptability to mainstream education and all its benefits. Extraordinarily accomplished people grew up in this world straddling both cultures, such as Bess Price, Alison Anderson and Noel Pearson.

No wonder the dream continues that a reconciliation of both worlds is still possible for today's troubled young Aboriginal people, as a remedy for their disaffection and their violence. There remains a yearning that the authority of wise elders who transmit law and traditional knowledge can be just as restorative today.[3] Hilary Bond's PhD thesis presents valuable research on the distinguished place of elders, noting that respect for elders is "an integral part of Aboriginal family life", and that elders, "as knowledgeable people, hold the keys to their people's well-being".[4] Moreover, their authority is embedded in law:

> As a political leader *Kulthangar* told me, "We leaders and that's a really big thing. We must be respected and heard. Respect that's a really big thing for us." The Elders expect their authority to be respected. They expect to be consulted with, because they are the gerontocracy. As the traditional authority figures of an Aboriginal community the Elders expect to be the leaders. In education, and matters of law, culture and society, they expect to be respected, consulted, heard and acknowledged, and they expect their wishes to be acted on, not so much because they feel the need, personally, for respect and to be heard and negotiated with, but because it is Aboriginal Law.[5]

---

3 Indeed, the wisdom and dignity of these elders mean that there is considerable respect for them among a large number of white people as well, making it a bit daunting to raise some critical notes.

4 Hilary Bond, *'We're the mob you should be listening to': Aboriginal Elders talk about school-community relationships on Mornington Island*, PhD thesis, School of Education, James Cook University, March 2004, 97: http://eprints.jcu.edu.au/971/2/02whole.pdf

5 Ibid, 99-100.

Ultimately, the well-being of young Aboriginal people entails more than the traditional world can give them. It entails full access to rights and freedoms that belong to a different, non-traditional world. Straddling both worlds for the young and powerless is just getting too hard. Disaffected young Aboriginal people seem to have less respect for their elders, while still taking advantage of tradition's greater acceptability of violence. They use violence against each other and against distraught elders, particularly when fuelled by alcohol and a desperate, at times suicidal sense of entitlement to get their own way in the family, often to get more poison spoils of mainstream life like cash for drink. At the same time, these young people are balking at restrictions that tradition places against access to mainstream's benefits such as personal freedom and achievement. In the resultant generational clash there are no winners, but the impact on young people is more tragic, and everyone grieves. This is my worry about the compliance idea, that if only the young people would sit down and listen to the wisdom of their elders and the old law, and follow what they have to say, all would be well. Certainly there are wise elders, and there are benefits for young people in receiving their caring attention and knowledge, such as helping them overcome substance abuse and its violent consequences. For example, elder-run camps aimed at reducing youth addiction to petrol sniffing can be very effective. Bond points to similar benefits:

> *Kulthangar* told me that the Elders are gradually "stopping drinking 'white man's grog' and stopping smoking 'white man's tobacco' [cigarettes]. We have to give a good example to the young people, show them our world is stronger than white man's world".[6]

Furthermore, there are clauses in codified Aboriginal laws submitted to the ALRC, which aim to replace some violent punishments with non-violent punishments, to increase the chance of formal integration

---

6 Ibid, 99.

of Aboriginal law into the mainstream law. While this moves in the right direction, highly restrictive and misogynist codes and violent punishments remain in these submissions. It is insufficient to transform violent punishment into a fine or imprisonment, when the so-called "crime", such as refusing a marriage promised at childhood, should not be classified as a crime.[7]

Despite Aboriginal submissions to the ALRC of modified law, there is resistance – akin to religious fundamentalism – to changing traditional law including its violence measures. Some elders urge that law is not man-made, man cannot change law, man's role is to follow and apply the law. Hence Aboriginal law is immutable, and traditional violent punishments cannot be changed. Ken Lechleitner, cross-cultural consultant of Anmatjere and western Arrernte heritage, draws on Christian comparisons to describe his point that "men do not make laws, we follow law".[8] In similar fashion, Warlpiri elder and Lajamanu leader Martin Johnson draws on the Old Testament. There are ancient, pre-Enlightenment precepts in Western culture in the Old Testament, from which traditional Aboriginal culture can draw additional validation (a troubling kind of "integration"?):

> I want to share from Genesis. "Whoever sheds the blood of man, by man shall his blood be shed. For in the image of God, God made man." In other words, we were never involved [*sic*], we don't believe that, we were created. In another place the bible says too, the law requires that nearly everything be cleansed with blood and without the shedding of blood is no forgiveness, and that is very true because even before the missionaries came we've lived that same law. No missionary told us that. But when we compare Warlpiri law to the bible, they're nearly the same.[9]

---

7 These submissions to the ALRC are discussed in more detail below.
8 Chris Bullock, reporter, "Old law, new ways", ABC RN, *Background Briefing*, 21 November 2010, transcript: http://www.abc.net.au/rn/backgroundbriefing/stories/2010/3067612.htm
9 Bullock, 21 November 2010.

Dave Price wrote of his dialogue with a Warlpiri elder:

> I suggested that there should be a change to the Law. He answered that he was trying to make such changes. It is such thoughtful, loving and worried men we should be supporting and talking with. We have to stop treating them like fools ... We have to give them deep thought and not be afraid to find and discuss the truth on a basis of real mutual respect, not shallow, cheer-squad type reverence.
>
> I've got a personal stake in all this. My wife's life has been directly threatened by drunk men armed with machetes and knives. They were never charged because the police adopted old Sir Baldwin's approach: Let the wild natives sort it out their own way. But this happened in the middle of Alice Springs in broad daylight. Being a whitefella, I don't have the right to "have my payback." In fact, almost all adult kin close to me, my loved ones, have been both victims and/or perpetrators of illegal violence. All involved believed they were adhering to the Law.
>
> The answer lies in dialogue, not "education" – that hasn't worked too well. Let's enter into dialogue with the old ones who are asking us to recognize their law. All cultures adapt. In the year the First Fleet left England a young Irish woman was publicly burned to death at Newgate for counterfeiting the coin of the realm. They don't do that in London anymore ... I have faith in Aboriginal people's ability to adapt, because they've been doing it massively for two centuries ... I have personally seen very significant changes made to the rituals around death and mourning, surely among the last to change in any society. I have seen Warlpiri people introduce innovation to respond to new circumstances, rationally and amicably, without dissent and discord.[10]

Nevertheless, great commitment is needed to bring about essential cultural changes. There is much evidence that older Aboriginal people are among those upholding the instrument of violence in traditional punishment and as an enforcer of "rights" over others. Unless this can

---

10 Dave Price, 2009.

be addressed, compliance to elders as law custodians is no solution for young people against persistent, traditional violent practices and oppressions.

Listing some actual or depicted situations in which elders – whether through caring and gentle words, written code, or brutal enforcement – call for young people's compliance to tradition, illustrates this. In all the following cases, young people's human rights are betrayed, and all of us have a shared responsibility to find solutions.

- The rape of an under-age teenage girl by her traditionally promised husband in his fifties.[11]
- The abduction of an under-age teenage girl by her traditionally promised husband in his fifties, with the help of her own grandmother.[12]
- The continued practice of polygamy especially by older men, resulting in oppression, particularly of young women, and shortage of traditionally marriageable women for single young men. That honest but beguilingly sweet film *Ten Canoes*[13] depicts both the wise concern of an older brother, as well as the younger brother's aching heart, with the message, *young man in love, listen to your much older and wise brother's advice to you on the virtue of patience, and one day, when your older brother is killed or dies through sorcery, you can wed his third, now teenage wife, meanwhile, just be good and patiently wait for her (perhaps a decade or two?) in the separate single men's camp.*[14]
- Correct skin marriage, which is increasingly incompatible with modern, more natural patterns and freedoms regarding love and marriage partners. A generator of "Romeo-Juliet" style tragedy,

---

11  *The Queen v GJ* [2005]
12  *Hales v Jamilmira* [2003] NTCA 9.
13  de Heer, 2006.
14  My perspective and words.

correct skin marriage is called a form of incest taboo but this categorisation is imprecise or misleading. Correct skin marriage imposes tight, exacting limitations on who one can marry, more akin to religious, race, caste or class restrictions that cause suffering for young people the world over. Is this the ultimate message of that marvellous Chooky Dancers play *Wrong Skin*[15]: *do not go against the wrong skin marriage rule, bereft young man, it only causes more grief and untold violence, just surrender to the loving arms of your caring, wise elder, be obedient, and all will be well?*[16]

- The following Lajamanu rule, which adds even further restrictions on who young people are able to love:

  > 17. If a man make avoiding cousins through initiation of a little boy, he then mustn't make love to the little boy's sister, if he does he should pay heavy fine or imprisonment.[17]

- Dangerous, mutilating, enforced subincisions still carried out on young men and boys as part of initiation.[18]

- In the film *Samson and Delilah*, Delilah complied to her elders and to her culture, including her submission to traditional head-bashing punishment for her grandmother's natural death, when in fact Delilah was the only person who with great love and tenderness, took care of her very ill and disabled grandmother. To me, Delilah's tragedy was that she was compliance personified.[19]

- Avoidance laws such as *mirriri*, which if not complied with, can carry the threat of violent punishment particularly against women.[20]

---

15 Nigel Jamieson, 2010.
16 My perspective and words.
17 ALRC Report 31, 1986 ,"19. Aboriginal Customary Law Defences" (The Lajamanu Submission 1981).
18 Sutton, 2009, 146; Michael Connor, "Passion and Illusions: Anita Heiss's stories", *Quadrant*, Vol. LVI No. 6, June 2012 http://www.quadrant.org.au/magazine/issue/2012/6/passion-and-illusions-anita-heiss-s-stories
19 Warwick Thornton, Director, *Samson and Delilah*, 2009.
20 Kimm, 2004, 52-3.

- Traditional child-rearing practices, including "cruelling", and a tolerance of children's anger and fighting.[21]
- Violent punishment. A Mornington Island submission to the ALRC of codified traditional law offers some protection of young people against elders, but is sadly telling in the breach:

  > young men may have to defend themselves with a fighting stick against an elder (but no blows will be delivered to the body).[22]

- Misogynistic rules for women's place in society, such as this Lajamanu law submitted to the ALRC:

  > 11. If widow woman wants to marry again she must get permission from her son-in-law first and then from her late husband's brothers and there should be an agreement with close relatives, if there is no agreement then the widow should not marry again, but should be dealt with through the Court.[23]

The skin system for marriage was a repeated item in community submissions to the ALRC for recognition of codified Aboriginal laws, for instance, in the Roper River submission:

> If a person steals someone who is promised to another person in marriage, or if a person goes with a person of a different skin group, they should also be punished in our traditional way by the elders, and if necessary by physical punishment. We would also like traditional marriages to be recognised under European Law and for wives and husbands to have the rights and obligations which come from this recognition of traditional marriages. If at any time this recognition of traditional marriages, under European Law, creates conflict to our traditional culture, then these conflicts must be resolved by a meeting of our elders.[24]

"Correct skin" marriage remains a powerful traditional law. The

---

21 Sutton, 2009, 111-12.
22 ALRC Report 31, 1986, "19. Aboriginal Customary Law Defences" (The Mornington Island Submission, 1981).
23 Ibid, (The Lajamanu Submission, 1981).
24 Ibid, (The Roper River Submission, 1981).

traditional perspective argues that young people's non-compliance to correct skin law is contributing to community dysfunction and violence. From an Enlightenment perspective, young Aboriginal people's normal romantic and sexual partnering behaviours are oppressed by traditional, "correct skin" rules. While the following quotations capture a generational clash from pre-contact to present times, with young people's longings clashing with older authority a prevailing theme, it must surely be harder to bear today:

> I got speared in the leg, too, for being cheeky. I got hit in the head, too, by all my old people. The spear came out of the calf. My old father did that. I was a cheeky bloke. Fighting the other fellas over some silly things I been doing in my young days. I was going with the wrong girls. My skin group is Milangka. I was with someone from a wrong skin group ...
>
> After you've taken your punishment then people don't worry about you[25]

In his examination of pre-contact, traditional practices that oppressed women, Nowra writes:

> The kidnapping of women from other tribes can also be due to the fact that, because of the complex kinship structures in Aboriginal society which prevented relatives having children, a young man may have had only one or two available women to marry in his own tribe, and even then the elders had first choice.[26]

The dance performance *Wrong Skin* portrays the pain endured by today's Aboriginal young people "wrongly" in love. Young people on very remote traditional communities where English is not the main language, such as on Elcho Island, nevertheless feel the tug of Western

---

[25] Henry Long, q. on Creative Spirits, "Aboriginal Law and Justice: Tribal Punishment and Payback": http://www.creativespirits.info/aboriginalculture/law/tribal-punishment-customary-law-payback.html

[26] Nowra, 2007, 23.

freedoms. Director Nigel Jamieson identified a discord between young Elcho Islanders' attraction to mainstream freedoms and a traditionally defined ideal society:

> Jamieson says *Wrong Skin* illustrates how young people in remote communities "walk a tight rope between two cultures". Arranged marriage, he says, "is strictly adhered to today [on Elcho]. It's the very foundation of Yolngu society and culture."[27]

Some interviews in the Mullighan Inquiry indicate that on APY lands, "wrong way" is less enforced today.[28] However, "wrong way" emerges in the Inquiry as a factor in young APY people's sorrows and tragedies, and they fear their parents' wrath especially when a "wrong skin" pregnancy is involved. Here is one such tragedy:

> Aged 14, the girl had a "wrong way" marriage to an older teenager. The girl became pregnant and the youth committed suicide. Welfare records suggest that fear of punishment under traditional law for the "wrong way" relationship and pregnancy may have contributed to the youth's suicide. The girl was allegedly told that she would be punished when the child was born, or to a lesser extent if the pregnancy was terminated. The girl was considered responsible for the youth's death and an assault on her carer had occurred as part of payback.[29]

The Inquiry also notes:

> There was evidence that families wanted pregnancies terminated or babies adopted out because of their concern that it is the result of a "wrong way" relationship. In one such instance a health professional noted that the family were more concerned with the baby being "wrong skin" than the sexual exploitation of the girl.[30]

---

27 Neill, 2010.
28 Mullighan Inquiry, 2008, 68.
29 Ibid.
30 Ibid, 173.

Annette Hamilton has observed that changes in oppressive customs relating to marriage will require young people to assert their individual rights:

> Professor Hamilton observes that while opposition to promised marriages comes from some whites and also from younger Aboriginal people who seek freedom of choice, as they grow older Aboriginal men may still take second and third betrothed wives. She comments that only the concerted opposition of the young seems likely to modify the system, especially in areas such as Arnhem Land.[31]

It is clear that many traditional customs upheld by older Aboriginal people are now just too oppressive and no longer compatible with young Aboriginal people's well-being.

## Integrating with the Enlightenment

Given the NTER and IM outcomes, market forces are unlikely to play a major role in remote area people relocating to urban areas for employment. This poses a significant problem, especially given the high birth rate in remote communities. Stronger anti-violence norms are more readily acquired through immersion in everyday mainstream life, rather than through "top-down" attempts to teach or enforce non-violent norms in discrete minority cultures. Immigrants from East Asia are generally able to adapt their attitudes and behaviours in a short time to meet the norms and expectations of their new country.[32] Positive daily interaction and neighbourly help and kindness from ordinary people in mainstream society are reported by Hirsi Ali as

---

31 ALRC Report 31, 1986, "12. Aboriginal Marriages and Family Structures", 1986, referring to Annette Hamilton, "Gender and Power in Aboriginal Australia", in N. Grieve & P. Grimshaw (eds), *Australian Women*, Oxford University Press, Melbourne, 1981, 76. This ALRC/Hamilton passage is referred to in *Hales v Jamilmira* [2003] NTCA 9.

32 Natasha Mitchell, reporter, "Challenging stereotypes: culture, psychology and the Asian Self (part 2 of 2)", ABC RN, *All in the Mind*, 14 August 2010, transcript: http://www.abc.net.au/rn/allinthemind/stories/2010/2978652.htm

helping refugees integrate and experience belonging.[33] Even just acquiring knowledge about how mainstream culture works helps in the process of belonging or integration. This echoes a key problem that Bess Price has urged us to respond to:

> All I see is that they are hunters and gatherers and they were vulnerable then and they are vulnerable now. They know nothing about how everything else operates outside of their communities and how they need to change in order to keep up with the rest of the outside world. They need to be given the tools and the mechanism to move forward ... [34]

Care is needed when comparing the process of adaptation to majority culture among migrants and refugees, with that of Indigenous people. Research presented by John Ogbu and Herbert Simons primarily in America suggests that adjustment is harder for involuntary, including Indigenous minorities. Attitudes to mainstream education held by students from involuntary minority communities are illustrative:

> Like their parents and members of their community, the students have an abstract belief in the importance of "getting a good education". However, their attitudes and behaviors contradict their verbal assertions. The mixed feelings lead to reduced efforts, which manifest themselves in failure to pay attention in class, do homework, and keep up with school assignments, and in claims that the work is uninteresting and boring. Some students are openly defiant as they challenge the teachers' authority. They do not put much effort into learning standard English because they see it as separating them from their peers, family, and community, thus threatening their minority identity. There is a strong negative peer group influence that more or

---

[33] Hirsi Ali, 2010, 253-4. While the situation of asylum seekers in the Netherlands cannot be directly compared with Aboriginal Australians, there are lessons here regarding minority integration. Furthermore, it evokes the possibility that churches may again be needed, this time not on remote missions, but to assist Aboriginal people in an urban-based process of integration..

[34] Bess Price, 2009.

less stigmatizes academic success and using standard English as "acting white." All of these attitudes and behaviors lead inevitably to poor academic performance.[35]

Nevertheless, Aboriginal Australians when given the opportunity have, particularly since the 1950s, displayed great capacity for cultural adaptation including educational achievement, and many thousands of Aboriginal Australians live successful, violence-free, well-adapted lives. Indeed, most Aboriginal people now form families with non-Aboriginal people, and increasingly so, which is not at all an inevitable situation among minority populations. Also, achievements in tertiary education among Aboriginal people over the last few decades are impressive. Research undertaken by the late Indigenous education leader Maria Lane and her husband, teacher and education researcher Joe Lane, demonstrates that when Aboriginal people are not segregated from the mainstream, their adaptation, including educational achievement, approaches mainstream levels. In his CIS paper, "Indigenous Participation in University Education", Joe Lane documents positive trends in Indigenous tertiary education.[36] Maria Lane found that when participating in mainstream life, Aboriginal people's progress through the generations is much like any migrant group in Australia, and from the 1950s, when they migrated from "the settlements" to urban areas, to the present, most Aboriginal people have developed into an "Open Society Population":

> The comparison with the experience of migrant groups is inescapable: although migrants from Greece and Italy and Yugoslavia and Lebanon in the fifties and sixties were expected

---

35 John Ogbu and Herbert Simons, "Voluntary and Involuntary Minorities: A Cultural-Ecological Theory of School Performance with Some Implications for Education", *Anthropology & Education Quarterly* 29(2), 1998, 179: http://faculty.washington.edu/rsoder/EDUC310/OgbuSimonsvoluntaryinvoluntary.pdf

36 Joe Lane, "Indigenous Participation in University Education", *Issue Analysis* No. 110, CIS, 27 May 2009.

to be content with employment in factories and on farms, they also did not expect their children to follow them: very often, in the second generation, their children have gone straight onto tertiary education and professional employment. I am suggesting that a high proportion of Indigenous people have followed a similar path.[37]

Joe and Maria Lane signal that separatist and differential strategies inhibit positive, mainstream progress. Welfare and segregation policies arising in the 1970s – including in the cities – have resulted in what Maria Lane described as "the Congealing of an Embedded, or Encapsulated, Welfare-Oriented Population", posing for her the question, "Two diverging populations?"[38] Here, we see the harm of well-intentioned but misplaced policy. It is separatist policy, not the presence of an intractable Aboriginal opposition, that is the fundamental barrier, resulting in many thousands of young Aboriginal Australians lacking enough opportunities to reach this high potential for cultural adaptation.

Overseas research on segregation and trust has further relevant insights. Political scientist Eric Uslaner undertook research in numerous countries regarding residential segregation's impact on inter-group trust. He found that "in a cross-national hierarchical model of trust at the individual level, residential segregation leads to lower trust, while the conventional measure of diversity does not"[39]:

> If people of different backgrounds don't live near each other, the chances that there will be sufficient interaction, among either adults or especially among children (who don't have the resources to travel to meet people unlike themselves), are small. We are less likely to trust people of different backgrounds

---

37 Maria Lane, *Two Indigenous Populations? Two Diverging Populations?* 12 March 2007 (unpublished paper).
38 Ibid.
39 Eric M. Uslaner, "Trust, diversity, and segregation", 2009, 4: http://www.bsos.umd.edu/gvpt/uslaner/uslanertrustdiversitysegregation.pdf

if we don't have the opportunity to interact with them and to understand their cultures.[40]

Moreover:

> When people of different backgrounds live apart from each other, they will not – indeed, cannot – develop the sorts of ties – or the sorts of attitudes – that lead us to trust people who are different from ourselves. Concentrated minorities are more likely to develop a strong identity that supersedes a national sense of identification (trust in people who are different from oneself) and to build local institutions and political bodies that enhance this sense of separateness.[41]

Perhaps the permit system is a symbol for this truth. In the light of Uslaner's findings, we need to consider that decades of separatist policies have reduced trust of mainstream Australia among young Aboriginal people, thereby harming their adaptation to mainstream culture and ways of life, and hence, trapping them into submission to traditional interpersonal violence. If so, liberating Aboriginal people from traditional violence entails that we restore the trust lost through decades of separation.

In *The Queen v GJ* case of the young woman taken with violent force as a promised bride, her greater intolerance of traditional, misogynist violence had developed at least in part because she knew about the freedom from such oppression available to young non-Indigenous women, perhaps observed when she attended school in Darwin.[42] Such violent, misogynist practices are not culturally validated by the everyday mainstream settings of a Western city. The effectiveness of this process may be first signalled with the emergence of courageous Aboriginal victims' resistance and calls for their right to Western justice and protection.

---

40 Ibid, 5.
41 Ibid, 9.
42 *The Queen v GJ* [2005]; Rogers on *Lateline*, 15 June 2006.

As is clear in *The Queen v GJ* however, the acquisition of new norms among young women is not without dangers. Warin tells of a terrible incident in 1985 when a young woman became severely disfigured by serious burns caused by

> her promised husband and his first wife placing her in a ring of spinifex and lighting it. This was because, as she told me, she didn't want to marry an old man and become his second wife. Her insights did not save her.[43]

While there are young Aboriginal women adopting mainstream ways, there are Aboriginal men who still claim these modern young girls as their promised possession, and have cars, guns, outstations and kin to help them secure and punish these resistant girls, well away from public purview. Without a whole raft of additional supportive responses, in particular police, judiciary, and a permanent safe place for these young girls to reside and live in freedom, a man's traditional sense of entitlement, and use of violence to enforce it, can still triumph over the emancipation of a young Aboriginal woman's mind.

Above all, Aboriginal victims of violence need policies or pathways that secure for them a positive, productive and safer life. I have categorised some necessary changes under two broad headings. Group One addresses the need to ensure that our legal, policy and program responses to Aboriginal violence are not diluted or weakened by overzealous allowance for cultural difference: Aboriginal victims need exemplary, mainstream law enforcement and protection. Group Two arises in the light of the limited success of the Intervention's market forces in encouraging remote Aboriginal people towards mainstream life. Hence we need creative policies that provide Aboriginal people with greater opportunities to experience and adopt the positive aspects

---

43 Warin with Franklin, 2007, 2.

of mainstream life, especially its less tolerant attitudes to violence. Both Groups One and Two point to areas crying out for change. Whatever our guilt, whatever our despair, in order to liberate Aboriginal people from violence, we must embark on the following.

### Group One: Aboriginal people deserve the best from the nation and from themselves

#### 1. *Professional insistence that Enlightenment values are universal and non-negotiable*

Upholding individual rights requires that we be compassionate Enlightenment ambassadors amidst all peoples, and Hirsi Ali's concept, "a campaign of enlightenment"[44] needs to be a core aspect of engagement with Australia's Aboriginal communities. A barrier to overcome is the strange, recent offspring of liberal-democratic thinking. This is the justified aversion to Western imperialism, but naïvely expressed as an uncritical, romantic commitment to traditional cultures. In so doing, we risk betraying Aboriginal victims of violence.

For ideological and pragmatic reasons, some scholars and professionals condone traditional norms that are antithetic to Enlightenment values. Rather than engage with the Aboriginal community on their need to shed violent norms and practices, some Western professionals validate maladaptive norms by praising the traditional idea of violence as healing in some circumstances, and when "correctly" applied as punishment, essential to prevent drawn-out retribution. But that is tantamount to saying, "It's okay that you think like that, that you behave that way", and traditional Aboriginal people can then think, "There's no need for us to change, we are getting them to accommodate to our way." What has happened to these professionals? Shouldn't they be appalled at the very portent of

---

[44] See Hirsi Ali, 2010, 205; and 209-12 for her encounter with and summary of the five Enlightenment principles.

irrational long-term retribution? How are children expected to thrive under such fearful conditions? The discrete Aboriginal community seems to be the pyrrhic "winner" in the culture wars here, but there are no winners, only victims, and a weakened mainstream polity.

Professionals need to be compassionate ambassadors of Enlightenment culture and skilfully engage, indeed argue in the spirit of respect and friendship, with these communities on the need to shed maladaptive practices. This is particularly so in remote communities where professionals are a main source of face-to-face engagement with Westerners. That such respectful challenge is not happening enough however, might indicate a professional surrender to the reality that cultural adaptation to mainstream ways is too difficult in most remote community settings. In such circumstances, to ensure that Aboriginal men, women and children receive their full Enlightenment rights might require encouragement and assistance from professionals to relocate to mainstream centres.

At the very least, Western professionals must "hold their nerve"[45] when they are on beautiful remote country and in the midst of ancient, at times beautiful traditional Aboriginal cultures which, as Etherington has poignantly described, symbolise our own unreachable, edenic longings.[46] Aboriginal people need us to "hold our nerve" and confidently, proudly, be the Enlightenment ambassadors that we should be in all places, amidst all cultures. Perhaps this is the core of what good missions were doing before self-determination came along.

Feminism is an important aspect of Enlightenment thought that has also lost confidence. Aboriginal victims need a strong feminism to assist their emancipation, rather than the present silence and

---

45 Warin documents another observation of non-Aboriginal "melting". "A friend of mine asks 'Why do people melt around Aboriginal people?' I guess she means why don't non-Aboriginal people take Aboriginal people as people, with much the same needs and hopes as themselves?" Warin with Franklin, 2007, 10.

46 Etherington, 2007, 6-8.

surrender to the scant hope that most Aboriginal women can liberate themselves, with the Western feminist role being to listen and to help only when asked. "We have left it in their hands", "this is as much as we can do" and "all we can do is support them" are three expressions of this white reluctance to intervene in Aboriginal violence that I heard during my field work. Violence against women is the misuse of male power to control women, to curtail women's personhood. It is very difficult for victims of oppressive, culturally endorsed, male abuses to speak out about their subjugation. Sometimes the victims' own tolerance for violence means that they cannot name it as a problem, and frequently they are terrorised into remaining silent by some members of their community. As Enlightenment feminists, we need to advocate confidently and assertively for Aboriginal victims of violence, including being staunch critics of practices that oppress women.

## 2. Equal rights under one law, and the need to accept that violence against Aboriginal women is steeped in tradition

Somewhat paradoxically, along with the unhelpful professional adaptation to violence within Aboriginal culture, are attempts to deny the traditional drivers of violence against Aboriginal women. This blunts our ability to comprehend just how dangerous traditional settings are for Aboriginal women. We have for years used the "culture" argument to reduce sentences for Aboriginal men who have committed heinous acts against women. The legal system needs to address the moral hazard regarding more lenient sentences, in that if Aboriginal culture allows men to be violent against women, violent traditional Aboriginal men might be more recidivist and dangerous, because they see their actions as legitimate. By reducing sentences on this basis, we accommodate traditional law, giving the message that we have some tolerance for misogynist customs, thereby further endangering Aboriginal women. These men are Australian citizens, subject to Western law, and if they do not know that, then self-determination policies are to blame. All Aboriginal people, all communities, should be told, clearly, repeatedly, in their first language, that they are subject to the same law as all Australians. That is the nation's duty. Aboriginal citizens have a right to know they have equal rights and responsibilities under the law, and to know that it is non-negotiable.

The factor of culture in Aboriginal men's violence against women renders Aboriginal women particularly vulnerable, compliant, silent victims, requiring a *stronger* application of Enlightenment principles, and *additional*, not less, police, judicial and other service assistance and protection, particularly in remote, traditional communities. Instead, particularly before the Intervention, we have delivered to Aboriginal people the opposite, with remote communities typically having scant access to police help. What a grave act of sexism on our part: all feminists should be loud in their condemnation. Cultural relativism blurs into raw racism too. Western Australian police and other services received desperate calls for help from an Aboriginal mother of eight, but she repeatedly failed to get the needed protection. Two bereaved relatives, her brother and her cousin, spoke of their pain at the lack of service response. The victim's cousin expressed his concern that her Aboriginality was a factor in why she got no service help. As stated by McGlade:

> The homicide rate for Aboriginal women is ten times that for non-Aboriginal women. So, you know, the risk is clearly much more serious and yet the way that people were treating [this mother] and treat Aboriginal women as if it's not really that risk, but it should be the opposite.[47]

We betray both Aboriginal women and our Enlightenment polity here. Again, there are no winners.

---

47 Hamish Fitzsimmons, reporter, "Systemic failure leads to domestic murder", ABC, *Lateline*, 2 September 2010, transcript: http://www.abc.net.au/lateline/content/2010/s3001223.htm Victim's first name in original.

## 3. Equal rights under one law, and children are more important than culture

Where there is abuse and neglect of children, no matter how oppressed or disadvantaged their parents or carers are, those adults must be held responsible and accountable for that abuse and neglect. The state has a duty to provide parent assistance, education or mentoring, but must ultimately insist on better parenting. If, after quality help, lack of interest or capacity in a family or community to care adequately for its children persists, the state has a responsibility to intervene. We hear complaints about too much intervention, but if we acted to protect Aboriginal women and children as much as we do to protect white women and children in similar circumstances, Aboriginal interventions would be even greater. Remember Ken Henry's delineation of seven conditions needed by children for adequate educational attainment, including a violence-free home, and that in many communities not one of the seven conditions was present. The nation has an immediate duty of care to these children by ensuring that they no longer live in a violent home or violence-ridden community or in chronic neglect. In his article, "Pathetic excuses perpetuate this fraud on vulnerable children", Tony Koch presents the stark policy implications of widespread community child neglect:

> If the laws that apply to the rest of this nation were applied to Aboriginal and some island communities, children would be taken from their parents and put into care by the truckload.
>
> The most serious abuse that occurs is not sexual or physical violence – although they are certainly occurring in horrendous numbers – but sheer physical neglect ...
>
> Yet argument bogs down on whether it is "culturally appropriate" for indigenous children to be placed in the care of human beings who have lighter skin.
>
> How pathetic. How disingenuous. Ask a starving child whether he or she cares who gives them a sandwich, or a safe house, or who clears up their clogged ears and weeping skin diseases, and

see what the answer is. The argument should never be about skin colour or "culture", but about the welfare of little children.[48]

In words that echo Johns,[49] Koch writes, "[t]he 'culture' can come later, if the child lives long enough".

If we keep to policies that lock Aboriginal people out of mainstream life, we will keep having to face the dilemma of leaving neglected Aboriginal children to suffer in their dysfunctional families and communities, or of taking the children to safety, away from their birth family, away from their kin community. The core argument here is that to avoid such a heartbreak policy choice, we need to shift to Group Two of recommendations, which is to provide whole families, not just children, a safer life.

### 4. Barriers to shifts from violence are too high in many remote communities

Despite exemplary projects and model communities since the beginning of the self-determination years, in most remote, traditional settings, cultural practices and other behaviours maladaptive to mainstream life are more often affirmed than challenged. This is inevitable when communities are shielded, both geographically and with welfare, from the mainstream's values, demands and law enforcement. Even input from brave professionals guided by Enlightenment principles may not be enough, though the situation would be worse without them.

It is easy to be beguiled into false optimism or, its close cousin, a sense of guilt for being critical here. I get beguiled into optimism and guilt when I hear about the glorious culture emanating from the Yolngu people and the remarkable Central Australian men's campaign against violence. And then I remember the terrible violence, overcrowding,

---

48 Tony Koch, "Pathetic excuses perpetuate this fraud on vulnerable children", *The Weekend Australian*, 24-25 July 2010, 4.

49 Gary Johns, "The Northern Territory Intervention in Aboriginal Affairs: Wicked Problem or Wicked Policy?", *Agenda*, Volume 15, No. 2, 2008 (2008b), 70: http://epress.anu.edu.au/agenda/015/02/pdf/15-2-CO-1.pdf

crippling traditional superstitions, even wife-lending for cash, on Elcho Island, a heartland of Yolngu culture.[50] I recall the persistent high rate of violence against women across Central Australia's communities despite years of actions including by the NPYWC, and the depth of traditional culture reaffirming violence as a normal part of life in these communities. And I recall the silence and secrecy surrounding remote community violence; and how hard, even dangerous it is for the voices of powerless victims to be heard, to alert us to their suffering and to get protection, particularly with the "permit" system in place. That, as Rothwell noted, "[t]here is a striking correlation between the levels of violence in a community and the tightness of its closure"[51] should ring our alarm bells very loud.

There are good community leaders, but there are also dangerous community leaders, and to assume that all is well if we hear no complaints is to put silent victims at critical risk. Governments must assert their authority, their right to know what is happening on all remote communities, and their right and duty to protect individuals – men, women, the elderly, young people, children and infants – from violence. In particular, governments must not allow villains to hide behind the "cultural rights" shield, and must insist on protecting individual rights.

The example of Oombulgurri in Western Australia teaches us a sorry lesson. While it shows the success that dedicated policing can yield and how policing in remote communities was previously under-resourced and inadequate, it also shows that remoteness mixed with a community's non-recognition of the human rights of young women is just too dangerous. Lack of permanent police presence also made the "voluntary liquor agreement" a mere farce. As reported by *The West Australian*, weeks after the NTER was launched, police commenced a crackdown on child abuse in remote Western Australia, including

---

50 Rothwell, 2010.
51 Rothwell, q. in Nowra, 2007, 68.

acting on a "tip off about a sex-for-cigarettes trade between teenage girls and local indigenous leaders":

> It was during this time that Det-Sgt Tom Doyle began hearing rumours that sex abuse was rife in other communities, including Oombulgurri. Det-Sgt Doyle and other detectives began visiting Oombulgurri and after slowly earning the trust of older women in the community, the information started to flow.
>
> But the senior Aboriginal leaders of Oombulgurri, who had effectively been presiding over a closed community for many years, did not take well to police being there ...
>
> "They threw young girls' underwear at the front of the police station door, about six or seven pairs ... it was in our face, signifying that it [sexual abuse] was happening here but you're not going to find it [and] victims won't talk," Det-Sgt Doyle said ...
>
> In the same month that an inquest into five deaths in the community between 2005 and 2006 started, three Oombulgurri community leaders were charged with child sex offences.
>
> Just a few weeks before the charges were laid, former community chairman Darren [Darryl] Morgan had boasted in *The West Australian* that Oombulgurri was not plagued by the sexual abuse that racked other Aboriginal communities.
>
> Yesterday, he was sentenced to 10 years for sexually abusing two young girls. His 38-year-old wife, Shirley Ann Veronica Bulsey, was jailed for abusing one of the same girls.[52]

In her article on the NTER, anthropologist Francesca Merlan writes that the Intervention and the drama surrounding its declaration,

> established a boundary: a moment beyond which an earlier situation was declared intolerable, and a move towards something else. Of course it matters what comes after, but one may ask: was such a boundary-making exercise useful

---

52 Jessica Strutt and Gabrielle Knowles, "Sad day of reckoning for Fantasy Island", *The West Australian*, 2 June 2010: http://au.news.yahoo.com/thewest/a/-/wa/7329149/sad-day-of-reckoning-for-fantasy-island/

or desirable? The anthropologist Peter Sutton sees its effect on Aboriginal communities and people as useful and, indeed, necessary. Nothing besides a declaration of a state of emergency would cause people to sit up and take notice; nothing else would have convinced those who drink, and those who assert strong, negative influences on daily Aboriginal community life, that the government was serious about its intentions to make change happen.[53]

Langton too, recognises the Intervention as necessary. As a key historian in the television series *The First Australians*[54], Langton's commitment to educating Australians about the cruelties of white settlers against Aboriginal people is clear. This does not prevent her from regarding the Intervention as a needed strategy to improve lives on today's Aboriginal communities, especially for women and children.[55]

Still, there are those who criticise the Intervention. Barry Morris and Andrew Lattas in their article "Embedded Anthropology and the Intervention" wrote that its "dramatic military-style take over of Indigenous communities was orchestrated around a moral panic concerning allegations of pedophile rings and the sexual abuse of children". Directing their critique particularly at Merlan and Sutton, Morris and Lattas speak of the "scandal of contemporary anthropology ... twist[ing] its theory to legitimise these new forms of racial hegemony":

> As it unfolds, the Intervention has become a new form of racial governance, which seeks to assimilate and rediscipline

---

[53] Francesca Merlan, "More than rights", *Inside Story: Current Affairs and Culture*, March 11 2009: http://inside.org.au/more-than-rights/ See also Sutton, 2009, 9, where he argues a similar point.

[54] Rachel Perkins, Director, *The First Australians*, SBS Television, 2008.

[55] For example, Langton, "The end of 'big men' politics", 2008; and Marcia Langton, "Stop the abuse of children", *The Australian*, 12 December 2007: http://blogs.theaustralian.news.com.au/yoursay/index.php/theaustralian/comments/stop_the_abuse_of_children/

Aboriginal families by transforming their everyday practices and cultural disposition ...

In Australian history the protection of Indigenous women and children has often provided the humanitarian language that has legitimised extraordinary interventions seeking control of Indigenous people's lives.[56]

My question to Morris and Lattas: how much control did the abused young women of Oombulgurri have over their individual lives? Koch's words, "How pathetic. How disingenuous", come to mind.

**Group Two: Pathways to the mainstream**

1. *Opening up remote area communities to the mainstream world*

Small, remote Aboriginal communities share some of the problems that small, remote, mainstream townships face regarding social isolation and economic viability. Even when they derive income from local natural resources or from tourism, typically neither source provides enough opportunity for their children's social, educational and career needs. However, remote non-Aboriginal children's stronger orientation to mainstream culture assists their adjustment to life in the broader economy and society. For small remote Aboriginal communities, isolation from the mainstream is intensified by those traditional norms that are maladaptive to mainstream demands, and by the permit system. The permit system can be an instrument of control for community "leaders", as it limits the access of vulnerable community members such as young women to outside ideas, friendship and help.

In organisations such as Indigenous Community Volunteers, volunteers work on partnership projects with remote Aboriginal communities.[57] There are probably many mainstream Australians

---

[56] Barry Morris and Andrew Lattas, "Embedded Anthropology and the Intervention", *Arena*, September 2010: http://www.arena.org.au/2010/09/embedded-anthropology-and-the-intervention/

[57] Indigenous Community Volunteers: Reconciliation in Action: http://www.icv.com.au/home/

who would value spending time in remote communities as volunteers, who in a spirit of equity, offer assistance and expertise to remote area Aboriginal people, or just as visitors offering kindness and friendship. One study found great interest among "grey nomads" to volunteer on Indigenous projects[58] While there were challenges associated with volunteering in mainstream rural and remote towns, opportunities were found.[59] Unfortunately, the barriers for grey nomad volunteering on Indigenous communities were seemingly insurmountable, with one author reporting that "[g]oing into communities is fraught, almost impossible without a sponsor, and often a waste of effort given the lack of mutual understanding, lack of resourcing and lack of follow-up of a particular project."[60]

This situation illustrates how alienated remote Aboriginal people can become from mainstream outsiders, reflecting Uslaner's finding of the harm that segregation can do to trust. To allow communities to "win" by keeping grey nomads out is a sad, pyrrhic victory. Community mistrust and withdrawal are doing no good at all, keeping out the outside world that they depend upon but cannot fully participate in because of cultural, lifestyle and skill gulfs that we have allowed to develop. Outsiders must be allowed legal access to communities, even those on community-owned land (of course, not to private houses or yards unless invited by the occupants), as isolation from mainstream Australians, particularly from those offering friendship and assistance, is debilitating and dangerous. We owe it to the most vulnerable on these communities to remove a community's right to keep outsiders out. In the most respectful and compassionate manner, we must

---

58 Jenny Onyx, Rosemary Leonard and Helen Hayward Brown, *Grey Nomads: New Partnerships Between Grey Nomads and Rural Towns in Australia*, Cosmopolitan Civil Societies Research Centre, University of Western Sydney, Volunteering Australia, and Social Justice and Social Change Research, January 2010: http://www.aag.asn.au/filelib/Grey_Nomad_Volunteers.pdf

59 Ibid, see their Conclusion.

60 Jenny Onyx, pers. comm., September 2010.

bravely overcome such barriers, recognise our common humanity and say, "We're here for a little while, and if there are tasks we can help with, or things to chat about, just let us know."[61]

Such contact has potential as a two-way non-threatening, enjoyable, enduring bridge to mainstream life, trust and friendship. The "grey nomads" in their own city could support a remote Aboriginal family to have a city holiday. Shared outings might include educational days on the essentials of living in the city. Organisations such as grey nomads' umbrella groups and churches might arrange groups to undertake it simultaneously, adding to the community spirit and fun. This mainstream–remote exchange concept could be extended into programs such as urban–remote "sister" communities, parishes and schools. These would be based on mutual support, holidays and friendship. These exchanges are not about facilitating transitory lifestyles or providing on-demand cheap city accommodation for remote area people. Rather, they would provide remote Aboriginal people with a trusted, enriching long-term connection with mainstream urban people.

The concept is a bridging process rather than an end in itself, and it might need to operate for years, to provide a much-needed counterpoint to the damaging isolation imposed by self-determination. It is important that we do not limit such schemes to a few communities, content that a few "model projects" are happening. As most communities have suffered under the isolating "self-determination" regime for decades, such opening up of remote Aboriginal communities to the mainstream and its universal rights values,[62] in a spirit of friendship and welcome, is needed on a vast scale across the nation.

---

61 Of course, safety both for communities and visitors must be assured, but whether or not outsiders are present, remote communities must receive their right to adequate police protection from community violence.

62 See Hirsi Ali, 2010, 205-209, for her concept of "a campaign of *enlightenment*" (her italics).

## 2. Getting to the cities

Encouraging Aboriginal people to leave remote settlements for a positive, safer future is probably the most important task, but it is also a troubling and challenging one. Remote Aboriginal people are particularly vulnerable to changes in government funding policies, as there is little private economy to cushion their exposure. With a paucity of independent modes of livelihood across much of remote Aboriginal Australia, the ability of Aboriginal people to live in remote Australia is both highly dependent upon government support for income, housing, education and other services, highly vulnerable to collapse when government reduces such support, and a long way from alternative solutions. Given this, I cannot see how a reduction in government funds necessary to keep these communities going can be made without significant pain of loss and resultant protest, and my heart is in my throat when I approach the subject.

I take strength from Etherington's plea and plan to help the necessary process of leaving for the cities in the most compassionate way possible. From decades of dedicated work with remote Aboriginal people, Etherington has argued that lack of jobs is the key to Aboriginal suffering, including violence and child abuse, in remote areas. After his examination of the limits and barriers to employment in the communities themselves, shifting to town for education and mainstream work emerges as the main chance of escape from their present suffering. Please read his article, because it captures the desperate need for supporting moves away from remote areas, it includes practical and compassionate ways to achieve this, particularly regarding education and employment and housing, and it expresses the angst that many of us feel when we take on the role of messenger. He writes:

> This is not about a forced long march. This is not about stealing wages, land or resources. This is not even about assimilation. It is unashamedly about integration: integration into a set of rights

and capacities and opportunities ... where the individual is given the same range of choices and the same freedom as every other citizen.

And don't back off. It is hard to stick to your guns when people say you're some sort of monster. Okay, maybe they are simply shooting the messenger, but it still hurts. And to some extent, even talking about this makes me feel like a monster. Shouldn't I just tiptoe away? But I have to ask myself: What will this kind of workplace engagement do to their mental health? Well, what is happening to their mental health now? That's a good argument, but I don't argue much anymore. Think of the kids. I think of the kids whose funerals I've had to conduct. But mostly I think of living kids.[63]

Etherington's distinction between 'assimilation' and 'integration' is important. Assimilation was the promotion of, or the insistent requirement for, conformity to the Anglo-Australian dominant culture, as if it were desirable for immigrants and Aboriginal people to lose all their culture and language in order to become "Anglo clones." No-one is arguing for that. Integration involves access to, and embracing, opportunities in mainstream society, with a necessary learning of certain skills and a necessary discarding of maladaptive aspects of the traditional culture. It does not involve any distancing from all those aspects of culture that have no conflict with human rights, such as language and knowledge of country.[64] There are remote area people who will want to move to urban and regional areas where there is mainstream employment, but who lack the confidence and resources to do so. For them, the main policy task is to assist them, financially and with education, training and employment mentoring, into safe, good quality, affordable urban housing in good employment and education centres. There are exemplary training and employment programs in place to assist Aboriginal people into mainstream employment such

---

63 Etherington, 2007, 11.
64 I thank James Franklin for his assistance regarding this passage.

as Generation One,[65] and the Aboriginal Employment Strategy[66] established by cotton farmer Dick Estens. This need is great. At present even trained, employed people on Aboriginal communities might be under-equipped for mainstream life and locations. Alison Anderson has pointed to an apartheid in remote-area Aboriginal education, training and employment that has reduced their mobility by essentially trapping them on remote areas. Aboriginal rangers, community police, teaching assistants and community health workers can have skill sets and qualifications well below non-Aboriginal park rangers, police officers, teachers and nurses. Addressing this inequality would help towards successful mobility including to urban, mainstream life.[67]

Some remote Aboriginal people who want to move will need other forms of support, such as welcome programs that help Aboriginal families settle into everyday town and suburban life. The Aboriginal-initiated Family Resettlement Program of the 1970s, Australian programs assisting new overseas migrants, and the welcome given to Hirsi Ali and other refugees by the kind parishioners of Ede in Holland, could be good models here.

Ian Mitchell's important article about the Family Resettlement Program laments the ideological pressure that closed it despite its clear success:

> The Resettlement Program of sponsoring Aboriginal families to move from the "fractured communities" occupying reserves, where there are minimal prospects for employment, housing, education and reasonable health, to cities where these quality of life factors were maximised, was instituted in the early 1970s and continued for several years.[68]

---

65 See the *Generation One* website: http://generationone.org.au/about
66 See the Aboriginal Employment Strategy website: http://www.aes.org.au/
67 Alison Anderson, "Separate but not equal", ABC RN, *Life Matters*, 11 November 2011, audio: http://www.abc.net.au/rn/lifematters/stories/2010/3062851.htm
68 Ian Mitchell, "Quality of Life or Querulous Betrayal? The Aboriginal sponsored migration program of the 1970s" (in "Abstract" section), Conference Paper, *The Bennelong Society Conference 2006: Leaving Remote Communities*.

Several community–city schemes were involved. Mitchell's article examines the migration of 17 families (102 people) from Bourke to Newcastle. The article urges that "resettlement" is not meant to evoke anything like the forced resettlements of earlier Australia or those still occurring overseas. The idea for the scheme was an Aboriginal initiative, and included the following principles:

- the participants must be volunteers
- maximum assistance must be provided that allows the migrants many more benefits than they experienced in their original places of living
- there must be means of escape for those dissatisfied with the move.[69]

The program's counsellor worked closely with each family, helping them settle into their place of work, getting their house and appliances running, helping parents and children with enrolling and settling in to school, getting a good local doctor, shopping, budgeting, and so on. With its daily visits by counsellors, weekend barbecues where the families were brought together, transport arranged to attend local sport and other activities, the scheme was quickly working:

> It was labour intensive, with minimal caseload, and therefore expensive. But after the first few months, most families gradually assumed responsibility for their own affairs and became less a burden on the organisation and counsellor. Concomitantly, the costs to government reduced dramatically. There were no welfare payments, the wage earners began paying taxes, the families themselves gradually bore the costs of living, the children settled quickly and willingly into school and health expenses plunged. None came to the notice of the police.
>
> The expectation, which proved correct, was that after a few families had successfully integrated into their new lifestyles, there would be a chain migration effect. Indeed, once this had begun, the "old" families acted as counsellors to the new.[70]

---

69 Ibid, (in "A View of the World" section).
70 Ibid, (in "Moving" section).

Despite this extraordinary success and despite its Aboriginal-initiated origins, ideological opposition on the basis that it was assimilationist and a threat to Aboriginal identity caused government funding and hence the program to cease. Today we surely know better, and we must loudly call for the widespread re-establishment of such a scheme.

Etherington emphasises the need for specialised urban housing. Some remote Aboriginal people, committed to creating a better, violence-free life for themselves and their children in an urban centre, will require specialised protected housing to achieve this goal. For instance, some young women might want escape and freedom, but their abusers cling to traditional "rights" over them. Etherington's blueprint to meet various housing needs and to manage likely problems is well worth considering:

> Provide massive funds for three tiers of housing in urban centres (I'm modelling from Darwin):
> - Long-term training hostels for those in work, especially young men and women apprentices or trainees ... Make living there a contract relationship between employer, trainee and government overlap
> - Government-supplied rental housing, which needs massive funding to allow for
>   - some gated communities, with their own security fence and guards, requiring non-residents to be there with consent ...
>   - staffing to allow management of those in separate housing, as is the current model, including a system of identity cards for residents and patrols to remove and, if needs be, charge any resident caught in a house without a resident's permit ...
> - A support programme for home buyers. As long as Australian law allows race as a category, we should use it to provide government underwriting of loans to employed indigenous people.[71]

---

71 Etherington, 2007, 9-10

A central goal is to extend the mainstream principle sought by many Aboriginal people seeking a better, safer life – that individuals and nuclear families have a right to control who lives in their home – against a cultural principle of "demand-sharing" to provide shelter to kin. This can threaten, at times violently, even urban Aboriginal women such as single mothers trying to establish a safe, more mainstream lifestyle in a non-crowded, orderly house in a quiet suburb,[72] just right for her and her children, and fulfilling all seven parameters for children's good education as listed by Henry.[73]

There are Aboriginal people who want to remain on remote communities. They might prefer non-urban life and have the capacity to provide on remote country a healthy, safe life for themselves, their children, and their children's future. They might include Aboriginal people with a rich affinity to country and commitment to ceremony, but through a modern, reformed, non-traditional but still distinctly Aboriginal culture, that has shed dangerous and oppressive practices and replaced them with universal rights principles of individual equity and non-violence. Such Aboriginal people may have lived a typical mainstream lifestyle, or perhaps have seen the human universality and applicability of Enlightenment values and adopted them after minimal contact with mainstream people.

These Aboriginal people will have the core values essential for a safe and beneficial life. Even if the lifestyle might be markedly different, perhaps in terms of a less materialist lifestyle and a spiritual attachment to country, it is integrated with the Australian community and polity because it shares its individual human rights values. Hence there is no polygamy, no promised marriage, no child brides, no forced skin rules regarding marriage, no avoidance relationships, no humbugging, no deferred blaming and payback, no

---

72 Field work, mid 1990s.
73 Henry, 2007, 8-9.

sorcery, no cruelling, and no legitimised use of violence of any form among these Aboriginal people.[74] They, including their children and young people, will derive meaning and richness from this alternative, integrated Aboriginal lifestyle and have no "need" for alcohol, kava, petrol sniffing and other substance abuse, nor gambling addiction, nor pornographic films. These communities will be safe, non-crowded, open and positive places, have a modern, non-fatalistic approach to health and disease, have no permit system, and have no need for heightened attention from the law. Their young people will not suffer the high levels of vulnerability, resignation and despair that lead to ill-health, crime and suicide. These people will have the flexibility and capacity to provide the same opportunities for their children as those enjoyed by Aboriginal people living a mainstream lifestyle and by non-Aboriginal children, securing quality primary, secondary and tertiary education for them, and ensuring that their children have the full mainstream choice and capability for a career, to be what they want to be, and to live wherever they want to live, when they grow up. For this integrated group, remote life on beloved lands could be a rich and noble choice.

After many years, however, self-determination is a proven poor generator of such remote area cultural reform and positive adaptation. Among those resistant to shifting to cities would include many dysfunctional, violent families and communities: indeed, the families and communities with the fewest skills for adjustment to mainstream urban life. It is for these that the policy courage must start, that policies both difficult and compassionate must be made and implemented. We must shun compulsion[75] unless the safety of children and young

---

74 As Nowra wrote, Indigenous communities "need to accept that certain aspects of their traditional culture and customs – such as promised marriages, polygamy, violence towards women and male aggression – are best forgotten" (2007, 92).

75 See Etherington, 2007, 2: "Aboriginal people will suffer even more if movement to these centres is compelled. Instead, the growing desire on the part of many motivated remote area people to move into urban centres should be supported and informed".

people – especially immediate safety – depends on it. Voluntary-based schemes should be the focus, but this is a challenging path. The most vulnerable remote people are those with a high tolerance for suffering and violence, so there is little market push to get out. The pull of cities would be minimal for this most vulnerable group, for whom even cities with more goodwill than racism could be experienced as alien and unwelcoming places.

It is hard to avoid the necessity of phasing out public provision of housing in those remote communities and towns with rampant violence and limited prospects for children and young people. Such phasing out is a fraught undertaking, requiring expertise and compassion. One outcome of freezing remote area public housing stock would be more overcrowding into existing houses, a likely occurrence given humbugging and high tolerance for discomfort and suffering on many communities. There are justified grounds to keep existing houses well-maintained, particularly for older people who would find adjustment to the city too upsetting, too late. The avoidance of housing programs that would encourage young families to remain in a remote violent place with no prospects is essential.[76] Is government housing policy already heading this way? The federal government has ceased housing funding for Northern Territory outstations/homelands. Larger centres with predominantly Aboriginal populations such as Galiwinku, Hermannsburg, Lajamanu, Nguiu and Wadeye have become the focus for housing, services and other infrastructure funding.[77] Economies of scale regarding services and infrastructure, perhaps even enough opportunities for real employment might result. But the core element – daily, friendly interaction with mainstream culture – is mostly absent from these larger centres. Many are dysfunctional and violent places,

---

76 See Johns, 2011, 262-73; and Gary Johns, *No Job, No House: An Economically Strategic Approach to Remote Aboriginal Housing*, The Menzies Research Centre Ltd, January 2009, and sponsored by the Ian Wilson Liberal Foundation Inc: http://www.mrcltd.org.au/research/indigenous-reports/No_Job_No_House.pdf

77 Northern Territory Government, "Territory Growth Towns."

and hence in turn, unlikely to attract a large enough mainstream population to counter this. Regarding the key issue of reducing violence and increasing safety, little seems achievable through this strategy.

If charities or the communities themselves start building houses on homelands in response to government retreat from homeland housing provision,[78] community freedom from violence still needs to be assured. People must have full access to mainstream police protection at mainstream levels. In particular, all children have a right to child protection at the highest national standard. There must be no more adaptations by child protection workers to lower standards of care and intervention for remote Aboriginal children.[79] In some instances, if whole communities are too violent and unsafe for children and young people to live in, whole families must be helped to shift out for the safety of their children. If parents are unable to protect their children from community violence and refuse to leave, or if the parent or parents themselves are abusing or neglecting their own children, protection workers must use national benchmark standards to secure child health and safety. If this can only be achieved by helping the non-abusing parent or another caring relative or carer from the community to leave with the children for a location offering long-term safety and life prospects, or by removing the children from family and community, then these measures sadly become mandatory.

In other words, if families want to stay on remote locations but the culture of violence and resultant at-risk children remains, the government has no option but to be constantly, highly interventionist and this, surely, is not the long-term option any of us are looking for.

---

78 For example, The Jack Thompson Foundation, "Vision: To house homeland communities in the future", 2008: http://www.jackthompsonfoundation.com/index.php?option=com_content&view=article&id= 2&Itemid=29

79 For example, Natasha Robinson, "One little boy's anguish as culture put before safety", *The Weekend Australian*, 24-25 July 2010, 9.

Furthermore, access to quality education from the first years of primary school through to Year 12 is every child's right, and must be provided. Some communities can facilitate this, at least for the primary years. It is not always feasible, however, to provide even satisfactory primary education on some communities due to economies of scale and distance, or because families – perhaps through no fault of their own – cannot provide a satisfactory environment. In such circumstances, families are obliged – as all of us would be – to either shift for their children's sake, or board their children with trusted families near adequate schooling, or with mainstream boarding schools,[80] with all the support that the children and their families need, given the inevitable homesickness and different cultural expectations.

It is worth keeping in mind that limited options about where people live, due to the reluctance of government to provide housing, education and other services in places of few industry and employment opportunities, are a normal aspect of mainstream life. I am not advocating anything different for remote Aboriginal people than we would all face if for whatever reasons, including deep spiritual reasons, we wanted to live without adequate personal resources in a remote location. The irony is, while most Australians would find remote bush life very hard, non-Aboriginal people's integration with mainstream culture and its Enlightenment principles tends to better equip them for a more positive, healthier and less violent life in remote locations compared with remote Aboriginal people through traditional, Aboriginal cultures.

Given that it is our nation's policies which have trapped Aboriginal people on distant, closed communities and so deprived them of engagement with mainstream values, lifestyles, education and

---

[80] See Johns' insights on the barriers to school achievement located outside school, in particular, when "adults fail to recognise the links between schooling and work": Johns, 2006. See also Northern Territory Government, "Outstations/homelands policy…"

employment, there is scope for generous relocation assistance.[81] Above all, we need to be generous in our welcoming to Aboriginal people who decide to leave the remote lands, so that they have every chance of establishing a positive life in towns and cities for themselves and their children.

### 3. *Together in the cities and beyond*

Across a range of key indices, Aboriginal people in major cities have better lives compared with Aboriginal people in remote areas. Urban Aboriginal people have higher literacy,[82] are better educated, employed, housed, and commit less violence against each other.[83] Of course, city life is not a panacea. Life in mainstream centres – from small towns to capital cities – is not always positive for Aboriginal people, whether they are long-term residents or recent arrivals, and

---

81 I have argued against affirmative action elsewhere, because it can debilitate personal confidence and incentive, harm race relations, and increase the sense of difference or right to special treatment based on race. In this case, targeted extra assistance is warranted to facilitate the process of adjustment, because the obstacle of long-term separation has unfairly set them so far behind. For a valuable perspective on the negative consequences of emphasising special needs based on race, see Anthony Dillon, "Defining racism", *On Line Opinion*, 9 March 2012: http://www.onlineopinion.com.au:80/view.asp?article=13353&page=2

82 The Indigenous Literacy Foundation notes that "In the Northern Territory, only one in five children living in very remote Indigenous communities can read at the accepted minimum standard. By Year 7, just 15% achieved this benchmark, 47 percentage points behind their urban Indigenous peers and 74 percent less than non-Indigenous students." (DEET NT 2006.)

83 Examples: Pink and Albion, 2008, regarding Indigenous Australians: "In 2006, almost one-third (31%) of those living in major cities had completed Year 12 compared with ... 14% in remote areas" (pp.7-8); "participation in full-time work and/or study was higher among people in non-remote than remote areas (38% compared with 18%)" (p.19). "Dwellings in remote and very remote areas tended to be in the poorest condition, with 9% requiring replacement compared with 4% of dwellings in non-remote areas" (p.43); and p.39, "Health problems related to inadequate housing and infrastructure in remote areas of Australia include infectious diseases such as skin infections and infestations, respiratory infections, eye and ear infections, diarrhoeal diseases and rheumatic fever (Menzies School of Health Research 2000)". See also Johns, 2011, Figure 12, p.269: in major cities less than 10% of Indigenous homes need an extra bedroom, while in very remote areas, the figure is more than 40% (ABS 2006 figures).

life for the average Aboriginal person in the city is still not as healthy or as safe as it is for non-Aboriginal residents. Hence while the safety and other benefits of the city for Aboriginal people are substantial, much needs to be done to enable urban Aboriginal people to receive the full benefits of mainstream urban life.

One major problem is that despite the high level of intermarriage, Aboriginal and non-Aboriginal people frequently have not integrated with each other in the cities. Certainly, cities bring Aboriginal people into friendship with non-Aboriginal people. But racial segregation affects much of daily public life including leisure activities, education and community services. Policy addiction to racial separation and distinctiveness has blunted uptake of the beneficial aspects of mainstream culture such as its focus on the individual and the nuclear family, and its lower tolerance for personal violence. For disaffected, non-integrated young Aboriginal people, cities can be simply a plentiful supply of the worst aspects of mainstream life, particularly its alcohol, drug, petrol and gambling outlets, and more opportunities to obtain desirable consumer goods through threats and violence. Fringe camps, ghettoisation and racism – and these reinforce each other – are further negative manifestations of segregation in the city.

Many, perhaps most, Aboriginal people living in cities have found pathways to full participation in mainstream life's benefits, including less tolerance for violence. The more vulnerable and disaffected however have not, and so remain trapped in harmful cultural and lifestyle behaviours which create further racial distance. To help this vulnerable, disaffected group achieve a positive adjustment to mainstream life we need to reverse policies and structures that have emphasised racial difference and distance in cities too. For these people, we need a broadscale process of desegregation and welcoming.

Another critical consideration is that such welcoming probably cannot occur in every town on the level necessary for Aboriginal people's positive adjustment. Regional cities, while they may contain mainstream populations of goodwill, are often segregated in many ways, the violence among the Aboriginal population often remains under-challenged, and such towns often suffer significant inter-racial fear and resentment. Moreover, while non-Aboriginal populations express their wish for less racial segregation, town Aboriginal populations seem less open, preferring the familiarity of being with other Aboriginal people.

With a broadscale move away from financial support for institutional and other public activities based on separate races, a shift of these funds to "welcome" and "together" programs, including making mainstream services and organisations into welcoming places for both Aboriginal and non-Aboriginal people, resistance should decline over time. The Family Resettlement Program's effectiveness arose from the recognition that some towns and cities are more amenable to integrating Aboriginal people than others. Town selection and program design for very remote, more traditional people would need additional considerations and resources. But even for less remote Aboriginal people, adjustment to urban life can be too difficult in one location, while the same Aboriginal people might thrive in another. As Mitchell records, at the time of the Family Resettlement Program, there was a great deal of Aboriginal community dysfunction in their town of origin, and its white community then contained a debilitating amount of racism. In Newcastle, "there were abundant opportunities for unskilled labourers", and while there was some "antagonism" among the city's non-Aboriginal residents,

> [i]n fact, there were many more welcomes from neighbours than there were rejections. Furthermore, gradually the settlers developed many new relationships with long-term residents, whom they met in clubs, jobs, sporting occasions or school meetings.[84]

---

84 Mitchell, 2006, in "Freedom or Fiasco? (What is the downside?)".

Indeed, this lack of racism was a crucial factor, a major source of self-esteem and a boost to successful integration. Mitchell points out that had they remained in their troubled town,

> they would have drawn unemployment benefits, incurred health and community expenses, received inadequate education and been regarded as second-class citizens by the majority population.
> In the host town, they enjoyed status, competed equally with whites, were subject to less discrimination, yet continued to identify themselves as indigenous ...
> Not surprisingly, the self-esteem felt by the migrants was greatest among the children ...
> Overall, all of the families expressed the strong belief that they experienced far less racism in Newcastle than they believed possible. In turn, this created a sense of self-value as Australians.[85]

Reducing Aboriginal violence requires a cultural shift, and such a cultural shift occurs through daily, positive experiences of friendship and belonging within the mainstream culture. With core emphasis on generating positive, trust-building, daily interaction between Aboriginal and non-Aboriginal people and on assisting Aboriginal people to acquire full, equal and non-segregated participation and success in mainstream life, programs similar to the wonderful Family Resettlement Program warrant broadscale consideration and support. Aboriginal knowledge and customs compatible with mainstream values might in turn be more proudly, confidently shared to enrich us all. Surely such positive integration is better than yet more dangerous decades of self-determination, segregation and failed, demoralising interventions. Surely such positive integration is better than the resigned, accommodating surrenders to the violence and suffering endured by Aboriginal people, surrenders sadly made in the name of recognising cultural difference and in appeasement for our guilty past.

---

85 Mitchell, 2006, in "Results" section.

# Bibliography

Aboriginal Employment Strategy, undated, *Aboriginal Employment Strategy* website. www.aes.org.au/

Aboriginal Resource and Development Services, 2008. *An Absence of Mutual Respect (Baynu Nayanu-Dapmaranhamirr Rom ga Norra).* www.ards.com.au/print/Absence_of_Mutual_Respect-FINAL.pdf

*Advertiser, The,* 2010. "Tackling the Gangs of Adelaide." Editorial, *The Advertiser,* 9 April.

*Age, The,* 2002. "Yunupingu's Son Jailed for Killing." *The Age,* 24 June. www.theage.com.au/articles/2002/06/24/1023864547058.html

*Alderson v The Queen* [2002] NTCCA 10.

Ali, A. H. 2010. *Nomad: A Personal Journey Through the Clash of Civilizations.* Sydney: Fourth Estate Harper Collins.

Altman, J. 2010. "Closing the Gap Between Rhetoric and Reality." *ABC The Drum Unleashed,* 17 May. www.abc.net.au/unleashed/34484.html

Al-Yaman, F., M. Van Doeland, and M. Wallis, 2006. *Family Violence Among Aboriginal and Torres Strait Islander Peoples,* Cat. No. IHW 17. Canberra: Australian Institute of Health and Welfare (AIHW). www.aihw.gov.au/publications/ihw/fvaatsip/fvaatsip.pdf

Anderson, A. 2011. "Separate But Not Equal." *ABC Life Matters,* 11 November. Audio. www.abc.net.au/rn/lifematters/stories/2010/3062851.htm

*Ashley v Materna* [1997] No. JA1/1997. NTSC.

Atkinson, J. 1990. "Violence in Aboriginal Australia Part 2." *The Aboriginal and Islander Health Worker* 14 (3), September.

Atkinson, R. 2009. "A Message from Commissioner of Police." Queensland Police Service, Queensland Government. www.police.qld.gov.au/programs/crimePrevention/dv/

Attorney-General's Department, 2008. *Night Patrol Services - Frequently Asked Questions.* Indigenous Justice and Legal Assistance Division. Link at: www.ag.gov.au

Australian Broadcasting Commission, 2002. "Nurses Warned of Working Risks in East Arnhem Land." *ABC NewsOnLine,* 19 January. www.abc.net.au/news/newsitems/200201/s461982.htm

Australian Broadcasting Commission, 2008. "Man Dies Following Riots on Elcho Island." *ABC News,* 11 February. www.abc.net.au/news/stories/2008/02/11/2159634.htm

Australian Broadcasting Commission, 2008. "Port Augusta Pushes Ahead with Dog Patrols Trial." *ABC News,* 26 November. www.abc.net.au/news/stories/2008/11/26/2430255.htm

Australian Broadcasting Commission, 2009. "Customary Law No Defence for

Accused Wife-Stabber." *ABC News*, 9 June. www.abc.net.au/news/stories/2009/06/09/2593332.htm

Australian Broadcasting Commission, 2009. "Indigenous Leaders Urge Recognition of Traditional Punishments." *ABC News*, 28 November. www.abc.net.au/news/stories/2009/11/28/2756266.htm

Australian Broadcasting Commission, 2009. "Jail a "Rite of Passage" for Indigenous Youth." *ABC Online News*, 23 September. On Youth Affairs Network Queensland, at: www.yanq.org.au/our-work/projects/mynq/2065-jail-a-rite-of-passage-for-indigenous-youth

Australian Broadcasting Commission, 2009. "Liquor Bans Blamed for Fitzroy Crossing Decline." *ABC News*, 11 September. www.abc.net.au/news/stories/2009/09/11/2683110.htm

Australian Broadcasting Commission, 2010. "SA Scores '1 Out of 10' on Youth Crime Fight." *ABC News*, 4 June. www.abc.net.au/news/stories/2010/06/03/2916932.htm

Australian Broadcasting Commission, 2011. "Many Indigenous Too Scared to Report Abuse." *ABC News*, 21 January. www.abc.net.au/news/stories/2011/01/21/3118796.htm

Australian Bureau of Statistics, 2004. *National Aboriginal and Torres Strait Islander Social Survey, 2002*, 4714.0.

Australian Bureau of Statistics, 2007. *2006 Census Quickstats: Hermannsburg (L) (Urban Centre/Locality)*.

Australian Bureau of Statistics, 2008. *National Regional Profile: Lajamanu (CGC) (Local Government Area)*.

Australian Bureau of Statistics, 2008 Reissue. *Regional Statistics, Northern Territory*, 1362.7.

Australian Bureau of Statistics, 2009. *New South Wales State and Regional Indicators September 2009*, 1338.1.

Australian Bureau of Statistics, 2009. *Population by Age and Sex, Regions of Australia, 2008*, 3235.0.

Australian Bureau of Statistics, 2009. *Recorded Crime - Offenders, Selected States and Territories, 2007-08*, 4519.0.

Australian Bureau of Statistics, 2010. *Causes of Death, Australia, 2008*, 3303.0.

Australian Bureau of Statistics, 2010. *National Aboriginal and Torres Strait Islander Social Survey, 2008*, 4714.0.

Australian Bureau of Statistics, 2010 Reissue. *Population Characteristics, Aboriginal and Torres Strait Islander Australians 2006*, 4713.0.

Australian Bureau of Statistics, 2011. Regional Population Growth, Australia, 3218.0.

Australian Database of Indigenous Violence. http://indigenousviolence.org

Australian Human Rights Commission, 2008. "Appendix 2: A Statistical Overview of Aboriginal and Torres Strait Islander Peoples in Australia." *Social Justice Report*, 2008. www.hreoc.gov.au/social_justice/sj_report/sjreport08/

downloads/appendix2.pdf

Australian Law Reform Commission (ALRC), 1986. *Recognition of Aboriginal Customary Laws*. ALRC Report 31. www.alrc.gov.au/publications/report-31

Bardon, J. 2010. "Dry Areas Just Send Grog Elsewhere: Study." *ABC News*, 13 December. www.abc.net.au/news/stories/2010/12/13/3091747.htm

Bates, D. 1985 edition. *The Native Tribes of Western Australia.* Isobel White (ed) 1985. Canberra: National Library of Australia.

Bell, D. and T.N. Nelson, 1989. "Speaking about Rape is Everyone's Business." *Women's Studies International Forum*, 12 (4).

Bennett, G. 1929. *The Earliest Inhabitants: Aboriginal Tribes of Dungog, Port Stephens and Gresford.* Sourced from Roberts, D. A., H. M. Carey and V. Grieves, *Awaba, A Database of Historical Materials Relating to the Aborigines of the Newcastle - Lake Macquarie Region*, University of Newcastle. Roberts, Carey and Grieves list this document as follows: "Bennett, Gordon. *The Port Stephens Blacks. The Recollections of William Scott.* Dungog: Dungog Chronicle, 1929." Link at: www.newcastle.edu.au/group/amrhd/awaba/bibliography/index.html

Berndt, R.M. and C.H. Berndt, 1981 second edition. *The World of the First Australians*. Sydney: Lansdowne Press.

Betts, A. 2010. "Parents Tug Kids Out of Lawless School." *Northern Territory News*, 14 May. www.ntnews.com.au/article/2010/05/14/147561_ntnews.html

Biddle, N. and B. Hunter, 2006. "Selected Methodological Issues for Analysis of the 2002 NATSISS." In Hunter, B. H. (ed.) *Assessing the Evidence on Indigenous Socioeconomic Outcomes: A Focus on the 2002 NATSISS*. Canberra: Centre for Aboriginal Economic Policy Research Monograph No. 26, 2006. http://epress.anu.edu.au/caepr_series/no_26/pdf/c26-whole.pdf

Blainey, G. 1976. *Triumph of the Nomads: A History of Ancient Australia*. South Melbourne: Sun Books. First published 1975.

Blokland, J. 2009. "Current Legal Issues in the Northern Territory Concerning Indigenous People and the Criminal Justice System." *National Indigenous Legal Conference*. nilcsa2009.com/JennyBlokland.pdf

Bolger, A. 1991. *Aboriginal Women and Violence*. A Report for the Criminology Research Council and Northern Territory Commissioner of Police. Darwin: Australian National University Research Unit.

Bond, H. 2004. *"We're the Mob You Should Be Listening to": Aboriginal Elders Talk About School-Community Relationships on Mornington Island*. Doctoral thesis, School of Education James Cook University. http://eprints.jcu.edu.au/971/2/02whole.pdf

Bowden, C. interviewed by K. Garrett. 2011. "Murderous Mexico." ABC RN, *Background Briefing*, 7 August. www.abc.net.au/radionational/programs/backgroundbriefing/murderous-mexico/2934362

Bradbury, D. 1991. *State of Shock* (movie).

Brady, M. 1990. "Alcohol Use and its Effects Upon Aboriginal Women." *Australian Institute of Criminology*. www.aic.gov.au/publications/previous%20series/proceedings/1-20/~/media/publications/proceedings/01/brady.ashx

Brennan, A. 2008. "Indigenous Men Apologise for Violence." *ABC Lateline*, 3 July. Transcript. www.abc.net.au/lateline/content/2008/s2293873.htm

Brough, M. interviewed by T. Jones. 2006. "Pedophile Rings Operate in Remote Communities: Brough." *ABC Lateline*, 15 May. Transcript. www.abc.net.au/lateline/content/2006/s1640148.htm

Brown, J. 2010. "Antidote to Welfare Dependency." *The Australian*, 19 January. www.theaustralian.com.au/news/opinion/antidote-to-welfare-dependency/story-e6frg6zo-1225820989453

Brunton, R. 1993. *Black Suffering, White Guilt: Aboriginal Disadvantage and the Royal Commission into Aboriginal Deaths in Custody*. Institute of Public Affairs.

Brunton, R. 2007. *A Bombshell in the Centre of Perth: An Anthropologist Considers the Single Noongar Judgment*. The Bennelong Society Occasional Papers, January.

Bullock, C. 2010. "Old Law, New Ways." *ABC Background Briefing*, 21 November. Transcript. www.abc.net.au/rn/backgroundbriefing/stories/2010/3067612.htm

Burbank, V. 1994. *Fighting Women: Anger and Aggression in Aboriginal Australia*. Berkeley: University of California Press.

Calma, T. 2006. *Ending Family Violence and Abuse in Aboriginal and Torres Strait Islander Communities - Key Issues: An Overview Paper of Research by the Human Rights and Equal Opportunity Commission*, 2001-2006. HREOC, June. www.humanrights.gov.au/social_justice/familyviolence

Calma, T. 2007. *Social Justice Report 2007*. HREOC. Link at: www.hreoc.gov.au/social_justice/sj_report/index.html

Cappo, D. 2007. *To Break the Cycle: Prevention and Rehabilitation Responses to Serious Repeat Offending by Young People*. www.socialinclusion.sa.gov.au/files/breakthecycle2007.pdf

Cavanagh, R. 2009. "Grog Runners Use Kids to Hide Booze." *NT News*, 9 September. www.ntnews.com.au/article/2009/09/09/83011_ntnews.html

Central Australian Aboriginal Congress Inc. 2008. "Taking Care of Our Children, Taking the Next Steps." *Aboriginal Male Health Summit 2008*. www.caac.org.au/malehealthinfo

Central Australian Aboriginal Congress Inc. 2010. "Stop the Violence." *Inteyerrkwe Journey of Family Violence Prevention Workshop*, 10-14 May. www.caac.org.au/stoptheviolence/

Central Land Council, 2008. *Reviewing the Northern Territory Emergency Response: Perspectives from Six Communities*. www.clc.org.au/Media/issues/intervention/CLC%20_REPORTweb.pdf

Centrelink, 2009. *Parenting Payment – Eligibility*. As updated on 16 November. www.centrelink.gov.au/internet/internet.nsf/payments/parenting_eligible.htm

Centrelink, 2010. *Income Management in the Northern Territory*, 16 August. www.centrelink.gov.au/internet/internet.nsf/individuals/income_mgt_nt.htm

Chagnon, N. 1996. "Chronic Problems in Understanding Tribal Violence and Warfare." In Bock, G. and J. Goode (eds). *Genetics of Criminal and Anti-social Behaviour*, (1995 Ciba Symposium). New York: Wiley, Chichester.

*Chambers v Kerr* [2007] NTMC 055.

Chief Minister's Department, Australian Capital Territory, 2004. *A Social and Cultural Profile of Aboriginal and Torres Strait Islander People in Canberra*. Authorised by Lincoln Hawkins, Chief Minister's Department, Canberra, August. www.actdgp.asn.au/content/Document/Social%20and%20cultural%20profile%20of%20Aboriginal%20and%20Torres%20Strait%20Islander%20people%20in%20Canberra.pdf

Chikritzhs, T. and M. Brady, 2006. "Substance Use in the 2002 NATSISS." In Hunter, B. H. (ed.) *Assessing the Evidence on Indigenous Socioeconomic Outcomes: A Focus on the 2002 NATSISS*. Canberra: Centre for Aboriginal Economic Policy Research Monograph No. 26, 2006.
http://epress.anu.edu.au/caepr_series/no_26/pdf/c26-whole.pdf

Chikritzhs, T., D. Gray, Z. Lyons, and S. Saggers, 2007. *Restrictions on the Sale and Supply of Alcohol: Evidence and Outcomes*, National Drug Research Institute Curtin University of Technology, Perth.
http://ndri.curtin.edu.au/local/docs/pdf/publications/R207.pdf

Chooky Dancers, The, and N. Jamieson, 2010. *Ngurrumilmarrmiriyu (Wrong Skin)* (theatre performance).

Christie, M. and J. Greatorex, 2006. "Yolngu Life in the Northern Territory of Australia: The Significance of Community and Social Capital, Inter-Networking-Communities." *ICT and Remote Capacity Building*, School of Australian Indigenous Knowledge Systems, Charles Darwin University.
www.cdu.edu.au/centres/inc/pdf/Yolngulife.pdf

Commonwealth Consolidated Acts, 2007. Northern Territory National Emergency Response Act 2007 – *Sect 90*.
www.austlii.edu.au/au/legis/cth/consol_act/ntnera2007531/s90.html

Commonwealth Consolidated Acts, 2007. *Northern Territory National Emergency Response Act 2007 – Sect 91*.
www.austlii.edu.au/au/legis/cth/consol_act/ntnera2007531/s91.html

Conigrave, K., E. Proude, and P. d'Abbs, 2007. *Evaluation of the Groote Eylandt and Bickerton Island Alcohol Management System*. A Report for the Department of Justice, Northern Territory Government, 31 July.
www.nt.gov.au/justice/licenreg/documents/reports/Groote%20Eylandt%20Alcohol%20Management%20Evaluation%20Report.pdf

Connor, M. 2012. "Passion and Illusions: Anita Heiss's stories." *Quadrant* Vol. LVI No. 6, June. www.quadrant.org.au/magazine/issue/2012/6/passion-and-illusions-anita-heiss-s-stories

Cook, J. and B. Wunungmurra, c.2006-2007. "Communities in Action for Crime Prevention." East Arnhem Harmony Mawaya Mala Inc. www.sitebuilder.yodelaustralia.com.au/sites/5530/John%20Cook%20and%20 Banambi%20Wunungmurra.doc

Council of Australian Governments. 2006. *Council of Australian Governments Meeting Outcomes*, 14 July: Indigenous Issues. www.coag.gov.au/coag_meeting_outcomes/2006-07-14/index.cfm#indigenous

Cowlishaw, G. 1978. "Infanticide in Aboriginal Australia." *Oceania* Vol. 48 (4), June.

Cowlishaw, G. 2009. *The City's Outback*. Sydney: University of New South Wales Press Ltd.

Creative Spirits, undated. "Aboriginal Law and Justice: Tribal Punishment and Payback." www.creativespirits.info/aboriginalculture/law/tribal-punishment-customary-law-payback.html

Cribb, R. 2005. *Indigenous People and Mental Health on Cape York Peninsula*. Individual Submission from Dr Roger Cribb, Submission to Senate Select Committee, 12 May. www.aph.gov.au/senate/committee/mentalhealth_ctte/submissions/sub261.pdf

Cripps, K., C. Bennett, L. Gurrin and D. Studdert, 2009. "Victims of Violence Among Indigenous Mothers Living with Dependent Children." *Medical Journal of Australia*, 191 (9). www.mja.com.au/public/issues/191_09_021109/cri10621_fm.html

Daniels, A. 2007. "The Outstation of Balma: Gapuwiyak Day Four". *ABC Darwin*, 17 November. www.abc.net.au/local/stories/2007/11/17/2095948.htm?site=darwin&microsite=gapuwiyak&section=latest

Dearden, J. and J. Payne, 2009. "Alcohol and Homicide in Australia." *Trends and Issues in Crime and Justice* No.372, July. AIC. Link at: www.aic.gov.au

de Heer, R. 2006. *Ten Canoes* (movie).

Department of Families, Housing, Community Services and Indigenous Affairs (FaHCSIA). 2008. "Section 1: Overview of the Northern Territory Emergency Response." *Submission of Background Material to the Northern Territory Emergency Response Review Board*. www.fahcsia.gov.au/sa/indigenous/pubs/nter_reports/Documents/nter_review_submission/sec1.htm

Department of Families, Housing, Community Services and Indigenous Affairs, undated. *Closing the Gap in the Northern Territory Monitoring Report, July – December 2009, Part One*. www.fahcsia.gov.au/sa/indigenous/pubs/nter_reports/closing_gap_NT_jul_dec_2009/Documents/closing_gap_NT_part_1.pdf

Department of Families, Housing, Community Services and Indigenous Affairs. 2010. *Income Management in the Northern Territory Emergency Response*.

www.fahcsia.gov.au/SA/INDIGENOUS/PROGSERV/NTRESPONSE/Pages/default.aspx

Department of Families, Housing, Community Services and Indigenous Affairs, 2010. *Indigenous Family Safety Agenda*, July.
www.fahcsia.gov.au/sa/indigenous/pubs/families/Documents/indig_family_safety_agenda.pdf

Department of Health and Ageing, and Hunter Institute of Mental Health, 2009. "Overview of Suicide in Australia." *Response Ability*, an initiative of the Australian Government Department of Health and Ageing.
www.responseability.org/site/index.cfm?display=134569

Department of Housing, Local Government and Regional Services, 2011. *Wait Times*. Northern Territory Government. www.territoryhousing.nt.gov.au/public_housing/new_tenants/wait

Department of Local Government and Housing, 2009. *Priority Public Housing*. Fact Sheet December, Northern Territory Government.
www.territoryhousing.nt.gov.au/__data/assets/pdf_file/0007/7099/priority_housing_web.pdf

Dillon, A. 2012. "Defining racism." *On Line Opinion*, 9 March. www.onlineopinion.com.au:80/view.asp?article=13353&page=2

Dodson, M. 2003. "Violence Dysfunction Aboriginality." *Address to the National Press Club*, 11 June. http://law.anu.edu.au/anuiia/dodson.pdf

Dodson, M. and B. Hunter, 2006. "Crime and Justice Issues." In Hunter, B. H. (ed.) 2006. *Assessing the Evidence on Indigenous Socioeconomic Outcomes: A Focus on the 2002 NATSISS*. Canberra: Centre for Aboriginal Economic Policy Research Monograph No. 26.
http://epress.anu.edu.au/caepr_series/no_26/pdf/c26-whole.pdf

Douglas, H. 2002. "Justice Kriewaldt, Aboriginal Identity and the Criminal Law." *Criminal Law Journal* Vol. 26, August. www.law.uq.edu.au/documents/kriewaldt/analysis/Justice-Kriewaldt-Aboriginal-Identity-and-the-Criminal-Law.pdf

Dowdell, A. 2009. "Port Augusta Elder Warns of Explosion of Gang Violence." *The Advertiser*, 4 September. www.adelaidenow.com.au/news/in-depth/port-augusta-elder-warns-of-explosion-of-gang-violence/story-fn31yuc0-1225769553231

Durack, M. 1969. *The Rock and the Sand*. London: Constable.

Eames, G. M. 1992. "Aboriginal Homicide: Customary Law Defences or Customary Lawyers' Defences?" In Strang, H. and S-A. Gerull (eds) 1993. *Homicide: Patterns, Prevention and Control: Proceedings of a Conference Held 12-14 May 1992*. Canberra: Australian Institute of Criminology.
www.aic.gov.au/publications/previous%20series/proceedings/1-27/~/media/publications/proceedings/17/eames.ashx

Edgerton, R. 1992. *Sick Societies: Challenging the Myth of Primitive Harmony*. New York: The Free Press.

Eszenyi, D. 2006. "Court Sentence Rules Must be Fair for All." *The Advertiser*, 3 July.

Etherington, S. 2001. "The Most Threatened People in Australia: The Remote Aboriginal Minority." In Johns, G. (ed) 2001. *Waking Up to Dreamtime: The Illusion of Aboriginal Self-Determination.* Singapore: Media Masters.

Etherington, S. 2007. *Coming Ready or Not! Aborigines are Heading for Town.* The Bennelong Society Occasional Paper, October.

Eyre, E.J. 1845. *An Account of the Manners and Customs of the Aborigines and the State of Their Relations with Europeans.* Made available by eBooks@Adelaide, 2004. http://ebooks.adelaide.edu.au/e/eyre/edward_john/e98m/complete.html

Family Violence Professional Education Task Force, 1991. *Family Violence: Everybody's Business, Somebody's Life.* Leichhardt: The Federation Press.

Fawcett, J.W. 1898. "Notes on the Customs and Dialect of the Wonnah-Ruah Tribe." *Science,* 22 August 1898. Sourced from D.A. Roberts, H.M. Carey and V. Grieves, *Awaba, A Database of Historical Materials Relating to the Aborigines of the Newcastle - Lake Macquarie Region,* University of Newcastle. Link at: www.newcastle.edu.au/group/amrhd/awaba/bibliography/index.html

Fawcett, J.W. 1898. "Customs of the Wannah-Ruah Tribe and Their Dialect or Vocabulary." *Science,* 21 September, 1898. Sourced from D.A. Roberts, H.M. Carey and V. Grieves, *Awaba, A Database of Historical Materials Relating to the Aborigines of the Newcastle - Lake Macquarie Region,* University of Newcastle. Link at: www.newcastle.edu.au/group/amrhd/awaba/bibliography/index.html

Fewster, S., J. Schriever, and K. McGregor, 2009. "Spirit of Gang of 49 on Show Outside Court." *The Advertiser,* 13 October.

Fitzsimmons, H. 2010. "Systemic Failure Leads to Domestic Murder." *ABC Lateline,* 2 September. Transcript. www.abc.net.au/lateline/content/2010/s3001223.htm

Franklin, J. 2008. "The Cultural Roots of Aboriginal Violence." *Quadrant* Vol LII No. 11, November.

Franklin, J. 2012. "The Missionary with 150 Wives". *Quadrant* Vol. LIV, No. 7-8, July-August.

Fraser, F. 1883. "The Aborigines of New South Wales." *Journal and Proceedings of the Royal Society of NSW for the year 1882.* Sydney: Thomas Richards. Sourced from Roberts, D. A., H. M. Carey and V. Grieves, *Awaba, A Database of Historical Materials Relating to the Aborigines of the Newcastle – Lake Macquarie Region,* University of Newcastle. Link at: www.newcastle.edu.au/group/amrhd/awaba/bibliography/index.html

Gage, N. 2009. "Petition to Save Dog Patrols." *The Transcontinental,* 25 March. www.transcontinental.com.au/article.aspx?id=1469570

Generation One, undated. *Generation One* website. generationone.org.au/about

Gillespie, N. 2008. (Letter from Gillespie as Aboriginal Legal Rights Movement CEO). *Your Legal Rights.* Edition 14, June. www.alrm.org.au/newsletter/SD.YLR.June%202008.pdf

Gordon, S., K. Callahan, and D. Henry, 2002. *Putting the Picture Together, Inquiry*

into the *Response by Government Agencies to Complaints of Family Violence and Child Abuse in Aboriginal Communities.* Department of Premier and Cabinet, Western Australia.
www.slp.wa.gov.au/publications/publications.nsf/DocByAgency/FEB7D71FB3A6AF1948256C160018F8FE/$file/Gordon+Inquiry+Final.pdf

Greatorex, J. 2008. *Submission on Regional and Remote Indigenous Communities.* www.aph.gov.au/Senate/Committee/indig_ctte/submissions/sub79.pdf

Gsell, F.X. 1956. *"The Bishop with 150 Wives": Fifty Years as a Missionary.* Sydney: Angus and Robertson

*Hales v Jamilmira* [2003] NTCA 9.

Hall, L. and P. Karvelas, 2010. "Violence to Rage for Years: Top Judge." *The Australian,* 28 May. www.theaustralian.com.au/news/nation/violence-to-rage-for-years-top-judge/story-e6frg6nf-1225872295169

Hamilton, A. 1978. "The role of women in Aboriginal marriage arrangements." In Fay Gale (ed). *Women's Role in Aboriginal Society.* Canberra: Australian Institute of Aboriginal Studies.

Hanssens, L. 2009. " 'Echo Clusters' - Are They a Unique Phenomenon of Indigenous Attempted and Completed Suicide?" *Paper presented at the 2nd Postvention Conference May 2009,* Melbourne. Forming part of Hanssens, L., *Submission to the Senate Community Affairs Committee Inquiry into Suicide in Australia 2009.* www.aph.gov.au/Senate/committee/clac_ctte/suicide/submissions/sub83a.pdf

Hanssens, L. and P. Hanssens, 2007. "Research into the Clustering Effect of Suicide Within Indigenous Communities, Northern Territory, Australia." *Paper Presented at Postvention Conference May 24-26th Sydney.*
www.whatsworking.com.au/WomenforWik/pdfs/Cluster_suicides.pdf

Harris, M. 1991. "Black violence: why whites shouldn't feel so guilty." *Herald (Spectrum),* 16 February.

Hazlehurst, K. 1994. *A Healing Place: Indigenous Voices for Personal Empowerment and Community Recovery.* Rockhampton: Central Queensland University Press.

Henry, K. 2007. "Addressing Extreme Disadvantage Through Investment in Capability Development." Keynote Address to the *Australian Institute of Health and Welfare Conference on Australia's Welfare 2007.* Canberra, 6 December. www.treasury.gov.au/documents/1327/PDF/Health_and_Welfare_Conference.pdf

House of Representatives Standing Committee on Aboriginal Affairs, 1987. *Return to Country: The Aboriginal Homelands Movement in Australia.* Canberra: Australian Government Publishing Service, March.

Howe, A. 2009. "R. v Wunungmurra: 'Culture' as Usual in the Courts." *The Australian Feminist Law Journal,* June.
http://findarticles.com/p/articles/mi_7466/is_200906/ai_n39235223/

Howson, P. 2002. "Why we desperately need new Aboriginal policies." *The Age,* 10 May 2002. www.theage.com.au/articles/2002/05/09/1020914030021.html

Hughes, H. 2007. *Lands of Shame: Aboriginal and Torres Strait Islander "Homelands" in Transition*. St Leonards: Centre for Independent Studies.

Human Rights and Equal Opportunity Commission, 1997. *Bringing them Home: Report of the National Inquiry into the Separation of Aboriginal and Torres Strait Islander Children from Their Families*. http://www.humanrights.gov.au/pdf/social_justice/bringing_them_home_report.pdf

Human Rights and Equal Opportunity Commission, undated. *Welfare to Work Submission*. Submission of the Human Rights and Equal Opportunity Commission to the Senate Community Affairs Legislation Committee Inquiry on the *Employment and Workplace Relations Legislation Amendment (Welfare to Work) Bill 2005*. www.hreoc.gov.au/disability_rights/employment_inquiry/w2wsub.htm

Human Rights Law Resource Centre, 2008. *Practical Implications of the Northern Territory Emergency Response*. Submission to the Northern Territory Emergency Response Review Board, August. www.hrlrc.org.au/files/YE0PPFCQTT/HRLRC%20Submission%20on%20NTER.pdf

Humphris, K. 2009. "Police Finally on the Beat in Galiwinku." *ABC 105.7 Darwin*, 10 March. www.abc.net.au/local/photos/2009/03/10/2512466.htm

Hunter, E. 1993. *Aboriginal Health and History: Power and Prejudice in Remote Australia*. Cambridge: Cambridge University Press.

iDIDj Australia, undated. "Education – profiles." Links at www.ididj.com.au/education/profiles.html

iDIDJ Australia, undated. "iDIDJ Philanthropy." www.ididj.com.au/ididjphilanthropy.html

Indigenous Community Volunteers, undated. *Indigenous Community Volunteers: Reconciliation in Action*. www.icv.com.au/home/

Indigenous Literacy Foundation, undated. "Indigenous Literacy". www.indigenousliteracyfoundation.org.au/about/indigenousliteracy

Jackson, Liz. 2001. "The Shame: Assessing the Impact of Violence on Aboriginal Communities." *ABC Four Corners*, 3 September. Transcript. www.abc.net.au/4corners/stories/s357126.htm

Jack Thompson Foundation, 2008. *The Jack Thompson Foundation* website. www.jackthompsonfoundation.com/index.php?option=com_content&view=article&id=2&Itemid=29

Jamieson, L. M., J. E. Harrison and J. G. Berry, 2008. "Hospitalisation for Head Injury Due to Assault Among Indigenous and non-Indigenous Australians, July 1999-June 2005." *Medical Journal of Australia*, Vol. 188, No. 10, 19 May. www.mja.com.au/public/issues/188_10_190508/jam11393_fm.html

*Jamilmira v Hales* [2004]. HCA Trans 18 (13 February 2004)

Jarrett, S. 1997. *"We Have Left it in Their Hands": a Critical Assessment of Legal and Policy Responses to Aboriginal Domestic Violence: a Location Study*. Doctoral thesis, Department of Geography and Department of Politics University of Adelaide.

Jarrett, S. 2001. " 'This is as Much as We Can Do': Aboriginal Domestic Violence." In Johns, G. (ed ) 2001. *Waking Up to Dreamtime: The Illusion of Aboriginal Self-Determination.* Singapore: Media Masters.

Jarrett, S. 2009. *Violence: An Inseparable Part of Traditional Aboriginal Culture.* Occasional Paper 3, Bennelong Society.

Jenkin, G. 1985. *The Conquest of the Ngarrindjeri.* Point McLeay: Raukkan Publishers.

Johns, G. 2006. *Aboriginal Education: Remote Schools and the Real Economy.* Menzies Research Centre, May.

Johns, G. 2008. "The Northern Territory Intervention in Aboriginal Affairs: Wicked Problem or Wicked Policy?" *Agenda,* Vol. 15, No. 2. http://epress.anu.edu.au/agenda/015/02/pdf/15-2-CO-1.pdf

Johns, G. 2009. *No Job, No House: an Economically Strategic Approach to Remote Aboriginal Housing.* The Menzies Research Centre. www.mrcltd.org.au/research/indigenous-reports/No_Job_No_House.pdf

Johns, G. 2011. *Aboriginal Self-Determination: The Whiteman's Dream.* Ballan: Connor Court.

Johnston QC, E. 1991. *National Report, Royal Commission into Aboriginal Deaths in Custody.* Canberra: Australian Government Publishing Service.

Kaberry, P. 2004 edition. *Aboriginal Woman Sacred and Profane.* London: Routledge.

Karvelas, P. 2010. "Fetal Alcohol Study Set Up." *The Weekend Australian,* 17-18 July.

Kelton, G. 2009. "Put Culprits Behind Bars for as Long as We Can." *The Advertiser,* 13 October.

*KF. (Inquest into the death of KF\*)* [2009] NTMC 024. (\*full name in source)

Kimm, J. 1999. *A Fatal Conjunction: Two Laws and Two Cultures: Issues of Gender, Culture and the Law (for Aboriginal Women).* Master of Laws thesis, Monash University.

Kimm, J. 2004. *A Fatal Conjunction: Two Laws Two Cultures.* Sydney: The Federation Press.

Kirby, M. 1980-1. "T.G.H. Strehlow and Aboriginal Customary Laws." *The Adelaide Law Review,* Vol. 7.

Koch, T. 2010. "Pathetic Excuses Perpetuate This Fraud on Vulnerable Children." *The Weekend Australian,* 24-25 July.

Lane, J. 2009. "Indigenous Participation in University Education." *Issue Analysis* No. 110, The Centre for Independent Studies, 27 May.

Lane, M. 2007. *Two Indigenous Populations? Two Diverging Populations?* Unpublished paper.

Langton, M. 2007. "Stop the abuse of children", *The Australian,* 12 December. blogs.theaustralian.news.com.au/yoursay/index.php/theaustralian/comments/stop_the_abuse_of_children/

Langton, M. 2008. "The end of 'big men' politics", Griffith Review Edition 22 *MoneySexPower,* 16 September. https://griffithreview.com/edition-22-moneysexpower/the-end-of-big-men-politics

Law Reform Commission of Western Australia, 2006. *Aboriginal Customary Laws Discussion Paper Part V - Aboriginal Customary Law and the Criminal Justice System*. www.lrc.justice.wa.gov.au/2publications/reports/ACL/DP/Part_05B.pdf

Littlely, B. 2010. "Crime Club: Inside the Gang of 49." Special Investigation, *The Advertiser*, 9 April.

Littlely, B. 2010. "Gangs Crime and Bloodshed." *The Advertiser*, 9 April.

Littlely, B. 2010. "Elders Plea to Be Involved in Curbing Gang Crime." *The Advertiser*, 10 April. www.adelaidenow.com.au/news/south-australia/elders-plea-to-be-involved-in-curbing-gang-crime/story-e6frea83-1225852031542

Littlely, B. 2010. "Behind the Door of Gang Central." *The Advertiser*, 12 April. Also, "Power to the People of Croydon," one of the *Comments* on this Littlely article. www.adelaidenow.com.au/news/south-australia/behind-the-door-of-gang-central/story-e6frea83-1225852460424

Lloyd, J. 2008. "Domestic Violence Related Homicide Cases in Central Australia." Australian Crime Commission. Paper given at *The International Conference on Homicide - Domestic-Related Homicide*, 3-5 December. www.aic.gov.au/events/aic%20upcoming%20events/2008/~/media/conferences/2008-homicide/lloyd.ashx

Lockwood, D. 1964 edition. *I, The Aboriginal*. London: Readers Book Club in association with The Companion Book Club.

Lunn, S. 2010. "Shame of 'Susso' to Spread: ACOSS." *The Australian*, 11 March. www.theaustralian.com.au/news/nation/shame-of-susso-to-spread-acoss/story-e6frg6nf-1225839328237

McCormack, D. 2006. "The Substance of Australia"s First Men." *A Presentation to the National Mental Health and Homelessness Advisory Committee of St. Vincent de Paul Society*, Darwin, 20 July. www.bowden-mccormack.com.au/uploads/articles-papers/substance-first-men.pdf

McGlade, H. 2006. "Aboriginal Women, Girls and Sexual Assault: The Long Road to Equality Within the Criminal Justice System." *Australian Institute of Family Studies, ACSSA Newsletter* No. 12, September. www.aifs.gov.au/acssa/pubs/newsletter/acssa_news12.pdf

McGlade, H. 2012. *Our Greatest Challenge, Aboriginal Children and Human Rights*. Canberra: Aboriginal Studies Press.

Macklin, J. 2010. "Closing the Gap, Building Momentum." Statement by FaHCSIA Minister, 11 May. www.aph.gov.au/budget/2010-11/content/ministerial_statements/indigenous/download/ms_indigenous.pdf

Macklin, J., M. McCarthy, and W. Snowdon, 2009. "Doors Begin to Open on Safe Places Across the NT." *Media Releases* (joint media release), 30 January. www.jennymacklin.fahcsia.gov.au/mediareleases/2009/Pages/safe_places_30jan09.aspx

McKnight, D. 2002. *From Hunting to Drinking: The Devastating Effects of Alcohol in an Australian Aboriginal Community*. London: Routledge.

McKnight, D. 2005. *Of Marriage, Violence and Sorcery: The Quest for Power in Northern Queensland*. Aldershot: Ashgate Publishing.

Malik, K. 2008. "Identity is That Which is Given." www.kenanmalik.com/essays/butterflies_identity.html (first published on butterfliesandwheels.com, 9 July 2008).

Malik, K. 2008. "Mistaken Identity." www.kenanmalik.com/essays/humanist_culture.html (first published in *New Humanist*, July/August 2008).

Marland, S. 2010. "Healthy Homelands." Amnesty International Australia, 11 March. www.amnesty.org.au/poverty/comments/22681/

Martin, B. 2007. "Customary Law - Northern Territory." *JCA Colloquium*, October. www.supremecourt.nt.gov.au/documents/speeches/commonwealth_intervention.pdf

Measey, M-A. L., Shu, Q. L., R. Parker, and Zhiqiang W. 2005. "Suicide in the Northern Territory, 1981 – 2002." *Medical Journal of Australia*, 185(6). www.mja.com.au/public/issues/185_06_180906/mea10056_fm.html

Meggitt, M. J. 1962. *Desert People: A Study of the Walbiri Aborigines of Central Australia*. Angus and Robertson, Sydney.

*Melpi v The Queen* [2009] NTCCA 13.

Melŋurr Gapu Dhularrpa Gawiya Raypirri ŋärra'ŋur Romgurr Mägayakurr. 2005. 3 September. Sourced at ARDS, www.ards.com.au/yolngu_law.htm

Memmott, R., R. Stacy, C. Chambers and C. Keys. 2001. *Violence in Aboriginal Communities*. Canberra: Report to the Crime Prevention Branch of the Attorney General's Department. www.ema.gov.au/agd/www/rwpattach.nsf/viewasattachmentPersonal/(E24C1D4325451B61DE7F4F2B1E155715)~violenceindigenous.pdf/$file/violenceindigenous.pdf

Merlan, F. 2009. "More than Rights." *Inside Story: Current Affairs and Culture*, 11 March. inside.org.au/more-than-rights/

Merritt, C. 2010. " 'End Ban on Customary Law in Sentencing,' Urges Law Council." *The Australian*, 18 February. : www.theaustralian.com.au/business/legal-affairs/end-ban-on-customary-law-in-sentencing-urges-law-council/story-e6frg97x-1225831554796

Middleton, A. 2011. "Domestic violence escape route lacks transport", *ABC News*, 18 April. www.abc.net.au/news/stories/2011/04/18/3194517.htm

Mitchell, I. 2006. "Quality of Life or Querulous Betrayal? The Aboriginal Sponsored Migration Program of the 1970s." *The Bennelong Society Conference 2006: Leaving Remote Communities*.

Mitchell, N. 2010. "Challenging Stereotypes: Culture, Psychology and the Asian Self (part 2 of 2)." *ABC All in the Mind*, 14 August. Transcript. www.abc.net.au/rn/allinthemind/stories/2010/2978652.htm

Morphy, F. 2005. *The Future of Homelands in North-East Arnhem Land*. Centre for Aboriginal Economic and Policy Research (CAEPR), Australian National University,

5 December. http://caepr.anu.edu.au/system/files/cck_misc_documents/2010/06/Homelands_future_FMorphy.pdf

Morris, B. and A. Lattas, 2010. "Embedded Anthropology and the Intervention." *Arena*, September. www.arena.org.au/2010/09/embedded-anthropology-and-the-intervention/

Mulholland, E. 2008. "Improving Health in East Arnhem Land." *Issues* Volume 83, June. issues.control.com.au/issues2008/bi83.shtml

Mullighan, E. P. 2008. *Children on Anangu Pitjantjatjara Yankunytjatjara (APY) Lands: Commission of Inquiry: A Report into Sexual Abuse.* www.sa.gov.au/subject/Crime,+justice+and+the+law/Mullighan+Inquiry/Children+on+the+APY+Lands#Commission

Murdoch, L. 2008. "Celebration spirals into tragedy." *The Age*, 30 July.

Murdoch, L. 2008. "Wrong Side of the Great Divide." *The Sydney Morning Herald*, 27 September. www.smh.com.au/articles/2008/09/26/1222217517616.html

Murdoch, L. 2009. "We Want to Live on Our Homelands." *The Age*, 28 September. www.theage.com.au/national/we-want-to-live-on-our-homelands20090927-g7py.html

Murdoch, L. 2009. "All-in Communities Will be Death of the Yolngu, Elder Says." *The Sydney Morning Herald*, 17 October. www.smh.com.au/national/allin-communities-will-be-the-death-of-the-yolngu-elder-says-20091016-h14x.html

Murdoch, L. 2009. "Living in Fear of Losing Everything." *The Age*, 17 Oct. www.theage.com.au/national/living-in-fear-of-losing-everything-20091016-h17l.html

Murdoch, L. 2009. "Saving the Yolngu People." *The Age*, 7 November. www.theage.com.au/national/saving-the-yolngu-people.20091106-i28q.html

National Indigenous Times, 2009. "Five Men Charged Over Alice Springs Murder." *National Indigenous Times*, 6 August. www.nit.com.au/news/story.aspx?id=18381

National Welfare Rights Network (NWRN), 2009. "NT Intervention Shows Claims for Some Centrelink Payments Up 30%." *NWRN Media Release*, 1 November. www.welfarerights.org.au

Neill, R. 1994. "Our Shame: How Aboriginal Women and Children are Bashed in their Own Community – Then Ignored." *The Weekend Australian Review*, 18-19 June.

Neill, R. 2002. *White Out: How Politics is Killing Black Australia.* Crows Nest: Allen and Unwin.

Neill, R. 2009. "Untruth by Omission." *Mission and Justice: Justice and Peace News from the Asia Pacific Region*, 11 July. www.missionandjustice.org/untruth-by-omission/

Neill, R. 2010. "From Elcho, an Affair to Remember." *The Australian*, 5 March. www.theaustralian.com.au/news/arts/from-elcho-an-affair-to-remember/story-e6frg8n6-1225837098543

Ngaanyatjarra Pitjantjatjara Yankunytjatjara Women's Council, 1990. *Minyma Tjuta Tjunguringkula Kunpuringanyi: Women Growing Strong Together*, NPYWC 1980-1990. Pitjantjatjara Council.

Ngaanyatjarra Pitjantjatjara Yankunytjatjara Women's Council (Aboriginal Corporation), 2007. "About Us." www.npywc.org.au/html/about_us.html

Nomad, The, 2008. "Security in Ceduna." *The Nomad Archives*, 11 July. www.thegreynomads.com.au

North Australian Aboriginal Justice Agency, 2008. *Submission by the North Australian Aboriginal Justice Agency*. Northern Territory Emergency Response Review, Department of Families, Community Services and Indigenous Affairs, 23 October. www.nterreview.gov.au/subs/nter_review_report/105_naaja/105_NAAJA.htm

Northern Territory Department of Justice. *Correctional Services Annual Statistics*. (for example, the years 2006-07). www.nt.gov.au/justice/policycoord/documents/statistics/ntcsannual statistics2006-07_EBook.pdf

Northern Territory Department of Justice, 2009. *NT Quarterly Crime and Justice Statistics*. Issue 29 September Quarter – Facts Sheets. www.nt.gov.au/justice/policycoord/documents/statistics/29/Issue-29_Fact%20Sheets.pdf

Northern Territory Emergency Response Review, 2007. "Section A – Summary of Task Force Findings as at September 2007." Northern Territory Emergency Response Review. nterreview.gov.au/subs/nter_review_report/177_drug_free/177_Drug_Free_2.htm

Northern Territory Emergency Response, Review Submission, 2008. "Section 1: Overview of the Northern Territory Emergency Response." *Submission of Background Material to the Northern Territory Emergency Response Review Board*, 2008. www.fahcsia.gov.au/sa/indigenous/pubs/nter_reports/Documents/nter_review_submission/sec1.htm

Northern Territory Government, 2006. *Regional Socio-economic Snapshots, Groote Eylandt Region*. www.nt.gov.au/dbe/documents/general/Groote_Snapshot_2008.pdf

Northern Territory Government, undated. "Homelands." *Working Future, A Territory Government Initiative*. www.workingfuture.nt.gov.au/Homelands/outstations.html

Northern Territory Government, 2009. "Outstations/Homelands Policy: Headline Policy Statement." *Working Future, A Territory Government Initiative*, May. www.workingfuture.nt.gov.au/Homelands/docs/Headline_Policy_Statement.pdf

Northern Territory Government, undated. "Territory Growth Towns." *Working Future, A Territory Government Initiative*. www.workingfuture.nt.gov.au/download/working_future_growth_towns.pdf

NTMC 044, No. D199/08. 2009. Coroner's Court, Nhulunbuy.

Northern Territory Police Fire and Emergency Services (NTPFES), 2008. "Disturbance – Ramingining." *NTPFES Media Release*, 21 April. www.nt.gov.au/pfes/index.cfm?fuseaction=viewMediaRelease&pID=8248&y=2008&mo=4

Northern Territory Police Fire and Emergency Services, 2010. "Disturbance –

Galiwinku." *NTPFES Media Release*, 22 December. www.nt.gov.au/pfes/index.cfm?fuseaction=viewMediaRelease&pID=11544&y=2010&mo=12

Northern Territory Police Fire and Emergency Services, 2010. "Disturbance – Ramingining." *NTPFES Media Release*, 12 July. www.nt.gov.au/pfes/index.cfm?fuseaction=viewMediaRelease&pID=10994&y=2010&mo=7

Nowra, L. 2007. *Bad Dreaming: Aboriginal Men's Violence Against Women and Children*. North Melbourne: Pluto Press Australia.

O'Connell, S. 2006. "Aboriginal Customary Law Under Siege." *National Indigenous Law Conference*, Sydney, 22-23 September. www.nswbar.asn.au/docs/professional/eo/indigenous/docs/NILC_paper1.pdf

Ogbu, J. and H. Simons, 1998. "Voluntary and Involuntary Minorities: A Cultural-Ecological Theory of School Performance with Some Implications for Education." *Anthropology & Education Quarterly* 29 (2). http://faculty.washington.edu/rsoder/EDUC310/OgbuSimonsvoluntaryinvoluntary.pdf

Onyx, J., R. Leonard, and H. Hayward Brown, 2010. *Grey Nomads: New Partnerships Between Grey Nomads and Rural Towns in Australia*. Cosmopolitan Civil Societies Research Centre, University of Western Sydney, Volunteering Australia, and Social Justice and Social Change Research, January. www.aag.asn.au/filelib/Grey_Nomad_Volunteers.pdf

Partington, G. 1996. *Hasluck Versus Coombs: White Politics and Australia's Aborigines*. Sydney: Quakers Hill Press.

Pearson, N. 2009. "The Welfare Pedestal." In N. Pearson, *Up From The Mission: Selected Writings*. Melbourne: Black Inc.

Perkins, R. 2008. *The First Australians*. SBS Television (television series).

Pink, B. and P. Albion, 2008. *The Health and Welfare of Australia's Aboriginal and Torres Strait Islander Peoples*. Canberra: Australian Bureau of Statistics - Australian Institute of Health and Welfare.

Pollard, D. 1988. *Give and Take: The Losing Partnership in Aboriginal Poverty*. Sydney: Hale and Iremonger.

Price, B. N. 2009. *Inaugural Peter Howson Lecture*, The Bennelong Society, 3 December.

Price, D. 2009. "Should Customary Law be Recognised by the Courts?" *Alice Online: Australia from the Inside Out*, 22 December. aliceonline.com.au/?p=380

Productivity Commission, 2007. *Overcoming Indigenous Disadvantage: Headline Indicators*. Link at: www.pc.gov.au/gsp

Productivity Commission, 2009. *Overcoming Indigenous Disadvantage: Key Indicators 2009*. Link at: www.pc.gov.au/gsp

Quinlan, F. 2006. *Submission to Senate Legal and Constitutional Affairs Committee*. Inquiry into the Crime Amendment (Bail and Sentencing) Bill 2006. 27 September. http://catholicsocialservices.org.au/system/files/Crime_Amendment_submission.pdf

Quinlan, F. 2006. "Sentencing Laws will Further Alienate Indigenous Australians."

*Eureka Street.com.au*, 16 October.
www.eurekastreet.com.au/article.aspx?aeid=1788
Ravens, T. 2008. "Aboriginal Men Say Sorry to Women." *Herald Sun*, 4 July.
www.heraldsun.com.au/news/national/aboriginal-men-say-sorry-to-women/story-e6frf7l6-1111116814778
Ravens, T. 2009. "Aboriginal Justice Group Calls for Federal Government to Allow Customary Law." *National Indigenous Times*, 12 June.
www.nit.com.au/story.aspx?id=17927
Reser, J. 1991. "Aboriginal Mental Health." In Reid, J. and P. Trompf (eds) 1991. *The Health of Aboriginal Australia*. Marrickville: Harcourt Brace Jovanovich Group (Australia) Pty Ltd.
Robertson, B. (ed). 1999. *Aboriginal and Torres Strait Islander Women's Task Force on Violence Report*. State of Queensland.
Robinson, N. 2008. "Secrets in the Shadows." *The Weekend Australian* Inquirer, 21-22 June.
Robinson, N. 2010. "Children in Remote Centres 'Starving'." *The Australian*, 3 August.
www.theaustralian.com.au/in-depth/aboriginal-australia/indigenous-children-in-remote-centres-starving/story-e6frgd9f-1225900257221
Robinson, N. 2010. "One Little Boy's Anguish as Culture Put Before Safety." *The Weekend Australian*, 24-25 July.
Rogers, N. interviewed by T. Jones. 2006. "Prosecutor Speaks Out About Abuse in Central Australia." *ABC Lateline*, 15 June. Transcript.
www.abc.net.au/lateline/content/2006/s1639127.htm
Rothwell, N. 2008. "Going Home - Line in the Sand - End of the Dream." *The Weekend Australian Magazine*, 6-7 December.
Rothwell, N. 2010. "And They Call It Failure to Thrive." *The Australian*, 8 May.
www.theaustralian.com.au/news/opinion/and-they-call-it-the-failure-to-thrive/story-e6frg6zo-1225863617761
Rubinstein, W.D. 2009. "The Biases of Genocide Studies." *Quadrant Online* Vol. LIII, No. 3, March. www.quadrant.org.au/magazine/issue/2009/3/the-biases-of-genocide-studies
*R v Ronnie Pangate Nelson* NTSC 64[2003].
Senior, K. 2004. *Boyfriends, Babies and Basketball: Present Lives and Future Aspirations of Young Women in Ngukurr*. naru.anu.edu.au/files/58_Senior.rtf
Sexton, J. and A. Wilson, 2006. "Fallout Over Four Wives." *The Australian*, 12 July.
www.kooriweb.org/foley/news/2006/july/aust12jul06.html
Skelton, R. 2007. "Violence Behind the Silence." *The Age*, 7 July.
www.theage.com.au/news/in-depth/violence-behind-the-silence/2007/07/06/1183351448912.html
Snowball, L. and D. Weatherburn, 2008. "Theories of Indigenous Violence: a Preliminary Empirical Assessment." *Australian and New Zealand Journal of Criminology* Vol. 41, No. 2.

Socom and Dodsonlane, 2009. *Our Home, Our Homeland, Community Engagement Report.* Northern Territory Government: Outstations Policy, January. www.workingfuture.nt.gov.au/Homelands/docs/Community_Engagement_Report.pdf

Songlines, 2009. " 'Peoples Abuse' – Why Jenny Macklin Must Now Resign as Minister for Indigenous Affairs." *Songlines: A Peoples Well-Being Movement*, 8 September. http://songlines.org.au/2009/09/08/peoples-abuse-why-jenny-macklin-should-now-resign-as-minister-for-indigenous-affairs/

South Australian Domestic Violence Council. 1987. *Report of the South Australian Domestic Violence Council.* South Australia: Women's Adviser's Office, Department of the Premier and Cabinet.

Sowell, T. 2004. *Race and Culture: A World View.* New York: BasicBooks.

Stanko, E. 1996. "Looking Back, Looking Forward: Two Decades and Shifting Perspectives on Familial Violence." In Sumner, C., M. Israel, M. O'Connell and R. Sarre (eds). *Proceedings of a Symposium Held 21-26 August 1994.* Canberra: Australian Institute of Criminology, January 1996. www.aic.gov.au/en/publications/previous%20series/proceedings/1-27/27.aspx

Statham, L. 2009. "Alcohol, Drugs Hidden in Dead Animals." *Adelaide Now.* 24 November. www.adelaidenow.com.au/national/alcohol-drugs-hidden-in-dead-animals/story-e6frea8c-1225803421275

Strehlow, K. 1991. *The Operation of Fear in Traditional Aboriginal Society in Central Australia.* Adelaide: The Strehlow Research Foundation.

Strutt, J. and G. Knowles, 2010. "Sad Day of Reckoning for Fantasy Island." *The West Australian*, 2 June. au.news.yahoo.com/thewest/a/-/wa/7329149/sad-day-of-reckoning-for-fantasy-island/

SuccessWorks, Courage Partners, and Morgan Disney Associates, 2005. *Evaluation of the Family Violence Regional Activities Program (FVRAP) Final Report*, Appendices. www.fahcsia.gov.au/sa/indigenous/pubs/families/fvrap/Documents/FRVAP_Final_Report_Appendices.pdf

Sutton, P. 2001. "The Politics of Suffering: Indigenous Policy in Australia Since the 1970s." *Anthropological Forum*, Vol. 11. No. 2.

Sutton, P. 2009. *The Politics of Suffering: Indigenous Australia and the End of the Liberal Consensus.* Carlton Victoria: Melbourne University Press.

Tatz, C. 1990. "Aboriginal Violence: a Return to Pessimism." *Australian Journal of Social Issues*, Vol. 25, No. 4, November.

Tatz, C. 1999. *Aboriginal Suicide is Different: Aboriginal Youth suicide in New South Wales, the Australian Capital Territory and New Zealand: Towards a Model of Explanation and Alleviation.* CRC funded reports, Criminology Research Council, 14 July. www.criminologyresearchcouncil.gov.au/reports/tatz/tatz.pdf

Taylor, P. 2009. "Violence Reports Surge After Grog Ban in Fitzroy Crossing." *The Australian*, 22 January. www.theaustralian.com.au/news/nation/violence-reports-surge-after-grog-ban/story-e6frg6pf-1111118629326

*The Queen v GJ* [2005] NTCCA 20.

*The Queen v Wunungmurra* [2009] NTSC 24.
Thornton, W. 2009. *Samson and Delilah* (movie).
Tlozek, E. 2008. "Apologetic Indigenous Men Not Accepting Total Blame." *ABC PM*, 3 July. Transcript. www.abc.net.au/pm/content/2008/s2294058.htm
Toohey, P. 2000. "Murder, Sorcery and Tribal Law Spill Bad Blood Between Native Leaders." *The Weekend Australian*, 25-26 November.
Toohey, P. 2009. "A New Lease of Life." *The Australian Weekend Magazine*, 10-11 January.
Toohey, P. 2009. "No End to Drug and Grog Runners." *The Australian*, 16 May.
www.theaustralian.com.au/news/no-end-to-drug-and-grog-runners/story-e6frg6po-1225712735544
Trudgen, T. 2000. *Why Warriors Lie Down and Die*. Darwin: ARDS.
United Nations, 2007. *The General Assembly, United Nations Declaration on the Rights of Indigenous Peoples.*
www.hreoc.gov.au/social_justice/declaration/assembly.html
Uslaner, E.M. 2009. "Trust, Diversity, and Segregation."
www.bsos.umd.edu/gvpt/uslaner/uslanertrustdiversitysegregation.pdf
von Struensee, V. 2005. "The Contribution of Polygamy to Women's Oppression and Impoverishment: An Argument for its Prohibition." *Murdoch University Electronic Journal of Law*. www.austlii.edu.au/au/journals/MurUEJL/2005/2.html
Wanganeen, R. 2009. "Profile: Rosemary Wanganeen." *ABC Bush Telegraph*, 9 March.
Warin, J. with J. Franklin, 2007. "Remote Aboriginal Communities: Why the Trade in Girls and Other Human Rights Abuses Remains Hidden." *The Bennelong Society Occasional Papers*, October.
Warner, W.L. 1958 revised edition. *A Black Civilization: a Social Study of an Australian Tribe*. New York and London: Harper and Brothers Publishers.
Webb, S. 1995. *Palaeopathology of Aboriginal Australians: Health and Disease Across a Hunter-Gatherer Continent*. Cambridge U.K: Cambridge University Press.
White, D., M. Alimankinni, and G. Alimankinni, 2006. *Indigenous Family Violence Offender Program: The Nguiu Experience*.
sitebuilder.yodelaustralia.com.au/sites/5530/Debra%20White.doc
Windschuttle, K. 2009. *The Fabrication of Aboriginal History. Volume Three: The Stolen Generations 1881-2008*. Sydney: Macleay Press.
Working Group for Aboriginal Rights (Australia), 2009. "Australian Government Supports UN Declaration on the Rights of Indigenous Peoples Friday April 3 Parliament House Canberra." *Working Group for Aboriginal Rights*, 4 April. wgar.wordpress.com/2009/04/04/
Wundersitz J. 2010. *Indigenous Perpetrators of Violence: Prevalence and Risk Factors for Offending*. Australian Institute of Criminology, Research and Public Policy Series no. 105. www.aic.gov.au/en/publications/current%20series/rpp/100-120/rpp105.aspx
Yirrkala Yidaki, undated. "Artists." www.yirrkala.com/yidaki/artists/index.html

# Index

Aboriginal Employment Strategy, 344

Aboriginal Family Violence Strategy, 273

Alawa people, 54, 107

Alcohol/Drunkenness
- canteen, 166, 175
- and domestic or other violence, 5, 24, 36, 43, 47-9, 55, 84, 119, 131, 148, 160-70, 188, 190, 191, 200, 201, 205, 216, 269, 289, 305, 316, 318,
- dry areas, dry communities, 183, 188
- foetal alcohol syndrome, 295,
- and homicide, 167-8
- as inadequate explanation for increase in violence, 47-9, 144, 160-71, 194, 269
- rates of alcohol consumption, 25, 32, 47-9, 167-8
- reduction programs, restrictions, 162-6, 171, 273, 276, 295, 304, 306
- smuggling, inflated prices, 8, 166
- and suicide, 200, 237-40, 242, 250,
- as town attraction, 175, 179, 182, 261, 353, See also Homelands, outstations
- See also Substance abuse

*Alderson v The Queen*, 191,

Ali Curung, 6-8

Alice Springs, v, vi, 186, 258, 280, 286, 318

Altman, Jon, 182, 199, 296-7

Anangu Pitjantjatjara Yankunytjatjara (APY) Lands, 47, 156-60

Anderson, Alison, 315, 344

Anger, 109, 122, 138, 321
- anger management, 144, 195,
- against victim for seeking help, 268,

Anthropological and other early accounts, 1, 12, 56-63, 77, 81-4, 99-119, 121-40, 170, 211-13, 214-5, 292-3

Apology for violence, CAAC men's, 279-294, 295

"Aranda" people, 105-11, 113

Araru outstation, 194-5

Arnhem Land, 111-12, 113, 118-9, 133, 149-152, 162-6, 173, 176, 197-253, 324

Atkinson, Bob, 42-3

Atkinson, Judy, 2

Australian Database of Indigenous Violence, 266

Australian Law Reform Commission (ALRC), 231, 317, 320, 321, 324,

Authority
- decline in elder traditional, 148, 184, 242, 314-5
- elder, as beneficial for, or clashing with, young people, 109, 175, 198, 315, 322
- (on) homelands, outstations, 175, 184, 198, 199-201, 253
- male right to, 121, 125, 149, 151

Avoidance relationship
- See also Brother-sister traditional relationship; Mirriri

375

Baluch, Joy, 264, 265,
Barkly, 207, 208
Beaumont, Kate, 307
Behrendt, Larissa, 94, 227, 230
Beliefs, continuation of traditional, 100, 116, 117-9, 141, 171, 193, 196, 239, 241,
- See also Traditional culture, customary law; Sorcery
Bell, Diane, 2-3, 170
Bennelong, 121-2
Bennelong Society, vii, viii
Bennett, Gordon, 81, 112, 126
Bennett, Mary, 126, 131-2, 232, 233, 234, 244,
Berndt, R.M. and C.H. Berndt, 106, 110, 113, 115, 128, 231
Biddle, Nicholas, 35
Blame
- irrational (incl. sorcery), 117, 138, 238, 240
- men's self-blame and suicide, 149
- resistance to blaming men, 44, 281-2
- victim-blaming, 9, 11, 44, 144, 229, See also Anger; Victims
- See also Guilt; Mirriri
Blokland, Jenny, CM, 11, 87, 89, 90
Bolger, Audrey, 3, 55, 74
Bond, Hilary, 315, 316
Boys
- as perpetrators, 19, 54, 158, 259
- as victims, 129, 158, 320,
Brady, Maggie, 47, 48-9
*Bringing Them Home* Report, 39

Brockman, Julius, 136
Brother-sister traditional relationship, 131, 221-4, 229, 321
- See also Avoidance relationship; Mirriri
Brown, Jessica, 308
Brunton, Ron, 14, 15, 18, 102, 128
Burbank, Victoria, 109, 116, 117, 118-9, 126, 146, 181-3, 188, 200, 223, 228, 229, 232

Cape York Peninsula, 70, 116, 161, 308,
Cappo, David, Monsignor, 265-6
Cash, negative impact, 261, 305-6, 311, 316, 336,
Catholic Social Services Australia (CSSA), 93-5
Ceduna, 262-3
Central Australian Aboriginal Congress (CAAC). See Apology for violence, CAAC Aboriginal men's.
Centre for Independent Studies (CIS), 308, 326,
Centrelink/Centrelink payments, 301-9
- See also Income Management
Chagnon, Napoleon, 101, 215, 218, 219, 229,
Chambers v Kerr, 11-12
Child abuse, Child neglect, 16, 39-40, 47, 56-7, 59-60, 66-7, 88, 100, 106-7, 127-129, 131-2, 133-6, 152-3, 155-60
Chooky Dancers/*Ngurrumilmarrmiriyu (Wrong Skin)*, 203, 247-8, 320,
Christians, Christianity, 116, 121, 124, 149-50, 317

- See also Catholic Social Services Australia; Missions
Christie, Michael, 199, 205, 213, 241-2
Cities/Towns/Urban
- violence and related issues, 76, 165, 175-6, 183, 186, 187, 198, 201, 205-7, 216, 220, 224, 255-272, 284,
- as part of solution to violence, 175, 342-55
Clans: and conflict, co-location, homelands, women, 147, 199, 201, 213-4, 216-9, 220-225, 236, 242, 244, 249, 252, 259, 287 See also Warfare
*Closing the Gap*, 295-7, 304, 309
Colonialism/Colonisation/Western impacts, 55, 69, 73-4, 79-80, 81-84, 96, 100, 101-3, 119, 123, 141, 144, 173-4, 198, 221, 227, 229, 251, 273, 280, 288-9, 314-5, 317, 322-3, 328, 330
- See also Missions
Compassion, as part of change process, 17, 253, 330, 331, 340, 342, 348, 349,
Competition over women, 126, 147, 234-5
- See also Marriage; Warfare
Cook, John, 203, 213, 216
Coombs, Nuggett/Coombsian, 14, 17, 176, 198
Council of Australian Governments (COAG), 85-6
Covenant on Civil and Political Rights, 72
Cowlishaw, Gillian, 119, 133-5, 223, 229, 267-8

Cribb, Roger, 70, 116-7
*Crime Amendment (Bail and Sentencing) Bill 2006* esp. Section 91, 75, 85-98, 226-7, 230
- See also *Northern Territory National Emergency Response Act*
Cripps, Kyllie, Catherine Bennett, Lyle Gurrin and David Studdert, 33, 35, 36-47, 49
"Cultural clash", 70, 247-8, 275, 304, 316, 322, 331 See also Hirsi Ali; Authority; Multiculturalism; Young People
Culture See Traditional culture
Darwin, 68-9, 150, 186, 192, 207, 246, 328, 346
Dawson, R., 126
Dearden, Jack, and Jason Payne, 161, 168-9
Department of Families, Housing, Community Services and Indigenous Affairs (FaHCSIA), 6, 27, 87, 274, 295, 296, 304, 305-6, 309
Dependence
- men's financial dependence on women, link to violence, 303-4
- (on) welfare, 12, 14, 21, 148, 171, 178-9, 200, 299, 301-4, 306-9
Dodson, Mick, 36, 128
Dog patrols, 262-4, 267
Domestic violence. See Marriage; Violence
Douglas, Heather, 83
Drug abuse. See Substance abuse

Eames, G. M., 70-3, 89, 96,

Edgerton, Robert, 100-1, 215,
Education, English language, Literacy, 3, 14, 17, 79-81, 116, 159, 171, 175, 185, 186, 189-90, 242, 245-6, 267, 287, 300-1, 322, 325-7, 342-3, 344, 347, 351
- educated women and vulnerability to violence, 141-2
- elder authority once helped children's western education, 315
- factors affecting education success, 79-81, 178-80, 200, 203, 245, 300-1, 334, 339, 342, 351, 352, 355
- (as) pathway to greater choice, 152, 300-1, 328, 348
- (and) understanding of Western law, 79
- See also Missions; Schools

Elcho Island, 90, 204, 210, 216, 220, 224, 246, 247, 302-3, 322-3, 336

Elder authority. See Authority; Education

'Embedded' and 'Open society' populations, 326-7
- See also Lane, Maria

Employment/Unemployment/Work, 17, 20, 58, 93, 116, 150, 152, 176, 177, 179-80, 187, 189-90, 201, 203, 238, 242, 251, 267, 268, 272, 281, 296, 299-303, 306-7, 308, 310, 311, 324, 326-7, 342-346, 349, 351-2, 355

Empowerment, 10, 12, 100, 240, 273, 277

Enlightenment. See Liberal-democracy

Eora people, 122,

Escape/Flee, from violence, 4, 51, 112, 124, 134, 144, 150, 173, 186, 235, 293, 309, 310, 342, 346,
- See also Missions

Estens, Dick, 344

Eszenyi, Deej, 85-6, 91-2, 96,

Etherington, Steve, viii, 80, 177-80, 200, 201, 229, 331, 342-3, 346, 348

Evans, Nathan, 237, 238, 239-40

Eyre, Edward John, 114, 122-3, 124, 125, 133, 136, 138-40

Family Resettlement Program, 344-6, 354-5
- See also Mitchell, Ian

Fathers
- power/traditional authority over daughters, 58, 82, 127, 129, 131, 221, 222, 229, 231,
- caring and protective role, 47, 58, 59, 129-30, 222, 279, 282

Fawcett, J.W., 126-7, 130, 136,

Fear in a "punitive culture"
- as traditional force of control, including sorcery, 105-119, 134
- of Aboriginal violence in mainstream towns, 268, 270-2, 354
- and suicide, sorcery, alcohol, 238-40, 242, 244
- of punishment incl. for reporting or fleeing violence; 9, 43-4, 99, 153-5, 157, 159, 272, 323 See also Rogers, Nanette

Feminist silence, reticence, 292, 333
See also Liberal democracy

Fights, physical, instances of, reasons for
- early accounts, 46, 54-5, 61-2, 82, 83, 127, 139-40, 147, 214, 222, 223, 231,

# INDEX

- recent accounts, 56, 146, 147-8, 174, 217-8, 228, 245, 270,
- brawls/gang violence, 8, 219-20, 258-61, 264-6
- children's fighting, 54, 321
- See also Gang; Injury; Payback; Violence; Weapons

Fitzroy Crossing, 161, 165-6

Franklin, James, vii, 18, 23, 25, 32, 33, 34-5, 39, 40-1, 51, 124, 145, 171, 235, 309, 329, 331, 343

Fraser, John, 136

Galiwinku, 204, 220, 224, 300, 349

Gallop, Justice, 72-3, 77-8

Gambling, 6, 131, 266, 272, 297, 298, 304, 305, 306, 348, 353

Gamurru-Gayurra, 188-90,

Gan Gan, 251

Gang of 49/Gangs/Gangsta, 7, 258-267

Generation One, 344,

Gillespie, Neil, 262, 263

Girls, incl. physical, sexual abuse; promised marriage, girls' resistance
- early accounts, 122, 123-4, 126, 128-9, 131-2, 134-5, 149, 231
- recent accounts, 47, 117, 145, 151, 152-3, 158-60, 233, 235, 329, 337
- See also Child abuse; Brother-sister traditional relationship; Mirriri; Women; Young people

Goinjimbe people, 133-5

Gordon Inquiry/Gordon, Sue, K. Callahan, and D. Henry, 5, 55-6, 57, 60-2

Gove Peninsula, 198, 237

Greatorex, John, 199-200, 205, 213, 237, 238, 241-2

Grey nomads, 340-1

Gringai, 112,

Groote Eylandt/Groote Eylandt and Bickerton Island Alcohol Management System, 161, 162-66

Gsell, F.X., 380

Guilt
- traditional determination of; communal, deferred, guilt, 110, 111, 115, 118-9, 136, 137-8, 219, 293, See also Blame; Payback; Punishment; Sorcery
- white, 7, 14-5, 39, 330, 335, 355

Gumana, Gawirrin, 199

Hamilton, Annette, 124, 324

Health clinics/Nurses and other health workers, v, 3, 132, 144, 153-5, 160, 173, 182, 197, 204, 212, 267, 283, 284-5, 290, 300, 303, 323, 344

Henry, Ken, 299-301

Hermannsburg, 108, 163, 349

Hinterland, 183, 188, 198, 261, 269

Hirsi Ali, Ayaan, including "cultural clash" and "Campaign of Enlightenment", 69, 275, 276, 291, 301, 313, 324-5, 330, 341, 344

Homelands, outstations, 8, 16, 34, 116, 157, 173-196, 197-203, 211, 214-6, 217, 219, 220, 224, 232, 235-7, 241-3, 248-52, 280, 288, 329, 349, 350, 351

Homicide/Execution//Killing/ Manslaughter/Murder, 4, 54, 76-7,

101, 154, 225-6, 229, 232, 239, 292, 319,
- early accounts, 55, 82, 84, 89, 106-112, 113, 114-5, 117, 122, 124, 126, 127, 130-1, 133, 135, 137, 139-40, 147, 178, 214, 215, 221, 222, 247, 293,
- recent accounts, v, 2, 9, 28, 30, 38, 45, 47, 50, 70, 71, 73, 145, 161, 167-8, 181, 187, 188, 190, 191, 194-5, 203, 206, 216-8, 255-6, 258, 281, 289, 291, 333
- See also Rates; Violence

Hospital/Hospitalisation for physical injury, 29, 30, 32, 35, 45, 46, 47, 50, 117, 119, 165, 166, 168, 177, 181, 187, 188, 207-8, 209-10, 249, 256, 284-5, 287
- See also Rates

Household, Income and Labour Dynamics in Australia (HILDA), 299

Housing/Household 12, 25, 30, 34, 41, 45, 50, 51, 144, 150, 153, 267, 272, 302,
- crowded housing, incl. house "humbugging", 309-11
- as issue of conflict, 184, 274
- issues related to remote provision of (incl. NTER), 175, 179, 186, 200, 201, 274,
- need for specialised, guard-protected urban, 346-7

Howard, John (Government), 174, 226

Howe, Adrian, 226-7, 230

Howitt, A.W., 128

Howson, Peter, 13, 80

Hughes, Helen, 16, 34, 78, 116, 131, 152-3, 192, 231

Human/Individual/Universal/Victim/Women's rights, vi, viii, 2, 4, 5, 12, 16, 56, 59, 65, 66-9, 72, 73-5, 85, 91, 95, 97, 101, 107, 131-2, 141, 145, 152-3, 157, 171, 192, 222, 227, 228, 229, 230, 234, 253, 263, 275, 288, 291-294
- See also Traditional culture, customary law; Liberal democracy

Human Rights Law Resource Centre (HRLRC), 92, 95-6

"Humbugging"/ "Demand sharing", 20, 36, 301, 303, 304, 306, 309-10, 347, 349,
- See also Cash; Housing; Income Management

Hunter, Boyd, 35, 36, 47,

Hunter, Ernest, 239, 242, 243, 247, 303

Hunter-gatherer, 99, 229, 244, 253, 325

Hunter River district, 126, 136

Identity, 14, 27, 53, 68, 83, 163, 243, 247, 298, 325, 328, 346

iDIDJ Australia, 248-9

Income Management (IM), 295-311, esp. 304-9
- See also Centrelink; Northern Territory Emergency Response

Indigenous Community Volunteers, 339

Indigenous Family Safety Program, 295

Infanticide, 119, 132, 133-6

Initiated male/Initiation/Uninitiated male, 60, 108, 110, 112, 159, 160, 190, 221, 260, 291, 320

Injury through violence, incl. gender patterns
- burns, 208, 318, 329
- cranial, facial, head, 9, 29, 43, 59-60, 67, 119, 123, 125, 126, 146, 154, 169-70, 191, 194-5, 216, 220, 223, 256, 260, 320, 322
- limb (arm, leg, thigh), 54, 62, 71, 123, 124, 138, 146, 169, 170, 195, 218, 219, 289, 290, 322,
- neck, 107, 109, 232
- shoulder, 139, 193, 290
- torso (abdominal, back, body, chest), 9, 62, 111, 193, 194, 195, 219, 232, 290
- See also Rape; Rates; Violence; Weapons

Integration, 3-5, 18, 20, 76, 143, 148, 176, 197, 201, 202, 246, 272, 274, 276, 301, 324-30, 331-55

Intervention(s), incl. need for; difficulties with; reluctance to; resistance to, 3, 5-6, 10, 90, 155, 224, 226, 237, 240, 252, 257, 273, 274-6, 296-8, 300, 311, 334, 339, 350, 355
- See also Northern Territory Emergency Response

Intervention, The. See Northern Territory Emergency Response

Inteyerrkwe/Inteyerrkwe Statement. See Apology for violence, CAAC Aboriginal men's.

Isolation, incl. as issue for safety, 4, 9, 44, 165, 179-80, 196, 211, 214, 224, 241, 243-4, 252, 339-41

Jabiru, 191
Jackson, Liz, 76, 157, 160
Jack Thompson Foundation, 350
Jamieson, Lisa M., James E. Harrison and Jesia G. Berry, 29, 169, 256, 320, 323
Jamieson, Nigel, 247,
Jealousy, 43, 45, 100, 113, 124, 285,
Johns, Gary, vii, 10, 13-14, 17, 23, 76, 78, 80, 157, 166, 192, 197, 201, 301, 335, 349, 351, 352
Jones, Tony, 173, 192, 193-4, 273,
Judicial responses/White law
- Aboriginal adaptation to/problems in adapting to, white law, v, 16, 79-85, 216-17, 224, 288-9, 318
- and Aboriginal perpetrators, 1, 3, 73-4, 76, 79, 87, 92, 96
- to Aboriginal violence, 65-98, 275
- and Aboriginal women victims, 1, 12, 65, 70-9, 91, 96-8, 328, 329
- and customary law, 65-79, 83-98
- defining 'ordinary' behaviour, 70-73
- legal aid, 92, 152
- white law is for all, 84-5, 333
- See also Police; Sentencing; Violence

Kaberry, Phyllis, 113, 114-5, 124-5, 132
Kaiadilt people, 147-8
Katherine, 192, 205, 206, 310 See also Barkly
Kimberley, 3, 124, 125, 132, 136, 239,
Kimm, Joan, 3, 5, 6, 8, 10, 12, 44, 56, 57, 75, 83, 95, 99, 102, 118, 119, 121, 123-4, 125, 136, 143, 188, 223, 224, 231, 234, 252, 320

Kin(ship), 15, 16-17, 20, 34, 51, 58, 109, 118, 134, 147, 152, 157, 160, 198, 212, 214, 218-9, 222, 224, 235, 242, 257, 259-60, 286-7, 290, 310, 318, 329, 335, 347

Koch, Tony, 334-5, 339

Kriewaldt, Justice, 83

Lajamanu, 6, 234, 288, 291, 317, 320, 321, 349

Lane, Joe, viii, 326-7

Lane, Maria, 326-7

Langton, Marcia, 76-7, 241, 338

Lattas, Andrew, 338-9

Laymba Laymba, Rosa, 224-6

Laynhapuy Homelands/Laynhapuy Homelands Association, 198, 251

Leibler, Mark, 127-8

Liberal democracy/Enlightenment/ Liberal democratic values, incl. regarding personal use of violence, 1-2, 15, 66, 67, 68, 69, 74, 76, 211, 218, 228-9, 275, 277, 291, 296, 298, 300, 314, 317, 322, 324, 330-2, 333, 335, 341, 347, 351,

- Enlightenment feminists, 331-2, 333

- post-Enlightenment, 2, 66,

- post-modernism, 101

- professionals should be "Ambassadors of Enlightenment", 291, 330-1

- relativism, 70, 73, 253, 333

- See also Hirsi Ali; Human Rights; Mainstream

Liddle, John, 279, 281, 282-5, 292 See also Apology for violence, CAAC men's

*Little Children are Sacred*, 7, 11, 174, 281, 283

- See also Stolen Generation

Littlely, Bryan, 259, 260, 261-2

Lloyd, Jane, 8, 9, 76, 157, 160, 194

Locals-outsiders, conflict and violence, 186, 272

- See also Clans, Tribes

Lockwood, Douglas, 54, 75, 107

Loy, Danielle, 289-91

Macklin, Jenny, 6, 66-7, 296

McLaren, Jock, 3

Mainstream, 4, 12, 102, 160, 162, 183, 186, 189, 196, 232, 255-72

- barriers to mainstream incl. violence; dangers in separation from mainstream, 4, 15, 80, 116, 118, 141, 148, 149, 175, 180, 185, 188, 200, 214, 237, 252, 267-72 See also Separatism

- modern-traditional clash, incl. for young people, 16, 70, 118, 141, 149, 192, 243, 245-6, 247, 251-2, 253, 322-3

- negative attractions of modernity, 251-2

- need for participation in, pathways to, immersion in, 14-15, 65-6, 180,

- positive, welcoming, contact as bridge to mainstream, 17, 201, See also Compassion

- reduction, suppression of violence and in tolerance for violence, 4, 18, 33, 52, 143-5, See also Violence

- values, incl. regarding violence, 10, 146, 192

- and women's emancipation, 328-9
- See also Integration; Liberal democracy; Missions; Strategies

Malik, Kenan, 53, 68-9, 70

Maningrida, 77, 88, 177, 188-90

Marriage, incl. marriage rules, 57, 58, 151, 171, 217, 244, 321, 324, 347, 348,
- adultery, 83, 130-1, 221-2,
- affection in; husbands protecting wife; marriage for love, elopement, 60-1, 127, 134-5, 246, 247,
- arranged, child, forced, promised, incl. female resistance to and punishment for, 4-5, 77, 82, 88, 122, 124, 125, 126, 127, 128-9, 131-2, 134-5, 149, 150, 151, 153, 159-60, 188, 190, 222, 229, 329,
- domestic violence in marriage, 58-60, 62-3, 144, 170, 194-5, 221, 225-6, 233, 234, 235, 252, 287, 293, 317,
- inter-racial marriage, 184, 246, 353
- polygamy/polygyny, incl. conflict between co-wives, 137, 229, 230-235, 244-5, 246, 252, 319,
- wife/girl/woman, male act of bartering/claiming/exchanging/ lending/kidnapping/killing to get/ raiding to get/stealing, 82, 122, 123, 126, 127, 128, 137, 147, 214, 223, 229, 231, 321, 322, 329, 336
- wrong skin, wrong way marriage, correct marriage, skin groups, 11, 55, 151, 222, 245, 246, 247, 252, 293, 319-20, 321-3, 347

Martin, Justice Brian, 78, 87, 90, 218

McGlade, Hannah, 75, 77, 78, 87, 90, 129, 157, 160, 188, 190, 192, 226, 333

McKnight, David, 18, 57, 99, 115, 116, 144, 147-9, 171, 200, 201

Meggitt, M. J., 46-7, 57-60, 61-2, 82-3, 125, 126, 128, 130

Memmott, Paul, Rachael Stacy, Catherine Chambers and Catherine Keys, 55, 56, 60

Mental abuse/Mental health issues, 40, 70, 112, 117, 209, 275, 298, 343
- See also Sorcery; Suicide

Mentors, mentoring, 285, 334, 343

Merlan, Francesca, 337, 338

Mildren, Justice, 88-9

Milingimbi, 204, 225

Minority groups, incl. issues of rights, viii, 10, 53, 67-70, 80, 102, 103, 267, 275, 294, 324, 326, 327-8
- "involuntary" minority, 325-6

*Mirriri*, 118-9, 222-4, 228, 229, 252, 293, 320
- See also Blame; Brother-Sister traditional relationship; Avoidance relationship; Punishment

Missions, missionaries, 17-18, 53-4, 79, 80, 107, 112, 115, 116, 124, 131, 135, 147-8, 149-50, 173, 186, 198, 199, 200-1, 212, 213, 223, 229, 232, 241, 242, 245, 251, 293, 299, 314-5, 317, 325, 331,
- See also Christians

Moorunde people, 138

Mornington Island, 115-6, 144, 147-9, 315-6, 321

Mothers, grandmothers, 33, 36-41, 58, 81, 82, 130, 136, 186, 191, 192-3, 195, 255, 264, 279, 302, 309, 319, 320, 333, 347,

- violence against due to parenting issues, 59, 108, 130, 222, 268,
- young age of Aboriginal mothers, 127, 131-2, 133-5, 150, 302-4

Mt Druitt, 267

Mulholland, Eddie, 197, 211-2

Mullighan Inquiry, 47, 117, 153, 155-60, 274, 303, 323

Multiculturalism, 68-70, 275

Mununggurr, Barayuwa, 198

Murdoch, Lindsay, 176, 199, 202, 205, 210, 213, 235-6, 237, 238, 240, 249, 251

"Murngin" people, 126, 130, 137-8, 214-5, 220, 221-3, 224, 226, 228, 243, 248

- See also Warner; Yolngu

Myths

- traditional/Dreamtime. See Punishment; Traditional culture; Women
- western, about traditional harmony, 100, 101, 144, 148, 153, 330

Nar-wij-jerook people, 138-40

National Aboriginal and Torres Strait Islander Social Survey, (NATSISS), 23-52, 60, 177, 256,

National Indigenous Legal Conference (NILC), 65, 87,

National Welfare Rights Network (NWRN), 306-7

Neighbours/Neighbourhood-community problems, 17, 24, 25-6, 29-32, 43, 50, 114, 136, 138, 256,

- neighbourliness, 313, 324-5, 354

Neill, Rosemary, 12-13, 15-16, 39-40, 237-8, 240, 245, 246, 247, 323,

Nelson, Topsy Napurrula, 2-3

Newcastle, 81, 112, 126, 345-6, 354-5

Ngaanyatjarra Pitjantjatjara Yankunytjatjara Women's Council (NPYWC), 8-10, 157, 336

Nguiu, 11, 124, 349

Ngukurr, 119, 149-152

*Ngurrumilmarrmiriyu (Wrong Skin)*. See Chooky Dancers

Nhulunbuy, 177, 205-6, 210, 212, 216, 250, 310

Night patrols, 6, 8, 12, 273, 276

Non-Aboriginal

- past norms and practices of equivalent violence, 121, 318
- (as) perpetrators of abuse, violence against Aboriginal people, 258,
- Aboriginal violence, and implications for race relations, 141-2, 271-2, 353-4,
- (as) victims of Aboriginal violence, 144, 257-8, 258-66, 272, 293,
- See also Colonialism; Judicial responses; Liberal-democracy; Marriage; Rates

Norms (including community, cultural, liberal-democratic, mainstream, violent) See Mainstream; Violence

Northern Australian Aboriginal Justice Agency (NAAJA), 86-7, 88, 226

Northern Territory Emergency Response (NTER)/The Intervention, 86, 174-5, 226, 237, 240, 274, 279-80, 281, 282-3, 285-8, 294, 295-311, 336-9 See also Income Management

# INDEX

*Northern Territory National Emergency Response Act (NTNERA) 2007 - Sect 91*, 85-99, 224-30
- See also *Crime Amendment (Bail and Sentencing) Bill 2006*

North Australian Aboriginal Legal Aid Service, 152

Nowra, Luis, 3-5, 57, 74, 75, 77, 78, 99, 121-2, 128-9, 154, 156, 192, 203, 322, 336, 348

O'Connell, Stewart, 65, 67-8, 73

Ogbu, John, 325-6

Oombulgurri, 336-7, 339

Palm Island, 70-3

Parents/Parenting See Fathers; Mothers

Partington, Geoffrey, 14, 17, 303-4

Payback/Feuding/Retaliation/ Retribution/Revenge/Vendetta, 7, 9, 33, 56, 61, 67-8, 82-3, 100, 109-10, 115, 117, 118, 121, 134, 135, 137, 138, 139, 147, 188, 214, 216, 217, 218, 235, 238, 239, 244, 259, 270, 287-91, 293, 318, 322, 323, 330-1, 347
- massacre, 106
- See also Fights; Victims; Violence

Pearson, Noel, 299, 308, 315

Permit system, 3, 4, 175, 211, 224, 328, 336, 339, 348

Perpetrators, community defence of, sympathy for, 10, 153-5, 268-9, 286
- See also Judicial Responses; Rates

Phillip, Governor Arthur, 121-2

Pitjantjatjara people, 55, 135, 156, 169 See also APY; Mullighan; NPYWC

Police (and Aboriginal violence), v, 3, 270, 291,
- Aboriginal calls on, 151, 219, 264, 333-4
- observations of, 42-3, 237, 289, 289,
- responses, 7, 8, 88, 115, 154, 162, 219, 220, 236, 250, 261, 264-5, 267, 270, 318, 333-4, 336-7
- records, reports, statistics, 28, 30, 32, 45, 47, 117, 162-5, 177, 187, 190, 195, 199, 205, 206-7,
- shortage of (incl. NTER addressing of), 175, 203-4, 295, 304, 329, 333, 336-7, 341, 350,
- under-reporting to, 9-10, 151, 153-55, 194
- See also Rates

Pollard, David, 14-15

Pornography, 131, 306, 348

Port Augusta, 186, 261, 262-5

Port Stephens, 81, 112, 126

Price, Bess, v, vii-viii, 79-80, 84, 291, 305, 315, 325

Price, Dave, 84-5, 291-2, 318

Prison/Arrest/Jail/Imprisonment, v, 11, 68, 76-8, 84, 87, 88, 92-3, 95, 97, 115, 163, 174, 188, 191, 195, 210-11, 216, 218-9, 238, 261, 262, 269, 284-5, 287, 288, 311, 314, 317, 320, 337,
- See also Rates; Homelands; Sentencing

Productivity Commission, 28, 45-8, 50, 145, 156, 161, 167, 177, 206, 215, 256, 258

Punishment See Fear; Judicial responses; Payback; Traditional culture; Sentencing; Violence

*Queen vs GJ,* 78, 79, 192-4, 319, 328-9
*Queen vs Dennis Wunungmurra,* 90, 225-6
*Queen vs Roddenby,* 87

Race relations, incl. violence impact on. See Non-Aboriginal
*Racial Discrimination Act,* 72, 291
Ramingining, 219, 248
Rape, 3, 57, 60, 72-3, 76-7, 78, 122, 127-9, 131-2, 154, 155, 158, 181, 229, 292, 319
Rates, incl. remote, non-remote
- assaults, violence, 2, 28, 29, 32, 42, 45, 46, 50, 162-6, 205-8, 256, 258
- child abuse/neglect, 156
- imprisonment and sentencing
- homicide, 9, 28, 45, 50, 145, 161, 215, 256, 258, 333
- hospitalisation for physical injury, 29, 46, 207-8, 256
- imprisonment/arrest, 163, 210-11
- injury, 29, 256
- sexual assault, 29, 32, 156, 256
- suicide, 208-10
- violence and alcohol, 161, 162-6, 166-9, 169-70
- See also National Aboriginal and Torres Strait Islander Social Survey (NATSISS)
Reconcile/Reconciliation Australia/ Decade for Reconciliation, 16, 21, 75, 127, 238, 240, 241, 244, 263, 246, 247, 263, 275, 315, 339 See also "cultural clash"
Remote, non-remote rates. See Rates

*Report of the South Australian Domestic Violence Council,* 42
Reser, Joseph, 239,
Roberts, Phillip (also named Waipuldanya), 54
Robertson, Boni, 55, 60
Robinson, Natasha, 155, 287-8, 297, 351
Rogers, Nanette, 173, 174, 193-4, 227, 273, 313, 328,
Rom, 202, 203, 221, 223-4, 236
Roper River, 54, 107, 321
Rothwell, Nicolas, 154, 233, 302-3, 336
*Royal Commission into Aboriginal Deaths in Custody (RCADC),* 14, 174, 183, 237, 240
Rubinstein, William, 135
Rudd, Kevin, 97, 249, 296

Safe house/Refuge/Women's shelter, 3, 5, 6, 7, 12, 51, 124, 268, 273, 276, 334 See also Housing
*Samson and Delilah,* 320
Schools, 6, 80, 149, 150, 152, 158, 159, 162, 178-80, 182, 192, 203, 212, 263, 267, 271, 296-7, 300, 301, 303, 305, 313, 314-5, 325, 328, 341, 345, 351, 354
- See also Education
Section 91. See *Northern Territory National Emergency Response Act*
Self-determination, 1, 2, 3, 4, 6, 10-11, 13-16, 17-18, 52, 66, 79-81, 84, 89, 95-98, 162, 166, 176, 177, 200-1, 203, 245, 251, 263, 267, 272, 274-7, 282, 298, 331, 332-3, 335, 341, 348, 355
- See also Homelands; Separatism

Self-esteem, 61, 200, 299, 355

Senior, Kate, 149-52

Sentencing, White law, esp. regarding Aboriginal violence, 223, 276, 337

- length; leniency in; mitigating factors incl. culture, 3, 67-8, 70, 72, 74, 75-9, 83, 84, 85-6, 89-91, 92-6, 191, 193, 226-7, 230, 281, 332

- home detention, parole, 182-3, 187, 188, 194-5

- Section 91 impact on sentencing See Northern Territory National Emergency Response Act

- See also Judicial responses

Separatism, segregation

- (in) cities and towns, 267, 271, 272, 353,

- (in) general, 1, 13, 18, 20, 276-7, 298, 327-8, 354,

- (through) remoteness, 176, 188, 251, 257, 313-4, 328, 344, 352

- See also Homelands/Outstations; Self-determination; Permit system

Sexual abuse/Sexual assault. See Boys; Child abuse; Girls; Marriage; Pornography; Rape; Rates; Women; Young People

Sexton, Jennifer, 231-3, 234

Shame/Shaming, 16, 76, 118, 223, 238, 268-9, 281-2, 285-7, 288-9, 309, 342

Silence/Silencing through threats, violence, of victims and witnesses, incl. under-reporting violence, 4, 6, 7, 10, 21, 30, 34, 38, 39-40, 44-5, 51-2, 126, 153-5, 155-60, 283, 333, 336

Simons, Herbert, 325-6,

Sisters. See Brother-sister traditional relationship; Mirriri

Skelton, Russell, 6, 7-8, 166,

Ski Beach, 177, 210, 216, 232, 236, 249

Skin group, correct, right, wrong. See Marriage

Snowball, Lucy, 23-6, 29, 32, 36, 38, 40, 48, 49, 161

Songlines, 66-7,

Sorcery/Cursing/Magic, 12, 57, 82-3, 106, 110, 112-8, 136, 137-8, 139, 148, 159, 171, 179, 216, 221, 238-40, 242, 244, 252, 293, 319, 347-8

- (as) "supernatural aggression", 116

Southwood, Justice Stephen, 226-7, 230

Sowell, Thomas, 102-3, 286-7

Spearing. See Payback; Punishment; Weapons

Spencer, Baldwin, 84

Spring Park, 191

Stanner, W.E.H., 124-5, 128

*State of Shock*, 281

Stolen generation/Removal from family as child, 25, 26, 36-41, 126, 144, 150, 281, 276, 350

- See also Child abuse

Strategies/remedies, 3, 6, 10, 13, 62, 84, 166, 183, 273-355 esp. 313-355

- See also Integration; Liberal-democracy; Mainstream

Strehlow, C., 113,

Strehlow, Kathleen, 99, 105-11, 113,

Strehlow, T. G. H. (Ted), 99, 105-10, 121, 293

Substance abuse/Drug abuse, v, 5, 12, 24, 32, 49, 94, 131, 144, 151, 166,

175, 190, 199, 200, 203, 207, 212, 242, 261-2, 266, 272, 276, 297, 298, 304-6, 310, 316, 348, 353
- petrol sniffing, 5, 47, 131, 175, 188, 200, 216, 248, 316, 348, 353
- See also Alcohol

Suicide, 5, 57, 60, 148, 149, 181, 188, 200, 203, 208-10, 211, 235-51, 314, 316, 323, 348,
- Self-harm, 203, 210, 248, 250

Sutton, Peter, 3, 12-13, 16-17, 19-20, 21, 99, 102, 125, 180-1, 200, 201, 214, 239, 246, 273, 276, 284, 286, 301, 309, 310, 320, 321, 338,

Swanson, Laura, 260

Tatz, Colin, 13, 148, 236-7, 240, 242, 247

Teachers, including their observations, 158, 178, 313, 325, 344
- See also Schools

Tench, Watkin, 121

*Ten Canoes*, 219, 248, 319,

Tennant Creek, 207

Theft/Robbery
- recent, 32, 154, 259-60, 262
- traditional society, of sacred objects, 108

To Break the Cycle, 265-6
- See also Cappo

Toohey, Paul, 77, 166, 175, 216-8

Traditional culture
- Cultural Theory, 23-4, 49
- customary law, 56-7, 65-98, 106, 105-19
- (and) interpersonal violence, 53-63, 121-40

- resilience of traditional culture, law, norms, 143-171
- See also Judicial responses; Mirriri; Payback; Sorcery; Violence; Women; Young people

Trudgen, Richard, 17-18, 199, 200, 201, 203, 205, 215-6, 242, 245, 248

Trust, factors affecting between-group trust, incl. segregation, 15, 201, 327-8, 337, 340, 341, 351, 355

United Nations Declaration on the Rights of Indigenous Peoples, 66, 97-8

Universal Declaration of Human Rights, 85

Uslaner, Eric M., 327-8

Victims
- tolerance for violence among, 10, 33, 143, 145, 151
- See also Blame; Boys; Child abuse; Fear; Girls; Marriage; Rates; Silence; Violence; Women; Young people

Violence, Aboriginal
  (a) attitudes to, incl. as acceptable/ justified/legitimate
- as "amusing", 268
- controlled violence, esp. traditional, incl. contemporary recognition of, 55, 59-60, 62, 129, 131-2, 134, 138-9, 146, 147, 169, 170, 289-90
- denial/downplay/evasion of pre-contact violence and continuity, 21, 53-63, 99-103, 129-32, 227-8, 280, 286, 294

- as "healing" or "virtue", 63, 65-70, 330
- as male right to punish/women's deserving, 33, 95, 149, 223, 227, 234, 268, 272
- as "necessary" punishment, incl. sacred realm, 105-119, 136
- suppression of violent practice by missions, white law, 53, 81-83, 115, 117, 213, 216, 239
- "zero tolerance", CAAC men's call for, 284

See also Abuse; Alcohol; Apology for violence; Boys; Brother-sister; Child Abuse; Cities; Girls; Homelands; Homicide; Injuries; Judicial responses; Mainstream; Marriage; Non-Aboriginal; Payback; Perpetrators; Rates; Silence; Suicide; Traditional culture; Victims; Weapons; Women; Young people

(b) property damage, 164-5

(c) public violence, anti-social behaviour, 258-267, 306 See also Fights; Neighbours

Volunteers/Volunteering, 339-40
- See also Indigenous Community Volunteers; Onyx

von Struensee, Vanessa, 230, 233, 234
- See also Polygamy

Wadeye, 176, 349

Waipuldanya (also named Phillip Roberts), 54-5, 75, 107,

Warlpiri/ "Walbiri" people, 46-7, 57-60, 80, 83, 126, 317-8

Wannah-Ruah people, 126, 130

War/Battles/Tribal conflict/ 101, 202
- early accounts, 54, 55, 114, 126, 127, 130, 136-40, 147, 212, 214-5, 244
- recent, 265, 268, 289
- See also Clans; Locals-outsiders; Payback

Warin, Jenness, 23, 34, 35-6, 44, 50-1, 90, 235, 329, 331

Warner, W. Lloyd, 57, 111-2, 118, 125, 126, 128, 129, 130-1, 137-8, 213-6, 220-3, 226, 228, 243, 244, 293

Warriors, 17, 127, 136, 147, 148, 213, 248, 249

Weapons, 63, 71, 83, 125, 139, 154, 219, 222, 225, 259, 260
- axes, 8, 154
- bats, 260
- boiling water, 195
- boomerang, 54-5, 59, 62, 170, 193, 290
- *bwirri*, 139
- club, 61, 62, 126
- fire, firebrands, 139, 329
- gun/rifle, 154, 189, 260, 329
- iron bar, 260
- knife, 62, 71, 154, 219, 224-6, 260, 318,
- machetes, 318
- *nulla nulla*, 8, 54, 55, 112, 290,
- rocks, 8, 154, 204, 217, 264
- screwdrivers, 260
- spear/spearing, 55, 62, 111, 115, 119, 123, 124, 134, 136, 138-9, 170,

216, 217, 218, 222-3, 287, 288-9, 322. See also Spearing
- star pickets, 154
- stick/digging sticks/fighting stick/yam stick, 54, 67, 119, 128, 139, 146, 154, 191, 193, 223, 228, 321
- tin can, 119
- *waddies*, 123
- *waltha*, 67

Weatherburn, Don, 23-6, 29, 32, 36, 38, 40, 48, 49, 161

Webb, Stephen, 99, 125

Welfare (Government)/Welfare dependency, 12, 14, 148, 171, 177, 200, 231, 271, 298-311, 327, 335, 345  See also Centrelink; Income Management

Wellesley Islands, 147

Western Australian Task Force on Domestic Violence, 42

Whistleblowers, 3, 4, 141, 155
- See also Silence; Victims

Wik people, 116-7, 181, 209

Wild, Rex, QC, 7, 90, 91, 283

Williams, Nancy, 117

Wilson, Ashleigh, 231-3, 234

Women
- continuity of traditional generators of violence against women, 70-3, 77-9, 117, 143-52, 159-60, 169-71, 129-132, 188-194, 220-235, 252, 268-9, 319-24
- subjection to violence in traditional gender roles, early accounts, 57-63, 118-9, 121-36, 220-3

- subjection to violence in traditional sacred life, 107, 110-12
- See also Escape; Girls; Brother-sister traditional relationship; Homicide; Human rights; Injury; Judicial responses; Marriage; Mirriri; Mothers; Parenting; Rape; Rates; Safe house; Silence; Traditional culture; Victims; Violence; Young people

Wunungmurra, Banambi, 203, 213, 216

Wunungmurra, Dennis, 90, 224-7, 230

Yarralin, 78, 192-4

Yengoyan, Aram, 135

Yidaki players; Yirrkala Yidaki, 248-9, 250-1

Yirrkala, 197-9, 200, 212, 234, 249

Yolngu people, 117, 118, 197-253, 323, 335-6
- See also 'Murngin' people

Yothu Yindi/Yothu Yindi Foundation, 202, 218, 237, 249

Young people
- (and) clash between traditional and mainstream culture, v, 176, 182-3, 188, 236, 241-9, 252-3, 313-6, 318-24, 348
- lack of power/vulnerability to punishment within traditional culture, 108-9, 110, 123-4, 126, 127-32, 133-6, 136-7
- See also Authority; Suicide; Warriors

Yuendumu, 273, 305

www.ingramcontent.com/pod-product-compliance
Lightning Source LLC
Chambersburg PA
CBHW052055300426
44117CB00013B/2129